English literary afterlives

MANCHEStER
1824

Manchester University Press

The
Manchester
Spenser

The Manchester Spenser is a monograph and text series devoted to historical and textual approaches to Edmund Spenser – to his life, times, places, works and contemporaries.

A growing body of work in Spenser and Renaissance studies, fresh with confidence and curiosity and based on solid historical research, is being written in response to a general sense that our ability to interpret texts is becoming limited without the excavation of further knowledge. So the importance of research in nearby disciplines is quickly being recognised, and interest renewed: history, archaeology, religious or theological history, book history, translation, lexicography, commentary and glossary – these require treatment for and by students of Spenser.

The Manchester Spenser, to feed, foster and build on these refreshed attitudes, aims to publish reference tools, critical, historical, biographical and archaeological monographs on or related to Spenser, from several disciplines, and to publish editions of primary sources and classroom texts of a more wide-ranging scope.

The Manchester Spenser consists of work with stamina, high standards of scholarship and research, adroit handling of evidence, rigour of argument, exposition and documentation.

The series will encourage and assist research into, and develop the readership of, one of the richest and most complex writers of the early modern period.

General Editors Joshua Reid, Kathryn Walls and Tamsin Badcoe
Editorial Board Sukanta Chaudhuri, Helen Cooper, Thomas Herron, J. B. Lethbridge, James Nohrnberg and Brian Vickers

Also available
Literary and visual Ralegh   Christopher M. Armitage (ed.)
Edmund Spenser and the romance of space   Tamsin Badcoe
The art of The Faerie Queene   Richard Danson Brown
A Concordance to the Rhymes of The Faerie Queene   Richard Danson Brown & J. B. Lethbridge
A Supplement of the Faery Queene: By Ralph Knevet   Christopher Burlinson & Andrew Zurcher (eds)
A Companion to Pastoral Poetry of the English Renaissance   Sukanta Chaudhuri
Pastoral poetry of the English Renaissance: An anthology   Sukanta Chaudhuri (ed.)
Spenserian allegory and Elizabethan biblical exegesis: A context for The Faerie Queene   Margaret Christian
Monsters and the poetic imagination in The Faerie Queene*: 'Most ugly shapes and horrible aspects'*   Maik Goth
Celebrating Mutabilitie: Essays on Edmund Spenser's Mutabilitie Cantos   Jane Grogan (ed.)
Spenserian satire: A tradition of indirection   Rachel E. Hile
Castles and Colonists: An archaeology of Elizabethan Ireland   Eric Klingelhofer
Shakespeare and Spenser: Attractive opposites   J. B. Lethbridge (ed.)
Dublin: Renaissance city of literature   Kathleen Miller and Crawford Gribben (eds)
A Fig for Fortune: By Anthony Copley   Susannah Brietz Monta
Spenser and Virgil: The pastoral poems   Syrithe Pugh
The Burley manuscript   Peter Redford (ed.)
Renaissance psychologies: Spenser and Shakespeare   Robert Lanier Reid
Spenser and Donne: Thinking poets   Yulia Ryzhik (ed.)
European erotic romance: Philhellene Protestantism, renaissance translation and English literary politics   Victor Skretkowicz
Rereading Chaucer and Spenser: Dan Geffrey with the New Poete   Rachel Stenner, Tamsin Badcoe and Gareth Griffith (eds)
God's only daughter: Spenser's Una as the invisible Church   Kathryn Walls
William Shakespeare and John Donne: Stages of the soul in early modern English poetry   Angelika Zirker

English literary afterlives

Greene, Sidney, Donne and the evolution of posthumous fame

ELISABETH CHAGHAFI

Manchester University Press

The right of Elisabeth Chaghafi to be identified as the author of this work has been asserted by her in accordance with the Copyright, Designs and Patents Act 1988.

Published by Manchester University Press
Altrincham Street, Manchester M1 7JA

www.manchesteruniversitypress.co.uk

British Library Cataloguing-in-Publication Data
A catalogue record for this book is available from the British Library

ISBN 978 1 5261 4495 9 hardback

First published 2020

The publisher has no responsibility for the persistence or accuracy of URLs for any external or third-party internet websites referred to in this book, and does not guarantee that any content on such websites is, or will remain, accurate or appropriate.

Typeset in Minion Pro by
Servis Filmsetting Ltd, Stockport, Cheshire

Contents

Figures

Acknowledgements

I am grateful to Bart van Es for his invaluable feedback during the early stages of the project. I also benefited from the assistance of knowledgeable librarians, especially Colin Harris and Bruce Barker-Benfield of the Bodleian Library, for letting me view the restricted pages of Aubrey's manuscripts, and Joe Marshall of Edinburgh University Library, for retrieving the Drummond manuscript in the nick of time before it was sent away for repairs. Useful feedback, suggestions and/or constructive criticism on various bits and pieces of the manuscript at various points were provided by Jean Brink, Megan Cook, Bill Engel, Tom Herron, Roger Kuin, Joe Loewenstein, Bill Oram, Anne Prescott, Syrithe Pugh, Cathy Shrank, Emma Smith, Rachel Stenner, Rob Stillman, Rémi Vuillemin and of course the two anonymous readers.

I would also like to thank Matthew Frost of Manchester University Press (MUP), and Tamsin Badcoe and Joshua Reid, of the Manchester Spenser series, as well as Zachary Leader, general editor of the *Oxford History of Life-Writing*, for putting up with half a dozen emails over the course of several years in which I kept badgering him about the publication date of the early modern volume of the series, and the Folger Shakespeare Library, for making thousands of pages' worth of rare books and manuscripts from their collections available online through their digital image collection.

Finally, I owe special thanks for general awesomeness and continued support to my mother (another knowledgeable librarian, and my longest-suffering reader by far), my cat Bonnie, and, last but not least, my long approoued and singular good friende, Mr I.B.L.

Note: an early version of the third chapter was published as '"Astrophel" and Spenser's 1595 Quarto', in *Explorations in Renaissance Culture*, 41 (2015).

Introduction

This is a book about the lives of dead poets.[1] It examines the ways in which an early modern network of individuals closely involved with literary production conceptualised ideas of authorship by reading, and summarily evaluating, the body of works of recently deceased authors. This process of retrospective assessment, sometimes aided by posthumous editions whose structure aimed to mimic the progression of the author's writing career, effectively resulted in the collective creation of literary life-narratives of sorts: 'literary' both because they were concerned with the life of the poet *as* a poet, and because they were substantially constructed from his own works. For this reason, this book addresses not only the question why in a period during which the idea of authorship underwent such crucial transformations there appeared to be so little interest in the lives and careers of authors; it also documents an important stage within the history of biographical reading and investigates the possibility of a pre-history of literary biography. Finally, it seeks to juxtapose and re-evaluate some misunderstood discourses of authorship and to challenge the common assumption that early modern authors primarily created themselves.

Although it is now several decades since the concept of the 'fashioned' self was formulated by Stephen Greenblatt, the New Historicist focus on the agency of poets in forging their own reputation has proved to have an enduring afterlife. Greenblatt defined self-fashioning as 'the power to impose a shape upon oneself [as] an aspect of the more general power to control identity – that of others at least as often as one's own'.[2] Yet despite his fairly broad definition, which does not associate the phenomenon of self-fashioning specifically with literary authorship, Greenblatt evidently thought of it as a literary concept. It is revealing that his monograph *Sir Walter Ralegh* (1973), in which he first developed this concept, begins by considering Ralegh in terms of his *vita activa* and his attempts to further it by 'bend[ing] art to the service of life', but increasingly focuses on Ralegh as a poet who transformed the crises and conflicts of his 'active' life into art.[3] Similarly, *Renaissance Self-Fashioning*, the book in which Greenblatt developed this concept further, begins with an introduction that

---

1 Throughout this study, I shall use the term 'poet' in the expansive sense that it has in Sidney's *Defence of Poesie*, where it includes authors of all imaginative literary works, regardless of genre. Sidney's concept of the author as a 'maker' creating a 'golden world' in his works famously extends even to 'Poets that neuer versified' (C4ᵃ), which he then illustrates by classifying *Utopia* as poetry.
2 Stephen Greenblatt, *Renaissance Self-Fashioning* (Chicago: University of Chicago Press, 1980), p. 1.
3 Stephen Greenblatt, *Sir Walter Ralegh* (New Haven, CT: Yale University Press, 1973), p. 59.

derives the book's title from the context (and the frequency) of the word 'fashion' in the works of Edmund Spenser, and Greenblatt's examples of self-fashioning figures also consist of poets and playwrights, whom he substantially views through their fictional writings. Even when writing about Sir Thomas More – who, as a political and religious (as well as a literary) figure, arguably embodied several areas of self-fashioning – Greenblatt's anchor point for his analysis is More's major fictional work, *Utopia*. 'Renaissance' self-fashioning as Greenblatt conceived it, and as it has traditionally been understood, is therefore effectively authorial self-fashioning.

It is not surprising, then, that the concept of self-fashioning has been a formative influence on academic debate about early modern authorship and literary careers. Modifying Greenblatt, a series of scholars have pictured a fashioned literary self that forms a constituent part of a professional career. In *Erasmus, Man of Letters* (1993), for example, Lisa Jardine argued that Erasmus's career as a public intellectual with an international reputation was the result of his efforts to construct a 'multidimensional cultural persona' for himself by manipulating his literary persona.[4] In her 1998 biography of Francis Bacon (coauthored by Alan Stewart), Jardine then expanded the concept of literary work as informing the writer's professional career, viewing Bacon's life as characterised by 'perpetual struggles with the demands of two possible careers' rather than treating his political career and his writing career as separate entities.[5] Richard Rambuss, in *Spenser's Secret Career* (1993), took a similar approach by 'tracing the various ligatures between Spenser's two careers' and particularly putting his career as a secretary back into focus.[6] Jason Scott-Warren, in *Sir John Harington and the Book as Gift* (2001), even went as far as to argue for the inseparability of his subject's careers as an author and courtier.[7] He concluded that Harington's writing for specific occasions and his creation of special presentation copies for particular dedicatees formed part of a strategy to further his career at court. Scott-Warren arrived at this conclusion through analysing both the circumstances of Harington's dedications of books as well as examining the presentation copies themselves. What unites those studies is that they largely view authors' writing careers as ancillary to projecting a selective professional image of themselves that was intended to signal their wider employability. While this school of criticism also regards authors' professional selves as connected to their literary careers, then, it takes a more pragmatic approach to it than Greenblatt's 'self-fashioning' model. This in turn links those studies to a second critical movement, which developed alongside New Historicism and had a significant impact on early modern authorship studies: the History of the Book.

One of the most prominent scholars of early modern authorship was Richard Helgerson, whose work on literary self-image shows the influence of both New Historicism and the History of the Book. It is characterised by a materialist focus on the author's relationship to patronage and the institution of print and argues for

4 Lisa Jardine, *Erasmus, Man of Letters: The Construction of Charisma in Print* (Princeton, NJ: Princeton University Press, 1993), p. 5
5 Lisa Jardine and Alan Stewart, *Hostage to Fortune: The Troubled Life of Francis Bacon* (London: Gollancz, 1998), p. 19.
6 Richard Rambuss, *Spenser's Secret Career* (Cambridge: Cambridge University Press, 1993), p. 2.
7 Jason Scott-Warren, *Sir John Harington and the Book as Gift* (Oxford: Oxford University Press, 2001).

authorship itself as an emergent professional field, leading early modern authors to define themselves as laureate or counter-laureate figures. Helgerson's first major study, *The Elizabethan Prodigals* (1976), examines the attempts of a generation of early modern writers to use the prodigal narratives that formed a staple of popular romance as a mirror for their own biography and to style themselves as 'prodigals', as a way of accounting for their own writing. In *Self-Crowned Laureates* (1983), he later contrasted the equally crafted efforts by two different groups of authors to convey a specific image of themselves, and position themselves in relation to the patron-age system, via claims made on title pages, in dedications to patrons, and sometimes within the actual works. Noting changes in early modern patronage structures, Helgerson proposed that the late sixteenth century saw the emergence of a new type of self-styled professional poet with the ambition to become a national poet. He suggested that the idea of the laureate poet who regarded the writing of poetry as a serious profession challenged the existing attitude towards poetry. This attitude dictated that the writing of poetry should be a courtly amateur pastime, whose results should be hidden and not published in print. Helgerson saw the beginnings of early modern laureate-ship in the 'laureate ambition' of Edmund Spenser's self-presentation as the 'new' poet in *The Shepheardes Calender*, followed by another defining moment in the history of authorship: Ben Jonson's *Works*. In editing his own collected works during his lifetime, Jonson effectively created his own literary monument, ensuring the perpetuation not only of his works but of his own views regarding their significance. Yet Jonson's decisions to declare his plays 'works' – for which he was mocked by some of his contemporaries – represent more than just an effort to fashion his authorial self. They also illustrate what Joseph Loewenstein has termed Jonson's 'possessive' authorship.[8] Examining the pre-history of copyright, Loewenstein argues for a connection between the phenomenon of print authorship and the growing desire among early modern print authors to retain control of their works even after publication. This model of authorship thus turns both the works and the authorial image fashioned through them into the author's 'property'.

The emphasis on the worldly goals of early modern authors has gone hand in hand with a more concrete engagement with the material text and has led to more attention being directed towards books in their physical form as well as the groups of people involved in their production – publishers, printers and compositors.[9] Representing

8 Joseph Loewenstein, *The Author's Due* (Chicago: University of Chicago Press, 2002) and *Ben Jonson and Possessive Authorship* (Cambridge: Cambridge University Press, 2002).
9 Broadly speaking, the distinction between the three roles is that booksellers provided the capital required for the production of books (which, depending on the type of book produced, could amount to a substantial investment) and subsequently sold them in their shops. Consequently, booksellers took the highest financial risk but also stood to gain most from the success of a book. The role of publisher, which did not strictly exist in the early modern book business, was effectively shared between book-sellers and printers, who owned the presses and were responsible for the physical production process. Compositors were employed by printers and set the type for printing, referring either to manuscripts or to earlier printed editions. They were essentially in charge of a book's layout, assembling text, blank space, illustrations and decorative devices (such as initials, borders of printers' flowers or decorative place-fillers) on the page in a practical – but ideally also aesthetically pleasing – fashion. This often involved 'reading' the texts they were setting in visual terms, to determine which were the elements requiring highlighting via layout or typography. In practice, however, these different roles were not

an effort to bridge the gap between two related but traditionally separate critical disciplines – literary criticism and bibliography – the History of the Book has had a prominent influence on early modern authorship studies, particularly since the 1990s. At the heart of it stands the notion that books as material objects are also carriers of meaning, and that literature cannot be considered exclusively as text and removed from its material publication context. One of the people to spearhead the movement during the 1970s was bibliographer D. F. McKenzie, who observed that the printing process for early modern books was not as mechanised and as regularised as literary scholars had been inclined to assume and that the production process itself deserved further attention. French structuralist Gérard Genette, on the other hand, approaching the issue from the angle of semantics during the 1980s argued in *Paratexts* that prefatory matter such as introductions or dedications, which do not form part of the text proper, nevertheless act as 'thresholds of meaning' and therefore should not be neglected by scholars.[10] Yet the theory that has proved the most influential for literary studies was that of cultural historian Roger Chartier, who proposed that to examine the transmission of meaning through literary works it is necessary to combine literary analysis with the study of books as material objects, as well as reception history and cultural practices of reading.

The influence of the History of the Book has also manifested itself in studies centring on the process of early modern literary production not only in print but also in manuscript form. One of the earliest studies in this field was Harold Love's *Scribal Publication* (1993). The title of its second, paperback edition, *The Culture and Commerce of Texts* (1998), further highlights the network-based aspect of its approach.[11] It is the original title, however, that best illustrates the starting-point for Love's key argument. Seventeenth-century manuscript miscellanies, he observes, were not always the product of individuals copying texts for their personal use. Instead, they were frequently the work of trained scribes, producing manuscripts on demand in scribal workshops. The conditions under which those manuscripts were created, Love argues, led to a sophisticated process of production that is comparable to print in terms of professionalisation – hence his use of the term 'scribal *publication*'. The 'scribal publication' model proposed by Love challenges assumptions

always strictly separate from each other, and there was some space within which early modern print professionals were able to define their own roles. So, for example, some printers also had their own bookshops – such as John Wolfe, who printed titles for other booksellers to begin with, but increasingly employed other printers to print titles for him as he became more successful. Some printers printed a vast range of different titles for a lot of different booksellers, while others were fortunate enough to secure the rights to lucrative titles that were reprinted at regular intervals, which allowed for an efficient use of their capacities – such as Thomas East, who during the 1580s printed every single edition of both parts of John Lyly's *Euphues*, one of the most successful titles of the decade (between 1578 and 1588, both parts were reprinted by East roughly once per year). At least some compositors moved into other roles, such as Henry Chettle, who wrote *Kind-Harts Dreame*, an attempt to fan the flames of the Harvey–Nashe quarrel and edited, co-wrote or perhaps even wrote *Greenes Groats-worth of Witte* (both discussed in Chapter 2).

10 Gérard Genette, *Paratexts: Thresholds of Interpretation*, trans. Jane E. Lewin (Cambridge: Cambridge University Press, 1997), originally published as *Seuils* (1987).

11 The second edition preserved the title of the first in its subtitle (its full title read *The Culture and Commerce of Texts: Scribal Publication in Seventeenth-Century England*). Nevertheless, the shift in emphasis is clear.

about the impact of print on manuscript circulation by suggesting that manuscripts were not simply replaced by printed books. Instead, print and manuscript publication were two coexisting industries catering for different markets. At the same time, the 'scribal publication' model challenges notions of single authorship, since it gives scribes a significant amount of control over the text in terms of both presentation and contents. Arthur Marotti's work occupies a middle ground in that it is concerned with both forms of 'publication'. His major study, *Manuscript, Print, and the English Renaissance Lyric* (1995) examines manuscript culture and print culture in their relation to each other and argues for a mutual influence. Peter Beal, whose 1996 Lyell lectures on bibliography were published as *In Praise of Scribes* in the same year as Love's *Culture and Commerce of Texts*, focuses not so much on the production process itself as on the group of people who produced the manuscripts and their role within early modern society. Noting that the modern marginalisation of seventeenth-century scribes forms a stark contrast to the way their role was perceived by their contemporaries, Beal argues that it is necessary to recognise them as significant figures and as 'key agents in the process of written communication and literary transmission'.[12]

As well as leading to new models for the process of literary production that acknowledge the role of manuscripts in relation to print, the influence of book history has also heightened critical awareness of the ways in which editing practices can affect readers' perception of texts and their authors. This is evident for example in Leah Marcus's *Unediting the Renaissance* (1996), which contained a plea to scholars of the early modern period to pay closer attention to the editions they worked with and not to trust 'authoritative' editions implicitly and mistake editorial choices for authorial intention. Jerome J. McGann, in *The Textual Condition* (1991) attributed even greater significance to the editing of texts, by arguing that 'producing editions is one of the ways we produce literary meaning'.[13] That heightened awareness of the editing process has not only made scholars warier of citing modern editions without also consulting the early modern editions they were based on, it has also led to a growing interest in early modern editions that is not purely bibliographical.

The evidence of printed editions and their power to shape an author has recently proved a fruitful area of research in Shakespeare criticism. For example, Margreta de Grazia's *Shakespeare Verbatim* and Andrew Murphy's *Shakespeare in Print* both make a persuasive case for the impact of late eighteenth-century Shakespeare editions on the development of both Shakespeare criticism and the perception of Shakespeare as an author figure. While a lot of emphasis has of course been placed on the impact of eighteenth- and nineteenth-century editions, the idea of 'Shakespeare' conveyed by early modern editions has also become the subject of investigation. This is reflected in new critical editions, such as a volume in the *Oxford Shakespeare* series, *The Complete Sonnets and Poems* (2002), edited by Colin Burrow. The edition's most radical aspect lies in Burrow's decision to include material of dubious authorship and even some that 'can be confidently attributed to other authors'.[14] Thus *The Complete Sonnets*

12 Peter Beal, *In Praise of Scribes* (Oxford: Clarendon Press, 1998), p. v.
13 Jerome J. McGann, *The Textual Condition* (Princeton, NJ: Princeton University Press, 1991), p. 33.
14 Colin Burrow (ed.), *The Complete Sonnets and Poems* (Oxford: Oxford University Press, 2002), p. 76.

and Poems contains not only an appendix of 'Poems Attributed to Shakespeare in the Seventeenth Century' (mostly gathered from manuscript miscellanies written after his death), it also reproduces the full text of *The Passionate Pilgrim*, a collection that assembled poems by several authors into a sonnet cycle and attributed it to Shakespeare. This is an unusual editorial approach; more commonly, composite early modern texts of mixed authorship are merely mined by editors for the contributions of specific authors rather than treated as a unit.[15] Arguably, in the case of *The Passionate Pilgrim*, the situation is further complicated by the fact that all of the poems it contains that are generally attributed to Shakespeare are modified versions of poems printed elsewhere (albeit later). Burrow, however, justifies the inclusion of non-Shakespearean material in a collection of Shakespeare's poetry by pointing out that irrespective of questions of authenticity or authorial intention, the falsely attributed poems and *The Passionate Pilgrim* in its entirety contributed to the textual presence of 'Shakespeare'. Moreover, he argues that they represent early readers' answers to the question he regards as central to his edition: 'What sort of poet was Shakespeare?'[16]

Yet Shakespeare is neither the only nor the first early modern author to have been 'fashioned' after his death through critical and editing conventions. Thomas Dabbs' *Reforming Marlowe*, published in the same year as de Grazia's *Shakespeare Verbatim*, presents a strong case for the theory that the canonisation of Christopher Marlowe as one of the major playwrights of the period was substantially brought about by the endeavours of nineteenth-century critics, who effectively created Marlowe as an author figure. At first sight, the date of his canonisation as an English classic would appear to make very little difference to our reading of Marlowe. After all, if his works are great, does it really matter whether he was recognised as a great playwright by his contemporaries? The answer to this question is of course that it does matter, though not only because scholars have a duty to distinguish 'bibliographical facts' from 'interpretive fictions', as Dabbs argues.[17] It also matters because those 'interpretive fictions' substitute for the biography of an author about whose life little is known – and much of what is known is of doubtful authority – and have thus themselves become an integral part of 'Marlowe'. As J. A. Downie notes in his essay 'Marlowe: Facts and Fictions', much has been extrapolated about Marlowe on the basis of very sparse evidence. One of the examples he uses to illustrate this point is the attribution history of *Tamburlaine*. Despite some contemporary allusions that could be read as identifying Marlowe as its author, it only became firmly attributed to Marlowe in the nineteenth century, through the endeavours of enterprising editor and forger John Payne Collier, who 'went to extraordinary lengths to "prove" that Marlowe wrote the

---

15 Chapter 3 contains a detailed discussion of another such text, Edmund Spenser's 'Astrophel' collection, which contains poetry by at least four other authors.
16 Burrow, *The Complete Sonnets and Poems*, p. 1. One of Burrow's declared aims is to readjust the focus that has traditionally been placed on Shakespeare as a playwright, at the expense of the poems and sonnets (partly as a result of their omission from the 1623 first folio). Pointing to the popularity of the poetry among Shakespeare's contemporaries, Burrow argues that the poetic works are in fact central to the idea of 'Shakespeare' in print.
17 Thomas Dabbs, *Reforming Marlowe* (London: Associated University Presses, 1991), p. 7.

play, down to forging an entry in Philip Henslowe's diary'.[18] Regardless of whether it is correct and when exactly it was made, the attribution of *Tamburlaine* to Marlowe matters not only because it affects our views of (to borrow Burrow's phrase) 'the sort of author' Marlowe was. It also indirectly affects the narrative of Marlowe the atheist. While few readers would go as far as to read the character of Tamburlaine as an authorial self-portrait, Marlowe's authorship of a play about a notorious atheist who dies unrepentant would seem to offer the most tangible evidence for his own alleged atheism (if slightly hampered by the fact that the play does not appear to have been among the evidence brought against him).

What the example of *Tamburlaine*'s attribution illustrates, then, is that the study of authorship and authorial personae is closely connected to biographical questions. Although traditionally associated with the approaches of early scholars such as Edmund Dowden (and consequently everything that was 'wrong' about nineteenth-century English studies), biography is once more becoming a legitimate focus for literary scholarship. This scholarly interest is illustrated not only by the critical biographies already mentioned but also by publications like the essay collection *Shakespeare, Marlowe, Jonson: New Directions in Biography* (2006) whose contributors, as the subtitle indicates, are all seeking new ways to utilise biography for literary criticism that go beyond mere biographical readings of texts. The same growing interest in biography manifests itself in a very different manner in collections such as *Constructing Christopher Marlowe* (2000), whose essays take the reverse approach by examining Marlowe's biography to discover how much of it was in fact 'constructed' by critical discourse about his works. Finally, there is the study of 'life-writing', whose growing significance is exemplified by the very scale of an ongoing project: the *Oxford History of Life-Writing* with its projected seven volumes.[19] That particular project is interesting in this context because its scope represents an emphatic statement about the significance of this field of research: stretching from antiquity to the present and surveying literary as well as non-literary biography, the declared aim of the project is to 'test and complicate' the received notion of a linear development of the genre.[20]

As far as the early modern period is concerned, however, one challenge is that the situation is already quite complicated. Biography (let alone literary biography) as a concept, did not exist at the time, so there is an inevitable overlap between the texts that, using a suitably broad definition of the term, could be regarded as early examples of 'literary life-writing' and those that form the subject of literary studies and authorship studies. This especially applies to paratextual material such as prefaces, dedications or prefatory authors' Lives: all of those may contain biographical information, but they nevertheless occur within the context of introducing works,

18 J. A. Downie, 'Marlowe: facts and fictions', in J. A. Downie and J. T. Parnell (eds), *Constructing Christopher Marlowe* (Cambridge: Cambridge University Press, 2000), pp. 13–29 (p. 19).

19 The first two volumes (including the early modern volume written by Alan Stewart) were published by Oxford University Press in 2018.

20 Since the series is indirectly modelled on the *Oxford English Literary History*, it proposes to place particular emphasis on the written lives of authors (an early working title was 'The Oxford History of Literary Life-Writing'), but without removing those lives from the context of other forms of life-writing that were contemporary to them.

and for that reason they are as much concerned with authorial presence and authorial control – both before and after death – as they are with 'biography'.

This study began with a broad focus on ghostly authorial presences between 1500 and 1700 and the birth of the dead author. During my research, however, it became apparent that there were moments within the period that I was investigating when the death of an author prompted a cluster of responses both among his immediate contemporaries and among the following generation. One of the concerns of those responses was the retrospective evaluation of both the lives and the works of the authors in question, and they frequently attempted to make connections between the two. Together, they formed intriguing networks of texts concerned not only with the authorial identity of particular writers but also with an overarching question: what defines the life of a poet and can it be retrieved from his works and narrated? This book, then, sets out to examine texts that could be regarded as biographical before the background of a simultaneous emergence of authorial presence and authorial control across the early modern period. This simultaneous emergence can be traced in a series of 'milestone' publishing events. It is therefore worthwhile at this point to take a brief historical overview of this ground.

Perhaps the earliest publishing milestone for the emergence of authorial presence during the early modern period was the publication of the verse miscellany *Songes and Sonettes written by the right honorable Lorde Henry Haward late Earle of Surrey, and other* in 1557. The preface to the reader, most probably written by printer and publisher Richard Tottel, set out the volume's double agenda – to promote national consciousness via the vehicle of vernacular poetry and to propagate this linguistic nationalism through identifying two particular poets as the figureheads of 'Englishe eloquence':

> That to haue wel written in verse, yea & in smal parcelles, deserueth great prayse, the workes of diuers Latines, Italians, and other, doe proue sufficiently. That our tong is able in that kynde to do as praise worthely as the rest, the honorable stile of the noble Earle of Surrey, and the weightinesse of the depe witted sir Thomas Wyat the elders verse, with seuerall graces in sundry good Englysh writers, do shew abundantly.[21]

The outcome of Tottel's endeavour to assemble 'those workes which the vngentle horders of such treasure, haue heretofore enuied [the reader]' (A.i[b]) was not only *Songes and Sonettes* itself but also the distinct authorial identities the preface refers to: 'noble' Surrey and 'depe witted' Wyatt, characterised respectively through the 'honorable stile' and 'weightinesse' of their writing.[22] Those authorial identities were reinforced not only by the title page, which presents Surrey as the main author, but also by

---

21 *Songes and Sonettes* (1557), A.i[b]. All quotations from early modern texts use the original spelling, punctuation and formatting.

22 In his preface to the first edition of Sidney's *Astrophel and Stella* (discussed in Chapter 3), Thomas Nashe adopts a similar stance, although his 'vngentle horders' are 'Ladyes' and the author his preface aims to introduce to a more general readership is not so much Sidney as 'Astrophel', the authorial identity created by his poetry – who consequently belonged to all readers, even as the Countess of Pembroke was trying to assert the family's right to control the posthumous reputation of Sidney himself.

some of the titles added to the poems. The titles attempted to construct a persona for 'Wiat' spanning several poems spread across the volume. So in *Songes and Sonettes*, the poem beginning with the line 'Mine old dere enmy, my froward maister', is given the title 'wiates complaint vpon Loue, to Reason: with Loues answere', while 'Syghes are my foode: my drink are my teares' becomes 'wiate being in prison, to Brian'. Additionally, the volume contains elegies for Wyatt – 'Of the death of sir Thomas wiate the elder' and 'Of the death of the same sir T. W.', followed by another poem 'Of the same' – as well as several references to Wyatt's poetry in poems by other authors (including a poem by Surrey that cites a line from 'wiate being in prison' but is printed before it).[23] Overall, however, the contents of the volume are less unified than the title suggests – which may explain why it continues to be better known as 'Tottel's Miscellany'. Nevertheless, *Songes and Sonettes* is significant as a publishing event because it represents a conscious effort to assemble miscellaneous verse into a body of literature attributable to a specific author.

A generation later, George Gascoigne's works constituted another early modern publishing milestone for the emergence of authorial presence in print. During Gascoigne's lifetime, two editions of his collected works were published within two years of each other. After Gascoigne's death, a third edition appeared. Although the arrangement of the contents varies between editions, perhaps the most significant difference between the editions is in the titles, which reflect a change in the way the contents and Gascoigne's authorship are being presented to readers. The title of the first edition, *A hundreth sundrie flowres bound vp in one small poesie* (1573), aimed to present the volume as a miscellany, and although he was named in the table of contents, the title page featured no mention of Gascoigne's name. In a sense, *A hundreth sundrie flowres* takes an approach to authorship that is the exact opposite of that of *Songes and Sonettes*. It is a body of works by a single author presented as a miscellany, whose title page even plays down its author's part in assembling the 'small poesie' by announcing that the contents have been 'gathered partely (by translation) in the fyne outlandish Gardins of Euripides, Ouid, Petrarke: and partly by inuention'. By contrast, the revised second edition of 1575 had a title that unambiguously assigned the authorship (and ownership) of the text to Gascoigne: *The Posies of George Gascoigne Esquire. Corrected, perfected, and augmented by the Authour*. The emphatic gesture of the 'Authour' regaining control of his printed text already indicated in the title of *Posies* was repeated both in the monumental structure that frames the title page and in the indignant author's preface that followed it. In this preface, Gascoigne not only aims to make it clear that he is fully in control of this edition and the choice to publish it was his own ('before I wade further in publishing of these Posies') but also lists the shortcomings of the previous edition and renounces all responsibility for it.[24] Finally, in 1587, ten years after Gascoigne's death, *Posies* was republished under the title *The whole woorkes of George Gascoigne Esquyre: Newlye compyled into one Volume*. Those claims were not strictly true – they were not his whole works, nor had

23 'Exhortacion to learn by others trouble' (E.ii.ᵇ) ends with the line 'But Wiat said true, the skarre doth ay endure'. This is an echo of the last line of 'Wiate being in prison' (L.iiiiᵃ), which reads: 'But yet alas, the skarre shall still remain'.
24 George Gascoigne, *The Posies of George Gascoigne Esquire* (1575), ijᵃ.

they been newly compiled; in fact, the *Whole woorkes* were little more than *Posies* republished with a new title page. Nevertheless, the misleading title page reveals a shift in terms of the strategies employed by publisher Richard Smith (who had also published the two previous versions) to promote the volume. The contrast to *A hundreth sundrie flowres* is particularly striking. On the title page of *A hundreth sundrie flowres*, the phrase 'bound vp in one small poesie' had served not only to reinforce the comparison between posies and 'poesie', it had also signified selection. That is, the phrase had been used to suggest to readers that they were being presented with only the choicest of 'flowres', regardless of the fact that at 445 pages, the collection was rather more substantial than the term 'small poesie' implied. By contrast, the corresponding phrase on the title page of the *Whole woorkes*, 'compyled into one Volume', attempts to convince readers of the exact opposite by creating an erroneous impression of completeness.[25]

The three different incarnations of Gascoigne's works between 1573 and 1587 show not only an early instance of an author practising 'possessive authorship' (to borrow Joseph Loewenstein's phrase), but also hint at a publisher's changing perception of authorship. Yet while the *Posies* only became the *Woorkes* after Gascoigne's death, two of the major publishing events of the early seventeenth century concerned poets who not only published collections of their works during their own lifetime but published them as their *Works*. The earlier of these events, the publication of *The Works of Samvel Daniel* in 1601, is remarkable partly because the act of a living author publishing his collected works and referring to them as his 'works' was almost unprecedented.[26] Yet it is also noteworthy because the uncommonness of this situation was so little remarked upon by Daniel's contemporaries – unlike the publication of Ben Jonson's works in 1616.

The title page design of *The Works of Samvel Daniel* is similar to that of Gascoigne's *Posies* in that it depicts a monumental structure framing the title (though in Daniel's case the structure is much more elaborate). Another characteristic the two title pages share is the claim that they have been 'augmented', although the implication of the word is different. On the title page of *Posies*, which aims to distinguish itself from *A hundreth sundrie flowres*, the word's role in the phrase 'Corrected, perfected and augmented by the Authour' highlights the author's involvement in the edition. Thus it serves to set the edition apart from the one that had preceded it, implicitly rendering *A hundreth sundrie flowres* not only unauthorised but also obsolete.[27] This of course does not apply to *The Works of Samvel Daniel*, because it had not been immediately preceded by an unauthorised edition. Instead, the claim on the title page that

25 At least one surviving copy of the *Whole woorkes* (STC 216:02) also had a woodcut of Gascoigne before a bookshelf – a copy of the portrait used in *The steele glas* (1575) – inserted to face the title page. In combination with the title, the portrait further reinforces the notion that the contents of the volume represent Gascoigne's complete works.

26 See John Pitcher, 'Editing Daniel' [based on a paper delivered in 1985], in W. Speed Hill (ed.), *New Ways of Looking at Old Texts* (Binghamton: Renaissance English Text Society, 1993), pp. 57–73. Pitcher argues that Daniel's *Works* represented 'an explicit claim on [the] succession' of Spenser, who had died two years earlier (p. 68).

27 A similar usage of the word 'augmented' occurs on the title page of the 1593 edition of Sidney's *Arcadia* (discussed in Chapter 3), which contains the phrase 'Now since the first edition augmented and ended'.

Daniel's works have been 'Newly augmented' above all emphasises the quality of the text, proclaiming it to be authoritative, while also acting as an incentive to owners of individual editions to buy the *Works* by implying that the volume represents the folio equivalent of a 'director's cut'. The fact that the phrase 'by the Authour' is missing here further highlights the confidence of the title page's claims, because it effectively takes Daniel's agency for granted: who else should be augmenting his works if not the author himself? The extent of Daniel's involvement in the production, as well as the presentation, of the *Works* is noted by John Pitcher, who observes that part of Daniel's agreement with his publisher was that 'the poet should receive a number of copies printed on large very high quality paper'.[28] This luxury edition of the *Works* was then used by Daniel for presentation copies, with specially printed dedicatory poems inserted. As in Gascoigne's case, however, Daniel's works did not become his 'whole' works until after his death. The title page of *The Whole Works of Samvel Daniel Esquire in Poetrie* (1623) is dominated by the word 'whole', which announces the volume to readers as – quite literally – the ultimate edition of Daniel's works, since they could no longer be 'augmented' by the author.

While the evident laureate pretensions of Daniel's poetic *Works* apparently went unchecked by his contemporaries, *The workes of Beniamin Ionson* (1616) did not. However, as Margreta de Grazia notes in her introduction to *Shakespeare Verbatim*, this was not because his readers questioned his status as the humanist 'English Horace' that entitled him to publish a folio of his works in an implicit bid to be seen as a living classic.[29] Instead, it was Jonson's unorthodox definition of 'works', indicated in the theatre-centred imagery of the title page and reinforced by the 'Catalogue' of contents, in which his major plays take precedence over his poetry, that was commented on. *Wits Recreations* (1640), an anonymously published miscellany of short poems (several of which have poetry or individual poets as their theme), contains two epigrams addressed to Jonson. The second of these, entitled '269. *To Mr. Ben. Iohnson demanding the reason why he call'd his playes works*', runs: 'Pray tell me, Ben, where doth the mistery lurke, | What others call a play you call a worke'. Within the context of *Wits Recreations*, the poem is of course little more than a good-humoured witticism. This is illustrated by the fact that its main function is to provide an opening for the punchline of the poem that follows it ('270. *Thus answer'd by a friend in Mr. Iohnsons defence*'): '*Bens* plays are works, when others works are plaies'.[30] Nevertheless, there is an implied barb in the assumption that the title of the *Works* requires a 'defence'. Moreover, it is unclear whether the two epigrams were originally intended to form a pair or whether the friend's reply was added at a later date, or perhaps even after Jonson's death in 1637. The publication of Jonson's *Works*, then, represents the final step towards authorial control. It is a publishing milestone because Jonson is not merely claiming the title 'works' for his writings during his own lifetime (as Daniel

---

28 Pitcher, 'Editing Daniel', p. 68.
29 Margreta de Grazia, *Shakespeare Verbatim* (Oxford: Clarendon Press, 1991), pp. 33–4.
30 *Wits Recreations. Selected from the finest Fancies of Moderne Muses* (1640), both G3ᵇ. The first of the two epigrams, '22. *To Mr. Beniamin Iohnson*' (B4ᵇ) mockingly praises Jonson for having his Roman characters speak with such eloquence that it exceeds that of actual Roman orators.

had already done fifteen years earlier). More significantly, he is claiming the right to impose his own definition on the term.

Thus runs the conventional narrative of the emergence of 'self-fashioned' authorial presence in print. The following section outlines the approach of this study in uncovering another narrative that unfolded before this background, concerning the emergence of authors who could no longer manipulate their own literary image because they were already dead.

The century and a half following the arrival of print in England, then, saw a major development in the emergence of new notions of authorship, alongside humanist ideas of the self. This has been well served by the critical movements outlined above, in a number of ground-breaking studies of authorship. However, one characteristic that those studies share is that they are all very focused on authorial creation during a writer's lifetime. While the History of the Book has been instrumental in bringing about a wider critical trend towards the study of networks of reception, there is still a natural tendency within authorship studies to view the emergence of the authorial persona predominantly as a product of self-fashioning. One of the more extreme manifestations of this is a strand of authorship studies sometimes referred to as 'career criticism'. The work of the most prominent 'career critic', Patrick Cheney, focuses on the concept of a deliberately crafted poetic career via a progression through different genres, and its origins in antiquity. He proposes that a number of widely known 'career models' for the ideal progression of authorship were available to early modern poets, who followed, adapted, combined or subverted them, while simultaneously responding to the careers of 'rival' contemporaries. Although the example of 'career criticism' may not be representative of authorship studies as a whole, it nevertheless serves as an illustration of the focus on authorial agency that is a result of its critical heritage. Traces of this can be found in most of the studies mentioned above.

Yet while the studies of Helgerson, Jardine, Loewenstein and others have successfully demonstrated how individual early modern authors shaped literary careers for themselves during their lifetime, the emphasis on the 'fashioning' author poses one problem: authorship is not only for the living. Even as authors such as Jonson or Spenser were crafting their own poetic careers, they never had the literary stage fully to themselves. Instead, they had to share it with a company of ghosts: authors who were already dead but who, through the reception of their works and attempts to trace the author's life and authorial identity in them, were embarking on posthumous careers. As a result, agency in the creation of authorial identity should not be assumed to lie purely with the living author but also with the people who read and interpreted his works after his death. The emergence of those authorial ghosts is a phenomenon that provides an ongoing counterpoint to the literary fashioning of living authors that took place alongside it.

This study is distinctive in that it examines a process less controlled than the milestone publishing events mentioned in the previous section: the process of posthumous fashioning of authorship and, occasionally, a 'life of the author' fashioned from his works. Although the emergence of authorship from manuscript to print is now central to literary conceptions of the period, the Renaissance treatment of the posthumous literary life is still an underresearched field. One trailblazing recent work is Gavin Alexander's *Writing After Sidney*, which traces not only the reception history of Sidney's works but also the beginnings of his posthumous literary career. Alexander notes Sidney's unique position as an early modern author whose birth as an author only occurred after his death, observing:

> Sidney as a major English author was the work of those who saw him into print. His life as a published author was posthumous and as such he was only to be found by new readers in his texts. If he was to be approached, addressed, or discussed as a writer, he had to be inferred or resurrected from the printed page.[31]

Yet while Alexander's main interest lies in outlining the findings of those 'new' readers and suggesting reasons why Sidney's works held such appeal for them, this study focuses on the process of 'inferring and resurrecting from the printed page' and its implications. By examining responses to a series of major literary figures among their contemporaries and the following generation of authors, it charts the pre-history of literary biography in the period. Overall, I argue for the gradual emergence of a linkage between the individual's literary output and the personal life, referring to biographies of early modern writers by current authors, as well as modern literary criticism, to illustrate the biographical problems posed by those lives.

One challenge biographers inevitably face when writing the lives of early modern authors is that there is a conspicuous gap between authors' works and the available information about their lives. This gap makes the established modern format of 'literary biography' – that is, biography that assumes a link between an author's life and his works and treats them as informing each other – all but impossible. Katherine Duncan-Jones, in the preface to her biography of Sir Philip Sidney, sums up the typical biographer's dilemma:

> Though Sidney is so well documented, there is, unfortunately, a wide gap between the letters, records and early memoirs, which are overwhelmingly concerned with his life as a courtier and soldier, and his imaginative literary works, which reflect many other preoccupations [...]. Complete integration of the outward and inward lives is impossible, for Sidney's public career is reflected only indirectly in his literary works.[32]

While this gap may be particularly conspicuous in Sidney's case, because his 'outward' life is uncommonly well documented, the same principle applies to his contemporaries. Biographers of Ben Jonson are in a relatively privileged position in this respect because some biographical material relating to his writing has survived, for example in the shape of his letters, the *Conversations with William Drummond* and *Discoveries*. It is therefore revealing that even Ian Donaldson, Jonson's most recent biographer (and coeditor of the seven-volume *Cambridge Jonson*), feels compelled to remind his readers that 'at times one is tempted to say [Jonson's] life is mainly

---

31 Gavin Alexander, *Writing After Sidney* (Oxford: Oxford University Press, 2006), p. xix.
32 Katherine Duncan-Jones, *Sir Philip Sidney, Courtier Poet* (London: Hamish Hamilton, 1991), p. x. I shall return to this passage in Chapter 3. It is worth noting, however, that Duncan-Jones does not rule out the possibility of crossing the biographical gap imaginatively, and her Shakespeare biographies in particular show her to be a firm believer in this practice.

a matter of gaps, interspersed by fragments of knowledge [...] [which], moreover, demand interpretation before they can be meaningfully pressed into service'.[33]

In the following chapters, such problems faced by modern biographers are set against a detailed analysis of contemporary responses to poets' lives shortly after their deaths. This is not only in the shape of written Lives, but also elegies, fictionalised and poeticised life-narratives, biographical readings of individual pieces and posthumous works editions arranged in a manner to suggest a quasi-biographical sequence of the contents. Essentially, this book is structured as a series of case studies around emerging ideas of authorship. In this, I am not concerned with charting the development of a specific category of authorship (such as laureates, amateurs or prodigals). Instead, the different chapters focus on an eclectic selection of literary writers whose authorial careers were substantially shaped by events and discourses following their deaths.

Robert Greene, Sir Philip Sidney, John Donne and George Herbert were selected for the case studies for two reasons. First, the ways in which they were shaped after their deaths were particularly complex and well documented, and involved multiple revisions and re-evaluations as well as attempts by early readers to make direct associations between an author's life and his printed works. Second, the chronological gap between the two contrasting pairs is helpful for highlighting the shift in attitude towards authors' lives and the differences in approach between Izaak Walton and the early readers and editors of Sidney and Greene.

The period that separates the two pairs of authors sees the publication of a number of posthumous collected editions of works by recently dead authors, including those of Spenser, Shakespeare and Donne. The best known format taken by these editions was the monumental folio – monumental both for its sheer bulk and for its purpose in acting as a memorial to immortalise a major author. Among the earliest examples of this format is the first collected edition of Edmund Spenser's works published by Matthew Lownes. The title page, dated 1611, echoes Ponsonby's 1598 'authorised' edition of Sidney's works both in its use of the same device to frame the title and in presenting what is effectively a complete works edition as an edition of the poet's best-known work plus extras.[34] Thus the Sidney folio is called *The Countesse of Pembrokes Arcadia [...] with sundry new additions of the same Author*, while the full title of the Spenser folio is *The Faerie Queen: The Shepheards Calendar: Together with the other Works of England's Arch-Poët. Collected into one Volume and carefully corrected.* Yet there the similarity ends. The Sidney folio was the result of his family's attempts to regain control of his posthumous reputation following the events outlined in Chapter 3, and sought to present readers with a stable, authorised, carefully edited text and an equally stable and authorised version of Sidney himself. The Spenser folio, however, is more problematic in this respect. Although the title page declares the contents have been 'carefully corrected', there is no front matter of any sort to support this claim, to provide additional information about the author and his works, or even to explain the label of 'Arch-Poët'. Furthermore, as Steven Galbraith has noted, the sequence

33 Ian Donaldson, *Ben Jonson: A Life* (Oxford: Oxford University Press, 2011), p. 9.
34 The device of had passed to Lownes along with the printing rights to Sidney's and Spenser's works after Ponsonby's death in 1604.

of contents varies between different copies, resulting in a 'bibliographically unstable' edition.[35] Galbraith concludes that the Spenser folio was essentially a 'consumer's product',[36] which allowed readers to buy sections separately and to assemble them into an edition in their preferred order. On closer inspection, then, the seemingly monumental Spenser folio turns out to be a cheaply produced collectors' edition issued by an enterprising publisher to sell already printed individual works, rather than an editorial tribute to a major author. It is perhaps no coincidence, however, that Lownes chose a title page recalling the most iconic monumental folio of the preceding decade to imply both that he had taken similar care over the text and the author in preparing his edition and that Spenser's poetic reputation was equal to Sidney's.

The 1620s, by contrast, saw the publication of a monumental folio that really was definitive for the posthumous reputation of its author: the 1623 first folio edition of Shakespeare's plays. As might be expected, the editors' preface addressed to 'the great Variety of Readers' stresses the 'care and paine' in producing an authoritative and comprehensive text, using imagery similar to that used by early Sidney editors. Thus John Heminge and Henry Condell declare that one of the purposes of their edition is to replace 'maimed and deformed' editions and present readers with the author's brainchildren 'perfect of their limbes; and [...] absolute in their numbers, as he conceiued thē' (A3ᵃ). Like the Sidney folio, *Mr William Shakespeares Comedies, Histories & Tragedies* also treats its author as a known entity who requires little introduction. Yet while in Sidney's case 'the author' evoked by the collected edition is a composite of the known public figure and his poetic personae, the 1623 folio presents readers with a notion of 'the author' that is almost entirely textual.[37] In this, the very first piece of writing in the volume, Ben Jonson's poem 'To the Reader', facing the portrait on the title page, which urges readers to 'looke | Not on his Picture, but his booke', sets a theme that recurs in the remaining poetic tributes that follow.[38] That theme is the equating of 'Shakespeare' and his (after)life with 'his book' and thus turning the author into his own monument: 'To the memory of my beloued, the author Mr. William Shakespeare: and what he hath left us', as indicated in its title, simultaneously addresses the author and the works; the 'life' referred to in 'Vpon the Lines and Life of the Famous Scenicke Poet, Master William Shakespeare' is the life within the lines; the last two poems, 'To the Memorie of the deceased Authour Maister W. Shakespeare'

---

35 Steven K. Galbraith, 'Spenser's First Folio: The Build-It-Yourself Edition', *Spenser Studies*, 21 (2006), 21–49. With some surviving copies, even the dating is problematic because some of the contents are dated to 1612 or 1613, while the title page states the publication date as 1611.

36 Galbraith, 'Spenser's First Folio', 23.

37 Magreta de Grazia even regards 'Shakespeare' in the 1623 folio as a 'bibliographical rubric' whose main function is to unify a diverse body of texts (*Shakespeare Verbatim*, p. 39).

38 Ironically, 'To the Reader' is printed on a left-hand page, so that in order to look 'on his booke', readers first had to turn to the author's picture. As a result, the poem's effect in its original printed context is to direct attention to the portrait as well as to the pages beyond it that constitute 'his booke'. During the period examined, the addition of authors' portraits at the beginning of editions became an increasingly popular phenomenon. With editions that lacked such portraits, some early book-owners even went to the trouble of pasting in authors' portraits themselves. The relationship between portraits, posthumous editions and biographical interest in authors following their deaths is a complex one, and in itself a worthy subject of future research.

and 'To the memorie of M.W. Shake-speare' respectively consider the author's survival in his 'wit-fraught Booke' and the book as a 'Re-entrance to a Plaudite'. The overall tenor of the commendatory poems, then, is that the edition is not only definitive in the version of Shakespeare it presents, but that it *is* 'Shakespeare'. The second folio edition of 1632, contains two further poems on the same theme, including the anonymous 'Vpon the Effigies of my worthy Friend, the Author Master William Shakespeare, and his Workes', which, perhaps through having been written after the first edition, places particular emphasis on the 'Workes' in their material form. In that poem, a reader is imagined discovering '*Shake-speare* to the life' through the act of turning the pages and reading the plays in succession. The dominance of the folio editions' Shakespeare summed up by 'his booke' can even be seen in *Poems Written by Wil. Shake-speare. Gent.* (published by John Benson in 1640), an octavo that is much more modest both in its appearance and in its claims to significance.[39] Benson's preface 'To the Reader' implicitly acknowledges the definitiveness of the folio editions in its account of the fate of the poems by stating that 'they had not the fortune [...] to have the due accomodatiō of proportionable glory, with the rest of his everliving Workes'.[40] Rather than claiming to have discovered a new or different Shakespeare in the supposedly neglected poems (as we might expect), Benson seems to be telling his readers that if they look closely enough at the poems, they will find the Shakespeare they already know – that is the Shakespeare of the folios.[41] Within this set-up, Benson's own edition can only claim to play a supporting role at best.[42]

The posthumous collections of John Donne's poetry published during the 1630s clearly do not have the same monumental aims as the posthumous folios of Spenser's and Shakespeare's works. This is unsurprising, as Donne's monumental folio, when it was published in 1640, of course contained a collection of his sermons. *Poems by J.D. with Elegies on the Authors Death* (1633), by contrast, has a plain title page which highlights its commemorative function: the title words printed in the largest font sizes are 'Poems' and 'Elegies'. This is followed by an almost absurdly understated preface 'to the Understanders' (as opposed to mere readers), in which publisher John Marriot makes a point of refusing to introduce the author or his poetry through praise. While this is in itself a trope of preface-writing, Marriot goes even further by refusing to portray himself as a conscientious publisher who took pains with the text or to promise 'more correctnesse, or enlargement in the next Edition', since to make such claims would belittle the power of Donne's poetry to shine even in mangled form.[43] One of the effects of Marriot's emphatic refusal to conform to the conventions

---

39 However, Margreta de Grazia argues that the 1640 *Poems* was nevertheless modelled on the folio editions in terms of its build-up and points out that it was even printed by Thomas Cotes, the printer of the 1632 folio (*Shakespeare Verbatim*, pp. 166–7).

40 *Poems Written by Wil. Shake-speare. Gent.* (1640), *2ᵃ.

41 Benson's edition was the first to reprint the sonnets and poems from *The Passionate Pilgrim* since their first editions some thirty years earlier, so he would have had some justification to present them to readers with something of a flourish.

42 The first of the two commendatory poems that follow (attributed to Leonard Digges, who also wrote one of the poems at the beginning of the 1623 folio) echoes this notion. The poem praises Shakespeare not for the poetry contained in the volume it prefaces but instead refers to a catalogue of plays.

43 *Poems by J.D. with Elegies on the Authors Death* (1633), A1ᵇ. As if to prove this point, the second edition, published two years later, concluded with an errata note.

of preface-writing is that the preface does not provide any introduction to the author or any explanation for the way in which the contents of the volume are arranged.[44] As a result, the impression that the first edition of *Poems by J.D.* conveys of Donne as an author is somewhat diffuse – except perhaps to Marriot's desired audience of 'Understanders'. While, as Ernest Sullivan has demonstrated, the 1633 edition was the early edition most frequently referred to by modern editors of Donne (even if it omits a number of poems and its textual authority on the poems included is dubious), it was the second edition, of 1635, that had the greatest influence on Donne's reputation as a poet. Compared to the first edition, the second edition of *Poems by J.D.* is much clearer in declaring its aim to present readers with a collection of the minor works of 'J.D.' to complement an as yet unpublished edition of Dr Donne's sermons. Facing the title page of the 1635 *Poems by J.D.* is a portrait of Donne at the age of eighteen, with a poem by Izaak Walton that maintains Donne's last days (rather than his youth) should be regarded as his 'golden age'.[45] The concluding couplet of that poem serves as a kind of thesis statement for the collection: 'Witnes this Booke ([Donne's] Embleme) which begins | With Love; but endes, with Sighes, & Teares for sins'. The 1635 text thus makes it clear from the outset that the order of contents is supposed to mirror the author's progress towards becoming Dr Donne, author of 'Divine Poëms' and subject of the elegies that conclude the volume.[46] Unsurprisingly, then, it is the 1635 version of *Poems by J.D.* that forms the basis for Walton's reading of Donne's poetry in his 'Life of Donne', which I shall discuss in Chapter 4.

This study begins with two authors' Lives that could be regarded as book-ending the period I am examining, before moving on to the posthumous careers of Greene, Sidney, Donne and Herbert. Chapter 1 frames the critical investigation in the ensuing chapters by contrasting examples of Lives written for authors who lived before and after my chosen period of specialisation, by contrasting two very different Lives of

---

44 The arrangement of contents may have been affected by other factors: Ernest Sullivan, in his essay on the 1633 edition of *Poems by J.D.*, points out that Donne's Satyres may have been 'relegated [...] to the very end of the volume' because the licensers' approval was delayed by censorship issues. Ernest W. Sullivan II, '1633 *Vndone*', *Text*, 7 (1994), 297–306 (p. 303). Sullivan also notes that for censorship reasons some of the poems – including some that had been very widely circulated in manuscript – were omitted from the edition.

45 The emblematic unit of the portrait and poem at the beginning of the 1635 *Poems by J.D.* form a counterpart to the portrait facing the title page of *Deaths Duell*, published two years earlier, which depicts a 'dead' Donne draped in his shroud, possibly based on the sick-bed drawing whose creation is described by Walton in the later versions of his *Life of Donne*. In the 1633 edition, John Marriot's poem 'Hexastichon Bibliopolae', acting as a textual substitute for a frontispiece portrait, had evoked both the *Deaths Duell* portrait and Donne's monument in St Paul's to argue for the superiority of his printed text in preserving the memory of Donne, using a true bookseller's pun on 'sheets': 'I see in his last preach'd, and printed booke, | His Picture in a sheete; in *Pauls* I looke, | And see his Statue in a sheete of stone, | And sure his body in the grave hath one: | Those sheetes present him dead, these if you buy, | You have him living to Eternity' (A2ᵇ). The title pages of the two posthumous editions of the *Devotions* (1634 and 1638) also show Donne's monument, framed by biblical scenes. For a detailed analysis of the portraits and their accompanying poems see Catherine J. Creswell, 'Giving a Face to an Author: Reading Donne's Portraits and the 1635 Edition', *Texas Studies in Literature and Language*, 37 (1995), 1–15.

46 Thus the order in which the contents are arranged follows a logical, though not necessarily strictly chronological, principle. The generic divisions introduced by the 1635 *Poems by J.D.* form the basis for the categories used in most modern editions.

1 Portrait of Donne aged 18, as a frontispiece of *Poems by J. D.* (1635), with a poem by Izaak Walton

2 Portrait of Donne in his shroud, as a frontispiece of *Deaths Duell* (1632)

3 Frontispiece of a later edition of Donne's *Devotions* (1638) featuring his monument at St Paul's, by the same engraver as the frontispiece of *Poems by J. D.* (1635)

English poets, dating to the 1590s and 1690s respectively. Thomas Speght's 'Life of Geffrey Chaucer', which was among the materials added to the 1598 edition of Chaucer's works, is often referred to as the first 'biography' of an English poet. It is a carefully structured text – even featuring its own table of contents – and unites typical features of the exemplary Life and the prefatory Life, while also demonstrating the dominance of the humanist idea of a life of public service (*vita activa*) within early modern life-narratives. Gerard Langbaine's 'Life of Abraham Cowley' (1691), on the other hand, forms part of a tradition of derivative biographical compilations particularly popular during the second half of the seventeenth century. Though not an original work, it stands out among the other Lives of the collection in which it was published through Langbaine's deliberate adoption of a different format that had recently been pioneered by Izaak Walton. Both these Lives, I argue, are not so much remarkable in themselves as because they reflect changed attitudes towards the writing of poets' lives as a result of wider discourses that the following chapters examine in more detail.

Chapter 2 focuses on the events following the 1592 death of Robert Greene, an author often described as the first 'professional' English writer who earned his living through churning out popular plays and pamphlets. Due to his reputation as a 'hack' writer, much of the existing criticism on Greene has focused on literary quality (as well as the apparent insult to Shakespeare as one of the addressees of the letter to the playwrights in *Greenes Groats-worth of Witte*), although there have recently been more varied approaches to Greene, for example in the articles of the collection *Writing Robert Greene* (2008). My chapter, however, is not so much concerned with Greene's career during his lifetime as with Greene's afterlife as a biographical phenomenon. I argue that Greene's notoriety as a prodigal scholar and a professional – if negatively perceived – poet figure is to a large extent a posthumous construct, created through his appearances as a ghostly character figuring in other people's works. Greene's ghostly afterlife was only made possible through a gradual fashioning of his body of works into a suitable life-narrative by other figures involved in the professionalisation of the English publishing industry during the 1590s. Vitally, however, this fashioned identity established the possibility of a newly close relation between the nature of literary output and personal life.

Chapter 3 is concerned with the problems involved in reconciling a poet's life-narrative with the *vita activa* model and examines the potential causes for the curious 'gap' between Sir Philip Sidney's public life and his works, which continues to pose a challenge for his modern biographers. For this I am considering the two 'waves' of responses to Sidney's death: first, the elegies published in the immediate aftermath of his death and funeral, which seek to establish him as an exemplary soldier and courtier, and second, the first portrayals of Sidney as an exemplary poet figure (often referred to as 'Astrophil' or 'Philisides'), following the printing of his works during the 1590s. For the most part, these two categories of life-narrative provided for Sidney remain distinct from each other, and there are few attempts to read his works biographically, beyond an 'identification' of Stella as Penelope Rich. Nevertheless, there is one remarkable exception: Edmund Spenser's 'Astrophel', which I argue should be read not as an unsuccessful belated elegy for Sidney but as a response to his rebirth in print and a highly innovative attempt to bridge the gap between the dead knight and the poet 'borne in *Arcady*'.

The interlude on Edmund Spenser's (lack of) afterlife in print forms a 'bridge' between Chapters 3 and 4. Surprisingly, considering that his status as one of the most eminent poets of his time was undisputed, Spenser's death in 1599 did not prompt many reactions in print, perhaps as a result of his long absence in Ireland. This section begins by examining the few known commemorative poems for Spenser and then proceeds to chart the emergence of a 'Life' of Spenser in the biographical compilations of the seventeenth century, culminating in the 'Summary of the Life of Mr. Edmond Spenser', a prefatory life published with the 1679 edition of his *Works*. Rather than merely checking them for factual errors, however (of which there are plenty), I focus on the ways in which the different accounts use and adapt anecdotes about Spenser. I argue that while they are very unlikely to be true, those anecdotes nevertheless have a narrative and structural function within the Lives and thus reveal the biographical compilers' attempts retrospectively to make sense of the life of a poet who had died several decades before.

The final section returns to the theme of poets' Lives by outlining the evolution of Izaak Walton's *Life of Donne*, stimulated by McGann's tenet that texts should not be studied in individual versions but need to be examined within the context of their entire 'life histories' of transformation through multiple editions and reproductions.[47] For this, I consider Walton's shifting emphasis in his account of Donne's career, towards a focus on moments of writing and on literary works as a reflection of an inner life. This shifting emphasis can be traced in Walton's use of Donne's writings, which develops across the different versions of his *Life of Donne* between 1640 and 1675, and which differs radically from the way in which quotation was commonly used by his contemporaries. His technique of using quotation in order to imitate the voice of his subject later allowed Walton to write the *Life of Herbert*, which, unlike the *Life of Donne* is not the Life of an exemplary clergyman that it set out to be, but the Life of a religious poet. This shift is particularly apparent in the way the *Life of Herbert* revisits the episode about the so-called anchor poems exchanged between Donne and Herbert, using it to convey a sense of their friendship as having been founded on shared poetic affinities and as having manifested itself through poetic dialogue. What I am arguing, then, is that the 'life history' of Walton's *Lives* led to his accidental discovery of a biographical technique that anticipates literary biography, which could not have happened without an awareness of the stealthy development of authorial afterlives.

As well as a chronological shift, Chapter 4 contains a shift in methodology compared to the earlier chapters, which grows out of differences in the source materials themselves. The starting-point for the earlier chapters was a thorough search of the English Short Title Catalogue (ESTC) database for biographical texts using a variety of keywords, including 'life', 'portrait', 'character' as well as 'works', 'plays' or 'poems'

---

47 McGann, *Textual Condition*, p. 9. Note that McGann's definition of 'reproduction' includes not only complete reprints but also shorter passages quoted in a different context – meaning that this footnote forms part of the transformation process of *The Textual Condition*.

(to locate biographical prefaces in collections). The search results were then grouped into broad categories by subject and form and became the basis for a chronology. Chapters 2 and 3, which chart the fashioning of biographical narratives for Sidney and Greene, show the gradual emergence of biographical assumptions about the author as a product of interaction between individual early readers with their own agendas. For this reason, excavating the use of life-details in posthumous editions as well as in modern biographies also forms part of my approach in those chapters. For the Greene chapter, the texts I examine all respond to Greene's death and retrospectively evaluate the phenomenon of his 'professional' writing career, trying to settle the question of whether it represents a pattern suitable for imitation.[48] While their authors did not write unified life-narratives any more than the early readers of Sidney did, the notion of Greene's works as forming part of his professional life offered a lot of potential for biographical readings. Even as they addressed biographical problems, such as the relative sinfulness of Greene's life, his repentance and his potential destination in the afterlife, the pamphlets written in the wake of Greene's death were above all readings of his works and considered his life in terms of his literary output. In the Sidney chapter, the evidence examined consists of texts written by Sidney's early readers responding to Sidney's death and subsequent rebirth in print, and drawing direct links between Sidney and his poetic personae. Those links were only made in individual points, and none of his early readers attempted to offer a complete reading or write a unified life-narrative for Sidney that might incorporate both the public figure and the poet. Nevertheless, those texts contain the germ of biographical reading and help to illuminate how the posthumous publication of Sidney's works in print transformed the ways in which Sidney was imagined by his readers. Both in Greene's and in Sidney's case, the collective result of the germinal biographical readings was a life-narrative of sorts which merged the author with his personae and thus effectively recreated him as a fictional character.

The closing Chapter 4 follows the evolutionary history of Walton's technique in his use of quotations from Donne's and Herbert's works, and is based on detailed comparisons between the different versions of Walton's *Lives*. At first sight, this shift in focus from the subjects of biography to the biographer may seem like an inconsistency. After all, the interest of Walton's *Lives* of Donne and Herbert lies partly in the fact that they are a phenomenon for which there is no precedent among the posthumous responses to earlier English authors. Nevertheless, Walton's *Lives* are not unconnected to the more heterogeneous and sketchy body of texts that I examine in the earlier chapters. None of those texts can in itself be called literary biography, but collectively, they contributed to create a new expectation of a connection between the life and works of an author on the part of his readers. Even Walton's own interpretation of the basic shape of Donne's life in the 1640 *Life* – that is, a teleological progression from Master Donne to Dr Donne – could be regarded as having been directly influenced by the biographically edited 1635 *Poems by J.D.*, mentioned earlier. In his

---

48 Despite this tendency of early responses to Greene's death to look back on his body of works collectively, however, Greene's reputation as a 'minor' Elizabethan writer (often included among the dismissively named 'university wits') meant that no collected editions of his works were published until the nineteenth century.

revisions of the *Life of Donne*, which were completed over a long period, Walton also entered into a dialogue with himself and his earlier readings, leading to a situation not dissimilar to the clusters of texts responding to each other's readings of Greene or Sidney examined in the earlier chapters.

One aspect this study does not cover, for reasons of space, is the influence of non-Anglophone life-writing – specifically the tradition of poets' and artists' lives that grew out of Italian humanism and that was already well established by the sixteenth century. At its beginning stood historiographic collections of great men's Lives harking back to the classical example of Suetonius or Plutarch. Initially, those collections restricted themselves to ancient subjects – as in Petrarch's *De viris illustribus*, written in the mid-fourteenth century – but soon they were expanded to include poets, as well as more recent subjects.[49] The first individual Life of a recent poet, Boccaccio's *Trattatello in laude di Dante* (begun in the 1350s and revised twice), also drew on classical precedents as well as medieval ones.[50] It was followed by a series of vernacular poets' Lives by a variety of authors, who focused particularly on the three poets by then established as the Italian 'modern classics', Dante, Petrarch and Boccaccio. Among those, the authors whose writings had perhaps the greatest impact on the development of literary biography were Leonardo Bruni and Alessandro Vellutello. Bruni, who began by translating select Lives from Plutarch into Latin at the beginning of the fifteenth century and later went on to write Lives of Dante and Petrarch, is notable for placing particular emphasis on documentary evidence.[51] Vellutello, writing in the early sixteenth century, took an approach to literary life-writing that was more firmly based on his subject's literary writings. In his 1525 edition of Petrarch's vernacular works, his rearranging of the order of the *Rime sparse* was central both to his reading of the poems as a sequence and to his reading of Petrarch's life, which he partially derived from it.[52] William Kennedy, in his study of early commentaries on Petrarch, singles out Vellutello's commentary as the first that 'develops as a narrative that seeks to confer continuity upon discontinuity, coherence upon incoherence [...] [and] constructs an alternative fiction to explain the record

49 As for example in Filippo Villani's brief Lives of famous citizens of Florence, written towards the end of the fourteenth century. For a detailed account of the structure of *De origine civitatis Florentie et de eiusdem famosis civibus* see Martin McLaughlin's essay 'Biography and Autobiography in the Italian Renaissance', in Peter France and William St Clair (eds), *Mapping Lives: The Uses of Biography* (Oxford: Oxford University Press, 2002), pp. 37–65 (p. 41). McLaughlin notes that one of the categories employed by Villani as a structuring device is called 'poets', although it is somewhat loosely defined and thus also includes 'theologians, jurists, physicians and rhetoricians'.

50 Dante had died only some thirty years before Boccaccio wrote the first version of the *Trattatello*. John Larner, in his article 'Traditions of Literary Biography in Boccaccio's *Life of Dante*' (*Bulletin of the John Rylands Library*, 72 (1990), 107–17), argues that Boccaccio was so heavily influenced by written Lives of Virgil he even adapted parts of his narrative so as to create parallels between Petrarch and Virgil.

51 For example, Bruni's Life of Dante contained quotations from letters that he claimed to have seen. McLaughlin observes that Bruni was also selective about which sources he considered to be trustworthy and decided against writing a Life of Boccaccio because he felt the biographical evidence available to him was too scant ('Biography and Autobiography in the Italian Renaissance', pp. 51–2).

52 The edition was published with a commentary and prefatory Life of Petrarch, accompanied by a counterpart Life of Laura, which attempts an identification based partly on 'evidence' found in the poems themselves.

of Petrarch's life, a version of the *Rime sparse* whose contestability draws every succeeding commentator into debate'.[53] Thus in many ways the development of Italian literary biography anticipated that of its English counterpart and can even be said to have indirectly contributed to the phenomena described in the following.

Although this study has a broadly chronological structure, the individual chapters are organised thematically and each chapter is concerned with a specific problem. One of my focal points is on tracing the way in which early modern authors' lives are narrativised both in the era itself and in the present. It is not my aim to write a history of authorship but to engage critically with modern biographical criticism, working backward to establish how the assumptions it makes came about, and scrutinising some of the narratives used in modern biography. My method is mainly based on bibliographical research, through comparing and distinguishing between editions, while paying particular attention to paratextual materials, such as dedications, prefaces and title pages. By investigating assumptions about individual authors, and also authorship in general, I hope to shed some light on a promising new area of early modern scholarship and direct greater scrutiny towards the assumptions brought into literary biography.

Using these methods, this book raises and addresses a number of questions concerning the posthumous careers of early modern authors: Did early modern readers have a coherent sense of the 'literary biography' of authors in living memory? Did publishers and editors programatically try to create biographical identities for authors whose works they were publishing posthumously? Was there a trend, specifically linked to print authorship, to view the 'whole' works of a recently deceased author not merely as his monument but as a reflection of his entire life, that is, a testament of sorts? And finally, is there a pre-history of literary biography that reaches back to the end of the sixteenth century?

---

53 William J. Kennedy, *Authorizing Petrarch* (Ithaca, NY: Cornell University Press, 1994), p. 47.

1

The complete author

Biographical readings

In 1903, Walter Raleigh, the first Professor of English at Oxford and one of the founding fathers of English literature as an academic discipline, wrote an article called 'Early Lives of the Poets'.[1] In this article he set out to trace what he called 'the late and gradual growth of an interest in the Lives of English Authors'.[2] Beginning with the sixteenth century, a period that he evidently considered to be the dark ages of English literary biography, Professor Raleigh noted that 'Elizabethan authors whose lives are fairly well known to us were always something more than mere authors'.[3] This has since become a commonplace. However, it is the observation with which Professor Raleigh followed up his point that is particularly interesting. Turning to his namesake Sir Walter Ralegh – a figure he liked to invoke, perhaps due to their shared name – he proceeded to contrast those two categories of Elizabethan authors ('mere' and 'more than mere') in terms of what survived of their life and work:

> We know more of Sir Walter Raleigh's career than of Shakespeare's and more of Essex than of Spenser. On the other hand, while the works of Shakespeare and Spenser have come down to us almost intact, most of the poems of Raleigh and Essex are lost.[4]

Professor Raleigh was responding to a historicist critical tradition that took a natural interest in the lives of authors (elsewhere in his article, he refers to biography as 'not the least valuable part of modern literary history'), yet did not necessarily draw a clear line between the career and the works of a writer.[5] That school of interpretation, which sparked projects like the *Dictionary of National Biography*, also produced what were effectively early psychoanalytical readings of poets' lives via their works. The pre-eminent example of this tradition is Edward Dowden's highly influential *Shakespeare: A Critical Study of his Mind and Art* (1875), which attempted to

---

1 The article was originally published in the very first issue of *Scottish Historical Review* (October 1903), but its main impact derived from its republication in the collection *Six Essays on Johnson* in 1910, which is the edition cited here. For the sake of clarity, I shall refer to this Walter Raleigh (who was knighted in 1911, just to add to the confusion) as 'Professor Raleigh' and use the spelling 'Ralegh' for his early modern namesake.
2 Walter Raleigh, 'Early Lives of the Poets', in *Six Essays on Johnson* (Oxford: Clarendon Press, 1910), pp. 98–127 (p. 98).
3 Raleigh, 'Early Lives of the Poets', p. 101.
4 Raleigh, 'Early Lives of the Poets', p. 101.
5 Raleigh, 'Early Lives of the Poets', p. 98.

reconstruct the dramatist's state of mind from his works by examining the plays in chronological order, to explore the development of 'the personality of the writer'.[6] Its main argument – which remained popular into the twentieth century – was that each of the plays mirrors a particular stage in Shakespeare's spiritual and emotional development.[7] Thus, according to Dowden, the sum of all plays was what he (in a perhaps unintentional bibliographical pun) called the 'complete Shakespeare'. Professor Raleigh, by contrast, is more careful in distinguishing between 'works' and 'career', which in his usage is almost synonymous with 'life'. After noting the lack of information about the careers of Shakespeare and Spenser, as well as the loss of most of Ralegh's and Essex's poetry, he moved on to interpret his observation by anticipating Richard Helgerson's division of early modern poets into 'amateurs' and 'laureates'. Thus Professor Raleigh argued that it was ultimately a question of class, and the loss of Ralegh's and Essex's poems was a result of the fact that 'men of position held professional authorship in some contempt'.[8] While the attitudes of 'men of position' might explain why Essex or Ralegh would not have aspired to see their poetry published in print, the medium of professional authorship, it nevertheless fails to account for the apparent lack of public interest in the lives of 'mere authors' after their deaths.

Professor Raleigh's conclusion perhaps oversimplified matters, yet I would argue that his initial observation – that there is a link between a relative absence of 'lives' and the presence of works – could provide a step towards an explanation for the scarcity of biographical material on the majority of early modern poets. Rather than an expression of elitist contempt or the difficulty of 'persuad[ing] man that his contemporaries are valuable and important persons', it could be an indication that interest in the lives of authors was transferred to their writings.[9] A significant part of sixteenth-century readers' interest in the lives of poets manifested itself in an engagement with their afterlives as authorial presences through biographical readings of their works. This phenomenon can be observed especially in sixteenth-century responses to recently dead authors. Thus an ideal starting-point for tracing the origins of early modern traditions of 'lives of the poets' and biographical reading can be found in the first collected works of an English author edited by one of his own contemporaries: *The workes of Sir Thomas More Knyght, sometym Chauncellour of England, written by him in the Englysh tonge* (1557).[10] Published during Mary's reign by More's nephew, William Rastell, *The workes of Sir Thomas More* shows signs of an editorial approach that could be termed 'biographical' editing. Though it was not a 'biography' of More, it arranged and framed More's English works in such a manner as to associate them with specific phases or events in More's life. Additionally, Rastell used introductory glosses both to create transitions between texts and to point out the biographical

---

6 Edward Dowden, *Shakespeare: A Critical Study of his Mind and Art* (London: Henry S. King, 1875), p. v.
7 As late as 1906, Lytton Strachey – Professor Raleigh's cousin and fellow founding father of English as an academic subject – criticised only Dowden's conclusion (in his essay 'Shakespeare's Final Period') but did not question the priciple of regarding the author as the sum of his characters.
8 Raleigh, 'Early Lives of the Poets', p. 101.
9 Raleigh, 'Early Lives of the Poets', p. 100.
10 It was also the first edition of *Works* of an English author to be published since the Henrician editions of Chaucer's works (some of which will be discussed in the next section of this chapter).

connections to his readers. The effect of this editorial strategy is to increase the authorial presence of More within the volume by turning his life – including his public life
– into a point of reference for reading the works.

Rastell's dedicatory epistle to the queen (trusting that 'it may please god to graunt
your highnes lo[n]g to reigne ouer us') reveals some of his motivations in publishing
the works of his 'dere vncle'.[11] The epistle praises the literary, moral and doctrinal
excellence of More's writing, while simultaneously stressing his Englishness: although
it is only two pages long, the epistle contains no fewer than eight words referring to
Englishness, of which seven are clustered on the first page.[12] Rastell is eager to portray
More not only as a Catholic martyr – which arguably would have been sufficient if
his sole motivation had been to further his own career through association with his
famous relative – but also as a distinguished author of national significance, worthy
of canonisation in both fields. By claiming that More's works are such as should be
'ioyously embrased and had in estymacion of all trew Englyshe hartes' (Cii^b), Rastell
is presenting appreciation of those works as a touchstone of 'trew' Englishness. He
even implicitly suggests that More the exemplary martyr may possess the ability to
convert heretics from beyond the grave through his 'worthy workes' (Cii^b), and thus
help to create a Catholic nation uniting all 'trew Englyshe hartes'.[13]

In *Writing the Nation in Reformation England* (2004), Cathy Shrank has argued
that humanism helped to shape not only the Reformation but also Tudor discourses
of nationhood, by equipping authors with the 'tools' for exploring ideas of national
identity. Shrank notes that in a sense this was an act of appropriation, pointing
out that they 'reapplied their learning to national ends, a shift away from Morean
or Erasmian humanism that also demonstrates the increasing secularization of
learning'.[14] *The Workes of Syr Thomas More* in a sense exemplifies this shift, since
Rastell is reapplying his learning both by defining More's significance through a
notion of Englishness and, conversely, defining Englishness through More's writings
and their nation-building powers. At the same time, however, it is a highly unusual
example. While Rastell's rhetoric closely resembles that of the Protestant nation-
writers Shrank's study focuses on, the England he is evoking in his epistle is a hypothetical one in which the effects of the Reformation have been reversed – effectively
a Catholic counter-nation.

It is remarkable that in his bid to have his 'dere vncle' recognised as an unof-
ficial patron saint of sorts, Rastell chose to portray him as an exemplary author in
'the Englysh tonge', as well as a martyr and an important political figure. In this,
his approach markedly differed from that of More's son-in-law William Roper,

---

11 *The Workes of Sir Thomas More* (1557), Cii^a. Rastell's hope that Mary stood at the beginning of a long
    reign was to be disappointed, however, since the queen died the following year.
12 The words are 'England', 'Englishman', 'Englyshe hartes' and 'the Englysh tonge'. Of these, the most
    frequently used is 'Englysh tonge', which Rastell mentions three times. Note also the double mention
    of 'England' / 'Englysh tonge' in the full title of the volume.
13 'I truste this boke shalbe moste acceptable […] for […] it beinge red of many, as it is likely to be, shall
    much helpe forwarde your Maiesties most godly purpose, in purging this youre realme of all wicked
    heresies' (Cii^b).
14 Cathy Shrank, *Writing the Nation in Reformation England, 1530–1580* (Oxford: Oxford University
    Press, 2004), p. 20.

whose *Mirrour of vertue in worldly greatnes, Or the life of Syr Thomas More Knight* was written in the same decade as Rastell's edition of More's works.[15] As historical studies of biography tend to point out, Roper's *Life of Syr Thomas More* does not aim to present its readers with the life of the author of *Utopia*. In his generic study, *The Nature of Biography*, Robert Gittings even termed Roper's omission of *Utopia* a 'notable and obvious [gap] [...] which a modern writer would never allow [since it is] the first thing a present-day reader would wish to hear about'.[16] In fact, the omission is 'obvious' in more than one sense: Roper's decision not to mention *Utopia* is not only the first thing a 'present-day reader' might notice about the *Life of Syr Thomas More*, it is equally 'obvious' given the life-writing conventions he was drawing on. As indicated by the full title of the *Life of Syr Thomas More*, Roper's account of More's life focuses on his 'worldly greatnes' and his 'vertue'. Consequently, it aims to present the life of a humanist exemplifying the concept of *vita activa* – not the life of a 'mere author'.

Rastell, on the other hand, is seeking to portray More the English author and his evolution over time, in parallel to More the exemplary humanist and politician (whom he considers to be sufficiently well known to need little introduction). He begins his *Workes of Sir Thomas More* with a group of comparatively frivolous texts that are not listed in the table of contents: 'fowre things [...] Mayster Thomas More wrote in his youth for his pastime'. Since Rastell otherwise arranges More's works in chronological order, the positioning of the 'fowre thinges' within the volume, along with their subheadings – which all repeat Rastell's claim they were written by 'Mayster' More 'in hys youth' – creates the impression that they are juvenilia. This impression may be misleading, however, since the only one of the four texts that can be safely dated must have been written by More when he was in his mid-twenties.[17] It is unlikely that Rastell is deliberately trying to mislead readers about More's age when he wrote the 'fowre thinges'. Nevertheless, he has clearly grouped them together to act as a prelude both to the works proper and to the mature More. Ascribing the lighter texts of the volume to More's youth allows Rastell to avert any suspicions that his collection might be treating him as (to borrow Professor Raleigh's phrase) a 'mere author'. At the same time, redefining the 'fowre thinges' as juvenilia allows him to incorporate the lighter side of More's character and his known fondness for 'mery iests' into the volume without causing any conflict with the more serious nature of the remaining texts or the figure of More the martyr.[18]

Rastell's way of introducing More's 'fowre thinges', then, serves to contextualise

---

15 It was not published in print until 1626, however.

16 Robert Gittings, *The Nature of Biography* (London: Heineman, 1978), pp. 24–5.

17 The text in question is an elegy for Henry VII's wife Elizabeth, who died in 1503. The remaining three 'thinges' are a 'mery iest' written in Skeltonic metre, a pageant about the ages of man and the 'preface to the book of fortune', a poem in three parts.

18 The early accounts of More's life contain references to pranks played by More (interestingly, they do not specify that these took place during his youth), and the play *Sir Thomas More* (*c.* 1593) contains several scenes highlighting More's playful nature. Although the anecdotes themselves may not be true (for example, one of the anecdotes in *Sir Thomas More* recycles an anecdote from John Foxe's account of the life of Thomas Cromwell), this nevertheless indicates that playfulness was regarded as one of More's prominent characteristics both by his contemporaries and by the following generation.

them and to provide a link between his works and his life. Throughout the *Workes of Sir Thomas More*, he continues to make such links, especially in the miscellaneous section at the end of the volume, which represents the final years of More's life. That section comprises 'deuout and vertuous instruccions, meditacions, and prayers' composed during his imprisonment, a number of letters by More intended to illustrate his character (for example his sense of justice in reimbursing his neighbour for the damage caused by a fire that had spread from one of More's barns) as well as his epitaph. Rastell includes these despite the fact that most of them were not originally written in 'the Englysh tonge'. They are reproduced both in Latin and in English translation and given a greater amount of contextualisation than the texts written before More's imprisonment, so that in some cases, the supplementary information provided by Rastell is longer than the text it is supplementing, as with More's epitaph. This epitaph perfectly illustrates what Greenblatt called 'the complex interplay in More's life and writings of self-fashioning and self-cancellation, the crafting of a public role and the desire to escape from the identity so crafted'.[19] More's epitaph was written shortly after he resigned as chancellor in 1532. It presents More's resignation as a renouncement of worldly life rather than as a political necessity, and the composing of an epitaph outlining his own lifetime achievements as a pious man's act of devotion to prepare himself for death and eternity. Through being placed outside its chronological context and grouped with later texts that were written during More's imprisonment, the epitaph acquires additional significance and thus becomes the epitaph of a saint who chose martyrdom rather than that of a politician who resigned out of protest.

I have outlined Rastell's editorial strategies in *The workes of Sir Thomas More* in some detail, because they show his interest in engaging with More the author as well as More the future saint.[20] By assuming prior knowledge of the key stages of More's life on his readers' part and using them as points of reference in his editorial glosses, Rastell creates a text that attempts to link More's life and works. Rastell's methods

---

19 Stephen Greenblatt, *Renaissance Self-Fashioning* (Chicago: University of Chicago Press, 1980), pp. 12–13. Greenblatt does not cite the epitaph as an example of this, however.

20 More is not a 'literary' writer of the kind I shall be examining in later chapters, and those among his works that could be classified as 'poetry' according to Sidney's definition only represent a fraction of his oeuvre. Nevertheless, it is important to note that More was persistently associated with imaginative writing both by his contemporaries and by the following generations, although the significance of this association shifted dramatically. During his lifetime, it was predominantly a negative association, used by More's opponents to discredit his arguments as mere rhetoric. In the 1583 edition of *Actes and Monuments*, for example, Foxe accuses More of supporting his 'heresies' by 'mighty argumentes, as big as milpostes, fet out of Utopia, from whence, thou must know reader, can come not fittons but all fine Poetrie' (p. 1008). For later generations, by contrast, treating More as a 'poet' offered a relatively safe way of acknowledging More's eminence and claiming him as a figure of national importance while avoiding the more problematic issue of his religious views. In the play *Sir Thomas More*, written some fifty years after More's execution, his life is portrayed as dominated by an inner conflict between More's 'poetic' nature and his political office that forces him to suppress it. As the play progresses and More withdraws from political life, he becomes increasingly poetified, increasingly speaks in verse and even refers to himself as a poet. In order to further highlight this conflict between poetry and politics, the authors of the play, in a deliberate anachronism, turn the character of Surrey into Surrey, the poet of *Tottels Miscellany* fame, who was still in his teens when More died (historically, the Surrey of *Sir Thomas More* should be Thomas Howard, the poet's father, who held the title until he became Duke of Norfolk).

are perhaps not the most effective. For the most part, his glosses do little more than gesture from More's writings towards the known facts about his life, and ultimately they fail to add up to the figure of More the author of national significance Rastell tries to evoke in his dedicatory epistle. Nevertheless, he confronts some of the key problems of biography and displays a degree of interest in More the author that is surprising in a mid-sixteenth-century context. In many ways, Rastell's strategy in proposing More as a national writer closely resembles the 'noisy protestations of [...] Englishness' Cathy Shrank has noted in the writings of his contemporary, Andrew Borde.[21] Yet while it was no doubt one of Rastell's aims to promote his own loyalty to the Catholic cause (and the Catholic queen) by proxy, his edition of More's work also suggests a notion of a complete life. The portrait of the 'Englysh' More that Rastell presents to his readers is not intended to replace that of the 'wyse and godlie' human-ist best remembered for his Latin writings, but to complement and enhance it, leading readers to a fuller understanding of More's greatness. For that reason, the *Workes of Thomas More* should be viewed not merely as a 'valuable resource, including mate-rial that would otherwise have been lost' (as Rastell's *DNB* entry calls it).[22] Instead, it should be treated as part of an early modern discourse of national literary conscious-ness, as well as an early example of biographical reading strategies that played an integral part in the pre-history of literary biography.

This chapter investigates the twin questions of what the established patterns of early modern life-writing are, and why they seem so inadequate when applied to the lives of poets. For this purpose, I shall first outline some problems of early modern 'biography' before moving on to examine in some detail two lives of poets written at the extreme ends of the period covered. Thomas Speght's 'Life of Geffrey Chaucer' (1598) and Gerard Langbaine's 'Life of Abraham Cowley' (1691) were both pub-lished considerably later than Rastell's edition of More's works and take constrast-ing approaches to narrativising the lives of their subjects. This raises two questions. First, what shifts in attitude towards the concept of authorship in general and literary authorship in particular do those two texts reflect? And second, what caused those shifts?

'Unrelated and fragmentary statements': early modern life-writing and Speght's 'Life of Chaucer'

Scholars of the history of biography face one major obstacle when writing about early modern biography: on close inspection, there is no such thing as early modern biography. While there are numerous texts about the lives of famous or remarkable people, referring to these texts as the term 'biographies' is nevertheless something of an anachronism.[23] More importantly, it is also too generic – which is misleading,

---

21 Shrank, *Writing the Nation*, p. 33.
22 J. H. Baker, 'Rastell, William (1508–1565)', *Oxford DNB*.
23 For most of the early modern period, the word 'life' was used in contexts where 'biography' would be used in modern English. The earliest examples of the word 'biography' in English begin to appear during the early 1660s (for example, John Fell's *The Life and Death of Dr. Thomas Fuller* (1661) and James Heath's *Flagellum, or the Life and Death, Birth and Burial of Oliver Cromwell* (1663), both refer

because the texts are too varied in length, content and form to be truly considered a genre.[24]

Grouping those texts loosely as 'life-writing' offers a partial solution to the generic problem, while also shifting the focus of attention away from questions of content and towards compositional aspects by removing the non-fictional connotations of the term 'biography'.[25] That is, by treating it as a piece of 'life-writing' rather than a 'biography', the question of whether a given written life is a 'true' account or not becomes less significant than questions about its writer and the way in which it is written. However, even the term 'life-writing' fails to convey an accurate sense of the diversity of texts included in this category.[26] This diversity is perhaps best illustrated by the detailed classification of the 'distinct, though overlapping, types' of early modern life-writing proposed by Thomas Mayer and D. R. Woolf. This classification system groups the texts according to their form and subject matter as well as the traditions that inform them (classical, humanist, ecclesiastical, hagiographic and Protestant).[27] Yet the problem of this classification system – one of the most comprehensive to date – lies in its very comprehensiveness: it consists of eighteen different categories, and definitively assigning a text to one of them proves far from simple in practice, because they are not in fact as clear-cut as they appear at first sight.

Since the notion of biography as a genre is absent from early modern life-writing, it is not surprising that 'lives' written during the sixteenth and seventeenth century fail to live up to modern expectations in terms of form and content. During the first

to themselves as biographies). Donald Stauffer consequently hypothesises that the word may have been 'imported from France at the time of the Restoration', although he notes with some dismay that 'no satisfactory appeal may be made to French lexicons as to whether the word _biographie_ was then in common use' (_English Biography Before 1700_ (Cambridge, MA: Harvard University Press, 1930), p. 219). The word does appear to have been current in French prior to the seventeenth century – Antoine du Verdier's _Biographie et Prosopographie des Roys de France_ was published in 1583 and reprinted only a few years later, although the word only featured in the title of the book, not in the book itself.

24 An ESTC search for titles between 1500 and 1700 containing the word 'life' produces numerous results, including extracts from chronicles charting the reigns of individual kings, saints' lives (usually translated from French or Spanish), guides to leading a good Christian life and funeral sermons (such as those for Katherine Brettergh and Katherine Stubbes, which were still reprinted up to forty years after their deaths and evidently used as instructional texts). Perhaps more surprisingly, however, early modern texts whose titles declare them to be 'lives' of some sort also include broadsheets and pamphlets recording the deeds of notorious criminals, romances and a number of plays. With these, the word 'life' in the title often seems to act as an indication that the play features central characters based on historical persons, such as Simon Eyre in Thomas Dekker's _The Shoo-Makers Holy-Day_, Vittoria Corombona in John Webster's _The White Diuel_ or the title characters of several of Shakespeare's history plays.

25 See Leon Edel's argument for the non-fictional status of biography in _Writing Lives: Principia Biographica_ (London: Norton, 1987), an approach to biography from a (twentieth-century) biographer's point of view: 'Are biographies a kind of fiction? Some critics hold this belief. But they are wrong. [...] Novelists have omniscience. Biographers never do' (p. 15).

26 For recent criticism of the category, see for example Debora Shuger's observation that even 'life-writing' is too much of a 'catchall label' for a group of texts that 'neither belong to a single genealogy nor establish an intertextual order among themselves' ('Life-writing in seventeenth-century England', in Patrick Coleman, Jayne Lewis and Jill Kowalik (eds), _Representations of the Self from the Renaissance to Romanticism_ (Cambridge: Cambridge University Press, 2000), pp. 63–78 (p. 63)).

27 Thomas F. Mayer and D. R. Woolf (eds), _The Rhetoric of Life-Writing in Early Modern Europe_ (Ann Arbor: University of Michigan Press, 1995), p. 13.

half of the twentieth century, the most common approach was to regard early modern life-writing either as failed attempts at or as crude precursors of biography.[28] In more recent studies, on the other hand, there has been a tendency to resolve the problem of the apparent non-existence of early modern biography (despite an abundance of 'lives') by proposing another narrative of emergence.[29] This approach can for example be found at the beginning of Kevin Sharpe and Steven N. Zwicker's preface to their jointly edited collection *Writing Lives*: 'Early modern England [was] the place and time in which what we recognise, and what contemporaries began to describe, as biography emerged from myriad forms of representing lives.'[30] This too would lead one to assume that early modern lives of poets would be exactly the right source to turn to in order to witness the emergence of the author in action. As an as yet unfixed category of writing, early modern life-writing might be expected to lend itself particularly well to recording changing attitudes towards the lives of its subjects. However, there is a conspicuous lack of early modern written lives of poets.

Until the late seventeenth century, authors' lives almost exclusively take the shape of biographical prefaces to their works (most commonly, these prefaces are found in editions of 'complete' works, especially those published posthumously). This could be a consequence of the inherently 'prefatory' nature of authors' lives: after all, their main function is to act as a supplement to a known body of works. Even in seventeenth-century authors' lives that were published separately from their works, there is often a close link to prefaces. Perhaps the best example of this is Izaak Walton's *Life of Donne*, whose development across several versions I shall trace in Chapter 4. It was initially conceived as a preface to a collection of Donne's sermons in 1640 and later expanded into the separately published version of 1658. Conversely, Walton's *Life of Herbert* was first published separately in 1670 but subsequently prefixed to all editions of Herbert's *The Temple* printed between 1674 and 1799.

Although this study focuses on the afterlives of early modern English poets, the key principles of biographical prefaces are in fact best illustrated by examining a text written by a Scottish publisher, to introduce the works of a Scottish author. In 1568, Edinburgh publisher Henry Charteris wrote a preface for his revised edition of the works of herald and historiographer Sir David Lyndsay, who had died in 1555. Charteris's preface is of particular interest here because it begins with a curiously self-reflexive passage in which he expresses his views on the established practices of preface-writing for collected works. This is done mainly to justify his decision to deviate from those practices, since Charteris goes on to argue that Lyndsay is still so well remembered that there is no need to introduce him to the reader in the established manner:

---

28 One of the most extreme positions is maintained by Harold Nicolson in *The Development of English Biography* (London: Hogarth Press, 1927). He dismisses all pre-Romantic life-writing as 'impure' (p. 8) and claims that while 'the seventeenth century [...] offered an immense opportunity [for biography], the opportunity was missed' (p. 38).

29 A notable counterexample is Alan Stewart's early modern volume of the *Oxford History of Life-Writing* (Oxford: Oxford University Press, 2018), which chooses instead to focus on fifteen case studies of lives or groups of lives.

30 Kevin Sharpe and Steven N. Zwicker (eds), *Writing Lives: Biography and Textuality, Identity and Representation in Early Modern England* (Oxford: Oxford University Press, 2008), pp. 1–2.

It is the common and accustomed manner [...] of those writing proems for another man's works mainly to concern themselves with two points. One is to explain the characteristics of the author, not only external, such as his parentage, birth, vocation, estate, strength, physical appearance [...] but also internal [...]. The other is to present his manner of writing, the utility of his works, and what benefits a diligent reader may gain from them.[31]

Charteris's outline of the 'commoun and accustomit maner' of preface-writing is relevant in this context because it illustrates two key aspects of the responses to recently dead authors and their works during the second half of the sixteenth century. First, through his list of the 'properteis' a prefatory life of an author could be expected to address, Charteris's account of preface-writing hints at a typical structure for a written life. Second, there is a clear separation between the 'twa pointis' of the author's life and his works, without any indication that a preface-writer could (or should) attempt to bridge them and write the life of the author *as an author*.

The type of prefatory life prefixed to a posthumous edition of works that Charteris describes in his preface to Lyndsay's works, then, represents a common form of life-narrative for print authors that existed during the late sixteenth and early seventeenth century. For authors of poetry, however, this treatment was initially less common. The earliest prefatory life of an English poet is Thomas Speght's 'Life of Chaucer', published with his 1598 edition of Chaucer's works.

It is fitting that the earliest life of a writer in English should be a life of Geoffrey Chaucer, as he is the most archetypal English author figure during the early modern period. As early as 1532, William Thynne, a royal clerk to Henry VIII and editor of the first complete printed edition of Chaucer's works, had acknowledged Chaucer's special role within English literary history by including a preface written by Brian Tuke (another senior clerk of Henry VIII's household).[32] Tuke's preface is an ambitious essay, which begins not with Chaucer but with the origins of language and the development of English, a process that Tuke portrays as a constant downward spiral – until the miraculous appearance of Chaucer in the midst of linguistic barbarism:

[I]t is moch to be maruayled, how in hys tyme, when doutlesse al good letters were layde a slepe throughoute the worlde, as the thynge whyche eyther by the dysposition and influence of the bodyes aboue, or by other ordinaunce of God, semed lyke and was in daunger to haue vtterly peryshed, such an excellent poete in our tonge shuld as it were nature repugnyng sprynge and aryse.[33]

---

31 Due to the different spelling conventions in sixteenth-century Scots, I have modernised this passage for ease of reference. The original reads: 'It is the commoun and accustomit maner [...] of all thame quhilk dois prohemiate vpon ony vther manis wark, cheiflie to trauel about twa pointis. The ane is, to declair the properteis of ye Authour, nocht onlie externall, as his originall, birth, vocatioun, estait, strenth, giftis of the bodie [...]: bot alswa internall [...]. The vther is, to declair his maner of wryting, the vtilitie of his warkis, & quhat frute, profite, and commoditie may ensew and follow to the diligent reidar.' *The warkis of the famous and vorthie Knicht Schir Dauid Lyndesay of the Mont* (Edinburgh, 1568), ✝ii^a. By 'internall [properteis]' Charteris essentially means personality traits.

32 For the attribution of the preface to Tuke rather than Thynne, see Greg Walker, *Writing Under Tyranny* (Oxford: Oxford University Press, 2005), pp. 60–5.

33 *The Workes of Geffray Chaucer newly printed* (1532), A.ii^b.

This is an early version of a narrative of authorial emergence, although 'extraction' may be a more appropriate term. Ultimately, Tuke is seeking to prove that Chaucer is not a medieval poet, and he praises him in terms that isolate him from his own historical period. This is particularly evident in the contrast between '*hys* tyme' and '*our* tonge' (emphases added). Tuke's sentence about the emergence of the 'excellent poet' clearly associates Chaucer with the latter, paradoxically implying that Chaucer is closer to his sixteenth-century readers than he was to his own contemporaries.

Yet although Tuke's preface to the 1532 edition stresses Chaucer's linguistic, even national, significance, it betrays no particular interest in his life.[34] Chaucer is defined through his body of work and his role as a messianic saviour of the English language, but Chaucer the historical figure appears to be peripheral to the narrative. This had clearly changed by the time Thomas Speght, a schoolmaster and antiquary, published his edition of Chaucer's works in 1598, with the help of veteran Chaucer editor John Stow (who had edited his own edition in 1561).[35] In fact, Speght's own contribution to the volume lay not so much in the editing of the texts as in the wealth of supplementary materials he added. These include the first substantial glossary to Chaucer's works (containing over 2,000 headwords, not all of which strictly required explanation) and a fifteen-page 'Life of our Learned *English Poet*, Geffrey Chaucer'.

While Speght's life of Chaucer is usually cited as the first life of an English writer, representing a milestone in the history of biography, scholars of biography tend to be less than enthusiastic about the life itself. Most modern scholars still essentially share Richard D. Altick's view of the text, voiced in 1965:

> [Speght] gathered all the facts then known, or what purported to be the facts, about Chaucer the man. This was the first 'life', in the English language, of a great English poet. It makes 1598 as good a year as any from which to date the beginnings of English literary biography.
>
> Nobody reads Speght today, for his biographical introduction is only a heap of unrelated and fragmentary statements on the topics listed.[36]

Altick is of course right to point out that Speght's 'Life of Chaucer' does not live up to the expectations a twentieth-century reader like him might have of the biography of a 'great English poet'. Nevertheless, he is perhaps too rash in dismissing it as a garbled heap of factual fragments that constitute a failed attempt to portray 'Chaucer the man'.

Contrary to what Altick's comment may suggest, Speght's life of Chaucer is in fact a very carefully structured text (see figure 1). It contains clear transitions between the individual parts and its shifts in focus show a progression, as the text moves from Chaucer's origins as a 'learned English Poet' (under the headings of 'Countrey',

---

34 See Greg Walker's argument that the edition had a political purpose and was intended as a 'subtly coded call for religious stability and consensus' (*Writing under Tyranny*, p. 56).

35 Stow is best known for his *Survay of London* (1598), a detailed topographical description of the city, but he also worked as a literary editor. He also edited the works of another major English poet, John Skelton, as *Pithy pleasaunt and profitable workes of maister Skelton, Poete Laureate* (1568).

36 Richard D. Altick, 'Literary Biography Before its Time', in *Lives and Letters: A History of Literary Biography in England and America* (New York: Alfred A. Knopf, 1965), pp. 3–4. Alan Stewart's volume on early modern life-writing refers to Speght's life of Chaucer, which he labels with the ambivalent adjective 'antiquarian', only once (*Oxford History of Life-writing*, p. 218).

'Parentage' and 'Education') to his private life as a wealthy landowner and head of family ('Mariage', 'Children' and 'Reuenues'), his public life at court ('Seruice', 'Reward' and 'Friends') and finally his posthumous fame and afterlife ('Books' and 'Death'). In the diagram on the first page of the 'Life', which acts as a table of contents, the same structure is replicated in miniature for Chaucer's children.

While it certainly charts a life, Speght's 'Life of Chaucer' is based on a concept of complete and exemplary life – that is, the kind of life worth recording – within which Chaucer's life as a poet is of little or no importance. Instead, Speght is concerned with associating Chaucer with a specific class and identifying him with certain social roles: the scholar, the patriarch and the esteemed servant of his king.

Speght devotes more than a page to the origin of Chaucer's family, seeking to refute claims that Chaucer's name implies that he came from a 'mean' family of recent immigrants.[37] For this purpose, he provides a reproduction of Chaucer's coat of arms to prove his point that any heralds who see it as an indication of his humble origins are wrong.[38] In the second edition of the *Workes of Geffrey Chaucer* (published in 1602), the title page specifically mentions that there have been 'in the life of Chaucer many things inserted', and the most substantial of those changes are in the section about Chaucer's parentage. Many of Speght's changes in the second edition, including those to 'the Life of Chaucer', were occasioned by the 1599 *Animauersions* of Francis Thynne, the Chaucer editor's son. These *Animaduersions* had used the format of a lengthy letter to the editor, in which Thynne had pointed out all the mistakes and inaccuracies he had found.[39] Partly in response to Thynne's criticism, Speght's efforts to ennoble Chaucer have become even more forceful in the second edition. He provides several additional sources to support his theory that by the time Chaucer was born his family had long been naturalised (before concluding with a flourish: 'But what need I to stand vpon the antiquitie or gentry of Chaucer, when the Role of Battle Abbey affirmeth Chaucer to haue come in with the Conqueror' (b.iii^a)). Additionally, Speght rephrases some of his earlier statements. For example, the speculative phrase 'I [...] rather must thinke', which had introduced the Speght's claim that 'the parents of Geffrey Chaucer were meere English, and he himselfe an Englishman borne' (b.ii^b) in the 1598 edition, becomes the confident assertion that '[m]oreouer *it is more likely* that the parents of Geffrey Chaucer were meere English, and he himselfe an Englishman borne' (b.iii^a) in the 1602 version (emphasis added).

Derek Pearsall regards this as an early instance of the 'plain snobbery among English biographers' concerning Chaucer's family origins, claiming that Speght was 'embarrassed at having the Father of English Poetry turn out to be the son of a wine merchant'.[40] However, Speght's defensiveness about Chaucer's origins need not be

---

37 'Chaucer' is a derivation of the French 'chausseur' ('shoemaker').
38 John Guillim's heraldic treatise *A Display of Heraldry* (1610) clearly shares Speght's view. It reproduces Chaucer's coat of arms as an example of a type of arms 'both honourable and ancient' and uses the explanatory text to compliment not only Chaucer, 'the most learned of Poets', but also Speght, 'the most learned of Antiquaries' (p. 274).
39 In reality, the length of the *Animaduersions* makes them more of a pamphlet: in the 1865 print edition published by the Early English Text Society, this 'letter' runs to nearly sixty pages.
40 Derek Pearsall, 'The Problems of Writing a Life of Chaucer', *Studies in the Age of Chaucer*, 13 (1991), 5–14 (p. 13).

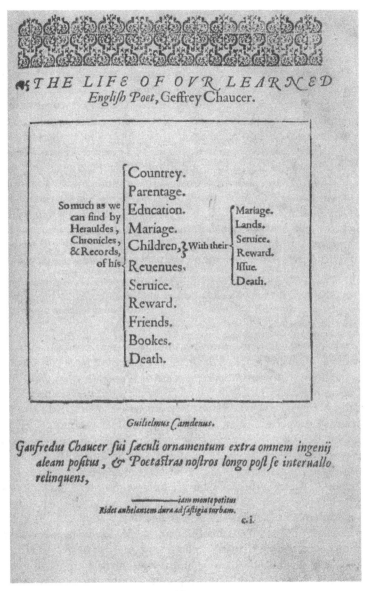

THE LIFE OF OVR LEARNED
Englifh Poet, Geffrey Chaucer.

| So much as we can find by Herauldes, Chronicles, & Records, of his | Countrey.
Parentage.
Education.
Mariage.
Children, With their
Reuenues.
Seruice.
Reward.
Friends.
Bookes.
Death. | Mariage.
Lands.
Seruice.
Reward.
Iſſue.
Death. |

Guilielmus Camdenus,

Gaufredus Chaucer ſui ſæculi ornamentum extra omnem ingenij
aleam poſitus, & Poetaſtras noſtros longo poſt ſe interuallo
relinquens,

——————*iam monte potitus*
Ridet anhelantem dura ad faſtigia turbam.
c.i.

4 Contents page of Speght's 'Life of Chaucer' (1598)

purely due to class snobbery. There is also an element of self-justification, as he was clearly aware that he was writing the life of someone who did not strictly fit among the people whose exemplary lives were generally considered worth writing (and reading) by his contemporaries. A similar form of self-justification can still be found much later, in Thomas Fuller's *History of the Worthies of England* (1662), which generally devotes very little space to poets. One of the few exceptions is Chaucer, and to justify his inclusion, Fuller particularly stresses Chaucer's 'laureate' status, which provided the poet with a royal seal of approval.[41] He is also eager to point out that this and 'many other boons' were a reward because '*Chaucer*, besides his poetical accomplishments, did the King service both in war and peace, as Souldier and Embassadour'.[42]

While Fuller names the 'poetical accomplishments' first, Speght presents Chaucer's poetry as tangential to an exemplary life rather than the reason why it should be considered exemplary, implying that Chaucer's fame as a poet alone would not be a sufficient reason for writing his life. Speght's 'Life of Chaucer' should therefore not merely be regarded as a clumsy attempt to write the life of a poet but as a conscious effort to ennoble that poet by portraying him not primarily as a poet but rather as someone who led an 'active' life and also wrote poetry. This attitude towards writing as ancillary to the biographies of writers can still be found in much later texts. In his preface to *Lives of the most Famous English Poets* (1686) – one of the seventeenth-century biographical compilations that I shall discuss in more detail in the next section of this chapter – William Winstanley defends his inclusion of people not primarily known as poets by implicitly acknowledging the superiority of their non-poetic achievements:

> It may likewise be objected that some of these Poets here mentioned, have been more famous in other kind of Studies than in Poetry, and therefore do not shine here as their proper sphere of fame; but what then, shall their general knowledge debar them from a particular notice of their Abilities in this most excellent Art?[43]

Winstanley is thus anxious to point out that he is merely proposing their poetic achievements as supplementary to their 'proper sphere of fame'. In Chaucer's case, the 'proper sphere' is of course his reputation as a poet, but Speght's 1598 'Life of Chaucer' nevertheless essentially corresponds to the pattern described as 'commoun and accustomit' by Henry Charteris thirty years earlier, which had placed emphasis on the 'externall properteis' of an author's life. The innovation of Speght's 'Life of Chaucer', then, lies not so much in its format as in the fact that it is being applied to a subject whose fame was exclusively owed to his poetic works. The limitations of the format with regard to narrating the lives of poets are apparent in the final section of Speght's text, 'His Death'. This is by far the longest section of the 'Life of Chaucer' and takes up five pages, which corresponds to a third of the 'Life'. Although it begins with a paragraph describing Chaucer's death and burial, the section is in fact mainly concerned with the aftermath of Chaucer's death, specifically its poetic aftermath.

In order to demonstrate Chaucer's literary significance to his readers, Speght in the final section of the 'Life of Chaucer' summarises the reception history of Chaucer among his fellow poets, from his contemporaries to the present day. After quoting Chaucer's epitaph and the inscription on his monument, Speght moves on to poetic tributes by contemporaries and near-contemporaries (mainly Hoccleve and Lydgate),

---

41 Fuller's later readers may have considered this achievement of Chaucer's even more impressive after the position had been revived and given a more official status with the appointment of John Dryden as poet laureate in 1668.
42 Thomas Fuller, *A History of the Worthies of England* (1662), p. 27.
43 William Winstanley, *The Lives of the Most famous English Poets* (1686), a3ª.

as well as 'men of later time' (c.iii[a]). Among the latter, he particularly highlights the two major English poets of the 1590s, Sir Philip Sidney and Edmund Spenser.[44] Speght's use of Spenser is especially interesting, because he reads Spenser's 'discourse of friendship' (Book IV of *The Faerie Queene*, which bears the subtitle 'of friendship' and had been published only two years earlier in the second edition of the poem) as a tribute to Chaucer, 'thinking himselfe most worthy to be Chaucer's friend, for his like naturall disposition that Chaucer had' (c.iii[a]).

Speght's account of Spenser's indebtedness to Chaucer for Book IV is a little misleading. While the book does begin by continuing the Squire's Tale, one of the fragmentary Canterbury Tales, most of it does not follow in the footing of Chaucer's feet. Nevertheless, Speght is evidently fascinated by the idea of a 'friendship' between the two great English poets. In order to illustrate this idea, he even reproduces a quatrain from *The Faerie Queene*, which on close inspection turns out to be a merging of the final couplets of two different stanzas:

> Dan Chaucer, Well of English vndefiled,
> On Fames eternal beadrole worthy to be filed.
> I follow here the footing of thy feet,
> That with thy meaning so I may the rather meet.[45]

By combining the two final couplets, Speght achieves the effect of making the address to Chaucer more direct and personal than it appears in its original context, turning it from the respectful acknowledging of a source into a testimony of the 'friendship' and like-mindedness of two great poets.[46] Nevertheless, Speght does not go as far as to suggest a literary influence of Chaucer on the poets he cites, and thus the final section of his 'Life of Chaucer' perhaps falls slightly short of what it sets out to do. The passages he cites and paraphrases primarily serve the function of proving Chaucer's exemplariness as a poet by demonstrating that he has always been held in high esteem by other poets, who have consistently 'carried this reuerend conceit of our Poet, and openly declared the same by writing' (c.iii[b]) throughout the centuries.

Yet it would be misleading to regard Speght's 'Life of Chaucer' merely in isolation, as an early (albeit disappointing) ancestor of literary biography. Despite its singular status as the first 'biography' of an English poet, the most significant aspect about the 'Life of Chaucer' is its timing, which indicates that it may in fact be the product of a wider phenomenon: the increased interest in authorship and authorial lives during the 1590s among both authors and professionals involved in book production. Speght's attempt to retrieve information about the life of a poet who had died nearly two centuries earlier and to present it to his readers as a valuable addition to his collected works is not the most remarkable manifestation of this. In fact, Speght's 'Life of Chaucer' could be regarded as an indirect consequence of debates during

44 Due to his peculiar afterlife (discussed in more detail in Chapter 3), I am treating Sidney as a poet of the 1590s.

45 The lines are the final couplets of *FQ* IV.ii.32 and 34.

46 For a more detailed account of the strategies employed by Speght in his edition to establish Chaucer and Spenser as a suitable pair, see my chapter 'Worthy Friends: Speght's Chaucer and Speght's Spenser' in the collection *Rereading Chaucer and Spenser: Dan Geffrey with the New Poete* (Manchester: Manchester University Press, 2019).

the 1590s about authors' lives and works, sparked by their deaths – debates whose participants struggled to reach a final verdict about the writing careers of recently deceased authors, and to define their approach to authorship retrospectively. Two of the most extensive and most interesting debates, centring on the two most prominent dead authors of the 1590s, Robert Greene and Sir Philip Sidney, will be discussed in the following chapters.

'Copying his picture from his writings': the biographical compilers and Langbaine's 'Life of Cowley'

To fast-forward to a point shortly after the period forming the main focus of this book, Gerard Langbaine (who belonged to the first post-Civil War generation) is a representative of a type of life-writing that grew increasingly popular during the second half of the seventeenth century: compilations of authors' lives gathered from a variety of earlier sources. The origins of those compilations can be traced back to anti-quarian bibliographies such as John Bale's *Illustrium Maioris Britanniae Scriptorum* (1548), which is essentially a catalogue of works supplemented with a modicum of biographical information, with the aim of placing authors both geographically and historically. Another influence on the compilations of authors' lives were themed biographical collections, such as Thomas Fuller's *History of the Worthies of England* (1662). Fuller is less concerned with compiling a comprehensive catalogue of names, and places greater emphasis on presenting the lives of individual 'worthies' in such a way as to show why they are deserving of that title. The most notable collections that focus specifically on the lives of authors are Edward Phillips's *Theatrum Poetarum* (1675), William Winstanley's *The Lives of the Most Famous English Poets* (1687) and Gerard Langbaine's *An Account of the English Dramatick Poets* (1691).

Those compilations of authors' lives do not constitute an original or innovative form of life-writing, and the compilers draw heavily on the work of their predecessors, which is why they do not tend to receive much attention within studies of biography. Modern scholars would perhaps not go as far as Professor Raleigh, who in 'Early Lives of the Poets' dismissed Winstanley as 'an industrious barber, who stole from Phillips as Phillips had stolen from Fuller'.[47] Yet the underlying assumption that compilers like Winstanley and Langbaine were effectively serial plagiarists and their contribution to the genre was therefore negligible, can be found in more recent works as well. Allan Pritchard, who argues for a more inclusive view of seventeeth-century life-writing that takes into account previously neglected forms, is uncharacteristically dismissive about the compilers' efforts, dubbing their collections 'rather slight productions' and *English Dramatick Poets* in particular 'really more a bibliographical than a biographical work'.[48] By contrast, Alan Stewart's strategy for dealing with the derivative nature of Phillips's, Langbaine's and Winstanley's efforts is mainly to avoid them and instead to pay greater attention to the authors of more 'original'

---

47 Raleigh, 'Early Lives of the Poets', p. 105.
48 Allan Pritchard, *English Biography in the Seventeenth Century* (Toronto: University of Toronto Press, 2005), p. 24.

compilations – such as Fuller, Anthony Wood or Samuel Clarke – and thus to focus on the sources rather than the compilers. When it does refer to the compilers, Stewart's book is less dismissive in tone than other studies of biography, although Stewart does echo Raleigh's sentiments about Winstanley in observing that he 'ransacked Fuller's *Worthies* and Phillips's collection to produce *The Lives of the Most Famous English Poets*'.[49]

The charge of plagiarism implicitly levelled against the seventeenth-century compilers because of their habitual copying and paraphrasing is not entirely fair, however. It is a judgement of their methods derived from notions of original authorship and good scholarly practice that were shared neither by the authors of those compilations nor by their seventeenth-century audience. There is no indication that the compilers had any intentions of misleading their readers about the derivative nature of their work (or indeed that any readers were misled). In fact, they frequently seem anxious not to be seen as claiming credit for the work of their predecessors. For example, Langbaine, in his preface to *English Dramatick Poets*, not only stresses his indebtedness to earlier compilations but even draws attention to the fact that in the main text, he has not always 'cited his authorities':

> I have collected all the material Passages of [the poets'] Lives, which I found scattered in Doctor *Fuller*, *Lloyd*, *à Wood*, &c. into One Volume, for the Ease of the *Reader*, and the Advantage to the Work. I have not indeed always cited my Authorities, to avoid loading the Page; tho' I here once for all make my publick Acknowledgment to the Foremention'd, as well as other worthy Writers, to whom I have been oblig'd in the compiling this *Treatise*.[50]

At first sight, this decision to omit references 'to avoid loading the Page' may seem at odds with the obligation to his predecessors that Langbaine professes. It also appears to contradict his disdain for 'our Modern *Plagiaries*', his term for derivative playwrights who recycle plots of earlier plays. Those 'plagiaries' are Langbaine's declared enemies, and he attacks them in several of his works. Consequently, in his 'Life of Cowley', which I discuss below, he is at pains to stress that Cowley '*is not an Author of that Stamp*'.[51] Yet it is important to note that Langbaine defines plagiarism only as passing off derivative material as original, meaning that the concept does not apply to compilations like his own, which are expected to be derivative.

However, even the knowledge that it would be anachronistic to accuse the seventeenth-century biographical compilers of plagiarism has not prevented modern scholars from feeling uneasy about their methods, which seem decidedly unscholarly by modern definitions. Richard Altick's description of the shortcomings of Phillips,

---

49 Stewart, *History of Life-Writing*, p. 213.
50 Gerard Langbaine, *An Account of the English Dramatick Poets* (1691), a5ᵃ–a5ᵇ. A revised edition was published in 1698, under the title *The Lives and Characters of the English Dramatick Poets: With an Account of all the Plays*.
51 Langbaine, *An Account of the English Dramatick Poets*, p. 82. As his authority, Langbaine cites extracts from an elegy by John Denham on Cowley's burial in Poets' Corner at Westminster Abbey. Denham's elegy compares Cowley favourably to his other poets buried there and stressed that unlike Ben Jonson – who 'did make bold | To plunder all the Roman Stores | Of Poets, and of Orators' – Cowley 'did not steal, but emulate' and 'what he writ was all his own' (Cited in Langbaine, *English Dramatick Poets*, p. 83).

Winstanley and Langbaine is particularly revealing in this respect. Altick notes with some indignation:

> It would not have been so bad if each compiler had copied verbatim from his sources; at least the original error would have been preserved in its pristine purity. However, [...] [s]tories were twisted, or merged, or transferred to another period, or grossly misinterpreted.[52]

Although Altick's wish for 'pristine' errors seems strange, it is clear from this passage that his main point of concern is a gradual corruption and falsification through the repeated collation process. Paradoxically, the reason why collections like Langbaine's *English Dramatick Poets* are receiving little critical attention today is also the reason they are of particular interest in the context of tracing a changing idea of authorship. Compiling is an act of reworking and re-evaluation, making the form ideally suited for a reshaping of earlier sources to fit new concepts of authorial lives and careers.

Of course, radical reshapings are not the norm in seventeenth-century biographical compilations; most entries are simply reproduced or slightly adapted from the corresponding entries in earlier compilations.[53] That is why Langbaine's 'Life of Cowley' stands out as something of an oddity. At the beginning of his entry for the poet Abraham Cowley, one of the most highly respected authors of the late seventeenth century, Langbaine rejects his predecessors' accounts of Cowley's life as inadequate, in a passage that is uncharacteristically vehement in tone:

> I have generally hitherto contented my self with giving a succinct Account of each Authors Affairs of Life, or Family: and chose rather to enlarge on their Works: but Mr. *Cowley* was a Person of so great Merit and Esteem in the world when Living; and his Memory so fresh in the minds of Learned Men, that I am oblig'd not to pass him slightly over. 'Tis true my Predecessors in this Work, I mean Mr. *Phillips* and Mr. *Winstanley*, have given but an imperfect account of Him, or his Writings: but as I propose not them for my Pattern in this Subject, so I must publickly own, that I have so great a Veneration for the Memory of this great Man, that methinks his very Name seems an Ornament to my Book, and deserves to be set in the best Light I can place it. Wherefore I shall be as careful in copying his Picture from his Writings, as an Artist would be in hitting the Features of his Sovereign.[54]

The main implication of Langbaine's 'I propose not them for my Pattern in this Subject' is not so much contempt for his predecessors' methods, as a firm belief that *this* subject, Abraham Cowley, deserves special treatment. Thus he is 'publickly' announcing his intention to make his own account of Cowley's life more thorough, although elsewhere he does take Phillips and Winstanley for his pattern and appears to see no fault in that. While Langbaine's book of course repeatedly – and sometimes gleefully – points out mistakes made by his two predecessors, this is a much more

---

52 Altick, *Lives and Letters*, p. 19.
53 The interlude between Chapters 3 and 4, which compares the accounts of Edmund Spenser's life in different biographical compilations, focuses on the differences between the accounts. On the whole, however, similarities and borrowings between the different compilations dominate.
54 Langbaine, *English Dramatick Poets*, pp. 77–8. The portrait of Cowley, the first of six portraits of relatively recent writers included in the volume, is inserted opposite p. 77.

fundamental form of criticism. In the case of Cowley, Langbaine is not merely noting minor factual inaccuracies but accusing Phillips and Winstanley of having failed in their task.

Perhaps surprisingly, given Langbaine's vehemence, there is nothing particularly remarkable about Edward Phillips's entry for Cowley in *Theatrum Poetarum*, which had been reproduced almost verbatim by William Winstanley in his *Lives of the Most Famous English Poets*. Phillips introduces Cowley as 'the most applauded Poet of our Nation both of the present and past Ages' and does not appear to 'pass him slightly over' – or at least no more so than he passes over any other poet.[55] Winstanley's book also contains a frontispiece that visually expresses the idea of Cowley's significance by depicting Winstanley framed by the monuments of two poets: Chaucer and Cowley (see figure 5). While the account of Cowley's life in *Theatrum Poetarum* is fairly brief at thirty-six lines, it is in fact one of the longer entries of the collection. Most of the lives in *Theatrum Poetarum*, including those of Chaucer, Shakespeare and Sidney, are shorter. Like many of Phillips's other entries, the entry for Cowley places greater emphasis on providing a catalogue of his works (with a nod at *The Works of Mr Abraham Cowley*, which had been published in 1668, shortly after the poet's death) than on his life. Phillips's (and Winstanley's) life of Cowley provides no biographical information about the author beyond noting that he began to write poetry in his early teens and was educated at Cambridge. To all purposes, then, the 'imperfect account' of Cowley's life that Langbaine objects to is a perfectly ordinary example of an entry in a late seventeenth-century biographical compilation – and most of Langbaine's own fall into the same category.

Yet it is this very ordinariness of Phillips's (and Winstanley's) version of Cowley's life that Langbaine objects to. Out of reverence for Cowley, his declared aim is to be more scrupulous in his approach than his predecessors. He illustrates this through an analogy that is both aptly chosen and more complex than it seems, by comparing himself to an artist drawing a portrait of his sovereign. Two elements of Langbaine's imagery at first do not appear to work. First, he seems to be comparing a mechanical, derivative task (copying and compiling) to a creative one (drawing a portrait). Second, he appears to be comparing the task of writing the life of a dead poet to drawing the portrait of a live model, which raises the question how Langbaine proposes to 'hit the features' of a dead subject while refusing to rely on earlier 'portraits'. Neither of those apparent contradictions becomes problematic, however, because Langbaine's true subject is not (to use Altick's phrase) 'Cowley the man' but the *dead* Cowley preserved within his body of work. The 'artist'-compiler's task consists of exercising good judgement in determining what the typical features of his 'sovereign' Cowley are, and to create a composite image by selecting those passages within his writings that exemplify those features. While the individual elements of the resulting portrait are the poet's work, however (just as the sovereign's features are his own and not created by the artist), the overall effect of a skilful portrait through selection is one that the poet could not have achieved himself, because it requires observation from a distance.

---

55 Edward Phillips, *Theatrum Poetarum* (1675), p. 1.

5 Frontispiece of Winstanley's *Lives of the Most Famous English Poets* (1687), depicting the author framed by Chaucer's and Cowley's monuments

Another function of the image of the artist drawing his sovereign is of course to ennoble Cowley – not so much through the word 'sovereign' as through the fact that he is deemed worthy of such special attention. This resembles Speght's ennobling of Chaucer not only by forcing the proof of his noble descent and stressing his association with the court of Edward III, but simply by deeming him worthy to be the subject of a written Life and 'set in the best light'. Purely by being singled out in this manner, then, the Abraham Cowley whose image Langbaine attempts to draw becomes a much more eminent poet than the Abraham Cowley of previous compilations.

In this context, it is important to note that Langbaine was only eleven years old when Cowley died in 1667. He cannot have had many (if any) personal memories of Cowley. Nevertheless, his opening paragraph suggests that he feels in a position to correct his predecessors, who, being some twenty-five years older than him, actually were Cowley's contemporaries. Langbaine's phrase 'his Memory so fresh in the minds of Learned Men' is ambiguous and equally includes the 'Learned Men' who had recollections of the poet while he was still alive, as well as those whose only acquaintance with Cowley was through his posthumous memory. Through blending the two meanings of 'memory' in his phrase, Langbaine is creating a situation in which Cowley's memory is effectively a collective memory. This in turn makes it possible for Langbaine's own 'memory' of Cowley to be of equal value as his predecessors', despite the fact that he belongs to a generation that mainly knew Cowley as a dead poet.

In terms of structure, Langbaine's 'Life of Cowley' is broadly similar to Speght's 'Life of Chaucer'. It begins with the poet's origins and education, lists his major works and ends with his death and testimonies of his posthumous fame, at which point Langbaine, like Speght, resorts to quoting from epitaphs and elegies. There are two points, however, in which Langbaine's 'Life of Chaucer' notably differs from Speght's 'Life of Chaucer': the role of 'service' and the discussion of the works.

The short section in Speght's 'Life of Chaucer' titled 'His Service' forms part of his legitimisation of Chaucer as the subject of a written life. It is primarily concerned with placing him at, or at least in the vicinity of, court and showing him employed on diplomatic missions. Langbaine, on the other hand, does not provide Cowley with a public life of service at court but instead uses the 'service' section of his 'Life of Cowley' to hint at his political leanings, through striving to associate him with Charles II as much as possible. This politicising of the notion of 'service' is not in itself remarkable. It occurs in other post-Restoration lives and is likely to be a direct response to the Civil War period, because the question of which faction a person had belonged to during the war assumed even greater significance after the interregnum. Thus Cowley's royalist credentials are a key ingredient in all posthumous accounts of his life. While Langbaine is not alone in seeking to highlight those royalist credentials, it is surprising that he attempts to trace Cowley's royalism in his works. In fact, Langbaine would not have needed to look far for evidence of Cowley's royalism, as becomes clear when comparing his account to that of Cowley's first biographer.

Shortly after Cowley's death, his friend and literary executor, Thomas Sprat, had edited an edition of his works, 'Consisting of those which were formerly Printed AND those which he Design'd for the Press', as the title page proclaims.[56] Sprat's edition of Cowley's works begins with a twenty-four-page bio-graphical preface called 'An Account of the Life and Writings of Mr Abraham Cowley'. Unlike Langbaine, Sprat is eager to stress that although Cowley chose to retreat from it, he led an active life in the service of the royal family, being employed on numerous diplomatic missions, serving the queen mother in exile for twelve years, and even at one point turning royal secretary, 'maintaining the constant correspondence between the late King and the Queen his Wife [...]. For he cypher'd and decypher'd with his own hand, the greatest part of all the letters that passed between them' (a^a).

Sprat's preface is one of Langbaine's main sources for his 'Life of Cowley', so Langbaine clearly had access to a wealth of biographical detail to illustrate Cowley's close association with the royal family.[57] Nevertheless, he chose to disregard Sprat's account in this point and instead attempted to prove Cowley a royalist through his writings. In Langbaine's version, the proof of Cowley's loyalty is in the history of his early comedy *The Guardian*. This play, Langbaine notes, had been written to be performed before Prince Charles on the occasion of a visit to Cambridge, and had enjoyed popularity beyond Cambridge in private performances during the prohibi-tion of the stage. Eventually, it was revised and performed under a new title 'at his Royal Highness's Theatre' after the Restoration (p. 81). Langbaine treats even the fact that the second incarnation of the play did not meet with universal approval as a confirmation of Cowley's loyalty, suggesting that it 'met with some Opposition [...] from some who envyed the Authors unshaken Loyalty to the Prince, and the Royal Cause, in the worst of Times' (p. 81).

Langbaine may never have seen or read the early version of *The Guardian*, yet its existence and its revisions evidently intrigued him. This is perhaps because Cowley's account of its hasty composition and performance before the prince in 1650 – 'neither *made* nor *acted*, but *rough-drawn* only' – strikes a chord with his own aim of 'copying the author's picture from his writings'.[58] Langbaine seems to regard the play in its early form as a lost character-sketch (and a lost source for his 'Life of Cowley'), although the poet himself was dismissive of it and 'accounted it only the hasty *first-sitting* of a Picture, and therefore like to resemble him accordingly' (p. 81). His inter-est in the compositional aspects of the play is at least partly an interest in the edited voice of the poet.

As far as its treatment of Cowley's works is concerned, one of the peculiarities of Langbaine's 'Life of Cowley' is that Langbaine shrinks away from providing descrip-tions or critical judgements of works, perhaps because it would conflict with his role as a compiler. Instead, he chooses to speak through the voices of others, especially that of his most trusted source, Thomas Sprat: 'I dare not presume to give a particular Character of his Works: therefore I shall refer them to the large Account of his Life

---

56 *The Works of Abraham Cowley* (1668). The implication is that whatever was not 'design'd for the press' has been omitted. Sprat's preface indirectly confirms this by stating he was instructed by Cowley not to 'let pass' anything he might deem inappropriate for publication (A^a).

57 Despite Langbaine's strategy of keeping references to a minimum 'to avoid loading the page', his 'Life of Cowley' contains three references to Sprat's 'Account of the Life and Writings', making it the most-cited text of the entry.

58 Cited in Langbaine, *English Dramatick Poets* (1691), p. 80.

written by the exact and ingenious author abovementioned, or to the Readers own judgement' (pp. 83–84). The only exception to this self-imposed reticence occurs in the final paragraph of the entry, when Langbaine chides his predecessors for what he considers blatant misattributions of works to Cowley.

While Langbaine considers it presumptuous to pass judgement on Cowley's literary quality, he is all the more eager to let Cowley speak for himself. As his declared intention is to 'copy his Picture from his Writings', Langbaine quotes extensively from Cowley's works and is keen to direct his readers' attention to this fact through parenthetical phrases like '(says the author)' or '(the author tells us)' (p. 80). The first source he cites is perhaps the most obvious one: an autobiographical essay called 'Of Myself'. From this, Langbaine extracts two anecdotes about Cowley's childhood, both of which relate to his early inclination towards poetry through his reading. By juxtaposing them to a catalogue of the works written by Cowley 'whilst he was yet but a *Westminster* Scholar' (p. 78), however, Langbaine creates an interesting effect. Through using the extracts from 'Of Myself' in this manner, he essentially transforms a simple anecdote about a precocious boy who read *The Faerie Queene* at the age of twelve, into a miniature portrait of the inner life of a young author, who had already written at least two plays and was to publish his first collection of poetry soon afterwards. For the remainder of his 'Life of Cowley', most of Langbaine's quotations from Cowley are not taken from the works proper but from prefaces and dedications. They are passages explaining Cowley's reasoning and the circumstances of the works' composition. In a sense, then, Langbaine's 'Life of Cowley' attempts to strike a balance between the author's life and his works, in order to portray him as an author at work.

Langbaine's 'Life of Cowley' resembles other lives from biographical compilations in that it is not an original piece. It avoids any discussion of Cowley's plays and is not so much concerned with portraying 'Cowley the man' as Cowley the author, using methods which may seem clumsy today. Nevertheless, it achieves its aim of capturing the memory (and fame) of the dead poet as his contemporaries and near-contemporaries saw it, and stressing his perceived eminence among English writers. The passages quoted are carefully chosen and well matched, and Langbaine's discussion of Cowley's revision of *The Guardian* in particular reveals an interest in the poet's life reflected in his works that is not present in Speght's 'Life of Chaucer' or in the lives of Cowley compiled by his predecessors.

What, then, happened during the century separating Speght's and Langbaine's 'Lives' that would explain the differences between them? Why does Langbaine, after his refusal to follow the 'pattern' of Phillips and Winstanley in his account of Cowley's life, declare his intention to '[copy] his Picture from his Writings'? In a sense, Pritchard's dismissal of the compilers' efforts as 'rather slight' is justified. Even in his 'Life of Cowley', Langbaine's approach is still derivative, and he evidently considers himself a compiler of 'scattered' lives from other sources, not an 'exact and ingenious author' like Thomas Sprat. Langbaine's 'Life of Cowley' – like Speght's 'Life of Chaucer' – is significant not so much because it is innovative in itself, but because it hints at a wider phenomenon: a changed attitude towards the writing of poets' lives. The uncommon format of the 'Life of Cowley' shows that by 1691, those changes had filtered down even into an established genre of life-writing that did not particularly lend itself to innovation, through its derivative nature and dependence on following 'accustomit' examples. As with Speght's 'Life of Chaucer', the source of change is located elsewhere and the 'Life of Cowley' represents a delayed response to it. In Langbaine's case, however, the change can be traced to a specific name: Izaak Walton. During the second half of the seventeenth century, Walton's *Lives*, written and rewritten over a period of thirty-five years, stood for a new strategy of writing the lives of authors, which allowed for closer links to their works. Walton's influence is apparent in Langbaine's technique of extensive quoting from Cowley's works to recreate the dead author's voice, as well as in the portrait metaphor with which he begins his 'Life of Cowley'. In fact, the popularity of Walton's *Lives* may even have been partly responsible for the demand for authors' lives that compilations like Langbaine's were trying to cater for.

While Walton's *Lives* were pivotal and transformative texts for the development of literary biography – an aspect about them which has yet to be fully recognised – they did not emerge out of a vacuum. Of course the generation of writers before Walton produced nothing as concrete as an attempt at literary biography, prompting Professor Raleigh to observe that 'the earliest notable English life of an English poet [Greville's *Life of Sidney*] is the life of a poet almost by accident'.[59] Nevertheless, the last decade of the sixteenth century in particular was haunted by the ghostly presences of recently deceased authors in posthumous publications and saw several remarkable attempts at grappling with the question that is central to literary biography. How can a reading of the works and the life be combined into a 'complete', unified portrait of the author that captures the internal life as well as the external?

59 Raleigh, 'Early Lives of the Poets', p. 101.

2

The posthumous career of Robert Greene

Robert Greene, 'celebrity author'?

As outlined in the previous chapter, 'literary biography' during the sixteenth and seventeenth centuries only exists in the form of a few scattered biographical texts describing the lives of poets. What unites those texts is that they all present their subjects' poetic careers as at best ancillary to their public careers. Yet while there seems to be a lack of interest in poets as the subjects of 'non-fictional' life-writing, fictional texts of the same period show an increasing engagement with the figure of the poet and his professional life. The beginnings of this development can be roughly dated to a series of apparently isolated events in the 1590s. First, there is the death of professional author Robert Greene in 1592 and his remarkable rebirth in numerous fictional and semi-fictional texts written in its wake. Second, we see the creation of Thomas Nashe's poet-figure Pierce Penilesse in 1593 (a figure that was subsequently taken up by several other writers and assumed something of a life of its own). Third, the decade witnesses the posthumous publication of a series of works by Sir Philip Sidney, including the *Defence of Poesie* in 1595.[1] Finally, the 1590s also saw the publication of a number of texts featuring prominent Henrician poet figures such as Skelton, More or Surrey as characters.[2] These texts show a marked interest in the identities of these individuals as poets, while stressing the potential for tension between their lives as poets and as public figures who lead a *vita activa*.[3]

As a rule, critical writing in the sixteenth century makes little connection between an author's life and his literary writing.[4] It therefore produces a challenge for modern biographers. Robert Greene's life, however, poses a different problem: ever since Greene's death, his life has been so closely associated with his works that separating the two is no easy task. Perhaps the closest parallel to this phenomenon is the

---

1 This phenomenon will be discussed in more detail in Chapter 3.
2 Skelton features most memorably as a character in the first of the two *Robert, Earl of Huntington* plays (published in 1601 and attributed to Anthony Munday and Henry Chettle), in which he is commissioned to write a Robin Hood play for performance at court and ends up playing the part of Friar Tuck himself. Unfortunately, Skelton's performance in the Robin Hood play is hampered by the fact that he is not an actor but a poet, so he frequently 'forgets himself' and slips out of character and into Skeltonics.
3 This particularly applies to the play *Sir Thomas More*, which presents the tensions between More's political office and his 'poetic' nature as the central conflict of his life.
4 For a detailed account of the characteristics of critical writing in the period, see Brian Vickers's introduction to his anthology *English Renaissance Literary Criticism* (Oxford: Clarendon Press, 1999), pp. 1–55.

posthumous notoriety of actor Richard Tarlton, who died almost exactly four years before Greene and was often compared to him.[5] Consequently, Peter Thomson's *DNB* article begins with the caveat that Tarlton 'became a legend in his own lifetime and was constantly reinvented after his death. As a result, fictions about his life have become inextricably tangled with its facts'.[6] Similarly, the story of Greene the scholar turned hack writer, who achieved notoriety during his lifetime and died miserable and destitute, is almost entirely derived from several of Greene's own writings, as well as Gabriel Harvey's letters, which were written after Greene's death. All of these are of questionable authority – the former because many of Greene's 'autobiographical' passages are embedded in otherwise clearly fictional texts, and the latter because Harvey not only held a personal grudge against Greene but actively denied knowing him personally. Even Harvey's famous description of Greene's destitute death is imagined and based on hearsay. It is merely a retelling of 'ascertayned reportes' Harvey claims to have gathered in London from Greene's 'hostisse *Isam*' and an unnamed gentleman.[7]

In 1986, Charles W. Crupi, one of the first Greene scholars, claimed that 'anyone who knows Greene's name at all knows something of his life'.[8] Nevertheless, there are only three facts relating to Greene's life that are certain: that he was university educated, that he wrote in a wide range of genres and his works were popular, and that he died in 1592.[9] Despite the impossibility of verifying any of it, however, Greene's 'biography' has attracted more attention than the works it is derived from. With the exception of a few recent studies, Greene criticism has primarily focused on his biography and questions directly relating to it, such as how autobiographical or how genuine his repentance tracts are, and whether (or why) he held a grudge against Shakespeare.[10] There are three main reasons for this interest in Greene's life. First, until around the second half of the twentieth century, quality of style and intrinsic literary value were still very dominant categories in literary criticism, and those categories were frequently used to justify critical interest. Using those criteria, Greene's works ranked towards the lowbrow end of the literary spectrum, making him a 'minor' writer and a counterexample at best.[11] Second – and perhaps more

---

5 Some sources even claim they died on the same day (3 September), but since the exact date of death cannot be established with complete certainty in either case, this is likely to be one of the parallels between their posthumous careers that were already drawn by contemporaries. The first known source to draw a link between the death of Tarlton and the death of Greene was Gabriel Harvey's *Foure Letters and Certeine Sonnets*, who claims to have been 'suddainely certified, that the king of the paper stage [...] had played his last part, & was gone to *Tarleton*'. Gabriel Harvey, *Foure Letters and Certeine Sonnets especially touching Robert Greene and other parties by him abused* (1592), p. 9.
6 Peter Thomson, 'Tarlton, Richard (d. 1588)', *Oxford DNB*.
7 Harvey, *Foure Letters and Certeine Sonnets*, pp. 10–11.
8 Charles W. Crupi, *Robert Greene* (Boston: Twayne, 1986), p. 2.
9 Although Lori Humphrey Newcomb's *DNB* article does of course contain more biographical detail than this, much of what is 'known' about Greene's life is in fact based on conjecture or derived from 'autobiographical' passages in his works.
10 The most notable exceptions to this are Steve Mentz, *Romance for Sale in Early Modern England: The Rise of Prose Fiction* (Aldershot: Ashgate, 2006) and Kirk Melnikoff and Edward Gieskes (eds), *Writing Robert Greene: New Essays on England's First Notorious Professional Writer* (Aldershot: Ashgate, 2008).
11 In literary histories, Greene is often grouped among the 'university wits', a category that is problematic because of its implications. As well as suggesting a lack of seriousness and substance in their writing

importantly – Greene's 'life' provides interest simply by virtue of being a story that is almost too good to resist. As early as 1691, Gerard Langbaine had remarked on the scarcity of sources for Greene's life and the list of his works, and seemed reluctant to refer to William Winstanley's earlier collection, *The Lives of the Most Famous English Poets* (1687), as his only authority:

> Robert GREEN
> This Author lived in the Reign of Queen *Elizabeth*, and was a Master of Arts at *Cambridge*: As to any further Account of him, I can meet with none, except what I am forc'd to borrow from Mr. *Winstanley*. But the truth is I dare not trust too much to him […]. However, for once I will venture to transcribe the following passage upon his Authority.[12]

Langbaine was right to doubt the reliability of Winstanley concerning the Greene entry, as *Lives of the Most Famous English Poets* merely paraphrases *Greenes Groatsworth of Witte*, which, as a highly fictionalised text, is hardly suitable as a direct source of biographical information. However, doubting Winstanley's authority did not deter Langbaine from using his material to retell the story of Greene's life; apart from a few sceptical insertions, the entry is a close paraphrase of Winstanley.[13] Crupi, in his account of Greene's reception history, notes that Langbaine's ambivalent response to Greene's biography was essentially the same that later scholars had: 'generations of scholars express uncertainty […] about the autobiographical pamphlets published just after Greene's death while relying on them for details of Greene's life'.[14] The third reason for the popularity of the story of Greene's 'life' is that it helps to bring some order to Greene's otherwise rather piecemeal oeuvre, by suggesting parallels between individual phases of his life and certain types of texts. Greene's list of publications shows a lack of a distinct pattern.[15] Greene wrote prolifically, and several of his works saw multiple editions within a short period. His works comprise plays and prose romances, as well as a number of 'coney-catching pamphlets'.[16] In addition to these, Greene also wrote several repentance tracts, in which the author renounces his loose life and loose writings.

However, instead of writing the repentance tracts after his pamphlets and romances (which would seem to be the most logical sequence), Greene appears to

---

(by dubbing this group of writers 'wits' rather than authors), the term also effectively classifies them as having remained in a state of literary adolescence and immaturity.

12 Gerard Langbaine, *English Dramatick Poets* (1691), p. 241.

13 Langbaine clearly did not feel comfortable relying exclusively on Winstanley's authority, however. In *The Lives and Characters of the English Poets* (1698), the revised edition of *English Dramatick Poets*, the paraphrase is missing. As a result, the section on Greene is considerably shorter and contains only the biographical and bibliographical facts that Langbaine felt he could verify, that is, that he 'liv'd and writ One Play and part of another in Queen *Elizabeth's* Reign, was Master of Arts in *Cambridge*, and has Published some other Pieces' (p. 66).

14 Crupi, *Robert Greene*, p. 1.

15 Steve Mentz solves this problem by dividing Greene's writing career into seven 'phases' which all overlap with each other, while noting that a chronology of Greene's works to provide an overview of his career progression is 'both required […] and suspect'. Steve Mentz, 'Forming Greene: Theorizing the Early Modern Author in the *Groatsworth of Wit*', in Melnikoff and Gieskes (eds), *Writing Robert Greene*, pp. 115–31 (pp. 123–4).

16 Those pamphlets are a cross between guidebooks and story collections: they combine information about tricks employed by contemporary con-artists with stories about famous 'coney-catchers'.

have alternated between seeking forgiveness for his written 'sins' and committing more of them. This has prompted some critical debate about the nature of his 'repentance'. The two most popular theories are: first, Greene's repentance was essentially a marketing ploy intended to promote his self-fashioned prodigal persona through exploiting another popular genre; and second, Greene's repentance was genuine, but due to his prodigal nature, its effects simply never lasted long. Lori Humphrey Newcomb takes an intermediate position by arguing that due to a lack of precedents, Greene's career was largely 'improvised' in nature. She suggests that this rather than calculated self-promotional strategies was the cause of what she terms his 'postponed repentance'.[17]

The problem of Greene's repentance has occupied criticism so much because it is more than merely a biographical detail. As Crupi notes, the attitudes that scholars take towards Greene's repentence are directly linked to how they view Greene's claims to moral motivations for his writings.[18] Yet perhaps more significantly, how one views Greene's repentance also has implications for how one views his authorial persona and the extent of his professionalism. Unfortunately, the matter is far from clear-cut, since the only available accounts of Greene's repentance – his own works and three posthumous pamphlets purporting to be by him – are unreliable as sources. Greene's prefaces suggest that he was very conscious of his authorial persona and encouraged autobiographical readings of his works. Nevertheless, it is important to bear in mind that Greene was not following an established career model for prodigal poets but shaping a career for himself as he went along, and he was thus forced to 'improvise', as Newcomb calls it.

The most important moment of Greene's career, however, was the point at which he ceased to be able to fashion it: his death and subsequent immortalisation in print. One thing that can be said with some certainty is that regardless of how far his career-shaping attempts actually went, Greene's life and works posed something of a puzzle to his contemporaries and to the following generation. Thus all the responses to Greene's death have one thing in common: they are struggling to draw a coherent picture of both Greene and his works, and they reach wildly different conclusions.

The fact that there is no clear consensus among the writers responding to Greene's death as to what to make of the author and his works, suggests that if Greene really did engage in conscious career-planning, he was only moderately successful. However, looking at Greene purely in terms of a professional career that he fashioned for himself during his lifetime, may be missing the point somewhat. There are of course numerous references to Greene as one of the most notorious and recognisable figures in London. It is this alleged notoriety that lies at the root of much of the critical interest in Greene and it has led to his reputation as 'England's first celebrity author'.[19] Nevertheless, it may not be a coincidence that nearly all of those references to his notoriety were made posthumously. Although his works were popular, there is little evidence that Greene's person attracted a lot of attention during his lifetime.

17 Lori Humphrey Newcomb, *Reading Popular Romance in Early Modern England* (New York: Columbia University Press, 2001), p. 28.
18 Crupi, *Robert Greene*, pp. 1–2.
19 L. H. Newcomb, 'Greene, Robert (*bap.* 1558, *d.* 1592)', *Oxford DNB*.

Interpretations of Greene's character are always closely linked to posthumous verdicts on his oeuvre and posthumous attempts to explain how its individual components relate to each other.

Greene's colourful 'biography' appears to be largely a product of posthumous readings of his works during the 1590s rather than the direct result of self-fashioning on Greene's part. This raises two questions: What prompted this uncommon interest in Greene's life so shortly after his death? And why is it that his early readers appear to have immediately turned to his works in order to satisfy this interest?

This chapter examines Greene's posthumous career during the 1590s as part of a wider debate about the nature of authorship and the potential links between personal life and printed works. The debate hinges on differing interpretations of Greene's life and his literary afterlife – exemplified in the Harvey–Nashe quarrel – and serves to cast light on competing conceptions of poetic careers towards the end of the sixteenth century. The following section considers the beginnings of the Harvey–Nashe quarrel in 1592 as a dispute between two authors advocating very different models of literary authorship. Within this dispute, Greene largely serves as a foil for the shining example of Edmund Spenser. The third section then looks at the continuation of this discourse on authorship in the three posthumous Greene pamphlets, also published in 1592. In the final section, I examine the twentieth-century debate about the 'authenticity' of *Greenes Groats-worth of Witte* and its implications for the Greene myth.

The beginnings of the Harvey–Nashe quarrel

One of the first people to attempt a posthumous portrait of Greene – albeit a particularly unflattering one – was Gabriel Harvey in his *Foure Letters and Certeine Sonnets, especially touching Robert Greene and other parties by him abused* (1592). As indicated by its title, *Foure Letters and Certeine Sonnets*, like Harvey's other published *Letters*, is a heterogeneous collection of texts, including a spiteful account of Greene's death, which Harvey himself did not witness.[20] Despite being mentioned in the title of the volume, Greene's name does not in fact feature very prominently among the contents listed in the index. This suggests that although Robert Greene and his death may have been the occasion of *Foure Letters and Certeine Sonnets*, its main protagonist is not Greene but Gabriel Harvey himself. Contrary to the claims made in the dedicatory epistle, *Foure Letters and Certeine Sonnets* is unlikely to be a selection of letters from Harvey's personal correspondence, which well-meaning friends had urged him to publish as they were. Just as the 'certeine sonnets' are arranged in a deliberate order to form a sequence, the letters are not spontaneous compositions: the third and fourth letter are even addressed to 'euery Reader', meaning the imagined readers of the final published volume. Like Harvey's other published *Letters*, then, they are deliberate and crafted pieces of writing whose purpose is academic self-fashioning. Thus Harvey's volumes of letters most resemble writing portfolios

---

20 I refer to Harvey's pamphlet by its full title rather than by the more commonly used short title *Foure Letters*, since it is part of my argument that the sonnets are part of Harvey's purpose and the text consequently needs to be read in its entirety and understood as a unit.

intended to display their author's rhetorical skill and wide knowledge, to show his character in a favourable light, and to advertise his services to potential patrons.

Why, then, if his main aim is self-promotion, would Harvey choose to make the death of Robert Greene, a man whom he claimed he hardly knew, the theme of his book? Ostensibly, the purpose of *Foure Letters and Certeine Sonnets* is to settle a score. The first edition of Greene's highly successful *A Quip for an Vpstart Courtier*, published earlier in 1592, had contained a passage mocking Harvey and his two brothers.[21] *Foure Letters and Certeine Sonnets* certainly contains elements of Harvey seeking revenge for the 'parties [...] abused', especially his youngest brother John, who had died shortly before the publication of *A Quip for an Vpstart Courtier*. Nevertheless, it would be wrong to read it purely as an angry counterattack intended to malign a man who had insulted his family. Although revenge may have been one of Harvey's motivations, his main reason for writing *Foure Letters and Certeine Sonnets* was to pursue a double agenda. His first aim was, as ever, to present himself in a favourable light, while his second was to use Greene's life and death as a foil, in order to propagate his own views on authorial careers.[22]

So how could *Foure Letters and Certeine Sonnets*, with its vitriolic attacks on a dead man, be regarded as a text that reflects favourably on its author? In order to answer this question, it is necessary to view the volume not as the result of spontaneous outrage, but in its entirety, as a text with a deliberate and crafted structure. Although especially Harvey's first two letters (i.e. the second and third letter in the book, which begins with a letter about rather than by Harvey) appear angry and vindictive, especially when read in isolation, they represent only the first step within a gradual journey towards the attitude of critical detachment portrayed in the final sonnet in the volume.[23] In fact, Harvey's attitude towards Greene does not remain unchanged throughout *Foure Letters and Certeine Sonnets*. The four letters span a period of just two weeks. The first, from Christopher Bird to Emmanuel Demetrius, to vouch for Harvey's character, is dated '29. of August 1592'.[24] The second, addressed from Harvey to Bird, and containing Harvey's most open gloating about the circumstances of Greene's death, is dated '5. of September', that is, shortly after Greene's death.[25] The third and fourth letters, dated '8. and 9. of September' and '11. and 12. of September' respectively, are addressed to the readers of Harvey's letters in print.[26]

---

21 The passage was removed in later editions, and in *Foure Letters and Certeine Sonnets*, Harvey maliciously hints that Greene's fear of its repercussions contributed to his death.

22 To an extent, this may serve to explain Harvey's seemingly hypocritical claim that he does not intend to 'conflict with Ghostes' (Gabriel Harvey, *Foure Letters and Certeine Sonnets* (1592), p. 12).

23 That is Spenser's sonnet 'To the Right Worshipfull, my singular good frend, M. Gabriell Haruey, Doctor of the Lawes', which I shall discuss in more detail below.

24 In *Strange Newes*, Nashe ridicules Harvey's somewhat contrived pretext for beginning the volume with a glowing character reference for himself by calling him a 'Fawneguest Messenger' (B4ᵃ) and questioning Bird's authorship: '[it] shoulde seeme by all reference or collation of stiles, to bee a Letter which M. *Birds* secretarie *Doctour Gabriell* indited for him in his owne praise, and got him to sette hand to when he had done. Or rather it is no letter, but a certificate (such as Rogues haue) [...] *that* Gabriel *is an excellent generall Scholler*' (C4ᵇ).

25 *The Repentance of Robert Greene* dates Greene's 'dying' letter to his wife to 2 September. This forms the basis for the widely held belief that Greene died on the following day.

26 The titles of the third and fourth letters are 'To euery Reader, fauorablie, or indifferently affected'

Of these, the third letter is by far the longest. It accounts for nearly half the length of *Foure Letters and Certeine Sonnets* and contains a shift in focus. Although Harvey does not quite 'bury the whole Legendary of [Greene's] Life & Death, in the Sepulchre of eternall Silence' (D2ᵇ), as he announces towards its beginning, he does move from malicious descriptions of Greene's death to considering his body of works, before moving on to wider questions of authorship and addressing himself to Nashe, whom he believes to be in need of career-related advice. Finally, the fourth letter, set apart from the others through italic type, shows a greater sense of detachment on Harvey's part, both from his own anger and from the initial narrative situation. In the fourth letter, Harvey is not only directly addressing his readers, but also explicitly imagines *Foure Letters and Certeine Sonnets* in its final printed form, by referring to it as 'this slender Pamflet', barely a week after Greene 'had played his last part'.[27]

Harvey's shift, from open attacks on Greene and joy at the circumstances of his death to considering him through his works and within a wider context of authorship, also results in a more measured tone, and a tendency to stress his own magnanimity rather than Greene's depravity. This is also evident in the short sonnet sequence at the end of the volume, titled 'Greenes Memoriall, or certaine Funerall Sonnets'.[28] One sonnet that particularly stands out is XVIII, entitled 'Iohn Harueys Welcome to Robert Greene':

> COME, fellow *Greene*, come to thy gaping graue:
> Bidd Vanity, and Foolery farewell:
> Thou ouer-long hast plaid the madbrain'd knaue:
> And ouer-loud hast rung the bawdy bell.
> Vermine to Vermine must repair at last:
> No fitter house for busy folke to dwell:
> Thy Conny-catching Pageants are past:
> Some other must those arrant Stories tell.
> These hungry wormes thinke longe for their repast:
> Come on: I pardon thy offence to me:
> It was thy liuing: be not so aghast:
> A Foole, and a Phisition may agree.
>   And for my Brothers, neuer vex thy selfe:
>   They are not to disease a buried Elfe.
>
> (*Foure Letters and Certeine Sonnets*, p. 71)

At first sight, the sonnet appears to contain yet more verbal abuse and ridicule directed against Greene. In quick succession, he is called a 'madbrain'd knaue', 'Vermine' and 'a Foole', while his writings are referred to as 'bawdy', as ephemeral 'Pageants' and as 'arrant Stories'. Greene's inclusion among the 'busy folke' in l. 6 can also be read as a thinly veiled insult, by labelling him a busy-body (as shown by his interference in the matters of the Harvey family), as well as mocking his 'business' both in his prolific writing and in his prodigality.

(p. 15) and 'To the same fauourable, or indifferent Reader' (p. 51). They are signed (respectively) '*The frend of his frendes, & foe of none*' (p. 50) and 'Your affectionate frend, G. H.' (p. 61).

27 Harvey, *Foure Letters and Certeine Sonnets*, p. 51 and p. 9.

28 The sequence contains twenty-two sonnets by Harvey as well as two short Latin poems on Greene and John Harvey and a final sonnet by Edmund Spenser, which I shall discuss in more detail below.

A typical example of this type of reading of sonnet XVIII is that proposed by Jennifer Richards in *Rhetoric and Courtliness in Early Modern Literature* (2003).[29] During her account of the pamphlet war between Harvey and Nashe, Richards singles out the sonnet as a particularly 'distasteful' example of Harvey's attacks on Greene. However, the 'distasteful' reading of the sonnet rests on certain assumptions about the situation described. Again, Richards's reading is typical here in that she quotes only the first and fifth line ('Come, fellow *Greene*, come to thy gaping graue: |… Vermine to Vermine must repaire at last'). This, however, disregards the fact that, as indicated by the title of the poem, the speaker is not Gabriel Harvey himself but his dead brother John, whom the first edition of *A Quip for an Vpstart Courtier* had dubbed 'a Physitian or a foole, but indeed a physitian'.[30] Harvey's sonnet playfully twists Greene's words by giving John the line 'A Foole, and a Phisition may agree'. Despite the 'distasteful' phrases, then, the situation depicted in the sonnet is essentially one of reconciliation after death. After playfully welcoming him among the 'Vermine', John generously forgives Greene for his 'offence' and tells him not to worry about the wrath of the surviving Harvey brothers.

When attributed to a speaker who is Greene's 'fellow' in death rather than a living speaker gloating about his death, the 'distasteful' imagery of the sonnet is transformed into macabre self-mockery by Gabriel as well as John Harvey. John, the speaker of the sonnet, implicitly includes himself among the 'Vermine' Greene is invited to join and even playfully twists the words of Greene's original 'offence' in l. 12. The sonnet's author, on the other hand, in the final couplet acknowlegdes his own helplessness against the 'buried Elfe'. Rather than an inappropriate celebration of Greene's death, sonnet XVIII is in fact a variation on the danse macabre motif. Ultimately, it is Gabriel Harvey himself, a vain fool left behind in a world of 'Vanity and Foolery', who becomes the butt of the joke in the realisation that the dead cannot be hurt through insults.

While the insult to his brothers and to himself may have been the occasion for Harvey to write *Foure Letters and Certeine Sonnets*, they are not the only thing by which he feels offended. Beyond the personal insult, Harvey also seems to object to Greene as a writer. One of the more puzzling features of *Foure Letters and Certeine Sonnets* is Harvey's insistence on his own unfamiliarity with Greene's person or his works. Thus he mocks Greene's appearance and loose life via hearsay, while professing he is 'altogether vnacquainted with the man & neuer once saluted him by name' (p. 9). Regarding Greene's works, Harvey declares that he 'will not condemne, or censure [them]' because he never so much as glanced at them but merely registered their presence 'in Stationers shops, and some other houses of my acquaintance' (p. 29).

---

29 Jennifer Richards, *Rhetoric and Courtliness in Early Modern Literature* (Cambridge: Cambridge University Press, 2003), p. 116. Like most commentators on the quarrel between Harvey and Nashe, Richards cannot fully conceal a certain partiality towards Nashe, who has the advantage of being the wittier of the two. One of the most differentiated accounts regarding Harvey's part in the quarrel remains that of R. B. McKerrow, appended to his edition of Nashe's collected works, which I shall refer to later in this section.
30 Robert Greene, *A Quip for an Vpstart Courtier* (1592), C3[b].

At first, Harvey's claim seems to be simply an excuse for having heard of such obvious examples of lowbrow writing at all (much like claiming only to have glanced at a trashy magazine at the hairdresser's because there was nothing better to read). However, on closer observation, the fact that Harvey stresses his lack of personal acquaintance with Greene and his works, would appear to weaken his own case against him. The terms in which Harvey finds fault with Greene's works are also revealing, because despite his initial protestations, he does of course go on to condemn and censure the works, and through them their author. Perhaps the most noticeable feature of Harvey's attack on Greene as an author is his readiness to draw conclusions about the character of the author on the basis of his works (or at least their titles). Harvey's claim never to have read any of Greene's 'famous' books may even be true. In *Foure Letters and Certeine Sonnets* he frequently alludes to titles by Greene but does not betray any detailed knowledge of their contents, except for the offending passage from *A Quip for an Vpstart Courtier*.[31]

One major factor that Harvey seems to disapprove of is the lack of unity within Greene's oeuvre, which frustrates his own attempts to make sense of it. Consequently, Harvey's explanation for the apparent disorder of Greene's works is that only a disturbed or confused personality could write so much and in so many different genres:

> Peruse his famous bookes: and in steede of *Omne tulit punctum, qui miscuit vtile dulci* (that forsooth was his professed Poesie) Loe a wilde head, ful of mad braine and a thousand crotchets: A scholler, a Discourser, a Courtier, a ruffian, a Gamester, a Louer, a Souldier, a Trauailer, a Merchaunt, a Broker, an Artificer, a Botcher, a Pettifogger, a Player, a Coosener, a Rayler, a beggar, an Omnigatherum, a Gay nothing: a Stoarehouse of bald and baggage stuffe, vnworth the aunswering. (*Foure Letters and Certeine Sonnets*, p. 25)

The vocabulary used by Harvey in this passage above all stresses disorder and lack of coherence, both among Greene's works and as a feature of his presumed personality. 'Wilde head', 'mad braine' and 'a thousand crotchets' all hint at the eccentricity or even mental illness indicated by the confusing number of roles assumed by the author, while the contrast between '*Omni*gatherum' – in other words, an all-inclusive muddle – and 'Gay *nothing*' (emphases added) suggests that Harvey in fact considers the scattered nature of Greene's oeuvre one of the causes of its worthlessness. In other words, he is not so much criticising Greene for writing in low genres as for not having had a more clearly patterned writing career.

After failing to do so via his body of works, Harvey attempts to make sense of Greene by turning him into a character. The 'king of the paper stage' (p. 9) whose image he is drawing, clearly does not represent an individual but a type with satirically exaggerated traits, which are worthy of censure or at least ridicule – a kind of anti-poet figure. In a sense, the lack of personal acquaintance with Greene turns into an advantage for Harvey here, because it means he is free to create a character he can then instrumentalise for his own purposes. As he portrays it, Greene's career stood in

---

31 In this, Harvey's approach differs radically from Nashe's in *Strange Newes*, his reply to *Foure Letters and Certeine Sonnets*. Nashe's method for discrediting the man and the works consists of examining nearly every line Harvey wrote in excruciating detail and then proceeding to turn his own words against him.

stark contrast not only to the career as a sage scholarly author Harvey envisioned for himself, but also to his idea of an ideal poetic career, exemplified in the career of his much-invoked friend, Edmund Spenser.

As indicated earlier in this section, Harvey did not write *Foure Letters and Certeine Sonnets* purely to vent his anger. He was also aiming to present himself as a magnanimous individual ultimately capable of forgiveness, even in the face of grave personal insults. This is certainly the note on which the book concludes. The final poem of the pamphlet is a sonnet by Edmund Spenser, 'To the Right Worshipfull, my singular good frend, M. Gabriell Haruey, Doctor of the Lawes'. The sonnet is dated 1586, clearly predating Greene's insult of the Harvey brothers, and is included by Harvey not because it bears any direct relation to his quarrel with the dead Robert Greene, but to act as a character reference of sorts. It praises Harvey's clear sense of judgement, his calm detachment in wielding his 'critique pen' and his immunity to the threats of 'faulty men' and thus encapsulates Harvey's character as he is seeking to portray it in *Foure Letters and Certeine Sonnets*.

As well as acting as a character reference, the sonnet also allows Harvey to conclude by gesturing towards the other positive author figure who features in the volume: 'Edmund Spencer'. One of Harvey's aims in his vilification of Greene is to portray him as a disgraced scholar who is unworthy even of the title 'Master of Arts', which appeared on the title pages of nearly all of his works.[32] His other intention is to portray Greene as having had the very opposite of an ideal authorial career. Thus the character of 'vile *Greene*' (p. 23) that Harvey is outlining in *Foure Letters and Certeine Sonnets*, is made to act as a foil not only for the Harvey brothers and their superior academic credentials, but also for Spenser (another Master of Arts, albeit not a scurvy one), whom Harvey regards as an ideal author. This is particularly apparent in the mock-crowning scene in which Harvey describes Greene the anti-laureate being posthumously crowned by his 'hostisse' – a scene that is unlikely to have occurred but encapsulates the contrast Harvey sees between Spenser and Greene in a powerful image:

> His sweet hostisse, for a tender farewell, crowned [Greene] with a Garland of Bayes: to shew, that a tenth Muse honoured him aliue. I know not whether *Skelton*, *Elderton*, or some like flourishing Poet were so enterred: it was his owne request, and his Nurses deuotion. (pp. 12–13)

Thirteen years earlier, Harvey had been presented to readers as a dedicatee of *The Shepheardes Calender* by virtue of being the addressee of the prefatory epistle.[33] Although it is uncertain to what extent Harvey was directly involved in the publication

32 Throughout the volume, Harvey is keen to stress his and his brothers' academic reputation, pointing not only to the Harveys' general respectability, but to the fact that they are 'vniuersally well reputed in both Vniuersities' (p. 4). He also uses the word 'doctor' repeatedly and pointedly, in order to emphasise the contrast between the 'scuruy Master of Art' (p. 4) and the more distinguished academic careers of the Harveys, noting that even John, the youngest, 'died not till the Vniuersitie of Cambridge had bestowed vpõ him a grace to bee a Doctor of his facultie' (p. 24).

33 While the title page of *The Shepheardes Calender* declares the volume to be 'entitled' to Philip Sidney – an ambiguous term, which could (and by some early readers was taken to) mean 'ascribed' – 'E.K.'s' epistle, placed where readers would expect to find the dedication, is addressed to Harvey. This effectively assigns the role of main dedicatee to him, even though the running titles only label it 'Epistle',

of the volume, he is a plausible candidate for the authorship of the glosses and possibly the epistle addressed to himself, partly because it praises Harvey's works so profusely. Regardless of whether he wrote or partially wrote it, however, the epistle's famous passage that predicts the New Poet's 'flight' to fame certainly echoes Harvey's views on poetic careers. The epistle of *The Shepheardes Calender* proposes that the New Poet has deliberately chosen 'base' pastoral for his debut in print as the first step to progressively greater poetic heights:

> [F]ollowing the example of the best & most auncient Poetes, which deuised this kind of wryting, being both so base for the matter, and homely for the manner, at the first to trye theyr habilities: and as young birdes, that be newly crept out of the nest, by little first to proue theyr tender wyngs, before they make a greater flyght. So flew Theocritus, as you may perceiue he was all ready full fledged. So flew Virgile, as not yet well feeling his winges. So flew Mantuane, as not being full somd. So Petrarque. So Boccace; So Marot, Sanazarus, and also diuers other excellent both Italian and French Poetes [...]. So finally flyeth this our new Poete.[34]

Commonly, this passage is cited to illustrate the beginnings of what Richard Helgerson has called Spenser's 'laureate ambition'. Helgerson himself regarded it as an indirect manifestation of that ambition, through 'E. K's' assurance to Harvey and other readers that his friend, the New Poet, is 'clearly beginning in the right way'.[35] For Patrick Cheney, on the other hand, the passage was an early example of Spenser's employment of the 'myth of the winged poet' in his endeavour to fashion a poetic career from several existing models.[36] Yet the passage's interest lies not only in the flourish with which the entry of the New Poet is announced, but also in the peculiar manner in which he is introduced to his readers.

Irrespective of the real identity of 'E. K.', his function as a figure within *The Shepheardes Calender* is to provide the elusive New Poet with a poetic life beyond the text itself. One of the strategies employed by 'E. K.' for this purpose is to hint at a substantial body of works already written, 'which slepe in silence' (iijᵃ). Additionally, 'E. K.' frequently invokes classical authors (including the English classic, Chaucer), and the glossed text provides a visual link to classical works. These elements create a somewhat paradoxical situation: the 'new' poet is effectively presented to his readers as a fully fledged classic, with an existing canon of works, which merely need to be 'woken' from obscurity. Although the New Poet is new to print, there is very little indication in 'E. K.'s' passages that he is a contemporary poet who is still in mid-flight, as it were. In fact, if it were not for his implicit claim at the end of the epistle to have recently spoken to the author, readers could be forgiven for concluding that the text had been edited posthumously.

I have mentioned the passage from *The Shepheardes Calender* because it echoes Gabriel Harvey's views regarding ideal poetic careers. Yet it is also of interest in the

never 'Epistle Dedicatorie', unlike the epistles prefacing 'Colin Clouts Come Home Againe' and 'The Ruines of Time'.
34 Edmund Spenser, *The Shepheardes Calender* (1579), iijᵃ.
35 Richard Helgerson, *Self-Crowned Laureates* (Berkeley: University of California Press, 1983), p. 68.
36 Patrick Cheney, *Spenser's Famous Flight: A Renaissance Idea of a Literary Career* (Toronto: University of Toronto Press, 1993), p. 12.

context of the Harvey–Nashe quarrel because of this paradox of introducing a living poet as a fixed authorial entity, whose life and works can be evaluated as a whole, and thus effectively treating him as a dead poet. During the Harvey–Nashe quarrel, both parties repeatedly use 'Immortall Spencer' as a point of reference in their arguments. Nevertheless, there is significant disagreement between Harvey and Nashe about their readings of Spenser's life and works and their assessment of what they signify. Harvey regards 'Mother Hubberds Tale' as an unfortunate generic slip that serves as proof that even Spenser is not infallible, while Nashe remembers it as the cause for 'sparks of displeasure' that were directed against its author. Similarly, Nashe disputes the existence of Spenser's friendship with Harvey, which forms an integral part of Harvey's account of Spenser's career (as well as his own).

Yet one thing that united Harvey and Nashe is that within their arguments they were both moulding Spenser's life and career to their purposes, while at the same time treating them as though they were fixed. What both were deliberately ignoring, however, is that unlike Greene, whose life and works could be given a final evaluation, Spenser was still very much alive and writing in 1592. Although Harvey and Nashe speak of Spenser as an established authorial entity with a known (and complete) oeuvre, it is worth bearing in mind that when they wrote their pamphlets, 'Spenser' did not have the same meaning as today: some of his major works had not yet been published, and *Complaints*, featuring the controversial 'Mother Hubberds Tale' at its centre, was his most recent work.[37] When Harvey and Nashe mention *The Faerie Queene* as Spenser's major work, they are thus thinking of a poem that comprises only three books, and when Nashe uses the name Colin Clout to refer to the author, he is alluding to a character that only exists within the confines of *The Shepheardes Calender*.[38] 'Colin Clouts Come Home Againe' and the second half of *The Faerie Queene* (including Colin's cameo in Book VI), which we would now naturally associate with the terms '*Faerie Queene*' and '*Colin Clout*', were still unpublished, perhaps even unwritten in 1592, which illustrates that Spenser's career was still in progress. Similarly, the sonnet at the end of *Foure Letters and Certeine Sonnets* is dated 1586 and consequently not by Spenser the celebrated author of *The Faerie Queene*, whom Harvey invokes at every opportunity, but by the as yet anonymous 'Immeritô', whose only published work had just seen its second reprint.[39]

37 *Complaints* consists of nine elements in total, of which 'Mother Hubberds Tale' is the fourth. However, since the different elements are of unequal length (the shortest, 'The Visions of Petrarch', is only three and a half pages long in the 1591 edition, while 'Mother Hubberds Tale' takes up a full five gatherings), readers who opened *Complaints* near its centre would have found themselves looking at 'Mother Hubberds Tale'.

38 *Foure Letters and Certeine Sonnets*, refers to Spenser's 'sweete Feary Queene' (p. 7), and *Strange Newes* invokes his 'gorgeous attired *Fayrie Queene*' (E^b) as well as '*Collin Clout*' (E3^b). Nashe is conflating the addressee of the letter he is quoting, 'M. Immeritô', and his fictional creation and refers to '[Harvey's] Epistles to *Collin Clout*'. This conflation of author and character is interesting because it is unlikely to be a mistake: Nashe accompanies his quotation of a passage in which Harvey appears to endorse satire with an exact (and correct) page and line reference, which suggests that he owned a copy of *Three Proper and Wittie Familiar Letters* (1580) and referred to it when writing *Strange Newes*.

39 The third quarto of *The Shepheardes Calender* was printed for John Harison the younger in 1586 by John Wolfe, who also published *Foure Letters and Certeine Sonnets* six years later. The *Familiar Letters* of 1580, which Nashe also attacked in *Strange Newes*, had contained two letters ascribed to 'Immeritô', although it was not strictly a work by him.

So how do Harvey and Nashe use Spenser in their debate? In *Foure Letters and Certeine Sonnets*, Spenser has a continued presence as a counterexample to Greene, as can be seen in the fact that the most outrageous title Harvey can imagine for a 'luxurious, and riotous' pamphlet of the sort Greene produced is '*Greenes* Faerie Queene'.[40] However, Spenser is also used as a positive example for Harvey's secondary target Thomas Nashe, whose retaliation in *Strange Newes* marks the start of his pamphlet war with Harvey.

As R. B. McKerrow, the editor of Nashe's collected works, observed in 1910, *Foure Letters and Certeine Sonnets* shows Harvey tackling his primary and secondary targets in a very different manner. While he vilifies Greene, 'Pierce' is merely treated as having strayed from the path and reproved in a somewhat patronising manner. Distancing himself from what he called the 'orthodox' view of the Harvey–Nashe quarrel, McKerrow argued that Harvey was by no means the vain, malevolent pedant depicted in Nashe's pamphlets and that the initial provocation perhaps did not warrant a response quite as harsh as *Strange Newes*: 'much of Harvey's attack upon Nashe is in truth rather to be regarded as a not unfriendly lecture on the futility of wasting time and talent on such fantastical subjects as *Pierce Penilesse*'.[41]

Somewhat ironically, considering his dismissive remarks about 'Euphuisme', Harvey in his 'not unfriendly lecture' is in fact adopting the part of Eubulus, the old gentleman of Naples, who appears at the beginning of John Lyly's *Euphues* (1578).[42] Noticing Euphues' 'pregnaunt wytte, his Eloquent tongue somewhat tauntinge, yet wyth delight [...] hys sayinges vaineglorious, yet pythie', Eubulus decides to admonish the young man, 'for hée well knewe that so rare a wytte woulde in tyme eyther bréede an intollerable trouble, or bringe an incomparable Treasure to the common weale'.[43] Unfortunately for Harvey, however, Nashe's response was much the same as that of his fictional counterpart, that is, to use his 'eloquent tongue' to lash out vehemently at his would-be mentor and to disregard his advice.

Yet while Eubulus' concerns for Euphues are of a moral nature, Harvey's concern for Nashe is literary. Unlike Greene, who in Harvey's view was beyond redemption because of the depths of literary (as well as moral) depravity he had sunk to before his death, 'his sworne brother, M. Pierce Pennilesse' (p. 28) may still be saved. However, in order to turn his 'golden talent' into the literary treasures he is capable of, he needs to be deterred from satire, which Harvey calls 'railing' and deems unsuitable for a poetic career:

---

40 Harvey, *Foure Letters and Certeine Sonnets*, p. 29. This is in allusion to Greene's *Menaphon* (1589), which was also published under the title *Greenes Arcadia*. Harvey does not appear to have read *Menaphon* but assumes it to be a reworking of Sidney's *Arcadia* for a lowbrow audience. He concludes that it must be a piece of 'mostrous newfanglednesse' (p. 29). The preface to *Menaphon* also happens to be the earliest known piece of writing by Nashe.

41 R. B. McKerrow (ed.), *The Works of Thomas Nashe*, 5 vols (London: Sidgwick & Jackson, 1910), v, 86.

42 Harvey, *Foure Letters and Certeine Sonnets*, p. 34. *Euphues* and the flowery rhetorical style associated with it had been very popular for most of the 1580s. By the end of the decade, however, it had already gone decidedly out of fashion, which explains why both Harvey and Nashe were eager to distance themselves from this style of writing in 1592. Harvey's use of 'Euphuisme' in *Foure Letters and Certeine Sonnets* is the earliest example in the *Oxford English Dictionary* (hereafter *OED*).

43 John Lyly, *Euphues: The Anatomy of Wyt* (1578), p. 2.

Good sweete Oratour, be a deuine Poet indeede: and vse heauenly Eloquence indeede: and employ thy golden talent with amounting vsance indeede: and with heroicall Cantoes honour right Vertue, & braue valour indeede: as noble Sir Philip Sidney and gentle Maister Spencer haue done, with immortal Fame: and I will bestow more complements of rare amplifications vpon thee, then euer any bestowed vppon them: or this Tounge euer affoorded.

(*Foure Letters and Certeine Sonnets*, p. 48)

Spenser is invoked by Harvey at this point not only as a positive example for Nashe to follow, but also to remind him that even a great poet may lose his footing and stray into satire. In an earlier passage in *Foure Letters and Certeine Sonnets* Harvey had talked of 'Mother Hubberds Tale' as Spenser's unfortunate brush with satire, in the context of explaining that even the best may err occasionally, externalising Spenser's 'failing' by attributing it to one of his characters, and thus avoiding direct criticism of Spenser himself: 'euen *Tully*, and *Horace* otherwhiles ouerreched: and I must needs say, Mother Hubbard, in heat of choller, forgetting the pure sanguine of her sweete Feary Queene, wilfully ouer-shott her malcontented selfe'.[44]

Nashe immediately retaliated with *Strange Newes*, which, as indicated in the heading that introduces the main text of the pamphlet, 'The foure Letters Confuted' (repeated as a running title until the end of the volume), is a comprehensive refutation of Harvey's points.[45] It is easy to read *Strange Newes* as a prolonged ad hominem attack due to its vehemence. Fundamentally, however, what Nashe is really challenging are Harvey's views regarding authorship. Nashe's strategy for discrediting Harvey's ideas – including his notion that satire is a dead end for literary careers and Nashe is therefore wasting his potential – is a methodical demolishing of the authorial role Harvey had crafted for himself in his writings.

Yet while Nashe is in disagreement with Harvey on nearly all points, there is one notable exception to this: the pre-eminence of Spenser. As far as Spenser's unchallenged status as the '*Virgil* of England' (*Strange Newes*, G3ᵃ) is concerned, Harvey and Nashe are in fact in perfect agreement. Nevertheless, Nashe turns even this point of agreement into a fundamental disagreement, by questioning the nature of Harvey's friendship with Spenser and accusing Harvey of shamelessly exploiting that friendship as a vehicle for self-promotion. As a result, Nashe spends more effort on defending Spenser against imagined insults by Harvey than he does on defending Greene against the very real insults of *Foure Letters and Certeine Sonnets*.[46]

Perhaps the best illustration of how Nashe manipulates his idea of Spenser's life and work to his own ends within the argument can be found in his reaction to Harvey's

---

44 Harvey, *Foure Letters and Certeine Sonnets*, p. 7. For Harvey, the word 'malcontent' is essentially synonymous with 'satirist'. In the fourth letter, he refers to Greene and Nashe as 'a Grashopper, and a Cricket, two pretty musitians, but silly creatures […] howsoeuer the Grashopper enraged, would bee no lesse then a greene Dragon: and the Cricket male-contented, not so little as a Blacke Bellwether: but the only Vnicorne of the Muses' (p. 52). This passage may have suggested the fable of the grasshopper who dies after writing his own epitaph in *Greenes Groats-worth of Witte*, which was probably published after Harvey's pamphlet.
45 Arguably, this makes *The Foure Letters Confuted* the 'true' title of the pamphlet.
46 Despite Harvey's allegations, Nashe is eager not to be seen as Greene's close associate and friend even while he defends him: 'What a *Calimunco* am I to plead for him, as though I were as neere to him as his own skinne. A thousand there bee that haue more reason to speake in his behalfe than I' (L4ᵇ).

labelling of 'Mother Hubberds Tale' as satire. Nashe's outburst is mainly known as one of the few pieces of contemporary evidence that the *Complaints* (1591) were 'called in', and that 'Mother Hubberds Tale' was the cause.[47] However, the passage is also of particular interest in the light of Nashe's claim that the 'friendship' of Spenser and Harvey is Harvey's invention, since he is doing more than just accusing him of reviving the memory of a literary scandal that had only just died down. Nashe is also accusing Harvey of lending credibility to rumours that 'Mother Hubberds Tale' was a satirical piece, and, more specifically, of convincing Nashe (against his will) that those rumours had not been merely slanderous and Spenser had in fact been guilty as charged. This is indicated in a peculiar change of pronouns during the relevant passage in *Strange Newes*: 'Besides, whereas before *I thought it* a made matter of some malitious moralizers against him, and no substance of slaunder in truth; now [...] *it cannot chuse but be suspected so indeed*' (E[b]; emphases added). Nashe's shift from the first person to an impersonal construction that implicitly includes himself indicates that he does to an extent believe what he so emphatically denies: that Harvey is 'the only familiar of [Spenser's] bosome, and therefore [should] know his secrets' (E[b]). Nevertheless, for the sake of refuting *Foure Letters and Certeine Sonnets*, Nashe paints an alternative image of the 'friendship', in which Spenser is merely unable to shake off Harvey after having humoured his vanity at the beginning of their acquaintance.

Why would Nashe be so eager to show that his reverence for Spenser exceeds Harvey's and to present himself as taking the former's part against the latter? As Richard McCabe has demonstrated, there was an element of 'cultural patronage' in the friendship of Harvey and Spenser, and in 1592, Harvey was more aware than ever that 'Edmund Spencer' was a name to conjure with.[48] McCabe's reading of the Harvey–Nashe quarrel as a 'contest between *two* would-be appropriators' over the right to associate their own name with the 'brand name' Spenser (p. 61) certainly rings true. Yet just as Harvey does not invoke Spenser's example in *Foure Letters and Certeine Sonnets* purely to enhance his own reputation, Nashe in *Strange Newes* does not challenge Harvey about his capitalising on Spenser's fame purely because he is hoping to capitalise on it himself.

Harvey's role as Spenser's respected and trusted friend formed an integral part of the authorial identity he had shaped for himself. Consequently, in order to demolish Harvey the author Nashe also needed to discredit the 'Hobbinol' myth on which Harvey had built much of his authority in print. In *Strange Newes*, Nashe strives to free 'Immortall *Spencer*' from 'the imputation of this Idiots friendship' (E[b]), even to the point of claiming that all instances of Spenser's praise that Harvey cites are forgeries or misunderstood satire: 'If euer he praisd thee, it was because he had pickt a fine vaine foole out of thee, and he would keepe thee still a foole by flattring thee' (L[a]). By attributing such a motivation to Spenser, Nashe is implicitly bringing him closer to his own position, while also suggesting that Spenser may be more inclined towards satire than his 'friend' Harvey would like to believe.

47 For an overview of the other pieces of evidence see Richard S. Peterson, 'Laurel Crown and Ape's Tail: New Light on Spenser's Career from Sir Thomas Tresham', *Spenser Studies*, 12 (1998), 1–35.
48 Richard McCabe, '"Thine owne nations frend / And Patrone": The Rhetoric of Petition in Harvey and Spenser', *Spenser Studies*, 22 (2007), 47–72.

It is uncertain whether Spenser himself (who was already living in Ireland by then) ever responded to the Harvey–Nashe quarrel in any way. However, there is a possible echo of Harvey's descriptions of Nashe's satirical writings in a passage of Book V ('Of Justice') that depicts a scene of censorship. Harvey's insult of choice for satire and satirists – which, at least by 1592, he disapproved of – had been 'railing', a term whose main meaning in early modern usage is angry, abusive ranting. In *The Faerie Queene*, Spenser consistently uses it in this sense; consequently, it is associated with Abessa and Corceca in Book I, Furor and Occasion, as well as Cymochles in Book II, Blandamour and Sclaundour in Book IV, Enuie in Book V and the Blatant Beast in Book VI. The only instance in which Spenser uses 'rayling' in the Harveyan sense to refer to a mode of writing is in V.ix.25, where Bonfont/Malfont's crimes against mercy (embodied by Mercilla) are described as including 'lewd poems', 'bold speaches' and 'rayling rymes'. The satirical poet is punished by having his name changed and his sharp tongue nailed to a post, which suggests Spenser's attitude towards satire was probably closer to Harvey's than to Nashe's – although in 1592, with 'Mother Hubberds Tale' as one of Spenser's most recent works, Nashe may have thought it possible that Spenser had turned towards satire.

While there may be a strategic element to Nashe's defence of Spenser, there is no reason to doubt that he does hold him in high regard as a poet and views his career as beyond reproach. One of the side-effects of Nashe's suggestion that *Three Proper and Wittie Familiar Letters* (1580) had been published purely on Harvey's initiative is that it absolves Spenser from the potential charge of having attempted to fashion an authorial career for himself in the same way as Harvey. This leaves Nashe free to disapprove of that practice and to contrast Harvey's career-fashioning and his approach to authorship unfavourably to Greene's:

> Hee made no account of winning credite by his workes as thou dost, that dost no good workes, but thinkes to be famosed by a strong faith in thy owne worthiness: his only care was to haue a spel in his purse to coniure vp a good cuppe of wine with at all times. (*Strange Newes*, E4^b)

What Nashe is describing in this passage is a model of professional authorship. Because Greene's pamphlets were popular and commercial, he argues, publishers were happy to 'pay him deare for the very dregs of his wit' (E4^b). This, in connection with what Harvey had called Greene's 'running Head, and [...] scribling Hand, that neuer linnes putting-forth new, newer, & newest bookes of the maker' allowed Greene to live by his pamphlets.[49] Nashe contrasts this with Harvey's lack of commercial success, claiming that rather than being paid for his efforts, he is reduced to 'bribing' publishers and stationer's shops to print and display his works (which amounts to accusing him of vanity publishing).[50] In *Strange Newes*, then, Nashe seeks

---

49 Harvey, *Foure Letters and Certeine Sonnets*, p. 23.
50 See also Act I, Scene 3 of the university play *The Second Part of the Return from Parnassus* (*c.* 1600), a scene that is clearly derived from *Strange Newes*. In this short scene, former scholar and poet-for-hire Ingenioso, a character based on Nashe, haggles with his publisher John Danter about the advance for his (as yet unwritten) 'Chronicle of Cambridge Cuckolds'. Although Danter initially refuses to pay more than the standard 40 shillings, pointing out that 'there is many a one that payes me largely for the printing of their inuentions' (ll. 342–3), Ingenioso eventually persuades him to 'haue it whatsoeuer it

to expose Harvey's authorial identity as the sage and impassionate scholarly author 'G. H.' as an elaborate self-deception on Harvey's part. In reality, he argues, Harvey has tried – and failed – both in achieving commercial success through his works and in securing patronage.

It is easy to view the pamphlet war between Harvey and Nashe as a destructive process in which two ambitious authors tried to further the authorial careers they had crafted for themselves by ruining each other's personal and professional reputations. Yet while destructiveness is certainly a prominent element of the Harvey–Nashe quarrel, and it arguably did wreck both their writing careers, there is a certain creative aspect to it as well. James P. Bednarz, in his study of the 'Poets' War' acted out on the English stage between 1599 and 1601, argued that 'despite the personal tone of Jonson's quarrel with Shakespeare, Marston and Dekker, the Poets' War was, on its most abstract level, a theoretical debate'.[51] Much the same can be said about the Harvey–Nashe quarrel, which despite the proliferation of personal insults in the pamphlets is fundamentally about notions of authorship. However, Harvey and Nashe not only defined their own roles as writers through their quarrel, they also sparked a wider debate among the relatively new but increasingly vocal group of 'professional' prose writers.

Edward Gieskes, in his study of rising professions in early modern England, described a broadening of the market for 'cultural products', which, he argues, 'enabled new categories of producers to develop and find an audience for their writing'.[52] Although the main focus of Gieskes' study is the way in which this development affected theatre, another category of 'new producers' that emerged were authors who were 'professionals' in more than one sense: they were simultaneously involved with other aspects of book-production, such as the printing, publishing and editing of texts. Nashe was one of the more prominent representatives of this group. His first two printed texts were editorial prefaces to works by other authors (Robert Greene and Sir Philip Sidney respectively), and he worked in close association with the printer and publisher John Danter. Another prominent print professional was Henry Chettle. As a stationer and compositor as well as a playwright, Chettle was involved in every step of commercial literary production from the writing to the selling of texts.[53] His contribution to the authorship debate triggered by the Harvey–Nashe quarrel was a pamphlet called *Kind-Harts Dreame* (1592), which not only contained his famous denial of authorship of *Greenes Groats-worth of Witte* but also identified itself as a direct response to *Foure Letters and Certeine Sonnets* both in the text and through its title page.[54]

Kind-Harts Dreame purports to be a collection of letters to posterity, which the

cost' (ll. 361–2). Both in *Strange Newes* and in *The Second Part of the Return from Parnassus*, the implication is that while pamphlet-writing may not be the most dignified of occupations, it is nevertheless a profitable way of making a living.

51 James P. Bednarz, *Shakespeare & the Poets' War* (New York: Columbia University Press, 2001), p. 7.
52 Edward Gieskes, *Representing the Professions: Administration, Law and Theater in Early Modern England* (Newark: University of Delaware Press, 2006), p. 217.
53 For a more detailed account of Chettle's role, see John Jowett, 'Henry Chettle: "Your old compositor"', *Text*, 15 (2003), 141–61.
54 *Kind-Harts Dreame* was licenced for print just four days after *Foure Letters and Certeine Sonnets*.

main character, Kind-Hart the barber, claims to have come by through unusual circumstances. After he has fallen asleep at an alehouse, six figures appear to him in
his dream. Of those, five are the ghosts of Kind-Hart's deceased friends, a ballad-
eer, a juggler, a physician and two 'personages not alltogether obscure' (B[a]): Richard
Tarlton and Robert Greene.[55] The sixth is the 'knight of the post' who has just returned
from delivering Pierce Penilesse's supplication to the devil.[56] When the knight refuses
to deliver the ghosts' letters of complaint to posterity, the ghosts settle for a different
method of delivery by forcing their letters on Kind-Hart, thus waking him from his
dream with their request to publish them in print.[57] What unites the ghosts' letters is
that their grievances all relate to people they believe to have brought their respective
'arts' into disrepute. *Kind-Harts Dreame* can be read as a humorous vindication of
different professions against detractors, but above all, it is directed against one particular detractor: Gabriel Harvey.

　　Greene's ghost stands out among the others because his letter to posterity has a
specific addressee (Pierce Penilesse) and because the cause of his restlessness is not
concern for his whole profession but concern for his personal reputation. Referring
to *Foure Letters and Certeine Sonnets*, Greene's ghost implores Nashe to avenge him –
or rather, he informs him that he would have implored him, had he been able to send
his letter sooner. Some commentators have been puzzled by what appears to be a
needless and belated attempt on Chettle's part to fan the flames of the Harvey–Nashe
quarrel. Since *Strange Newes* had already been published, Chettle would have been
aware that Nashe needed no further encouragement to 'reuenge [his] wrongs' (E2[a]).
The exhortation to Pierce is in fact framed by two clear indications that Greene's
ghost is relaying an obsolete message: 'My quiet Ghost […] *had once intended* thus to
have exclaimd' and 'All this *had I intended* to write'.[58] However, by placing Greene
in the company of the other professional ghosts, Chettle is doing more than merely
fanning the flames of an ongoing pamphlet war. *Kind-Harts Dreame* is both a commentary on and a contribution to the authorship debate triggered by the Harvey–
Nashe quarrel. It suggests to its readers that what is at stake here is not only Greene's
reputation but that of an entire profession, to which both Chettle and Nashe also
belong. When viewed in this light, the purpose of the exhortation to Nashe is perhaps
not so much to egg him on in his dispute with Harvey as to remind him that he too
is a professional writer, even if he had not chosen to portray himself in this manner
in *Strange Newes*.

　　Above all, however, *Kind-Harts Dreame* is a direct response to *Foure Letters and
Certeine Sonnets* in its own right. The clearest indication of this is its title page, which
features an emblem of snakes coiling about a palm tree, and a motto, which reads 'Il
vostro malignare non giova nulla' ('your malignity will be to no avail'). This device,

55　The fact that the two are grouped together echoes Harvey's quip that Greene had 'gone to Tarlton'.
56　In Thomas Nashe's *Pierce Penilesse*, impoverished writer Pierce uses a 'knight of the post' – another
　　term for a perjurer – as a messenger to deliver his petition for money to the devil, as perjurers are a
　　group of people who can be counted on to go to hell (and fast). The motif of the knight of the post going
　　to hell and taking messages along was picked up by several of Nashe's contemporaries.
57　Hence *Kind-Harts Dreame*'s subtitle, 'Deliuered by seuerall Ghosts vnto him to be publisht, after *Piers
　　Penilesse* Post had refused the carriage', which also highlights Nashe's pun on 'post'.
58　*Kind-Harts Dreame*, E[b]–E2[a]. Emphases added.

which was probably owned by John Wolfe, the printer of Harvey's pamphlets, had been used before, on the title pages of Wolfe's editions of Machiavelli's works.[59] Between 1592 and 1593, however, it was closely associated with Harvey. In addition to *Kind-Harts Dreame*, there were four other title pages that used the device during this period. Out of these, three featured the name 'Harvey' and the fourth the name 'Greene'.[60]

The image had been a fitting choice for *Foure Letters and Certeine Sonnets* because it encapsulated Harvey's sense of wounded integrity. Geffrey Whitney's *A Choice of Emblemes* (1586) had featured a similar image under the heading 'Inuidia integritatis affecla [*sic*]'.[61] The second verse of Whitney's 'moralizing' poem underneath, which interprets the emblem, begins:

When noble peeres, and men of high estate,
By iuste deserte, doe liue in honor greate:
Yet, Enuie still dothe waite on them as mate,
And does her worste, to vndermine their feate.[62]

In its new context, on the title page of *Kind-Harts Dreame*, the significance of the emblem is less clear than it had been on the title page of *Foure Letters and Certeine Sonnets*, as it is simultaneously referring to three different grievances. First, it can be applied to Chettle's defence against the accusation of having written *Greenes Groatsworth of Witte* and authored the contentious passages attacking the playwrights. At another level, the emblem represents the professional integrity that each of the entertainers whose ghosts visit Kind-Hart in his sleep claims is endangered by those 'that wake to commit mischiefe' (A4[b]). Finally, referring to Greene's dismay at being slandered by Harvey in *Foure Letters and Certeine Sonnets*, the use of the emblem can be seen as a subtle way of turning Harvey's own imagery against him. The title page of *Kind-Harts Dreame* thus effectively transforms him from 'gallant Palme' to poisonous serpent, while asserting the integrity of Greene's life and works, as well as those of Chettle and his fellow print professionals.

This authorship discourse sparked by the Harvey–Nashe quarrel was instrumental in creating a new category of authorship. Together, the participants 'wilfully forge[d] in their conceits a liuing Author'.[63] This in turn led to what might be termed the Greene myth: the story of bestselling author and his notorious life, which, according to Crupi, 'anyone who knows Greene's name at all' is familiar with. In a sense,

59 *I Discorsi di Nicolo Machiavelli* (1584), *Il Prencipe* (1584) and *Libro dell'arte della Guerra* (1587), all published under a false imprint. Wolfe was also one of the two printers involved in the printing of *Greenes Groats-worth of Witte* (the other was Nashe's printer and publisher, John Danter).

60 The three Harvey pamphlets are *Foure Letters and Certeine Sonnets* (1592), *Pierces Supererogation* (1593), as well as *Philadelphus* (1593) by Harvey's brother Richard. The Greene pamphlet is *Philomela* (1592), a posthumously published romance that does not contain any references to Greene's life or works.

61 'Invidia integritatis affecta' translates as 'integrity set upon by envy'.

62 Geffrey Witney, *A Choice of Emblemes, and other Deuises, for the moste parte gathered out of sundrie writers, Englished and moralized* (1586), p. 118.

63 *Kind-Harts Dreame*, A3[b]. Chettle uses this phrase to describe the playwrights' attempts to pin the authorship of *Greenes Groats-worth of Witte* on him, but it also serves as an apt phrase to describe the fashioning of Greene's authorial persona through the pamphlets.

then, Harvey and Nashe should be regarded not merely as the opponents in a personal quarrel but also as instrumental figures in the creation of 'Greene' and his posthumous career.

'All Greenes'? The posthumous Greene pamphlets

Within months of *Foure Letters and Certeine Sonnets*, three pamphlets were posthumously published under Greene's name, each purporting to be Greene's final work, written on his deathbed: *Greenes Groats-worth of Witte*, *The Repentance of Robert Greene Maister of Artes* and *Greenes Vision*. All of these were dated 1592, which illustrates the speed at which the debate about Greene's authorial career unfolded.[64]

Although the three pamphlets, unlike *Strange Newes*, are not direct responses to *Foure Letters and Certeine Sonnets*, they do respond to Harvey's points regarding Greene's authorial career, especially his claim that it lacks a discernible pattern. The one possible exception to this is *Greenes Groats-worth of Witte*, for which there is some indication that it may have been written in direct response to the early stages of the Harvey–Nashe quarrel. A passage in the letter to the playwrights is addressed to Nashe and gives 'yong *Iuuenal*, that byting Satyrist' the following advice:

> Sweet boy, might I aduise thee, be aduisde, and get not many enemies by bitter wordes: inueigh against vaine men, for thou canst do it, no man better, no man so well: thou hast a libertie to reprooue all, and name none; for one being spoken to, all are offended; none being blamed no man is iniured. Stop shallow water still running, it will rage, or tread on a worme and it will turne: then blame not Schollers vexed with sharpe lines, if they reproue thy too much liberty of reproofe. (F^a–F^b)

While this could of course be in reference to earlier clashes between Nashe and Harvey, the timing is peculiar, and the address 'Sweet boy' resembles Harvey's 'Good sweete Oratour'. Additionally, the image of the 'worme' can be regarded as an allusion to the snakes of the title emblem of *Foure Letters and Certeine Sonnets* (discussed above), and the phrase 'if they reproue thy too much liberty of reproofe' echoes a passage in which Harvey criticises the danger that satirists may 'ouer-reche': 'Oratours haue challenged a speciall Liberty: and Poets claimed an absolute Licence: but no Liberty without boundes: nor any Licence without limitation' (p. 6). It is thus possible to consider *Greenes Groats-worth of Witte* at least partly a response to *Foure Letters and Certeine Sonnets*.[65]

Regardless of whether the similarities between the addresses to Nashe in *Foure Letters and Certeine Sonnets* and *Greenes Groats-worth of Witte* are a sign that the latter is a response to the former, or just an odd coincidence, there are three

---

64 Greene had, after all, only died in September 1592. While the any books published between 1 January and 24 March 1593 would of course have been dated 1592 (according to the old style, the new year began on Lady Day (25 March) rather than on 1 January), this still means the books were all published over the space of just six months.

65 While it was licenced before *Foure Letters and Certeine Sonnets*, this need not mean that it was also printed first. Henry Chettle, who was instrumental in the publishing of *Greenes Groats-worth of Witte*, is generally believed to have written or at least edited it, so it would not have been impossible for him to include some allusions to *Foure Letters and Certeine Sonnets*.

characteristics that all of the posthumous Greene pamphlets share. First, each of them is presented to the reader as Greene's last work, written shortly before (or even 'at the instant of') his death. Second, all three pamphlets are concerned with outlining and evaluating Greene's literary career through looking back on his life. Finally, all three texts show signs of significant editing or even collaboration. This led to another type of authorship debate during the twentieth century, focusing on the authenticity of *Greenes Groats-worth of Witte*.

Greenes Groats-worth of Witte purports to represent Greene's voice speaking from beyond the grave, and several paratextual elements are framed to remind readers that the book is Greene's and that Greene is dead. The first of these reminders is on the title page, which, although it does not explicitly claim the book was written *by* Greene, emphasises the word 'Greenes' in the title through a particularly large font. Following the four-line synopsis of the pamphlet's contents, two lines describing the supposed circumstances of the text's publication simultaneously declare Greene the author of the text by speaking of '*his* death and [...] *his* dyeing request' (emphases added) and draw particular attention to the fact of his recent death (A1[a]). William Wright's preface, 'The Printer to the Gentle Readers', again reminds those readers that 'nowe hath death giuen a period to his pen' and urges them to 'accept [the pamphlet] fauourably because it was his last birth and not least worth' (A2[a]). The main part of the text, which tells the story of Roberto the usurer's son, is followed by several letters of farewell.

By contrast, *The Repentance of Robert Greene*, which is likely to be based on an earlier repentance tract by Greene, is framed as (without explicitly proclaiming to be) his last work through the way in which it is edited. The very first sentence of Cuthbert Burbie's preface touches upon what he clearly considers the text's three main selling points: its topicality due to Greene's recent death, the popularity of Greene's works and his interestingly 'loose' and 'lasciuious' life.[66]

> Gentlemen, I know you ar [*sic*] not vnacquainted with the death of *Robert Greene*, whose pen in his life time pleased you as well on the Stage, as in the Stationers shops: And to speake truth, although his loose life was odious to God and offensiue to men, yet forasmuch as at his last end he found it most grieuous to himselfe (as appeareth by this his repentant discourse) I doubt not but he shall for the same deserue fauour both of God and men.
>
> (*Repentance*, A2[a])

Above all, Burbie's preface hints at an increased interest in the story of Greene's life in the wake of his death. Although sometimes taken as a reference to Greene's notoriety as a known figure during his lifetime, the position of Burbie's claim that Greene's life was 'odious to God and offensiue to men' suggests that it is simply an attempt to stress its scandalous nature in order to generate interest among his readership. Although Burbie also refers to the pamphlet's possible moral benefits for its readers as the story of a penitent sinner, he adds this almost as an afterthought on the second page of his preface. It is thus reasonable to assume that Burbie's main motivation for

---

66 Burbie is more commonly known for two of his later publications, the quarto of Shakespeare's *Love's Labour's Lost* (1598) and the 'good' quarto of *Romeo and Juliet* (1599).

publishing the *Repentance* was not concern for readers' morals but to capitalise on the increased interest in Greene while it lasted.

Finally, although internal evidence suggests that *Greenes Vision* was in fact written two years earlier, its publisher Thomas Newman goes to some lengths to convince readers that it is Greene's last work.[67] In his dedication, Newman also stresses the text's authenticity: 'Manie haue published repentaunces vnder his name, but none more vnfeigned then this, being euerie word of his owne: his own phrase, his own method' (A3ª).[68] The pamphlets Newman indirectly accuses of having been 'feigned' or at least not containing 'euerie word of [Greene's] own' most likely include *Greenes Groats-worth of Witte*, whose authorship appears to have been questioned almost as soon as it was published.[69] The dedication is followed by a preface ('To the Gentlemen Readers, Health') signed 'Yours dying: *Robert Greene*', in which the author expresses his intent to rescue his posthumous reputation and not to let 'iniurious tongues triumph ouer a dead carcase' after his death (A4ª).[70] Interestingly, the preface portrays Greene as not so much seeking divine forgiveness for his life but forgiveness from his readers for his works, making the *Vision* a very different type of repentance. Although the preface to the *Vision* is paying lip-service to penitence of the kind found in the *Repentance* in the phrase 'God forgiue me all my misdemeanours', it is otherwise only concerned with what judgements readers might pass on the author on the basis of his works.

Why, then, were the publishers of *Greenes Groats-worth of Witte*, *The Repentance of Robert Greene* and *Greenes Vision* all so eager to stress that what they were presenting to their readers was Greene's final work? The most obvious explanation is that of topicality. Greene's death – or, more likely, Harvey's utilisation of it in *Foure Letters and Certeine Sonnets* – may have either caused an increased interest in Greene and his 'vile' life, or at least led publishers to anticipate such an interest and put whatever 'dregs of his wit' (*Strange Newes*, E4ᵇ) they still possessed into print. However, beyond the fact that during the last months of 1592 the name Greene was perhaps better known than ever before, the conceit of posthumously presenting the author's last work, written on his death-bed as a form of personal reckoning, has another function. It allows for a final evaluation of both the life and the works. This, again, is something that all three of the posthumous Greene pamphlets attempt to do, although they differ in their methods and conclusions.

---

67 The occasion of the pamphlet was the false attribution of a mock-Chaucerian romance called *The Cobler of Caunterburie*, which had been published in 1590, as an immediate reply to the anonymous *Tarltons Newes out of Purgatorie* (published in the same year and sometimes attributed to Tarlton's fellow actor Robert Armin).

68 Thomas Newman is an intriguing figure in the publishing scene of the early 1590s, albeit an elusive one, as is illustrated by an uncommonly sparse *DNB* entry. His best-known publication, which I shall discuss in the following chapter, is the 1591 quarto edition of Sidney's *Astrophel and Stella*, which in its first version contained a preface by Thomas Nashe.

69 Thomas Nashe emphatically denied being the author of *Greenes Groats-worth of Witte* in his preface to the second edition of *Pierce Penilesse* (1592), while Henry Chettle, who probably was involved in its writing, declared it to be 'all *Greenes*, not mine nor Maister *Nashes*' in *Kind-Harts Dreame* (1593), one of several pamphlets that did not claim to be by Greene but featured Greene as a ghost (A4ª).

70 As this preface is the only thing in the text to support Newman's claim that the *Vision* was one of Greene's last works, its authority is questionable, especially considering the clear references to *The Cobler of Caunterburie* as a newly published work.

The earliest and best known of the pamphlets, *Greenes Groats-worth of Witte*, is a curious mixture between biographical narrative and prose romance featuring a hero whose name, 'Roberto', is clearly intended to identify him as a recognisable fictional alter ego for Greene. Like *Foure Letters and Certeine Sonnets*, it is a volume consisting of several different components. Through blurring the distinctions between the pamphlet's author, its narrator figure and the principal character of the main narrative, however, it transforms the grotesquely depraved author portrayed by Harvey into a semi-fictional character. The beginning of this transformation can be seen even before the start of the main narrative. William Wright's preface is followed by another, unsigned, preface called 'To The Gentlemen Readers', which is written in Greene's voice, but contains a switch in perspective. The first third of the preface, which describes the following pamphlet as Greene's 'Swanne like songe', refers only to 'Greene' and 'he'. Then the perspective changes to the first person, when the preface introduces the possibility that the book may in fact not turn out to be a swan-song after all: 'yet if I recouer, you shall all see, more fresh sprigs, then euer sprang from me' (A3ᵇ). The three sentences that follow use the personal pronoun 'I' eight times. This includes one peculiar instance (not replicated in the second edition) in which the capital letter 'I' is set in roman type rather than the long italic type used throughout the rest of the preface, and thus effectively highlighted.

While this could be a simple mistake that happened because some italic 'I's were mixed in with the roman type at the print shop, throughout the rest of *Greenes Groats-worth of Witte* font changes are used only to highlight proper names and Latin phrases.[71] The only exception to this is the famous phrase 'Tygers hart wrapt in a Players hyde' (F1ᵇ) from the letter to the playwrights, which is set like a Latin phrase, perhaps to make it more easily recognisable as a modified quotation from Shakespeare's *Henry VI*.[72] The 'highlighted' I of the preface could well be coincidence, but it is a fitting illustration of the blurring of identities between 'Greene', 'Roberto', 'R. G.' and 'I' that occurs in the rest of the pamphlet. The frame narrative of *Greenes Groats-worth of Witte* (which is interrupted by tales and poems at several points) follows the story of the scholar-poet Roberto, the first of these identities.

In his essay 'Forming Greene', Steve Mentz proposes that *Greenes Groats-worth of Witte* should be read as a 'summatory response to Greene's twelve-year career in print' rather than as a disjointed text.[73] He argues that the different parts of the text 'lay out in full the seven genres that span Greene's prose career'.[74] Although Mentz is primarily concerned with explaining the structure of *Greenes Groats-worth of Witte*

---

71 There is one other instance of the wrong type of 'I' being used, in the word 'Incontinence' (on the same page, but separated from the other roman 'I' by three italic 'I's). In the second edition (1596), the preface 'To the Gentlemen Readers' is set in roman font, without any highlighting of the 'I'.

72 This quotation is the strongest piece of evidence in the case for the identification of Shakespeare as the 'vpstart Crow, beautified with our feathers' (with the additional twist that the passage is borrowing one of the crow's own feathers in order to make the accusation).

73 Steve Mentz, 'Forming Greene: Theorizing the Early Modern Author in the *Groatsworth of Wit*', in Melnikoff and Gieskes (eds), *Writing Robert Greene*, pp. 115–31 (p. 115).

74 Mentz, 'Forming Greene', p. 126. According to Mentz's classification, the seven genres are: Lylian romance, novella collections, Greek romances, farewells to folly, coney-catching, repentance tracts and satire/invective.

and the peculiar form of collaboration between a dead author and his editor, he is raising an important point here that applies to all three posthumous pamphlets. They are 'final' works taking a retrospective look at Greene's career and evaluating it. In the case of *Greenes Groats-worth of Witte*, this retrospective aspect is of particular interest in the light of the ironic subtext of the frame narrative, which tells the tale of Roberto.

At first sight, the story of the hapless poet Roberto appears to be a straightforward prodigal tale portraying the protagonist's descent into a dissolute state not unlike the one described by Harvey. However, some features in the text serve to undermine this prodigal tale from the outset. Roberto's moral and financial decline begins after his father Gorinio disinherits him on his deathbed. Instead of his inheritance, Roberto merely receives an old groat, 'wherewith I wish him to buy a groats-worth of wit' (B2[b]). Yet the reason Roberto is disinherited and turned from an idealistic scholar into a 'poore pennilesse Poet' is that he does not share his father's moral values. Gorinio is a miserly usurer, and Roberto refuses to follow in his footsteps, because he insists that usury is a sin. In order to contextualise Roberto's filial disobedience, it is thus revealing to see what sort of 'wit' Gorinio is hoping to pass on to his sons, exemplified in his advice to his favourite son, Roberto's younger brother: '*Luciano* if thou read well this booke (and with that hee reacht him Machiauels workes at large) thou shalt se, what tis to be so foole-holy as to make scruple of conscience where profit presents it selfe' (B3[b]).

As a result of this, the moral of the prodigal narrative is subverted from the start. When a miserable Roberto later regrets not having heeded his father's advice, he is effectively regretting that he allowed moral scruples to get in the way of a lucrative career as a money-lender and that he failed to transform his single groat into a fortune, as Gorinio did. After an unsuccessful attempt to cheat his brother out of his inheritance, Roberto falls into bad company – actors, drunkards and coney-catchers – and makes a miserable living as an 'Arch-plaimaking-poet' (E[b]) until he has lost everything but his father's groat. At this point he exclaims: 'O now it is too late, too late to buy witte with thee: and therefore will I see if I can sell to carelesse youth what I negligently forgot to buy' (E2[b]–E3[a]). 'Sell' is an unexpectedly materialistic choice of verb here, and it again indicates that Roberto's remorse is not primarily of a moral nature. Ultimately, he regrets his lack of prudence in monetary matters, which has driven him into poverty, rather than the fact that he has become 'hardened in wickednesse' (E2[a]).

As soon as Roberto realises that his very failure to make money could potentially be turned into profit by writing down and selling his story as a cautionary tale to benefit 'careless youth', the narrator interrupts the narrative:[75]

> Heere (Gentlemen) breake I off *Robertoes* speach; whose life in most partes agræing with mine, found one selfe punishment as I haue doone. Heereafter suppose me the saide

---

75 The narrator also interrupts and draws attention to his role on four other occasions during the narrative: 'Here by the way Gentlemen must I digresse', 'now returne, wee to sicke *Gorinius*' (both B2[b]), 'But that wee may keepe forme, you shall heare howe it fortuned' (B4[b]), '[Roberto,] whom we will follow, & leaue *Luciano* to the mercie of *Lamilia*' (D4[a]).

Roberto, and I will goe on with that hee promised: *Greene* will send you now his groats-worth of wit, that neuer shewed a mites-worth in his life: & though no man now bee by to doo mee good: yet ere I die I will by my repentaunce indeauour to doo all men good.

(*Groats-worth*, E3ᵃ)

Until the narrator's interruption, any identification of Roberto as Greene's alter ego must have been resting on loose similarities, that is their shared first name and similarities between their biographies. During Roberto's decline, for example, he takes to writing plays and associates with the kind of people described in Greene's coney-catching pamphlets. Now, however, it is the narrator who explicitly forces the comparison on his readers and simultaneously identifies himself as Greene by shifting from 'I' to '*Greene*' and back to 'I'. Through this confused reference, the passage actively blurs the distinctions between the three personae of 'Roberto', 'I' and 'Greene'.

The confusion of identities serves to obscure rather than explain the title of the pamphlet. The tale of the impoverished poet Roberto, who regrets not having heeded his father's advice to devote his life to material gain, is in fact a poor illustration of the speaker's professed altruistic intentions in his 'repentaunce'. If we are to 'suppose [him] the saide *Roberto*', then the 'groats-worth of wit' that he intends to sell to his readers is not the poet's lament over his 'blacke workes' and his materialistic variation on the ten commandments (E3ᵇ) that follow, but the paradoxical fact that a penniless poet may still make money out of his situation by selling a story about a penniless poet to a publisher. Rather than confirming Harvey's negative reading of Greene's career, then, *Greenes Groats-worth of Witte* represents an ironic celebration of a successful career as a professional writer able to turn 'the very dregs' – or a mere groat's-worth – of his wit into cash. Even the letter to the playwrights frames Greene's condemnation of professional play-writing in materialistic terms, and urges the playwrights to turn towards 'more profitable courses' (Fᵇ). 'Greene' thus seems as much concerned for their material as their spiritual welfare when he concludes by expressing his wish 'that [they] should liue' (F2ᵇ).

By contrast, *The Repentance of Robert Greene* evaluates Greene's authorial career not so much in material as in moral terms. It presents his works both as the main manifestation of Greene's wickedness and as his potential path to redemption. What links the two main sections of *The Repentance of Robert Greene*, 'The Repentance of Robert Greene' and 'The life and death of Robert Greene', is their common theme of Greene's life. However, while they are essentially covering the same ground (that is Greene's prodigal-like life and his repentance), they are approaching this theme from different angles. 'The Repentance of Robert Greene, Maister of Arts' deals almost entirely with Greene's spiritual life – or lack thereof – until 'checked by the mightie hand of God' through the sudden onset of sickness (B2ᵇ). This leads him to contemplate God and the afterlife and to conclude: '*Robin Greene* thou art damned' (B3ᵃ). 'The life and death of Robert Greene', on the other hand, focuses primarily on the details of Greene's sinful life. Curiously, this appears to be almost synonymous with his professional life.

In the two passages in the narrative that stress the depths of depravity to which Greene has sunk, the text pointedly refers to his writings. The first of those passages describes how, after having managed to alienate even his 'lewd' and waggish university friends, Greene moves to London and becomes 'an Author of Playes, and a penner of Loue Pamphlets [...] [and] soone grew famous in that qualitie' (C^b). This is immediately followed by his resolve that 'there was nothing bad, that was profitable: whereupon I grew so rooted in all mischiefe, that I had as great a delight in wickednesse, as sundrie hath in godlinesse' (C^b).[76] Through the text's association of professional writing with 'wickednesse', what is initially just a symptom of Greene's fall (his being reduced to writing cheap, 'profitable' popular texts to support his drunken, sinful lifestyle) is reinterpreted as a wicked action in itself and 'the first steppe to hell' (C2^a). As a result, the text appears to suggest that Greene's chief sin was writing.[77] This theme of Greene's writings precipitating his fall recurs in the second passage of the 'Life and death', which is concerned with Greene's writings. In this passage, the statement that his 'misdemeanors [are] too many to bee recited' (C3^b) is followed by a stock-taking of his writings and their detrimental effects. The continual 'penning of plaies' is interpreted as the cause of Greene's swearing and blaspheming, while the 'trifling Pamphlets [...] of Loue, and vaine fantasies' make him 'beloued of the more vainer sort of people' (both C3^b), who are even worse company than his former friends, the Cambridge wags.

However, while 'The life and death' portrays Greene's sins primarily as literary ones, it also conversely suggests the possibility of commercial writing as a form of atonement, when pointing out that there is one type of writing that Greene need not repent:

> But I thanke God, that hee put it in my head, to lay open the most horible coosenages of the common Cony-catchers, Cooseners, and Crosse-biters, which I haue indifferently handled in those my seuerall discourses already imprinted. And my trust is, that those discourses will doe great good, and bee very beneficiall to the Common-wealth of England. (*Repentance*, C3^b–C4^a)

In the above passage, Greene's stock-taking over his works, which began as self-accusation, has turned into what reads like a thinly veiled boast. The implication is that just as Greeene wrote himself out of God's grace, he might write himself – and his readers – back into it, which is of course the premise of *The Repentance of Robert Greene* as set out by the two prefaces.[78]

The Repentance of Robert Greene is the most overtly biographical of the posthumous

---

76 Note the difference between this use of the word 'profitable' and its much more positive connotations in *Greenes Groats-worth of Witte*.

77 Just over a decade earlier, Stephen Gosson had used a similar argument by portraying plays (and especially comedies) as corrupting influences not only on players and audiences but on the people who write them: 'Now if any man aske me why my selfe haue penned Comedyes in time paste, & inueigh so egerly against them here, let him knowe that *Semel insaniuimus omnes*: I haue sinned, and am sorry for my fault: [...] better late then neuer.' Stephen Gosson, *The Schoole of Abuse* (1579), C7^b. Note also the similarity of Gosson's 'better late then neuer' and 'sero sed serio', the motto of *Greenes Vision*, which translates to 'late but in earnest'.

78 A rather different take on the power of writing can be found in a 1593 pamphlet (not discussed here in detail), in which Greene's writings fail to convince either St Peter or the devil of his good (or bad) intentions, as is illustrated in its full title, *Greenes Newes both from Heauen and Hell Prohibited the first for writing of bookes, and banished out of the last for displaying of conny-catchers*.

Greene pamphlets, as well as the one that most clearly casts him as a prodigal figure. It is also the pamphlet in which Greene's works are most explicitly associated with his sins and the various phases of his life. As a result, Greene's works are given a sequence, which, though factually inaccurate, is the sequence that best accounts for the different genres in which he wrote, while also matching the tale of the prodigal who falls into ever lower company and eventually mends his ways. Thus *The Repentance of Robert Greene* suggests that Greene started out as a playwright, then wrote his 'Loue Pamphlets' (that is, his romances), followed by the coney-catching pamphlets and ultimately his repentance tracts.

The Repentance of Robert Greene attempts to establish a link between his life and works and therefore constitutes a posthumous reshaping of Greene's life and works by turning the prodigal narrative into a key to his writing career. The prodigal narrative with its associated writing phases helps to arrange Greene's works into a pattern and thus provide him with the authorial career that he lacked according to Harvey.

The third of the posthumous pamphlets, *Greenes Vision*, offers yet another reading of Greene's authorial career. It takes the form of a dream vision brought about by Greene's dismay at being 'burdened with the penning of the *Cobler of Canterbury*' (B^a). The false attribution leads Greene to question his own works and to regret the literary 'follies' that have earned him the reputation of someone who might be suspected of having written such a poor work as the *Cobler of Caunterburie*. He proceeds to write 'Greenes Ode, of the vanitie of wanton writings'. The ode takes its main argument, that 'wanton books infect the minds' (B2^b), to comical extremes by suggesting that Ovid's love poetry was solely responsible for the decline of Rome, and that he was banished because Augustus disapproved of this harmful use of poetic skill. Following a repentant prayer, Greene then falls asleep and has a dream vision of the ghosts of Chaucer and Gower, who tell him what they think of his works.[79]

The context in which Newman places the pamphlet by setting it up as Greene's last will and testament affects its meaning because it assigns a particular significance to it and encourages readers to regard it as a pamphlet à clef. A similar shift of meaning through labelling *Greenes Vision* Greene's final work can be seen in the motto on the title page, *Sero sed serio* ('late, but in earnest'). When placed at the beginning of a text purporting to have been written at the instant of its author's death, this motto assumes the rather more ominous-sounding additional meaning of '*too* late, but in earnest'.[80] For the character of Greene, the immediate effect of Newman's mislabelling of *Greenes Vision* is that his life and his works become more closely linked than they are in the other posthumous pamphlets. Greene's authorial identity becomes more prominent as a theme, as the text is ostensibly Greene's reflection on his life,

---

79 In this the *Vision* echoes not only Dante's *Purgatorio* but also John Skelton's 'Garlande of Laurel', a poem of some 1,600 lines in praise of John Skelton himself, in which a dreaming Skelton encounters the three English classics Chaucer, Gower and Lydgate, who welcome him as one of their own. In his pamphlets against Nashe, Gabriel Harvey repeatedly associates Skelton with Greene and Nashe as part of his attack on satire – conveniently forgetting that his friend 'M. Spencer' had derived the name of his alter ego Colin Clout from one of Skelton's satires.

80 The adjective 'serus' can have either meaning. See also *Greenes Neuer Too Late* (1590), which is referred to as 'my *Nunquam sera est*' in the *Vision* (it is the title which Greene claims he must finish before he can heed Gower's advice).

when in fact it is mainly a reflection on his works (and his concern that his readers may judge his life on the basis of those works). As a result, the reader is encouraged to view what is primarily a discussion of the relative merits of various genres of writing as a metaphor for Greene's life. 'Vain' writings become a substitute for, rather than a symptom of, the vanity of his life and his loose living.[81] Similarly, Greene's 'repentance' is triggered not by any spiritual experience – such as the 'mightie hand of God' of the *Repentance* – but merely by his mortification at being suspected of being the author of the *Cobler of Caunterburie.*

The key scene for the shaping of Greene in *Greenes Vision* is the scene that makes up the bulk of the pamphlet: Greene's encounter with Gower and Chaucer, which leads to a debate about the moral purpose of writing. The passage is of interest not only because of the poets' discussion of Greene's work but also because Gower and Chaucer themselves are examples of authorial ghosts whose 'lives' have been derived from their works. Their textual nature is made clear from the very beginning, as Greene identifies the two even before they introduce themselves, because they are bearing their own names as captions:

> These two ould men came to me, and sat downe by me, the one on the right hand, and the other on the left: looking vpon them earnestly, I spyed written on the ones brest *Chawcer*, and on the others *Gower.*
>
> (*Vision*, Cᵃ)

The poets' appearance and demeanour reflects their attitudes towards writing (which is of course in turn derived from a reading of their own works). Chaucer is 'blithe and merry' of countenance, while Gower is

> Of couller pale, and wan his looke,
> Such haue they that plyen their booke,
> [...]
> His visage graue, sterne and grim,
> *Cato* was most like to him.
>
> (*Vision*, Cᵃ–Cᵇ).

Unsurprisingly, Chaucer defends the romances, arguing that there is nothing inherently wrong with pleasant tales, while the austere Gower disapproves of them and urges Greene to adopt a more moral approach to writing. Just as Gower has managed to convince Greene to give up writing romances, a third figure appears. This third figure is the biblical king Salomon, who overrules the two others and authoritatively states that the only type of writing worth pursuing is theological writing. At this point, the author awakes and promises his readers to heed Salomon's advice in his future works if he possibly can.

The conclusion of *Greenes Vision* as well as Greene's submitting first to Gower's and then to Salomon's advice project a potential writing career for Greene that echoes that of the notorious prodigal scholar figure of the previous decade, John

---

81 'Now I am sick, and sorrow hath wholy seazd on me: vaine I haue beene, let not other men shewe themselues vaine in reproching my vanitie. I craue pradon of you all, if I haue offended any of you with laciuious Pamphleting. Many things I haue wrote to get money, which I could otherwise wish to be supprest' (*Vision*, A4ᵃ).

Lyly's *Euphues*. Like *Euphues*, Greene is to be imagined progressing from wantonness and misapplication of wit, which began during his years at university, to a wiser application of his faculties in the study of theology, with a brief flirtation with moral philosophy forming the intermediate stage. However, because of the way in which *Greenes Vision* is set up as the author's final legacy to his readers, written 'at the instant of his death', this projected writing career is of course destined to remain fictional and merely a '*vision* of vertue', as Newman calls it (A3ᵃ, emphasis added). In reality, the list of Greene's publications from 1590 onwards shows no shift towards theology, unless the coney-catching pamphlets are to be read as such. Nevertheless, as a posthumous publication and disguised as Greene's final work, *Greenes Vision* succeeds in achieving something it may not have if its context of publication had been different. It provides Greene with a patterned (if incomplete) writing career simply by offering readers a vision of what might have been. The mere promise of the 'fruites of [his] better laboures' (H4ᵃ), with which the pamphlet concludes, is thus turned into a substitute for the real thing.

Greenes Groats-worth of Witte and the Greene myth

The figure of Greene the notorious dissolute author continued to haunt print after his death. The three posthumous pamphlets were succeeded by two further pamphlets, which featured Greene's ghost as a protagonist: Henry Chettle's response to *Foure Letters and Certeine Sonnets*, *Kind-Harts Dreame* (1592) and *Greenes Newes From Both Heauen and Hell* (1593).[82] Nevertheless, his authorial identity remained as elusive as reliable facts about his life. This is exemplified in a second authorship debate involving Greene, which spanned the twentieth century and revolved around the first of the posthumous Greene pamphlets.

Much of the critical attention *Greenes Groats-worth of Witte* received, particularly during the first half of the twentieth century, owed less to Greene himself or to the text as a whole than to its most famous element: the letter to the playwrights. The letter, which urges 'those Gentlemen of [Greene's] Quondam acquaintance that spend their wits in making plaies' to find 'more profitable courses' (Fᵇ), provides an intriguing picture of early modern authorship. This is partly because the letter contains a sketch of a community of influential playwrights in the late sixteenth century, but also because it seems to offer descriptions of individual known playwrights. These notably include the 'famous Gracer of Tragedians' (E4ᵇ) – generally believed to be Marlowe – who is rebuked for his atheism, and the imitator who is referred to as the 'vpstart Crow, beautified with our feathers, that [...] beeing an absolute *Iohannes fac totum*, is in his owne conceit the only Shake-scene in a countrey' (Fᵇ). The latter of these references lent the text additional significance in the eyes of Shakespeare

---

82 Later resurrections of Greene included *Greene in Conceipt* (1598) and *Greenes Ghost Haunting Coney-Catchers* (1602), both of which draw on the character created through the debate following his death. The title page of *Greene in Conceipt* shows a literally resurrected Greene writing at his desk while still wrapped in his shroud.

scholars, who interpreted this passage as stating that Shakespeare underwent a career progression from player to playwright.[83]

As a result, the authorship of *Greenes Groats-worth of Witte*, which had been called into question straight after its publication, also gained in importance. The crux of the problem was outlined by Harold Jenkins in 1935, in response to an article that had cast serious doubt on Greene's authorship of the pamphlet and called it the product of either collusion or forgery:[84]

> An interest far exceeding its literary value has always attached to *The Repentance of Robert Greene*, because it supplies the basis of much of the generally accepted biography of Greene. An even greater notoriety envelops *Greene's Groatsworth of Wit*, which contains, apart from a certain autobiographical significance, the celebrated attack upon Shakespeare as an 'vpstart Crow'. It is therefore a matter of some moment when the authenticity of these two pamphlets is brought into question.[85]

Although Jenkins vehemently argued that both pamphlets are genuine works by Greene and should not even be classified as 'doubtful', the evidence he cites is perhaps not as conclusive as he might have wished. More recent Greene scholars tend to concede that *Greenes Groats-worth of Witte* is not 'Greenes' in the sense that Robert Greene was its sole author and the circumstances of its composition were exactly as described by the title page and paratextual materials. John Jowett concludes that it 'must, to all effects and purposes have been written by [Chettle]'.[86] D. Allen Carroll cautiously states that 'Greene *may* have had something to do with the writing of *Groatsworth*, Chettle *certainly* did'.[87] Steve Mentz regards it as a special case that 'does not fit existing models of collaboration any more than our models of single authorship'.[88] Katherine Duncan-Jones, on the other hand, considers Nashe 'by far the stronger suspect', arguing that the letter to the playwrights in particular would have been 'beyond the reach of the journeyman Chettle'.[89]

Nevertheless, the terminology used when discussing the authorship of *Greenes Groats-worth of Witte* is revealing. Often it betrays a sense of thinly veiled frustration that the text is not what it purports to be. For example, Lori Humphrey Newcomb, one of the foremost proponents of the view that Greene was an early example of a 'celebrity' author who fashioned an authorial persona for himself, in her article

83 For a less orthodox reading of the Shakespeare reference in *Groats-worth*, which challenges the notion of Shakespeare's career progression, see Bart van Es, '"Johannes fac Totum"? Shakespeare's First Contact with the Acting Companies', *Shakespeare Quarterly*, 61.4 (2010), 551–77.

84 That article was Chauncey Sanders, 'Robert Greene and his "Editors"', *PMLA*, 48 (1933), 392–417. Sanders points out that the attribution to Greene rests entirely on the authority of Henry Chettle, who was a doubtful source, since he had admitted to having carried out other forgeries.

85 Harold Jenkins, 'On the Authenticity of *Greene's Groatsworth of Wit* and *The Repentance of Robert Greene*', *Review of English Studies*, 11 (1935), 28–41 (p. 28).

86 John Jowett, 'Johannes Factotum: Henry Chettle and *Greene's Groatsworth of Wit*', *Bibliographical Society of America, Papers*, 87 (1993), pp. 453–86 (p. 466). As evidence for his claim Jowett cites Austin's authorship study (discussed below).

87 D. Allen Carroll (ed.), *Greene's Groatsworth of Wit* (Binghamton, NY: Center for Medieval and Early Renaissance Studies, State University of New York at Binghamton, 1994), p. x.

88 Mentz, 'Forming Greene', p. 118.

89 Katherine Duncan-Jones, *Ungentle Shakespeare: Scenes from his Life* (London: Thomson Learning, 2001), p. 44.

on Greene in the *DNB* calls *Greenes Groats-worth of Witte* 'largely an opportunistic forgery'. She then adds, with a hint of disapproval, that the attribution of the letter to the playwrights to Greene had 'far-reaching implications for Greene's reputation'. D. Allen Carroll, editor of the first – and so far the only – modern edition (1994), is clearly anxious to draw his readers' attention to the full circumstances of the authorship debate, of which he provides a detailed and well-balanced summary in his introduction.[90] Carroll is reluctant to pronounce a verdict, but he nevertheless seems to feel obliged to point out that attributing the text to Chettle would make it (at least in modern terms) a forgery. Nevertheless, he is particularly careful not to sound censorious: 'If the book is indeed Chettle's, or largely his, as few have believed and as the evidence seems to suggest, then it ranks as one of the most successful creative hoaxes in our culture' (p. x).

'Hoax' and 'opportunistic forgery' are very loaded terms to apply to what might be more neutrally described as an unusual case of collaborative authorship. This suggests that among recent Greene scholars there is still a certain reluctance to give up *Greenes Groats-worth of Witte* as 'Greenes', because it would cast some doubt on what Jenkins had called the 'generally accepted biography of Greene'.

That *Greenes Groats-worth of Witte* is a collaborative text (even if the extent of Chettle's involvement is uncertain) is evident from Chettle's defence against the charge of sole authorship in his preface to *Kind-Harts Dreame*, 'To the Gentlemen Readers'.[91] In order to justify himself, Chettle suggests misreadings of Greene's bad handwriting as the possible origin of any offences caused and outlines his own part in the pamphlet's publication as follows:

> At the perusing of *Greenes* Booke, [I] stroke out what then in conscience I thought he in some displeasure writ: or had it beene true, yet to publish it, was intollerable [...]. I had only in the copy this share, it was il written, as sometime *Greenes* hand was none of the best, licensd it must be, ere it could be printed which could neuer be if it might not be read. To be briefe I writ it ouer, and as neare as I could, followed the copy. (A4^a)

The language that Chettle is using to describe his own role in preparing the manuscript for print challenges modern conceptions of the distinction between copy-editing and writing. Especially the two key phrases 'it was il written' and 'to be briefe I writ it ouer' are ambiguous and could include anything from copying out the manuscript in a neater hand to major revisions of the text itself (equally, '[I] stroke out what [...] I thought he in some displeasure writ' could refer to the censoring of individual offensive words or to the deletion of substantial passages).

The importance assigned to the question of Greene's authorship of *Greenes Groats-worth of Witte* is evident in the fact that one of the first large-scale stylistic analyses to establish authorship is called *A Computer-aided Technique for Stylistic Discrimination: The Authorship of 'Greene's Groatsworth of Wit'* (1969). This study, hailed as a technological triumph by its author, Warren B. Austin, due to its use of a

---

90 The title page of Carroll's edition cautiously states that the text is '*attributed to* Henry Chettle and Robert Greene' (emphasis added).

91 This preface not only contains Chettle's denial of authorship, it is also the only source for the claim that some of the 'diuers play-makers' were offended by the letter addressed to them and 'wilfully forge[d] in their conceites a liuing Author' they could hold responsible for it (A3^b).

'high-speed' IBM computer, was funded by the US Department of Education, which again illustrates the importance assigned to settling this question. However, despite its confident conclusion that *Greenes Groats-worth of Witte* had in fact been written by Chettle, Austin's study nevertheless failed to prove Chettle's authorship beyond doubt. Its methods for determining stylistic markers, as well as the tacit assumption that the texts the pamphlet was being compared to could all be reliably (and solely) attributed to either Chettle or Greene, were subsequently challenged, most notably by Richard Westley in 2006.[92] This somewhat unsatisfying conclusion to the authorship debate aptly illustrates the problems involved in a search for single authors in a collaborative text.

Greenes Groats-worth of Witte is a text whose authorship was doubtful to begin with and whose most characteristic feature is its blurring of authorial identities. It presents Greene to his readers almost via a collection of fragments – or 'broken and confused lines' (E3[b]) – thrust into the world 'without shape' (A4[a]). There is, then, a certain irony in the fact that such a text should have come to be regarded as a prime source in a search for biographical facts and authorial identities of both Greene and the playwrights addressed in the letter.

Relinquishing the notion that *Greenes Groats-worth of Witte* is broadly what it claims to be – a collection of loosely autobiographical pieces written by a notorious author on his death-bed – would remove some of the basis for Greene's 'generally accepted' biography. This in turn might affect Greene's status as a 'celebrity author' of his time. Yet this would not necessarily devalue the text. Ultimately, the search for the author of *Greenes Groats-worth of Witte* and the search for Greene's biography both represent two sides of the same need to identify a single author figure. That much of authorship studies is, at its root, concerned with identifying single authors can be seen in influential studies such as Brian Vickers's *Shakespeare, Co-Author* (2002). One of Vickers's declared aims is to make readers more aware of collaboration as a common early modern phenomenon and to recontextualise the notion of Shakespeare as a 'solitary genius'.[93] Nevertheless, Vickers is driven by the desire to create a more 'authentic' picture of Shakespeare and his collaborators as single authors by extracting them from the collaborative plays. This is evident in his use of terms like 'fair', 'justice', 'recognition' or 'restitution', when speaking of the identification of collaborators through stylistic analysis, evoking modern notions of intellectual property:

> Plays were vehicles of entertainment, no doubt often ephemeral. But many great works have survived, and some extant masterpieces were produced by two or more co-authors. *It seems only fair* to try to identify which playwrights contributed which parts, if only – four hundred years after the event – to *give each the recognition they deserve*.[94]

92 Richard Westley, 'Computing Error: Reassessing Austin's Study of *Groatsworth of Wit*', *Literary and Linguistic Computing*, 21 (2006), 363–78.

93 Brian Vickers, *Shakespeare, Co-Author: A Historical Study of Five Collaborative Plays* (Oxford: Oxford University Press, 2002), p. vii.

94 *Shakespeare, Co-Author*, p. 43 (emphases added). Note, however, that since one of the purposes of Vickers's analysis is to highlight Shakespeare's stylistic superiority over his collaborators, there is also a qualitative undertone to the phrase 'the recognition they deserve'.

Although Vickers is of course concerned with collaboration among playwrights, his attitude towards collaboration as a literary phenomenon is very similar to that displayed in the twentieth-century debate about the 'authenticity' of *Greenes Groatsworth of Witte*. When viewed as a collaborative text pieced together, and perhaps even partially composed, after Greene's death, *Greenes Groats-worth of Witte* ceases to be a cornerstone of the Greene myth. However, this arguably turns it into something even more interesting: a posthumous reshaping of an authorial career that had already ended, by a network of people involved in book production, from 'broken and confused' literary remains. As such, it provides evidence of an interest in the role of the author that goes beyond mere self-fashioning concerns and may contribute towards a fuller view of the notion of professional authorship during the late sixteenth century.

So where does this leave Greene the celebrity author? I would suggest that Greene's interest need not be viewed as dependent on the truth of his 'generally accepted' biography. In order to appreciate his significance for the developing notions of professional authorship and a potential link between an author's life and his fictional works, it may be more helpful to envision Greene not so much as a clearly defined author figure but as a posthumous phenomenon. The evident appeal of Greene's colourful biography and the myth of his notoriety should not distract from the fact that they were merely the products of a fascinating discourse of authorship, which originated with the Harvey–Nashe quarrel during the 1590s. This discourse of authorship saw a number of different writers projecting their own ideas of authorship onto Greene's career. Had it not been for *Foure Letters and Certeine Sonnets* and its consequences, the posthumous Greene pamphlets may never have been published.

At first sight, Robert Greene and Sir Philip Sidney appear to have little in common, although they were both university educated and almost exact contemporaries.[95] They are positioned at opposite ends of the literary scene of the late sixteenth century. Greene's name has become almost synonymous with the lowest form of 'popular' author: a professional hack, whose livelihood depended on churning out plays and cheap printed pamphlets. Sidney, on the other hand, is one of the most canonical poets of his time and associated with high literary quality, partly because he is viewed as a highbrow 'amateur poet', who shunned the medium of print during his lifetime. Only the posthumous publication of Sidney's works in print during the 1590s made them more widely available. Nevertheless, their ensuing popularity was at least partly due to the air of exclusivity that still surrounded those works, which stemmed from the fact that they had originally been written for a manuscript readership. Nevertheless, Greene and Sidney do have two things in common. First, they both posthumously became major literary figures of the 1590s – albeit in very different ways – and second, autobiographical readings of their works played a crucial part in this process. Chapter 3 examines the reception history of Sidney and his works as a phenomenon similar to the 'meta-literary commentary' (to borrow Steve Mentz's phrase) in the aftermath of Greene's death.[96]

---

95 Sidney was four years Greene's senior and died six years before him.
96 Mentz, *Romance for Sale*, p. 207.

In both cases, we see a discourse seemingly centring on the the identity of a single author, which on closer examination turns out to be a debate about the nature of authorship, prompted by the death of a particular author and by the posthumous evaluation of his works.

3

'Borne in Arcady':
Sidney's literary rebirth

A failed elegy: Spenser's 'Astrophel'

Edmund Spenser's 'Astrophel', subtitled a 'Pastorall Elegie vpon the death of the most Noble and valorous Knight, Sir *Philip Sidney*', is an oddity. Historically, Spenser scholars (in particular those of the first half of the twentieth century) have bemoaned its failure as a work of commemoration. H. S. V. Jones's observation that it 'occupies no very distinguished place in the long tradition of the elegy' carries a note of regret that Spenser, an unquestionably great poet who in 1595 stood at the height of his powers, should have written a 'bad' elegy.[1] There has been – and still is – a strong impulse to find excuses for this. S. E. Winbolt tried to defend Spenser by arguing he only wrote an elegy for Sidney 'because it was expected of him [although] [h]is heart was, apparently, not in the work', while H. E. Cory proposed that Sidney's death had caused poetic trauma, so Spenser was 'chilled by his sadness to an unwonted and uneasy self-consciousness' and thus unable to write true to his usual form.[2] Michael O'Connell, on the other hand, argued that Spenser deliberately transferred all emotional involvement to the 'Lay of Clorinda', forming the second half of what he terms 'Spenser's double elegy'.[3]

The problem of 'Astrophel' lies partly in the tone of the poem, which has frequently been described as 'cold' and detached, and generally lacking the passion we might expect to see expressed in an elegy. This impression of detachment is compounded by the fact of 'Astrophel's' late publication – it was published in 1595, nine years after Sidney's death, when the initial flood of elegies had already become a trickle. Additionally, it was published alongside poems that had already appeared in print and been attributed to authors other than Spenser himself, one poem that the 1595 quarto attributes to another author, as well as a poem that had been entered into the Stationers' Register by another poet in 1587, the year of Sidney's funeral. Despite, or perhaps because of, its limitations as an elegy, 'Astrophel' is the most widely known poetic response to Sidney's death and continues to frustrate Spenser scholars with its failure to do what it says on the tin. Yet the oddness of 'Astrophel' is not limited to its timing and its un-elegiac tone; it also creates bibliographic problems, a fact illustrated

1 H. S. V. Jones, *A Spenser Handbook* (New York: F. S. Crofts, 1930), p. 330.
2 S. E. Winbolt, *Spenser and his Poetry* (London: George G. Harrap, 1912), p. 64. H. E. Cory, *Edmund Spenser: A Critical Study* (Berkeley: University of California Press, 1917), p. 215.
3 Michael O'Connell, '*Astrophel*: Spenser's Double Elegy', *Studies in English Literature*, 1 (1971), 27–35 (especially pp. 34–5).

by the lack of established naming conventions to describe the poem within its wider publication context. It is therefore useful at this point to describe the contents of the 1595 quarto in some detail.

Originally, 'Astrophel' forms part of a quarto volume published in 1595 that is usually referred to as *Colin Clouts Come Home Againe*, largely because the title page contains no mention of 'Astrophel' – or indeed any indication that the volume's contents are not entirely 'By Ed. Spencer'.[4] Following this title page, which would lead readers to expect a single poem called 'Colin Clouts Come Home Againe', is a dedication to Sir Walter Ralegh, dated to 1591 (A2ᵃ–A2ᵇ). On the next page, visually separated from the dedication by printer's flowers, there begins the title poem, a pastoral travel narrative of sorts, in which Colin tells his fellow shepherds of his encounter with the Shepherd of the Ocean (an easily identifiable pseudonym for the dedicatee of the volume) and his subsequent journey to the court of Cynthia.

Until this point, the makeup of the volume remains relatively unsurprising. However, rather than continuing until the final page, the poem concludes with the word 'Finis' halfway through the volume (E2ᵇ). This unexpected conclusion to the title poem is faced by a new title page (E3ᵃ) which announces the following content to be 'Astrophel', a 'Pastorall Elegie' on the death of Sir Philip Sidney in 1586, although the running title continues as 'Colin Clouts / come home againe' for a further nine pages.[5] This new poem, whose title is repeated in a large font size on E4ᵃ, tells the story of the death of the shepherd Astrophel and continues until F4ᵇ. It is then followed by yet another unexpected feature of the volume, what appears to be an untitled poem, which is framed by two borders of printer's flowers and attributed to Astrophel's sister Clorinda, and which begins on a new page with the first line 'Ay me, to whom shall I my case complaine'.[6]

After this untitled poem, there follow two more poems, whose titles are in the

---

4 For a contemporary counterexample to this practice, see the title page of the first quarto of Sidney's *Astrophel and Stella* (1591), which draws attention to the fact that some of the contents are not by 'Syr P. S.' with the following addition to the title, 'To the end of which are added, sundry other rare Sonnets of diuers Noble men and Gentlemen'.

5 The running title stops (in mid-title) on Gᵃ, where it is replaced by one of the borders of printer's flowers that frame the so-called 'Lay of Clorinda'. However, when the border ceases again on G3a (the transition to 'The Mourning Muse of Thestylis'), the running title does not recommence. Instead, the space is used for additional lines of verse. Thus 'The Mourning Muse of Thestylis' and 'A Pastorall Aeglogue' both have thirty-two lines per page, while 'Colin Clouts Come Home Againe' has only thirty. The first section of 'Astrophel' (which in addition to the space taken up by the running titles uses slightly more space because the poem is divided into stanzas of six lines) has twenty-six lines per page. The 'Lay of Clorinda', which has the neatest layout of all the poems in the volume, has four complete stanzas (i.e. twenty-four lines) on each page. Six of the eleven pages containing Roydon's 'Elegie' – which is also divided into stanzas of six lines, though metre and rhyme scheme are different – use the same layout, but it cannot be sustained because the first page of the poem requires additional space for the title and the overall number of stanzas is thirty-nine.

6 This poem is most commonly known under the title 'The Dolefull Lay of Clorinda', though this title is not in the original text and was only introduced in the Variorum edition of Spenser's works (which added the title and a corresponding entry in the table of contents, without alerting readers to the fact that neither the 1595 quarto nor Matthew Lownes's edition of Spenser's complete works (1611 onwards) feature a separate title for the poem, or even any unambiguous clues that it is indeed a separate poem. For the sake of clarity, I continue to use this title when referring to the stanzas supposed to be spoken by Clorinda, although I argue that they are in fact part of the poem 'Astrophel'.

same font size as the rest of the text. 'The Mourning Muse of Thestylis', is a pastoral commemorating Sidney the soldier, while 'A pastorall Aeglogue vpon the death of Sir Phillip Sidney Knight, &c' is a dialogue between two characters called Colin and Lycon, who are composing mourning verses for a third character called Philisides. As an additional surprise for an unsuspecting reader who thought he had bought a volume of poetry written exclusively by Spenser, the 'Pastorall Aeglogue' is signed 'L. B.', indicating that it was written either entirely by, or in collaboration with, Spenser's friend Lodowick Bryskett.[7]

The final section of the volume consists of a group of three further (unattributed) commemorative poems for Sidney, titled 'An Elegie, or friends passion, for his Astrophill', 'An Epitaph vpon the right Honourable sir Phillip Sidney knight' and 'Another of the same'. Those three poems had all previously been printed in the miscellany *The Phoenix Nest* (1593) and the authors of the first two had already been identified prior to their publication in print as Matthew Roydon and Sir Walter Ralegh.[8] After the three *Phoenix Nest* poems, the volume concludes with a second 'FINIS', followed by the printer's note 'London | Printed by T. C. for William Ponsonbie. | 1595'.[9]

Although the separate title page for 'Astrophel' effectively divides the volume into two halves, it is not a full title page: all bibliographic information (that is, the printer's emblem, publisher's and author's names, as well as the place and year of publication) is missing.[10] Francis Johnson's *Critical Bibliography*, in acknowledgement of this, refers to it as a 'sub-title'.[11] The wording of the sub-title itself further complicates matters, partly because of the tension between the pastoral persona and the known public figure whose name it invokes, and partly because it appears to refer only to the first of the poems which follow it. Nevertheless, the poem forms a unit not only with the 'Lay of Clorinda', but also with the poems by the other authors (which are introduced as the works of pastoral personae who feature in the first poem). This is indicated both visually and through the poems themselves. The two final stanzas of

7 'The mourning Muse of Thestylis' (G3a–H2a), also by Bryskett, had been entered into the Stationers' Register (although apparently not published) in 1587. Poetic collaboration is a theme that appears several times in the volume, perhaps most memorably in the section of 'Colin Clouts Come Home Againe' that describes Colin's duet with the Shepherd of the Ocean.

8 The 'Friend's Elegy' was attributed to Roydon by Thomas Nashe in 1589 (see the section on *The Phoenix Nest*), and *England's Parnassus* (1600) cited passages from it as examples of poetry by Roydon. The attribution of the 'Epitaph' to Ralegh rests mainly on the tag 'Petrarch of our time'. The earliest identification of Ralegh as its author is in the moral to book XVI of Sir John Harington's *Orlando Furioso* (1591): while discoursing on the subject of love poetry and its conventions, Harington quotes a version of sonnet 18 from *Astrophel and Stella* and refers to Sidney as 'our English *Petrarke, Sir Philip Sidney*, or (as *Sir Walter Raulegh* in his Epitaph worthely called him) the *Scipio* and the *Petrarke* of our time' (p. 126). The attribution of the third poem is less certain, but it has been variously attributed Sir Edward Dyer or to Fulke Greville.

9 The initials 'T. C.' stand for Thomas Creed, who also printed the fifth quarto edition of *The Shepheardes Calender* in 1597.

10 All of these features are included on the 'first' title page of the volume. By contrast, Spenser's *Complaints* (1591) contains four separate title pages, all of which contain full bibliographic information, possibly to strengthen the claim of the preface that Spenser did not intend to have them published in a single volume but that they were merely 'gathered togeather' as 'parcels' by his publisher, William Ponsonby (A2ᵃ).

11 Francis R. Johnson, *A Critical Bibliography of the Works of Edmund Spenser Printed Before 1700* (Baltimore, MD: Johns Hopkins University Press, 1933), p. 30.

'Astrophel', which function as a transition to the 'Lay of Clorinda', clearly show it is intended to be read alongside the 'Lay', whose final two stanzas in turn serve as a similar transition to the remaining poems. Additionally, the running title 'Colin Clouts / come home againe' continues well beyond the first 'FINIS' of the volume, while the second is followed by the impressum, which repeats the bibliographical information of the title page and forms a bracket linking the two halves.[12] As a result of this, the seemingly separate parts are visually made to form a larger unit.

These bibliographic peculiarities raise a number of questions. Is 'Astrophel' the title of the entire collection of Sidney-themed commemorative poems that constitute the second half of the volume, or merely the first of these poems (and if the latter, where precisely does this poem end)? Should the second half of the volume be read as distinct from the first or as part of a larger composite, which includes 'Colin Clouts Come Home Againe'?[13] And what are we to make of the confusion of dates? The poems of the second half are all introduced as spontaneous compositions 'upon' the death of Sidney (which implicitly dates them to 1586), yet three of them are exactly reproduced from a text printed in 1593. Similarly, the volume as a whole, whose publication date is twice given as 1595, begins with a dedication that is dated to 27 December 1591, without any explanatory note by the author, printer or publisher.[14]

This bibliographic ambiguity has added to the ambivalence towards *Astrophel*, which is reflected in modern editing practice. It is generally omitted from selections of Spenser's poetry, and whenever it is printed in collections, its contents tend to be reprinted selectively, resulting in dramatic changes to its form. The Variorum edition of Spenser's works, which placed a lot of emphasis on single authorship due to its declared aim of consolidating Spenser's status as a 'major' poet, was among the first to select only the sections written by Spenser for reprinting.[15] For the most part, this led to the omission of paratextual materials, such as the commendatory sonnets of *The Faerie Queene*, but the 1595 quarto is one of two texts changed beyond recognition

---

12 Cf. *Complaints*, in which the running titles change correctly.
13 Although the title page makes no mention of 'Astrophel', it is problematic in the light of its full list of contents to call it *Colin Clouts Come Home Againe*. I shall therefore be referring to the volume as whole as the 1595 quarto. Since I shall argue that the commemorative poems that comprise the second half of the volume are intended to be read as a collection of poems forming a unit, I shall use the title *Astrophel* to refer to this unit, so as to distinguish it from 'Astrophel', the first poem of the collection. Regarding the finishing point of 'Astrophel', as nearly all editions print l. 216 as the final line of the poem, I am following this convention when referring to it, for clarity's sake, even though I shall argue that ll. 205–16 are effectively a transition between 'Astrophel' and the 'Lay of Clorinda'.
14 The dating of the dedicatory epistle and the phrase 'I make you present of this simple pastorall' suggest that 'Colin Clouts Come Home Againe' was originally written as a New Year's gift to Ralegh, but this does not explain its publication in print four years later, whether or to what extent the poem was revised for print publication, or even whether 'simple pastorall' refers only to 'Colin Clouts Come Home Againe'.
15 General preface in Edwin Greenlaw (ed.), *The Works of Edmund Spenser: A Variorum Edition*, Charles Osgood and Frederick Padelford, 11 vols (Baltimore, MD: Johns Hopkins University Press, 1932–57), i, p. v: 'The present edition aims to furnish an accurate text of Spenser's poetry and prose and to make accessible in convenient form the fruits of all the significant scholarship and literary criticism which have contributed to the better understanding and appreciation of this major poet. [...] The number of scholars devoting themselves primarily to the study of Spenser has steadily increased for the last quarter of a century, and fresh studies appear with every volume of the learned journals. [T]his activity gives promise of continuing indefinitely.'

through this editing practice.[16] The Variorum text of *Astrophel* breaks off after the 'Lay of Clorinda', thus omitting the remaining five poems, which together comprise 647 lines, that is nearly twice as many as the first poem, 'Astrophel', and the 'Lay of Clorinda' combined (342 lines). The 'Dolefull Lay', however, is given particular prominence: it is listed separately in the index and notes and even receives a separate heading, which is not in the 1595 text.[17] None of these editorial changes in the Variorum edition are brought to the reader's attention.

While the latter may be somewhat at odds with good modern editing practice, the attitude towards *Astrophel* exemplified by the Variorum edition persists in more recent editions. The 1999 Penguin edition of Spenser's *Shorter Poems* at first sight appears to be very different from the Variorum edition in that it is much more careful about making editorial changes visible. While the index and notes list the 'Dolefull Lay of Clorinda' under a separate heading, the title is put in square brackets within the main body of the text, to identify it as an editorial addition. The five elegies that are not by Spenser are again omitted, but this time omission is noted and explained through the edition's intent to '[supply] only Spenser's contributions to the volume'.[18] The reader is then referred to the latest edition to reprint those poems: de Sélincourt's edition of 1910. So while McCabe is clearly much more at pains to lay open and justify his editorial decisions than the Variorum editors, the effect on the text is essentially the same. Both editions present a version of *Astrophel* that plays down the part of all elements not written by Spenser himself through omitting them, and gives a prominence to the 'Lay' that may not be wholly justifiable through its appearance in the 1595 text (though certainly through the critical attention it has received). As a result, readers of modern Spenser editions may initially be puzzled to see *Astrophel* – correctly – referred to as a collection.[19]

It is surprising that although the importance of the material nature of early printed texts has increasingly come to be acknowledged by early modern scholars, little attention has been paid to the makeup of the 1595 quarto in its entirety. 'Colin Clouts Come Home Againe' is now recognised as the 'pivotal work in Spenser's poetic corpus' as which Louis Montrose identified it in 1996 in his influential essay 'Spenser's Domestic Domain', which has shaped critical discussion of the poem for nearly two decades and played a crucial part in establishing it as an important text

---

16 The other text is *Three Proper and Wittie Familiar Letters / Two Other Very Commendable Letters* (1580), a collection of five 'familiar' letters written for publication, a format favoured by Spenser's friend Gabriel Harvey, whose contributions make up the bulk of the volume. The Variorum edition completely changes the nature of the text by culling Spenser's contributions from the *Letters* and presenting them as correspondence, while relegating Harvey's letters to an appendix, and it also tacitly changes the letter-writers' names (which in the original edition had been given only as 'G. H.' and 'Immeritô') to 'Harvey' and 'Spenser'. The Penguin edition of the *Shorter Poems* goes even further, by reproducing only the four poems that are embedded in the *Letters*.

17 In its original form, the 'Lay of Clorinda' is only distinguished from the first 'Astrophel' poem through the addition of decorative borders and a page break.

18 Richard McCabe (ed.), *Edmund Spenser: The Shorter Poems* (London: Penguin, 1999), p. 663.

19 As for example in Gavin Alexander, *Writing After Sidney* (Oxford: Oxford University Press, 2006) and Raphael Falco, 'Spenser's "Astrophel" and the Formation of Elizabethan Literary Genealogy', *Modern Philology*, 91 (1993), 1–25.

within the Spenser canon.[20] Nevertheless, this recognition of its importance is based on a reading that largely extracts 'Colin Clouts Come Home Againe' from its publication context and treats it as though it had been published on its own.[21] Consequently, Montrose's reading of 'Colin Clouts Come Home Againe' foregrounds its autobiographical elements and Spenser's construction of his own authorial persona. Yet this 'laureate' reading of the poem has come at the price of obscuring a more complex picture of authorship within the volume as a whole; in a sense, *Astrophel* has been sacrificed for Colin Clout.

'Astrophel' presents a challenge for Spenser scholars and editors alike. It is still primarily viewed as one of Spenser's minor works – an inexplicably 'bad' elegy by a great writer, which, in addition to its ineffectiveness as an elegy for Sidney is overshadowed by the apparently much more significant 'Colin Clouts Come Home Againe'. I would argue that the function of 'Astrophel' (and *Astrophel*) has been misunderstood, because the title 'A Pastorall Elegie vpon the death of [...] Sir *Philip Sidney*' has been taken too literally. This has resulted in a decontextualisation both reflected in and perpetuated by modern editing practice. 'Astrophel' has not only been extracted from *Astrophel* through the removal of poems by other authors, but also separated from 'Colin Clouts Come Home Againe', even though the appearance of Spenser's 1595 quarto strongly suggests that they were intended to be read together. In order to understand why it is a misconception to regard 'Astrophel' purely as an odd and unsuccessful elegy, it is therefore necessary to view it in its original publication context. 'Publication context' in this case should be taken both in the material sense (paired with the ambitious authorial fiction of 'Colin Clouts Come Home Againe' and accompanied by poems by other authors) and in the historical sense, as part of the print responses to Sidney's death during the 1580s and 1590s. McGann's observation that the 'life histories' of text 'exhibit a ceaseless process of textual development and mutation' through recontextualisation, reproduction or even quotation, is especially pertinent to those responses to Sidney's death, and it holds particularly true for Spenser's 1595 quarto.[22]

If taken as a whole, the 1595 quarto raises three questions. First, why should Spenser have chosen to publish his elegy so late? Second, what is the purpose of the other poems that accompanied it? And, above all, how does *Astrophel* relate to 'Colin Clouts Come Home Againe'? In addressing these questions, I shall argue that the reasons why the 1595 volume is so complex and seems so confusing to modern readers are linked to nearly a decade's-worth of published responses to the life of Sidney preceding its publication. Additionally, the decade in question did not only see the posthumous transformation of Sidney from soldier and unpublished coterie poet to quasi-laureate figure of national importance. The period of 1586 to 1595 was

20 Louis Montrose, 'Spenser's Domestic Domain: Poetry, Property, and the Early Modern Subject', in Margreta de Grazia, Maureen Quilligan and Peter Stallybrass (ed.), *Subject and Object in Renaissance Culture* (Cambridge: Cambridge University Press, 1996), pp. 83–130 (p. 97).
21 Montrose initially acknowledges that the volume is a poetic miscellany, introducing it as '[a poetry book] containing *Colin Clouts Come Home Againe*, as well as *Astrophel* and other elegies for Sidney', but then proceeds to analyse only 'Colin Clouts Come Home Againe' (p. 94).
22 Jerome J. McGann, *The Textual Condition* (Princeton, NJ: Princeton University Press, 1991), p. 9.

also of great significance for Spenser's own development as a poet, as the major part of Spenser poetic oeuvre was written and published during that time, in parallel to Sidney's.[23] Consequently, the underlying assumption of the 1595 quarto, that both Colin Clout and Spenser himself are known figures to the reader, is not without justification. Furthermore, the decade is one which has been of particular interest to studies in the evolving idea of authorship and poetic activity, and, as an exploration of poetic creativity and the ways in which poets are remembered after their deaths, the 1595 quarto forms an important part of this wider discourse. This chapter examines the reception history of Sidney and his works, arguing that this is confusing partly because it is in fact a complex reflection on the nature of poetic activity and the life (and afterlife) of a poet. Spenser's 1595 quarto therefore represents an important step within the history of nascent literary biography in the early modern period.

The two Sidneys

Although Sidney's life is well documented and there are numerous contemporary responses to his works, it continues to pose a challenge for his biographers, because the material effectively adds up to not one but two Sidneys: on the one hand Sidney the idealised courtier and soldier, and on the other Sidney the poet, with few links or correspondences between the two. Katherine Duncan-Jones outlines this problem in the preface to her 1991 Sidney biography:

> Though Sidney is so well documented, there is, unfortunately, a wide gap between the letters, records and early memoirs, which are overwhelmingly concerned with his life as a courtier and soldier, and his imaginative, literary works, which reflect many other preoccupations, emotional, aesthetic, erotic, religious. Complete integration of the outward and inward lives is impossible, for Sidney's public career is reflected only indirectly in his literary works.[24]

What is perhaps most interesting about this passage is Duncan-Jones's word choice, because it illustrates the literary biographer's implicit desire to overcome the 'wide gap' and achieve 'complete integration' of public and private life in order to present readers with a single, consistent, unified figure. Arguably, this is a problem similar to the one that Greene scholars face in the attempt to link his life to his known works.

---

23 The first editions of *Arcadia* and *The Faerie Queene* were both published in 1590; 1591 saw the publication of two editions of *Astrophel and Stella*, as well as *Complaints, Daphnaida* and the fourth edition of *The Shepheardes Calender*. In 1593, when the second version of Arcadia was published, Spenser appears to have been busy with other matters, though in 1595 he published the quarto discussed above, as well as *Amoretti*; in the same year, two different versions of *The Defence of Poesie* went on sale. Between 1596 and 1598, Spenser published the second version of *The Faerie Queene, Prothalamion, Foure Hymnes* and the fifth and final quarto edition of *The Shepheardes Calender*. During the same period, a revised version of *Astrophel and Stella* was published, followed by a folio edition of Sidney's complete works. The majority of these titles were printed for the same publisher, William Ponsonby, so for most of the 1590s Spenser's and Sidney's works would have been available at the same bookshop, quite possibly lying next to each other. Even after Ponsonby's death, the association between the works of the two poets did not cease; Matthew Lownes's edition of Spenser's works recycled the title page frame of the 1593 *Arcadia* edition (featuring the 'pig in marjoram' device discussed in the section on the two *Arcadia* editions) for the title page of *The Faerie Queene*.

24 Duncan-Jones, *Sir Philip Sidney, Courtier Poet*, p. x.

At the same time, however, the passage contains a hint of frustration not only at the general impossibility of this task, but also at the fact that so much of Sidney's life appears to be unrelated to the figure of Sidney the poet and his 'many other preoccupations'. Duncan-Jones resolves the problem by 'moving continually to and fro between Sidney's outward and inward lives, to suggest [...] connections' and claiming 'the freedom Sidney would call "poetical", identifying causes and connexions which make the narrative coherent, even if they cannot always be documented or clinchingly proved' (both p. xi). Other recent studies of Sidney have taken different approaches to the problem of the two Sidneys. For example, Alan Stewart's biography argues that the defining characteristic of Sidney's life is the contrast between his reputation at home and abroad, and accounts for his poetry as a by-product of the tension between the two roles.[25] Even scholars who are not writing biographies of Sidney are frequently forced to position themselves in relation to this problem. As a result, they are split into studies of Sidney's literary impact (such as Gavin Alexander's *Writing After Sidney*) and studies of the 'fashioned' author within the works (such as Edward Berry's *The Making of Sir Philip Sidney*).

What Duncan-Jones refers to as the 'gap' can be traced to the two waves of responses to Sidney's death: the first following his death and funeral and the second following his subsequent rebirth as a print author. Very few of Sidney's elegists tried to account for both Sidneys. Angel Day's elegy, which will be discussed below, is an unusual example of an early elegist acknowledging a 'gap' between Sidney the soldier and Sidney the poet. However, Day's elegy does not attempt to bridge this 'gap' (possibly because he is writing prior to the publication of Sidney's works), but instead offers his readers two distinct, coexisting versions of Sidney.

'Sydus *Sidnae* Britannum': Lant's Roll and the early elegies

Sidney's death, or, to be more precise, his spectacular funeral four months later, provoked an immediate poetic response in the shape of numerous elegies both in Latin and in English.[26] Additionally, four volumes of commemorative verse were published in quick succession by members of three universities – Cambridge, Leiden and Oxford (two separate collections, one of which only contained contributions by the members of New College).[27]

---

25 Alan Stewart, *Philip Sidney: A Double Life* (London: Chatto & Windus, 2000).
26 Although Sidney had died on 17 October 1586 and his body had been returned to England in early November, his funeral only took place in February, for financial reasons (see H. R. Woudhuysen, 'Sidney, Sir Philip (1554–1586)', *Oxford DNB*. Raphael Falco points out that before Sidney's death 'there [was] virtually no vernacular tradition of funeral elegy' ('Instant Artifacts: Vernacular Elegies for Philip Sidney', *Studies in Philology*, 89 1992), 1–19, p. 3). Nonetheless, it needs to be noted that most of the early commemorative verse for Sidney was still in Latin rather than English.
27 *Academiae Cantabrigiensis Lachrymae Tumulo Nobilissimi Equitis, D. Philippi Sidneij Sacratae* (Cambridge), *Peplus, Illustrissimi Viri D. Philippi Sidnaei Supremus Honoribus Dicatus* (New College), *Exequiae Illustrissimi Equitis, D. Philippi Sidnaei, gratissimae memoriae ac nomine impensae* (Oxford) and *Epitaphia in Mortem Nobilissimi et Fortissimi Viri D. Philippi Sidneij Equitis* (Leiden). All four collections contain predominantly Latin poems, although a few authors showed off by contributing poems written in ancient Greek or even Hebrew. *Exequiae* also contains some contributions written in novelty shapes, including wings that resemble George Herbert's 'Easter Wings', a funeral monument,

Most of the poems contained in the commemorative volumes are conventional, if not generic, examples of poetic mourning, written by authors who contributed poems because their university was publishing a collection, rather than because they knew Sidney well and felt personally grieved by his death.[28] Regarding the image they present of Sidney and his life, those poems are perhaps of more interest if taken in bulk rather than individually. That is to say, one of the most interesting aspects about collections such as *Lachrymae* is the recurring of topoi, because they reveal something about the received idea of Sidney as a public figure in the wake of the impact that his funeral had made. One thing which immediately strikes modern readers is that in the vast majority of the poems there is no mention of Sidney as a poet, even among those written by people close enough to Sidney's family circle to know, or know of, his works.

The most likely explanation for this phenomenon is that although they were poetic tributes, they were tributes to Sidney the public figure and worthy *subject* of poetry, who had been evoked by the imagery of the elaborate funeral procession in February 1587.[29] It is perhaps not a coincidence that the stately imagery of Lant's Roll – a pictorial representation of Sidney's funeral procession in a series of engravings by Thomas Lant, published in 1588 – acts as a visual counterpart to the early elegies.[30] Lant's Roll and the early elegies show similarities in the particular emphasis which they place on portraying Sidney as first, a military hero, second, an exemplary courtier and diplomat, and third, the 'star' of England, mourned by the entire nation. This can be seen from a comparison between Lant's Roll and the *Lachrymae* collection, which was the earliest to be published.

Sidney the 'knight' figures in the commemorative verse partly through concrete references to the campaign in the Low Countries and partly through numerous invocations of Mars. In this context, it is worth bearing in mind that the actual circumstances in which Sidney received his knighthood had little to do with his having distinguished himself either as a soldier or as a courtier. He was knighted as a matter of protocol, so he could act as a proxy for his friend, Prince Johann Casimir, when the Prince was presented with the Order of the Garter.[31] Nevertheless, his elegists are persistent in their usage of the word 'knight' to invoke the image of a 'verray parfait

---

columns and a 'pyramid' that looks eerily like a Christmas tree. The only English poem among them is the first poem of the *Lachrymae* collection, written by James VI of Scotland.

28 Alexander argues that the elegies for Sidney are mostly 'formulaic', adding that 'one suspects that some of the University men had the same themes for amplification suggested to them' (*Writing After Sidney*, pp. 57–8).

29 A number of elegies specifically mention the date of Sidney's funeral, and Alexander Neville's preface to *Lachrymae* is dated 'Londini, M.D.lxxxvj. Feb. xvj.'. This has sometimes been read as an indication that the publication of *Lachrymae* either did or was intended to coincide with the funeral itself. The book's ESTC entry consequently lists this as its publication date, correcting the year to 'M.D.lxxxvij' to match the new dating system. However, this is more likely to be a stylistic device used by Neville to create a sense of immediacy and thus link the poetic 'tears' of the contributors to the public outpour of grief at Sidney's funeral.

30 The roll itself is untitled, though it is sometimes referred to by its first words, 'Sequitur celebritas & pompa funeris'.

31 However, Alan Stewart points out that in a sense Sidney's knighthood did not constitute an elevation to a higher rank, since Johann Casimir's reason for nominating Sidney as his proxy was that 'in his eyes, Sidney was already suitably elevated' (*Philip Sidney: A Double Life*, p. 7).

6 Sidney's hearse on display at St Paul's, detail of Lant's Roll (1587), plate 2

gentil knyght', equally famed and accomplished in battle and at court. Although there
are some elegies that refer exclusively to Mars, he features more frequently as part of
a trio of classical deities, who claim Sidney as their own and mourn for his loss: Mars,
Minerva and Apollo.

Among those three deities invoked by the elegies, there is a clear hierarchy regarding the order in which they are mentioned, in accordance with their perceived relevance to Sidney's life. Mars, representing the military aspect of Sidney's career,
always takes precedence. While this may not be fully borne out by biographical facts
– contrary to what the invocations to Mars are trying to imply, Sidney only spent a
relatively short period of his life as a soldier – it corresponds to the prominent military imagery of Lant's Roll.

Minerva, on the other hand, is used by the commemorative poems to call to mind
Sidney's life as a significant political figure. This too may not fully correspond to
Sidney's importance at the English court (though Alan Stewart has made a strong
case for Sidney as a key figure at other European courts), but once again it corresponds perfectly to the stately imagery in the engravings of Lant's Roll. At the very
beginning of the Roll, for example, Sidney's hearse is depicted lying in state at St
Paul's. The rosette, which dominates the background of the image, calls to mind the
location and serving as visual proof of Sidney's national importance, giving the image
an almost regal air.

Finally, Apollo is used by elegists to represent Sidney's overall accomplishment in
all arts. However, much like the references to the muses, who also figure prominently

in *Lachrymae*, this should not be read as a specific allusion to Sidney's poetry, but as a general tribute to Sidney as an educated humanist and all-round paragon. The collective tears of the muses are not for Sidney the poet but for Sidney the 'phoenix', uniquely worthy of having poetry written about him, in order to spread his fame and preserve his memory as an example to others. This is essentially the same idea as that of Sidney as the 'star' of England, an image which seems to have appealed some of the early elegists, perhaps because of the potential for a Latin pun on 'sidus / Sidneius'. The foremost (though not the only) example of this is a poem by Alexander Neville, the editor of the *Lachrymae*. This poem, which praises Sidney's exemplary life and valorous death, is dominated by the recurring line 'dulce decus nostrum, *Sydus Sidnae Britannum*'.[32] In Lant's Roll, there is no single visual equivalent of Sidney the 'star', since the idea of Sidney as a paragon is what the funeral procession in its entirety is trying to convey. However, there is one engraving that shows an ensign trailing a star-covered banner, which may well be in reference to 'Sydus Sidnae Britannum' (although it has also been read as an allusion to Stella).

The early elegies for Sidney, then, largely repeat the images of Sidney conveyed by the funeral procession as it is documented through Lant's Roll. That is, they portray Sidney primarily as a hero and a paragon. Although some of the elegists betray an awareness of, if not familiarity with, his poetry, it is always Sidney's *vita activa* that takes precedence. There appears to be a consensus with Fulke Greville's view that Sidney's poetry was incidental to his life, and that he ought not to be remembered as a poet because it would belittle his true significance. Famously, Greville's posthumously published *Life of Sidney* only makes very few references to Sidney's writings.[33] When he does mention Sidney's *Arcadia*, however, Greville is at pains to stress that it does not make Sidney a poet in the strict sense of the word, and to discourage his readers from viewing him in that light:

> [Sidney] had that dexterity, even with the dashes of his pen to make the *Arcadian Antiques* beautifie the Margents of his works; yet the honour which (I beare him record) he never affected, I leave unto him, with this addition, that his end in them was not vanishing pleasure alone, but morall Images, and Examples (as directing threds) to guide every man through the confused *Labyrinth* of his own desires, and life: So that how soever I liked them not too well (even in that unperfected shape they were) to condescend that such delicate (though inferior) Pictures of himselfe, should be suppressed; yet

32 'Our sweet ornament, Sidney, the star of Britain'. The phrase 'dulce decus nostrum' is of course alluding to the famous line from Horace's *Odes* and serves to further highlight the patriotic element in Neville's poem.

33 Although the *Life of Sidney* was not published in printed form until 1652 – well after Sidney's and Greville's deaths in 1586 and 1628 respectively – it was written around 1612 and originally intended by Greville as a dedication to Sidney to preface an edition of his own works. Due to its publication context, it is sometimes referred to by its manuscript title, 'A Dedication to Sir Philip Sidney', and the accuracy of the 1652 title has been repeatedly questioned, usually to argue in favour of reading it as a dedication, as in John Gouws's article 'Fact and Anecdote in Fulke Greville's Account of Sidney's Last Days', in Jan van Dorsten, Dominic Baker-Smith, Arthur F. Kinney (eds), *Sir Philip Sidney: 1586 and the Creation of a Legend* (Leiden: Sir Thomas Browne Institute, 1986), pp. 62–82. A notable exception is Adriana McCrea's article 'Whose Life Is It, Anyway? Subject and Subjection in Fulke Greville's *Life of Sidney*', in Mayer and Woolf (eds), *The Rhetoric of Life-Writing in Early Modern Europe* (Ann Arbor: University of Michigan Press, 1995), pp. 299–320. McCrea refers to it as 'the so-called *Life*' and argues that it is not so much a biographical as an autobiographical text, whose true subject is Greville himself.

I do wish that work may be the last in this kind, presuming no man that followes can ever reach, much lesse go beyond that excellent intended patterne of his.[34]

Greville's choice of imagery here is revealing of how anxious he is to play down the significance of Sidney's writings compared to his (non-literary) 'works'. He views them as illustrations, both in the sense that they act as 'images and examples', which have an aesthetic as well as an explanatory function, and in the sense that they are to be treated as marginal.[35] Paradoxically, Greville is legitimising Sidney's writing by insisting that 'his end was not in his writing even while he wrote' but that he aimed 'to make himself, and others, not in words or opinion, but in life, and action, good and great' (both p. 21). In Greville's view, then, Sidney's poetic works constitute not a point of conflict between the different spheres of his life but an aspect of his *vita activa*. Greville is making the same point when he insists towards the beginning of his book that Sidney 'purposed no monuments of books to the world' (p. 13), that is, he tries to persuade his readers that Sidney himself did not wish to be remembered as a poet, hinting that readers who choose to remember him through 'monuments of books' have misunderstood him.

At the time when Greville was writing his *Life of Sidney* – some twenty-five years after his friend's death – he was evidently not expecting all of his readers to share his view that Sidney's poetry should be regarded as merely marginal to his 'real' works. Prior to Sidney's transition from manuscript to print author, however, Greville might not have needed to labour his point so much. This is illustrated by Angel Day's elegy (probably written in 1587), which is unusual in that it is uncommonly emphatic about Sidney's poetic achievements. Like many other elegies, *Vpon the life and death of the most worthy, and thrise renowned knight, Sir Phillip Sidney: A Comemoration of his worthines* opens with the 'tears of the muses' motif. However, Day specifically singles out three muses closely associated with poetry: Thalia, Erato and Calliope, whom he names in the first stanza. The remaining six muses appear to be absent. The seventh and eighth stanzas of the elegy not only show Sidney as a poet (note also the pun in 'Penbrooke'), but also contain an explanatory gloss naming *Arcadia* as one of Sidney's works.[36]

> *Archadia* now, where is thy soueraigne guide,
> Who stately *Penbrooke* erst did to thee knit,
> Where be the notes, his skill did earst deuide,
> In sondry meeters, wounde from finest wit.
> Which he so well in couert shapes could fit.
> Where be the pipes, the deintiest shepheards sound:
> That euer erst, within thy woods were found.

---

34 Fulke Greville, *The Life of the Renowned Sr Philip Sidney* (London, 1652), pp. 244–5.
35 See meanings 1a and 3 of the *OED* entry. During the seventeenth century in particular, the term 'illustration' could – among other things – be used to refer to explanatory glosses. One of the best-known examples of this usage occurs in a text that is almost exactly contemporary to Greville's *Life of Sidney*: Michael Drayton's chorographical poem *Poly-Olbion* (1612), which was published with marginal glosses by the antiquary John Selden, who termed his annotations 'illustrations'.
36 The gloss – the only one in the poem – reads: 'A book by him penned, called the Countesses of Pēbrooks Archadia' ([A]4ᵃ).

Sugred *Sidney*, *Sidney* sweete it was,
That to thy soile, did giue the greatest fame.
Whose honny dewes, that from his quil did passe,
With honny sweetes, aduaunst thy glorious name.
Who ere thee knewe, that knewe thy soyle to blame:
Far was it from the skill if any one,
To wade in thee, so far as he hath gone.

(Day, *Vpon the Life and Death*, [A]4[a])

Later in his elegy, however, Day abandons his praise of Sidney's 'honny dewes' in order to praise a very different kind of virtue in him. Line 156 somewhat abruptly announces, 'Thou mightie *Mauors* [Mars] knowest he was a Knight' (B[a]), which marks the (quite literally) martial turning-point of the poem, at which 'Sugred *Sidney*, *Sidney* sweete' is transformed into 'This worthie Knight Sir Phillip *Sidney* bold', who is likened to Hector, fresh out of battle, riding a gore-splattered horse (l. 171).

What is remarkable about Angel Day's elegy is that although he simultaneously presents his readers with two very different Sidney figures and maintains a roughly equal balance between them, he makes no attempt to reconcile the two into a single Sidney. There is merely an implied link via the idea that both are different manifestations of Sidney's noble character. In essence, then, Day's attitude towards Sidney's poetry is not so very different from Greville's: for Day, the 'sondry meeters, wounde from finest wit' merely represent an (as yet) underappreciated facet of Sidney's 'worthines' that deserves a mention. Unlike Greville, however, Day did not yet have to defend his view of Sidney as an exemplary hero against an audience of readers who, after having first encountered his works in print, thought of him primarily as a poet. Day's Sidney, unlike Greville's, is still very much a manuscript poet whose works are only circulated among a comparatively exclusive readership. This explains both the necessity to gloss the word '*Archadia*' and the necessity to be so emphatic about his merits as a poet.

However, the underappreciation of Sidney's 'worthiness' as a poet, which Day's elegy laments, soon ceased to be a problem. The second wave of responses to Sidney's death was occasioned by the appearance of his works in print during the 1590s. Between 1590 and 1597, multiple versions of *Arcadia*, *Astrophel and Stella* and *A Defence of Poesie* were printed, some of which were unauthorised. In the following sections, I shall first examine reactions to Sidney's sudden transformation from manuscript poet to printed author, as exemplified by the 1590 and 1593 *Arcadia* editions. Then I shall move on to the side-effects of Sidney's new role as a major literary figure of the 1590s: his gradual fictionalisation through association with his characters and narratives. For this, I shall primarily be looking at the first edition of *Astrophel and Stella* (1591) and its reception. After this, I shall turn to *The Phoenix Nest* (1593) as a particularly literary response to Sidney containing the idea of literary survival. Finally, I shall return to the starting-point of this chapter, that is Spenser's 'Astrophel', which at first sight appears to be merely another tribute to Sidney within the second wave of responses, but which is in fact part of Spenser's uniquely self-aware exploration not only of Sidney's death but also of its poetic consequences.

From manuscript to print: *Arcadia* (1590 and 1593)

While some of the early elegies, like Angel Day's cited above, mention Sidney's writing, they are primarily responses to Sidney the soldier and courtier. Sidney the poet figure only entered the public consciousness after the posthumous publication of his works, particularly *Astrophel and Stella* (read as a sonnet sequence featuring a principal character based on Sidney himself), and *A Defence of Poesie*. However, the first of Sidney's works to be printed was the (incomplete) revised *Arcadia* edition of 1590, edited by Fulke Greville and John Florio.[37]

All early editions betray an awareness of Sidney's recent and sudden transition from manuscript poet to print author. This awareness is perhaps most noticeable in the 1590 *Arcadia*, which begins with a dedication to the Countess of Pembroke. The dedication – which takes the form of a letter from Sidney to his sister – stresses the trifling nature of his 'idle worke', likens it to a deformed child, and expresses Sidney's intention to restrict its readership:

> Now, it is done onelie for you, onely to you: if you keep it to your selfe, or to such friendes, who will weigh errors in the ballaunce of good will, I hope, for the fathers sake, it will be pardoned, perchance made much of, though in it selfe it haue deformities. For indeede, for seuerer eyes it is not.[38]

At first sight, the fact that Sidney's letter is addressed to a close family member would seem to make it appear a piece of private correspondence.[39] Nevertheless its intimacy, much like its apologetic remarks regarding the quality of the text, is likely to be a trope to some extent. By giving his permission for manuscript copies of his unrevised text to be circulated, even while stressing that the text may only be passed on to a select, forgiving circle of friends, Sidney's dedicatory letter immediately qualifies its own initial claim that what follows is intended only for the Countess of Pembroke's eyes.

The reproduction of this letter, which, if genuine, would originally have been written for an audience of manuscript readers (including, but not necessarily limited to, the Countess of Pembroke), at the beginning of a printed text places it in a new context.[40] Paradoxically, this has the effect of enhancing rather than reducing the

---

37 I am following Gavin Alexander in avoiding the names 'Old Arcadia', 'New Arcadia' and 'The Countess of Pembroke's Arcadia' because they serve to confuse rather than clarify the matter (see *Writing After Sidney*, pp. xiii–xiv). Sidney's *Arcadia* exists in several different versions, both in print and in manuscript form, some of which use the title 'The Countess of Pembroke's Arcadia'. The three main versions are: first, the original, unrevised version (sometimes called the 'Old Arcadia'), circulated in manuscript form but not printed until 1926, after having been rediscovered by the scholar and manuscript collector Bertram Dobell towards the beginning of the twentieth century; second, the revised version (sometimes called the 'New Arcadia'), which is incomplete and breaks off in mid-sentence during Book III (this version was the first to be published, in 1590); and third, the composite, 'augmented and ended' version, which was published in 1593 and formed the basis for all further editions until the rediscovery of the unrevised manuscript version. As Hugh Sanford's preface points out, this version is 'the Countess of Pembroke's' in more than one sense, because she was in fact involved in its publication, and the preface even goes as far as to credit her with coauthorship.
38 Sir Philip Sidney, *Arcadia* (1590), A3^b.
39 The letter is addressed 'to my deare Ladie and Sister, the Countesse of Pembroke', a conventional form of address of the type that might be found on the address leaves of early modern letters.
40 No holograph version of this dedicatory epistle exists, so it is impossible to verify whether or when Sidney wrote it. The question of authenticity is irrelevant for my argument, however, because I am

element of privacy. In the context of manuscript circulation, Sidney's reference to the 'friendes, who will weigh errors in the ballaunce of good will' implicitly includes his entire readership: ideally, anyone reading the dedicatory letter would first have to have been vetted as a 'friend' who could be trusted to understand and value the text.[41] As a result, the sense of privacy conveyed by Sidney's letter in a manuscript context is an inclusive one, as it automatically places its readers in a position of trust: that trust is what has made them eligible to become readers of the manuscript in the first place. By contrast, the readership of the same dedicatory letter prefixed to a printed text is placed in a very different position. In the context of a printed text, Sidney's wish to restrict its audience on the one hand increases the value of the text by making it appear exclusive and desirable. On the other hand, however, through a dedicatory letter that is clearly aimed at a manuscript audience, the reader of the printed *Arcadia* is also made aware of the fact that he is not part of its intended audience and, strictly speaking, should not be reading it. While the dedicatory letter thus allows the readers of the printed *Arcadia* a more intimate glimpse into the life of its author than they might otherwise have had (unless they had previously been manuscript readers), it also puts them firmly in their place.

What is peculiar about the 1590 *Arcadia* is not so much the fact that it is incomplete as the fact that this incompleteness is hardly commented on. The only clear indication that it is unfinished – other than the text's breaking off in mid-sentence – is the ellipsis formed by three asterisks, which replaces the word 'finis' on the last page.[42] The title page makes no mention of the text's incompleteness, though, and the editor's note on A4^b (probably written by Greville) only mentions it in passing, while outlining the changes he has made to the presentation of the text:

> The diuision and summing of the Chapters was not of Sir *Philip Sidneis* dooing, but aduentured by the ouer-seer of the print, for the more ease of the Readers. He therefore submits himselfe to their iudgement [...]. As also if any defect be found in the Eclogues, which although they were of Sir *Phillip Sidneis* writing, yet were they not perused by him, but left till the worke had bene finished, that then choise should haue bene made, which should haue bene taken, and in what manner brought in. At this time they haue bene chosen and disposed as the ouer-seer thought best.
>
> (1590 *Arcadia*, A4^b)

Only the use of the subjunctive mood in the penultimate sentence – 'till the worke *had bene* finished'; 'choice *should haue bene* made'; 'which *should haue bene* taken' – indicates that the condition for Sidney's selecting of the eclogues, that is the completion of the work, was not fulfilled.

---

concerned with how the letter shapes the text and readers' expectations in a print context, authorised by the Countess of Pembroke.

41 This is not to say that this conceit of readers as 'friendes' reflects the reality of early modern manuscript circulation. William Ponsonby obtained the rights to the book after he contacted Sidney's family and informed them he had been offered an illicit copy. Regardless of whether this copy really existed – if it did, it has not survived – Ponsonby's story was evidently considered plausible, which suggests that in reality it was much harder to limit the readership of manuscripts to an intimate audience than in the idealised version that Sidney's letter presents.

42 This is, however, followed by an impressum at the bottom of the page, which gives a false impression of closure.

While Greville himself remains largely silent on the matter of the 1590 *Arcadia*'s incompleteness, his decision to prefix it with Sidney's letter to the Countess of Pembroke has one ingenious side-effect. By removing the letter from its original context and attaching it to a printed edition of the incomplete revised 'New' *Arcadia* manuscript, Greville is effectively making Sidney himself apologise for the state of the text.[43] As a result of this changed context, the image of the text as a deformed child (see the passage quoted above) subtly shifts in meaning. Instead of referring only to stylistic 'flaws' or the general 'trifling' nature of the work, the image now also implicitly refers to the incompleteness of the 1590 *Arcadia*. Paradoxically, Sidney's overdue brain-child, which 'if it had not ben in some way delivered, would have grown a monster', has, in its printed form, turned into something more closely resembling a premature birth, an image also used to describe an incomplete work in the preface to *Greenes Groats-worth of Witte* (1592), which dubs the contents of the volume 'an Embrion [which] without shape, I feare me will be thrust into the world. If I liue to end it, it shall be otherwise' (*Groats-worth*, A3^b–A4^a).

In his *Life of Sir Philip Sidney*, Greville uses a hybrid of these two images of incompleteness and unpolishedness, in referring to 'this *Arcadia* of his' as an 'unpolished Embrio' (pp. 19–20). Arguably, this combined imagery has been intentionally chosen by Greville because the vagueness of reference allows him to speak of 'this' *Arcadia* as a single text. However, by the time Greville wrote the *Life of Sidney*, 'his' *Arcadia* – the 1590 edition, which had been based on the manuscript in his possession – was no longer the only version. The 1593 *Arcadia* presented an open challenge not only to the editorial methods used by Greville to transform the manuscript into a printed text, but also to Greville's reading of Sidney. Seeking to replace the older version, it asserted that as a result of editorial 'defectes' the 1590 edition had projected a false image of Sidney the 'Authour' as well as Sidney the exemplar.

While the 1590 *Arcadia* makes surprisingly little reference to the fact that the text it presents to readers is incomplete, the 1593 edition, by contrast, is very emphatic about its own completeness. The title page of the 1593 *Arcadia* declares it to be 'now since the first edition augmented and ended', and the preface 'To the Reader' devotes a significant amount of space to an elaboration on this claim. In that preface, Hugh Sanford, secretary to the Earl of Pembroke and one of the people involved in the 'augmenting' of the text, takes up Sidney's image of the deformed child. In his version, however, some of the flaws were in fact 'spottes' added by the previous edition. He refers to the editorial changes by using a composite imagery, which suggests a curious mixture of beauty treatment and home improvement:

> The disfigured face, gentle Reader, wherewith this worke not long since appeared to the common view, moued that noble Lady, to whose Honour consecrated, to whose protection it was committed, to take in hand the wiping away those spottes wherewith the beauties thereof were vnworthely blemished. But as often in repairing a ruinous house,

---

43 If the letter was intended to preface a manuscript version of *Arcadia* presented to the Countess of Pembroke, it is unlikely that it would have been a version that ended in mid-sentence as the 1590 *Arcadia* does. More plausibly, the letter would have been prefixed to a perhaps unpolished but essentially complete version, similar to the 'Old' *Arcadia* manuscript that was rediscovered at the beginning of the twentieth century and is now held by the Folger Shakespeare Library.

the mending of some olde part occasioneth the making of some new: so here her honourable labour begonne in correcting the faults, ended in supplying the defectes; by the view of what was ill done guided to the consideration of what was not done. Which part with what aduise entred into, with what successe it hath beene passed through, most by her doing, all by her directing, if they may be entreated not to define, which are vnfurnisht of meanes to discerne, the rest (it is hoped) will fauourably censure. But this they shall, for theyr better satisfaction, vnderstand, that though they finde not here what might be expected, they may finde neuerthelesse as much as was intended, the conclusion, not the perfection of *Arcadia*: and that no further then the Authours own writings, or knowen determinations could direct. Whereof who sees not the reason, must consider there may be reason which hee sees not.[44]

The image used in the first sentence of Sanford's preface is one of restoration by rather simple means. The face of the 'vnworthely blemished' *Arcadia* is restored to its true beauty by the Countess of Pembroke's judicious wiping. Among the blemishes wiped away are the chapter divisions and summaries introduced by Greville. Thus the first edition, which Sanford evidently considers deeply flawed in its approach to Sidney, is being replaced with a new, more authoritative one. However, the second sentence contains a shift of imagery, alerting the reader to the fact that not all blemishes could be as easily remedied and there was need for some more radical treatment. As the preface continues, the editorial process which was initially likened to a light skin treatment, begins to sound increasingly like corrective surgery that requires justification.

When Sanford turns to the previous editors and other 'worthless Reader[s]', his tone is hostile, bordering on aggressive. He calls them 'vnfurnisht of meanes to discerne' and denies them any right to criticise the current edition. A similar attack on Greville and Florio is implied in the emblem on the title page. It shows a pig facing a marjoram plant, superscribed with the motto 'SPIRO NON TIBI' ('my scent is not for you'). The implied accusation is that the editors' lack of critical discernment made them impervious to the true moral qualities of *Arcadia*, and that this led them to produce such an inferior, 'blemished' text.[45] Nevertheless, the overall tenor of the preface is one of justification, sometimes verging on the defensive. Sanford brandishes the image of the Countess of Pembroke as an authoritative, goddess-like figure in relation to the text like a shield to deflect potential criticism. Interestingly, as Sanford presents it, this authority is derived not so much from her close connection with the deceased author (who is only named as her brother in the penultimate line of the preface) and an implied superior knowledge of his 'determinations', as from her indisputable ownership of the text. When viewed in this context, even the dedicatory letter, which is reprinted and precedes the preface, acquires the function of a document proving that ownership. The Countess of Pembroke as presented by the 1593 *Arcadia* is not merely the goddess possessively guarding a text that has been

44 *Arcadia* (1593), ¶4ᵃ. Albert Feuillerat's edition, which does not contain the 1593 edition in its entirety but only has 'The Last Part of Sir Philip Sidney's *Arcadia*, from the folio of 1593' as a separate second volume, omits this preface from the second volume. Instead, it is only reproduced as an alternate preface in the notes to the 1590 edition in the first volume.
45 See Margery Corbett and Ronald Lightbown, *The Comely Frontispiece* (London, Boston: Routledge & Kegan Paul, 1979), pp. 58–65, for a more detailed description and an account of this emblem's history.

'consecrated' to her; she has effectively become its author by right. By the final paragraph of Sanford's preface, she has acquired such a degree of authority over the text that instead of having the text consecrated to her honour, she is in a position to consecrate it back to its original author:[46]

> [C]onsidering the fathers vntimely death preuented the timely birth of the childe, it may happily seeme a thanke-woorthy labour, that the defects being so few, so small, and in no principall part, yet the greatest vnlikenes is rather in defect then in deformity. But howsoeuer it is, it is now by more then one interest *The Countesse of Pembrokes Arcadia*: done, as it was, for her: as it is, by her. Neither shall these pains be the last […] which the euerlasting loue of her excellent brother, will make her consecrate to his memory.
>
> (1593 *Arcadia*, ¶4ᵇ)

The reason I have discussed the editorial conflict surrounding the two earliest printed *Arcadia* editions at some length is that it illustrates two closely linked phenomena in relation to the printing of Sidney's works. These phenomena are the demand for closure on the one hand, and on the other hand the idea of a single authoritative text, reflecting an accurate (and officially sanctioned) view of Sidney himself.

The 1593 *Arcadia* edition, then, is inspired by an idea of single authorship and aims to provide an authoritative printed text to serve as a template for later editions. This is of course in stark contrast to manuscript circulation, which is characterised by a blurring of the concept of authorship, since textual variations and incompleteness through selection by scribes who effectively act as coauthors are to be expected. As can be seen from William Ringler's and H. R. Woudhuysen's inventories of manuscripts known to contain Sidney's poetry, 'complete' manuscript copies are uncommon compared to those containing selections based on the preference of the manuscripts' original owners, as well as perhaps the availability and the state of the texts they copied.

Of course a prose narrative like *Arcadia* would lend itself less to partial copying than poetry. Nevertheless, the more fluid nature of texts as part of a manuscript culture may explain why Greville apparently saw no need to explain, let alone justify, the state of the text in his *Arcadia* edition of 1590. Even as he was editing *Arcadia* for print, Greville still viewed Sidney essentially as a manuscript poet, and himself as an editor whose task was to reproduce a manuscript that was authentic but would not necessarily be expected to be a complete or definitive version of the text.

Sanford's hostility towards the earlier editors, on the other hand, can be partly explained through the fact that to him, writing only three years after Greville's edition, Sidney was already a poet associated with the medium of print. Consequently, Sanford's goal as an editor was to finalise both the text and Sidney's image as a poet, which left no room for textual variation or lack of closure. Thus the differences between the 1590 and 1593 *Arcadia* illustrate the speed of Sidney's transformation from manuscript poet to print author, as well as the changing attitude towards him as a consequence of this.

---

46 Sidney himself, on the other hand is almost feminised at this point by being presented as having died in childbirth. For a detailed discussion of the father and child imagery in Sidney's letter and Sanford's preface see Andrew Fleck's article 'The Father's Living Monument: Textual Progeny and the Birth of the Author in Sidney's "Arcadias"', *Studies in Philology*, 107 (2010), 520–47.

Sanford's 1593 *Arcadia* edition later formed the basis for the 1598 folio edition, whose title suggests a definitive version of *Arcadia*, but which is effectively a collection of Sidney's complete works. In a sense, the need for a similarly unified Sidney is a product of Sidney's transition into print authorship, much like the desire of Sidney's family (whose interests Sandford's edition represented) to control his image through issuing authorised and authoritative editions of his works.

Interestingly, however, the readers of the early editions showed little inclination to seek such a unification by attempting to unite Sidney the hero and Sidney the newly published poet. A possible explanation is that this would have appeared to belittle Sidney's public life and achievements (also expressed in Greville's insistence in the *Life of Sidney* that 'his end was not in writing, even while he wrote' (p. 21)). Responses to Sidney during the 1590s therefore took a very different turn, by eschewing associations of Sidney the hero with Sidney the poet and instead seeking to unite Sidney the poet with his works. This resulted in a semi-fictionalised Sidney figure, derived from his own writings.[47] The starting point of this association was the character Philisides, Sidney's miniature self-portrait in *Arcadia*. However, while there were some references to Sidney as 'Philisides' following the publication of *Arcadia*, with Edmund Spenser's 'The Ruines of Time' (*Complaints*, 1591) being the earliest example, it was another name that came to be applied more frequently to Sidney as a poet figure: 'Astrophel', or occasionally 'Astrophil'.[48] In the following section, I shall examine the role of the early editions of *Astrophel and Stella* for the emergence of Sidney's semi-fictionalised life-narrative as 'Astrophel'. In this, I shall be focusing primarily on the first edition. This is not so much because it was the most influential edition – in fact, it had to be withdrawn shortly after publication, making it unlikely that many copies were sold and read – but because its prefaces constitute perhaps the earliest responses to Sidney's works by readers who had first encountered them in print (and who were themselves print professionals).

The liberation of Astrophel: the first quarto of *Astrophel and Stella*

Astrophel and Stella has often been viewed as a partially autobiographic text. The three key assumptions that form the basis of this reading are first, that the sonnets and songs constitute a sequence forming a loose narrative; second, that the protagonist of that narrative and speaker of the majority of poems is called 'Astrophel' (or 'Astrophil'); and third, that this protagonist is a fictional alter ego of Sidney himself.

To some extent, these assumptions are ingrained within the text itself. For example, as Ringler and others have noted, there are indications that Sidney intended the speaker 'Astrophel' to be as identifiably like himself as possible.[49] However, this

---

47 See Gavin Alexander's observation that 'Sidney becomes his personae after his death' (*Writing After Sidney*, p. xxxviii).

48 Ringler argued that for etymological reasons the character's name should be spelt 'Astrophil'. In contemporary sources, however, 'Astrophel' is the more common spelling, which may indicate the influence of the print edition.

49 In one sonnet, for example, a comparison is made between the speaker and a sparrow, the bird traditionally associated with the name 'Philip'. The association is heightened by the fact that the sparrow in the poem is referred to by the dismissive diminutive 'Sir Phip'.

narrativisation of Sidney as 'Astrophel' is not fully reflected in the way in which
the poems appear in early manuscripts. While there are surviving manuscripts that
contain nearly all of the poems of *Astrophel and Stella*, far more contain selections
of only a few poems, which may indicate that some early manuscript readers viewed
it as a collection rather than as a narrative sequence. Similarly, the title *Astrophel
and Stella*, which is crucial for the identification of the speaker of the sonnets as the
'Astrophel' of songs viii and ix, rarely occurs in manuscripts.[50]

One manuscript, University of Edinburgh MS De.5.96, is of particular interest
in this context. This manuscript was originally owned by Sidney's contemporary
Edward Dymoke and had the title *Astrophel and Stella* subsequently added by its later
owner, Scottish poet William Drummond of Hawthornden. The manner in which
Drummond added the title suggests it was in imitation of the title pages of a printed
book. The manuscript contains two added titles by Drummond: first, 'ASTROPHEL
and STELLA written by Sr Philip Sidny Knight' on the first page of the manuscript,
along with his own dedication of the manuscript to the library, and second, 'S. P.
Sidneys Astrophell and Stella', facing the first page of sonnets (this is written on the
verso of Dymoke's elegy for Sidney, which precedes the text of *Astrophel and Stella*).
Additionally, Drummond amended the first and second line of the first sonnet by
inserting the words 'my loue' and changing 'the deare She' to 'she (deare She)'. That
is, he effectively corrected the lines to read 'Louing in truth, and faine in verse my
loue to show | That she (deare she) might take some pleasure of my paine', as they do
in print editions from 1598 onwards.[51] While Drummond did not make very many
additions to the manuscript, then, those changes he did make suggest that he thought
of the printed text as the original and that his aim was to ensure the manuscript more
closely resembled the text he knew before he donated it to the 'Colledge of Edenb.'.
This is consistent with the fact that Drummond was born one year before Sidney's
death and thus belonged to the first generation of readers who had only encountered
Sidney as a print author. An additional side-effect of Drummond's added titles is to
give greater prominence to the name 'Astrophel': in the title he added to the first page
of the manuscript 'ASTROPHEL' is written twice as large as 'STELLA' – and indeed
twice as large as 'Sidny'. There is, then, some evidence that the assumptions which
form the basis for most readings of *Astrophel and Stella* – that it forms a narrative,
whose protagonist 'Astrophel' is a fictional self-portrait of Sidney – may owe more to
early printed editions than to the text as it was circulated in manuscript form.

Before its inclusion in the 1598 folio of Sidney's works, which became the definitive
version for Drummond, as well as other readers, *Astrophel and Stella* had appeared
in three different quarto editions.[52] In the following, I shall focus on the first of these
quartos. As noted in the previous section, this was not the most influential edition of

---

50   The name 'Astrophel' appears only three times within the text: twice in song viii and once in song ix.
      However, according to the list of manuscripts containing poems from *Astrophel and Stella* compiled
      by William Ringler, the songs seem to have been copied particularly frequently.
51   Ringler concludes that 'Those additions are taken from [the 1598 folio] or a later folio, probably the
      1599 Edinburgh edition, which are the only texts with the reading "she (deare She)" in AS I.2.' (William
      Ringler (ed.), *The Poems of Sir Philip Sidney* (Oxford: Clarendon Press, 1962), p. 540).
52   Q1 and Q2 are both dated 1591, Q3 is most likely to have been published in 1597.

the text. Q1 famously had to be withdrawn shortly after its publication and survives in only two copies.[53] Nevertheless, Q1 is of particular interest for the purpose of examining early responses to Sidney's appearance in print: on the one hand because it was the first of Sidney's works to be printed after the 1590 *Arcadia* and on the other hand because it contains a dedicatory epistle and a preface to the readers, unlike the two later quartos.[54]

The writers of the epistle and preface were both representatives of the printing industry who already figured in my previous chapter; printer and publisher Thomas Newman and professional pamphleteer Thomas Nashe. Newman's epistle and Nashe's preface are both characterised by two themes: Sidney's poetic survival through the medium of print, and a narrativised reading of the work that effectively merges Sidney with his poetry.

Sidney and his works, Newman and Nashe argue, are under threat. In their view, the danger is not so much that Sidney's works may be forgotten as that they may be misremembered due to the corrupting influence of manuscript publication. Although the Q1 text bears little resemblance to that of the authoritative 1598 quarto edition and tends to be regarded by Sidney scholars as a garbled, perhaps even pirated, version of the text, Newman's epistle specifically stresses that it is a carefully edited and printed text. Despite his delight at having 'lighted vpon' the text, which he describes as 'famous [...] [among] all men of iudgement', Newman claims, he did not simply print it as it was but attempted to reverse corruptions to the text caused by its popularity in manuscript:

> For my part, I haue beene very carefull in the Printing of it, and where as being spred abroad in written Coppies, it had gathered much corruption by ill Writers: I haue vsed their helpe and aduice in correcting & restoring it to his first dignitie, that I knowe were of skill and experience in those matters.[55]

It is of course impossible to tell whether Newman was simply lying about this careful editing process or whether he had wasted his labours on a version of the text that had indeed been corrupted beyond recognition. Given his similarly questionable claims regarding his own scrupulousness in *Greenes Vision*, we may be inclined to disbelieve his protestations. Nevertheless, Newman's epistle shows that he at least wished to *appear* to be taking great pains not only for the sake of the text but out of respect for its author.[56] The epistle's distinction between Sidney and his works is blurred, and

---

53 The reasons for Q1's withdrawal are unclear. The two most common theories are first, that Sidney's family objected to the unauthorised publication, and second, that Samuel Daniel objected to to the inclusion of an early version of his *Delia* sonnets. Finally, Germaine Warkentin has suggested that it was Newman's dedication to Francis Flower which caused offence, stressing that having already printed copies recalled and destroyed was an uncommonly harsh punishment for a printer and that 'the usual penalty for cases of disorderly printing was simply a fine'. Germaine Warkentin, 'Patrons and Profiteers: Thomas Newman and the "Violent enlargement" of *Astrophil and Stella*', *Book Collector*, 34 (1985), 461–87 (p. 464). None of those three hypotheses has been conclusively proven, however.

54 These survive only in the British Library copy.

55 *Syr P.S. His Astrophel and Stella [...] to the end of which are added, sundry and rare Sonnets of diuers Noble men and Gentlemen* (1591), A2ᵇ.

56 Additionally, Newman of course had a professional interest in portraying himself as a careful restorer of texts to their 'first dignitie', because giving his readers the – possibly misleading – impression that

the grammatical ambiguity of 'his first dignitie' in the passage cited above serves to highlight this. In a sense, Newman is suggesting that not merely the text but Sidney himself is being threatened by the textual corruption caused by manuscript transmission through 'ill Writers', and that consequently it is not only the text but Sidney who needs to be rescued and restored.

Newman's professed concern for Sidney's poetic survival should perhaps not be taken entirely at face value. As a printer and publisher, he obviously had a vested commercial interest in advocating the printing of Sidney's works. It is therefore unlikely that Newman's desire to rescue Sidney from manuscript publication was caused purely by his concern for Sidney's 'dignitie'. Nevertheless, Newman's point that Sidney should be remembered for, and through, his works is an interesting one: 'I thought it pittie anie thing proceeding from so rare a man, shoulde bee obscured, or that his fame should not still be nourisht in his works, whom the works with one vnited griefe bewailed' ([Q1] *Astrophel and Stella*, A2ᵇ).

No doubt the early responses to Sidney's death would have agreed with Newman's judgement of him as 'so rare a man'. They might even have supported his claim that 'all men of iudgement' considered *Astrophel and Stella* 'one of the rarest things that euer any Englishman set abroach' (Aiiᵃ).[57] However, Newman's view that the exceptional character of the work constitutes a significant part of Sidney's own 'rarity', and that it should therefore be made public and contribute to his posthumous fame, was still uncommon in 1591. Even Angel Day's elegy discussed above had merely treated Sidney's poetic achievements as one relatively unknown facet of a man rightly famous for other things. Newman, on the other hand, presents Sidney's works as both the source of Sidney's fame and the instrument for its perpetuation. The second use of 'works' in the passage quoted above is probably an error on the compositor's part; 'world' would make more sense in this context. Nevertheless it is a revealing error to occur at this particular point, because the odd image of Sidney's works bewailing their author in fact aptly illustrates Newman's point that Sidney should be viewed through his poetic works.

Yet the most remarkable aspect about Q1 is the fact that Newman's epistle and Nashe's preface are perhaps the earliest recorded readings of Sidney as a print author, by people who had not previously been part of his manuscript readership.[58] Their eagerness to claim him for print and to portray Sidney the manuscript poet as merely an inferior, corrupted version of the true Sidney can of course be explained through professional bias. However, their peculiar tendency to blur the distinctions between the author and the works may reveal something about the way in which early readers responded to Sidney's rebirth in print.

Nashe's casually titled preface 'Somewhat to reade for them that list' approaches

---

the text was of higher quality than manuscript versions served his strategy to present print as the superior medium.

57 The first page of the book, containing the first half of Newman's dedicatory epistle is irregularly marked in this format. All subsequent pages are marked in the format A3, A4, B1 etc.

58 Although Newman and Nashe must of course have obtained and read a manuscript of *Astrophel and Stella* to prepare their edition, they did so with a view to publishing it in print. Thus they were already envisioning Sidney as a (prospective) print author.

Astrophel and Stella from an unexpected angle, treating the arrival of 'Astrophel' as a pivotal moment in the drama of the history of poetry. Nashe begins his effusive praise of Sidney as a poet by adapting a line from Ovid's *Amores* (III.2, 44) to create the impression of Ovid having to yield his position as the chief author of love poetry: *'Tempus adest plausus aurea pompa venit*, so endes the Sceane of Idiots, and enter *Astrophel* in pompe' (A3ᵃ).[59] The poem from which Nashe has borrowed this line is set at a circus, where Ovid's speaker attempts to seduce a young woman while simultaneously commenting on the progress of an ongoing chariot race. The 'golden procession' with effigies of the gods takes place before the start of the race. By placing 'Astrophel' at the centre of the 'pompe', Nashe is thus effectively deifying him, while relegating Ovid to the less dignified position of the (ultimately unsuccessful) lover. He then elaborates on his claim that Ovid was – quite literally – only the opening act for this superior poet, by comparing scenes from the *Metamorphoses* to a puppet play.[60] Nashe continues the theatre imagery by presenting *Astrophel and Stella* as a tragedy (or rather a tragicomedy):

> [H]ere you shal find a paper stage streud with pearle, an artificial heau'n to ouershadow the faire frame, & christal wals to encounter your curious eyes, while the tragicommody of loue is performed by starlight. The chiefe Actor here is *Melpomene*, whose dusky robes dipt in the ynke of teares as yet seeme to drop when I view them neere. The argument cruell chastitie, the Prologue hope, the Epilogue dispaire, *videte queso et linguis animisque fauete.* (A3ᵃ)[61]

Nashe's insistence on using theatre imagery in the preface to a poetic text appears an odd choice at first sight. Nevertheless, it serves a clear purpose: to encourage a 'dramatic' reading of the text as a coherent narrative sequence featuring a protagonist called 'Astrophel'. Although the title of the work may support such a reading, it is worth noting that outside the title, the name 'Astrophel' only occurs in two of the songs, which in Q1 are called 'Syr P.S. his Other Sonnets of variable verse' and separated from the rest of *Astrophel and Stella*. Since Q1 contains an abridged version of song viii, the second mention of the name 'Astrophel' in that song is omitted. As a result, the name that Nashe is applying both to the work as a whole and to its author occurs only twice within the text proper, but five times in Nashe's preface.

The dramatic reading proposed by Nashe is crucial for establishing 'Astrophel' as a character, which in turn is a prerequisite for Nashe's fictionalising of Sidney by merging him with this character. Similarly, the numerous Ovid references serve to establish 'Astrophel' as a writer of love poetry, but the comparison also invites readers to draw parallels to Ovid's love poetry, which was read as containing a

---

59 Literally: 'Now is the time to applaud, the golden procession is coming'.
60 'Gentlemen that haue seene a thousand lines of folly drawn forth *ex vno puncto impudentiae*, [...] that haue seene *Pan* sitting in his bower of delights, & a number of *Midasses* to admire his miserable hornpipes, let not your surfeted sight, new come fro[m] such puppet play, think scorne to turn aside into this Theater of pleasure' (A3ᵃ).
61 The final sentence (which roughly translates as 'watch, I ask you, and applaud') is an adaptation of another Ovidian phrase, which occurs in several places, including just before the line from *Amores* quoted in the opening sentence of Nashe's preface.

semi-autobiographical narrative similar to that which 'identified' Stella as Penelope Rich.[62]

One thing that is missing both from Newman's dedicatory epistle and from Nashe's preface is any direct mention of Sidney's name (although Nashe names the Countess of Pembroke once). While he is of course identified on the title page, in the running titles and at the end of the *Astrophel and Stella* poems as 'Syr P.S.', Newman refers to him only once, as 'so rare a man'. Nashe's praise is both more lavish and more elaborately phrased; his preface portrays Sidney as a messianic figure for poetry whose arrival lights up the dark that has descended on Parnassus. However, while ascribing to Sidney (and specifically Sidney's *name*) powers bordering on the supernatural, Nashe also carefully avoids mentioning that name. Instead, he refers to him as 'so excellent a Poet (the least sillable of whose name sounded in the eares of iudgement, is able to giue the meanest line he writes a dowry of immortality)' (A3ᵃ) or merely 'the Author' (A4ᵇ). At the same time, Nashe cleverly conflates *Astrophel and Stella*, the poet figure of the sonnets, as well as their author into 'Astrophel', blurring the distinctions between the poet and his work:

> I hope [readers] wil also hold me excused though I open the gate to his glory, & inuite idle eares to the admiration of his melancholy.
> *Quid petitur sacris nisi tantum fama poetis.*[63]
> Which although it be oftentimes imprisoned in Ladyes casks, & the president bookes of such as cannot see without another mans spectacles, yet at length it breakes foorth in spight of his keepers, and vseth some priuate penne (in steed of a picklock) to procure his violent enlargement. (A3ᵃ)

The blurring between author and work is particularly noticeable in Nashe's use of pronouns in this passage, shifting from Sidney to 'Astrophel' even within the same sentence. In the first sentence, 'his glory' clearly refers to the author whose work he is introducing, while 'his melancholy' should, strictly speaking, refer to the speaker of the poems. Similarly, when Nashe is describing the book's escape into print, his use of pronouns is ambiguous: 'it' may equally refer to the poet's (or the protagonist's) melancholy of the first sentence, to the posthumous fame implicitly desired by the poet or to the book itself, all of which are – more or less literally – 'imprisoned' in the process of manuscript circulation. In the second half of the sentence, the pronoun 'his' (which in early modern usage may mean 'its' as well as 'his') further heightens the ambiguity of reference in the passage. In combination with the personification of the third sentence, this ambiguity implies that it is not only *Astrophel and Stella* but 'Astrophel' himself who has escaped into print. Furthermore, through placing this sentence after the quotation from Ovid, and by using the image of the pen serving as a picklock, Nashe is suggesting that this 'liberation' of Sidney's works is both in the author's interest and, in a sense, the author's own doing, as it will contribute to his fame. This reading makes the printing of *Astrophel and Stella* not only a resurrection

---

62 I.e. 'Corinna', the name of the poet's mistress was read as a pseudonym for Augustus' daughter Julia, whom Ovid was believed to have been in love with.
63 Another line from Ovid, this time quoting *Ars Amatoria*: 'What do the sacred poets seek if not fame?'

of the author but an act of self-resurrection, an image that is repeated in the phoenix analogy, which occurs slightly later in the preface:[64]

> Deare *Astrophel*, that in the ashes of thy Loue, liuest againe like the *Phoenix*; ô might thy bodie (as thy name) liue againe likewise here amongst vs: but the earth, the mother of mortalitie, hath snatcht thee too soone into her chilled cold armes, and will not let thee by any meanes, be drawne from her deadly imbrace [...]. Therefore mayest thou neuer returne from the *Elisian* fieldes like *Orpheus*, therefore must we euer mourne for our *Orpheus*.
>
> Fayne would a second spring of passion heere spende it selfe on his sweet remembrance: but Religion that rebuketh prophane lamentation, drinkes in the riuers of those dispaireful teares, which languorous ruth hath outdwelled, & bids me looke back to the house of honor, where fro[m] one & the selfe same roote of renowne, I shal find many goodly branches deriued.

(Q1 Astrophel and Stella, A3^b–A4^a).

This passage stands out mainly for two reasons: the first is Nashe's mythologising of Sidney when describing his death, the second is Nashe's apparent refusal to do what 'we euer must' do and mourn the dead poet. Finally, the comparison to Orpheus completes the process of fictionalising Sidney as well as his recasting as an archetypal poet figure. Nashe's dismissal of continued mourning of Sidney as 'prophane lamentation' at first sight seems like a forced transition to the praise of the most prominent of the 'goodly branches', the Countess of Pembroke. However, as it is framed by the image of the phoenix and the reference to the Countess of Pembroke, the decision not to mourn for Sidney could be read as an encouragement not to dwell on Sidney's death but to look towards the 'living' poet present in his works, still guarded by the 'second *Minerua*' (A4ᵃ) yet on the verge of escaping into print.

It may be an exaggeration to claim that the narrative of 'Astrophel' the emerging poet figure originates with the first quarto edition of *Astrophel and Stella*, or to credit that edition with substantially shaping readers' perceptions of the text. However, Newman's dedicatory epistle and Nashe's preface to the reader offer an intriguing insight into the way in which Sidney's early readers perceived his works immediately after their publication in print. The epistle and preface suggest an unprecedented interest in considering Sidney not as the familiar public hero of the 1580s, but as a new poet figure and hero of his own works. Yet in choosing the word 'pompe' to denote the splendour of 'Astrophel's' arrival, Nashe is not only evoking Ovid, but also the 'pompe' of Sidney's funeral a few years previously, which his readers would most likely have recalled, and perhaps even witnessed at the time. He is merging the seemingly opposed ideas of *pompa funeris* and *pompa aurea* and presenting 'Astrophel's'

---

64 In addition to rebirth, the image of the phoenix of course suggests uniqueness, thus stressing again Sidney's 'rarity'. Even before the poetic miscellany *The Phoenix Nest*, which will be discussed in the next section of this chapter, the likening of Sidney to a phoenix was a popular trope among his elegists. See for example John Phillips's account of Sidney's funeral, *The Life and Death of Sir Phillip Sidney* (1587): 'This *Phenix* sweet *Sidney* was the flower of curtesie, who in his life time gaue a perfect light in his conuersation to leade men to virtue' (p. 2); and Nicholas Breton's poem 'A most singular and sweete Discourse of the life and death of S.P.S. Knight', published in *Brittons Bowre of Delights* (1591): 'Yet while I liue in all this miserie, | Let me go quarrel with this cruell fate, | Why death should do so great an iniurie, | [...] To kill a *Phoenix* when there were no mo' (A3ᵇ).

first procession as mirroring the spectacle of Sidney's last. Thus Nashe is implicitly depicting the figure of 'Astrophel' arriving on the public stage 'in pompe' in order to replace 'Syr P.S.' who had just vacated it in similar pomp. It is this new 'Astrophel' figure that forms the basis for the Sidney tributes of *The Phoenix Nest*, which in turn is the source of three of the seven *Astrophel* poems.

'Yet in his Poesies when we reede': *The Phoenix Nest*

Like many early modern miscellanies, *The Phoenix Nest* (1593) is difficult to classify precisely because of the miscellaneous nature of its contents. As with Spenser's *Complaints* (1591), which functions as a miscellany by a single author (and is introduced as such in the printer's preface), it is possible to identify certain broad themes within *The Phoenix Nest*. Those themes include elegy, lover's complaint, pastoral, the sonnet form or dream-poetry. However, it is not possible to apply any one of those themes to the volume as a whole without having to stretch that single 'theme' beyond its limits. To an extent, this is also true for the theme that most forces itself on readers of *The Phoenix Nest*: the theme of tributes to Sir Philip Sidney.

The Phoenix Nest begins with a cluster of Sidney-themed texts, which together account for nearly one fifth of the volume, including Matthew Roydon's elegy, the only poem of the miscellany to contain a direct phoenix-reference. The remaining contents of the volume feature several Sidneyan echoes, especially of *Astrophel and Stella*, which had been published two years earlier. Nevertheless, although the editor 'R. S.' clearly intended the Sidney theme to be noticed by readers of the volume, it would be hard to argue that, for example, the 'excellent Dialogue betweene Constancie and Inconstancie [...] presented to hir Maiestie, in the last Progresse' is about Sidney. In this section, I shall therefore not attempt to account for every element in *The Phoenix Nest* via the Sidney theme. Instead, I would like to examine how *The Phoenix Nest* establishes and explores this theme within its first few texts, and what image of Sidney it may be trying to convey.

One peculiarity about the cluster of four overtly Sidney-themed texts at the beginning of the volume is that they are all indirectly dated and all appear to be several years out of date. 'The dead mans Right', a posthumous counterpart to Sidney's 'Defence of the Earl of Leicester' – an open letter circulated in manuscript and possibly printed and distributed as a pamphlet – is introduced as having been written on the occasion of Leicester's death in 1588. Similarly, the three poems that follow this second defence of Leicester are grouped together in the index as 'An excellent Elegie, with two speciall Epitaphes vpon the death of sir Philip Sydney', dating them to 1586.[65]

Yet despite their emphasis on an early date, the three commemorative poems for Sidney assert 'the dead mans right' in a way that differs markedly from the tenor of the *Lachrymae* elegies. The subheading of Matthew Roydon's 'Elegie, or friends passion, for his Astrophill' and Walter Ralegh's 'Epitaph' both invoke 'the right Honourable sir Philip Sidney knight, Lord gouernor of Flushing', and this is implicitly echoed in the second epitaph's title 'Another of the same'. However, the main subject of the

---

65 For the use of 'upon' to indicate a precise moment, see meanings 6a and 7 in the *OED*.

three poems is not Sidney the knight but Sidney the poet, along with 'the dead mans write', as it were.

There is no reason to doubt the dating of the poems, and even some evidence to support it. Roydon, Ralegh and Greville (or Dyer) could easily have had access to Sidney's poetry in manuscript, and an 'Epitaph [by Roydon] on his beloued *Astrophel*' had been mentioned by Thomas Nashe in his first published piece, the preface to Greene's *Menaphon*, in 1589.[66] The poems, then, may well have been initially written in 1586. Nevertheless, their moment of publication in 1593, as well as their positioning at the beginning of a poetic miscellany that mostly consists of love-sonnets and pastoral poetry must have given them at least the appearance of being a response to the publication of *Astrophel and Stella* and the first, or perhaps both, of the two *Arcadia* editions. This particularly applies to Matthew Roydon's 'Elegie', which is set in a fictional pastoral landscape that gestured towards *Arcadia* ('these woods of Arcadie', l. 91). That fictional landscape is populated mainly by birds and mythical beasts – including a phoenix – which form a circle 'like to an Ampitheater' (l. 24) around the 'friend' of the title, who is mourning for 'his Astrophill'. Roydon is thus placing a fictionalised version of himself within a poetic landscape with Sidneyan references, in order to mourn Sidney's fictional alter ego. If the poem was indeed written shortly after Sidney's death, this would have signalled a degree of intimacy by implying that the writer of the poem belonged to the inner circle who had read his works during his lifetime – the 'friendes' mentioned in Sidney's dedicatory letter to his sister. The elegy, then, would have been as much about advertising Roydon's own status as a 'friend' as about lamenting Sidney's death.

By 1593, however, as the editor of *The Phoenix Nest* (if not Roydon himself) must have been aware, those references to Sidney's works had been given a different significance in the light of the recent publication of *Arcadia* and *Astrophel and Stella*. As a consequence, what may well have been initially written as a personal response to Sidney's life and death is effectively transformed into a literary one. Even stanza 24, which is addressed to Stella, and the poem's most direct reference to *Astrophel and Stella*, shifts in meaning. In 1593, 'we', the readers of Sidney's 'Poesies' constituted a much wider audience than in 1586:

> Although thy beautie do exceede,
> In common sight of eu'rie eie,
> Yet in his Poesies when we reede,
> It is apparent more thereby (ll. 139–42)

What is peculiar about Roydon's elegy is that although Athena and Mars each receive a mention (it is Astrophill's donning of Pallas' armour that provokes Mars' jealousy and thus causes the hero's death by thunderbolt), the main emphasis of the poem is on Astrophill's poetic perfection. Even Astrophill's love for Stella is only described in terms of its poetic consequences, that is, the perpetuation of her 'short liud beautie'

---

66 Note, however, that since *The Phoenix Nest* is the earliest source for the poems, it is not possible to establish whether they were reproduced as they had originally been written.

through verse, almost creating the impression that poetry was the sole aim of this love, as well as its only outcome.[67]

Roydon's elegy, then, despite its apparently early date of composition, responds primarily to Sidney as a poet, by portraying his persona 'Astrophill' as a poet figure. This resonates particularly strongly in the context of *The Phoenix Nest*'s publication shortly after *Astrophel and Stella*'s appearance in print in 1591, which had made Sidney's 'Poesies', as well as the figure of Astrophel, publicly accessible. Instead of addressing only a relatively small and exclusive readership able to understand references to his writings prior to their publication, Roydon's poem at the beginning of *The Phoenix Nest* creates a common point of reference for all Sidney readers, especially readers who had not known Sidney and were only familiar with him through his works. This, somewhat ironically, makes Roydon's elegy the most inclusive Sidney-themed text of the miscellany.

While the two epitaphs that follow Roydon's elegy also respond to Sidney's poetry, they do so in a more indirect manner. For example, both poems implicitly praise Sidney's poetic skill by suggesting that he would have written a better epitaph for himself. The first epitaph, written by Walter Ralegh, contains a brief account of Sidney's public life and praises him as a military hero, yet this life narrative is framed within a narrative of poetry. The first three stanzas express the speaker's awareness that, in the light of Sidney's superior 'wit', any effort to mourn him poetically can amount to little more than a gesture of 'friendly care' (l. 6). That the phrase 'wit high, pure, diuine' (l. 2) of the first stanza alludes to Sidney's poetic skill is apparent not only in the fact that it is contrasted with 'the powre of mortall line' (l. 3), but also in the poem's conclusion. The final stanza dubs Sidney the 'Scipio, Cicero, and Petrarch of our time' (l. 58). Ralegh's use of the epithet 'Petrarch of our time' here is illustrative of the importance that he assigns to Sidney's poetic activities. It is the final element of a tripartite praise, implying that it is the most significant of the three. Through its position in the line, 'Petrarch' rather than 'Scipio' or 'Cicero' (both of which would be suitable names to associate with Sidney's *vita activa*) becomes the ultimate praise.

The second epitaph, which has been variously attributed to Greville or Dyer, features a very similar passage. In this passage, the speaker states that Sidney was 'Declaring in his thoughts, his life, and that he writ, | Highest conceits, longest foresights, and deepest works of wit' (l. 15–16). As in the passage from Ralegh's epitaph, the third element in each line of the couplet is given particular emphasis through its position. Additionally, the rhyme establishes a direct link between 'what he writ' and the 'deepest works of wit', which suggests that 'works' is intended to be read as 'writings'. The second epitaph is not so much concerned with eulogising Sidney's life as with the poetry resulting from his death, that is the 'sundry sorts [of laments by] ech liuing wight' (l. 12), which include the speaker's own attempt to convert grief into *furor poeticus*.

What links all three Sidney-themed poems of *The Phoenix Nest*, then, is that they

---

67 Since no earlier version of Roydon's elegy survives, however, it is possible that he revised it before (if not for) its publication in *The Phoenix Nest*, for example by reducing the part of Mars, whose appearance in the poem is as sudden and brief as Astrophill's subsequent death.

all consider Sidney through his poetic remains and explore the theme of his survival through poetry – both in 'his Poesies', which in 1593 reveal him to a wider audience as the 'Petrarch of our time' and through the numerous epitaphs and elegies lamenting 'his lacke'. This, then, was the original publication context of the three Sidney elegies in *The Phoenix Nest*, before Spenser included them in his *Astrophel* collection two years later. The following section returns to *Astrophel* and examines it in the light of the responses to Sidney's death outlined so far, focusing especially on how *Astrophel* works as a collection and as a counterpart to 'Colin Clouts Come Home Againe'.

A poets' poet: Spenser's 1595 quarto

The reception of Sidney and his works over the first years following his death was a complex process that unfolded in different phases. The first elegies, which had been strongly influenced by the iconography of the spectacular funeral procession in 1587, primarily focused on Sidney's public life as a courtier and soldier. With the publication of his first works in print between 1590 and 1593, the perception of his life shifted towards one that incorporated his poetic activity in an increasingly dominant function. Thomas Nashe's preface to Q1 of *Astrophel and Stella* (1591) presented Sidney not as 'Syr P. S.' but as the poet figure 'Astrophel', who had recently emerged on the public stage with the publication of his poetry, while *The Phoenix Nest* (1593) considered Sidney mainly in terms of poetic impact, following the publication of his works.

I would like to propose, then, that Spenser's 'Astrophel' should not be viewed in isolation, as an elegy lacking in passion, but within the context of the second wave of responses to Sidney's death. Additionally, it should be read within its original publication context, as a collection forming a unit with 'Colin Clouts Come Home Againe'. Its true subject is not the 'Sir *Philip Sidney*, knight' commemorated in the funeral procession of 1587 and in the early elegies, but Astrophel, the 'Gentle Shepheard borne in *Arcady*' – in short, Sidney the poet figure, who had entered the public consciousness with the posthumous publication of his works during the 1590s.

One way of reading Spenser's delayed response to Sidney's death is as an indication that his chief interest in the 1595 quarto was not in Sidney the public hero, or even Sidney the literary patron, but in Sidney the poet, who had posthumously emerged. Although passages in *Three Proper and Wittie Familiar Letters* (1580) suggest that Spenser was aware of the existence of Sidney's poetic writings, the degree of his familiarity with Sidney at which the letters hint is not corroborated by Sidney himself.[68] Spenser's first specific reference to one of Sidney's works was in 'The Ruines of Time', published in 1591, one year after the first *Arcadia* edition.[69] It appears likely,

---

68 In his two letters, Immeritô hints at intimacy with Sidney and Dyer, though the only interaction described is that Immeritô received Sidney's old copy of Drant's rules of quantitative verse, which contained some annotations (these annotations do not feature in the discussion of quantitative verse that follows, however, and it is unclear how detailed they were). Sidney only acknowledged Spenser indirectly, via the rather lukewarm praise for 'The *Sheapheards Kalender*' in *Defence of Poesie*, as containing 'much Poetrie in his Eglogues: indeede worthy the reading if I be not deceiued', which hardly suggests a great deal of poetic exchange with its author and is followed by open disapproval for its archaisms (I4ᵇ).

69 'Yet will I sing, but who can better sing, | Than thou thy selfe, thine owne selfes valiance, | That whilest

then, that while Sidney was still alive, Spenser had only been an outside observer of his poetic activities. After Sidney had posthumously 'slipt into the title of a Poet' in the early 1590s, however, which had led him to be perceived as a major literary figure, Spenser was able to respond to Sidney as a fellow print author with whom he effectively shared his role as the most renowned English poet of the decade.[70] The timing of the 1595 quarto is crucial, because Spenser is portraying Astrophel as a 'shepheards boy', that is, Sidney the posthumous literary phenomenon and published poet equally 'knowen' for his songs as Spenser's own alter ego Colin Clout. This would not have been possible in the 1580s, directly following Sidney's death.

Although the sub-title clearly identifies the subject of 'Astrophel' as Sidney and most of the subsequent poems repeat this identification, the *Astrophel* collection as a whole seeks to portray him primarily as a shepherd among shepherds. Sidney the 'knight' and known public figure acts as a point of reference throughout, yet this Sidney merely functions as an ongoing subtext to the narrative of Astrophel the pastoral poet and his poetic survival both in his own works and in the 'dolefull lays' composed by his fellow shepherds.

The first three stanzas of 'Astrophel', which function both as an introduction to the poem and to the collection as a whole, are addressed to a specific audience – a community of shepherds:[71]

Shepheards that wont on pipes of oaten reed
Oft times to plaine your loues concealed smart:
[...]
Hearken ye gentle shepheards to my song,
And place my dolefull plaint your plaints emong. (ll. 1–6)

The overt reason given for addressing the shepherds is that 'the rymes bene rudely dight' (l. 12), and consequently only suitable for an equally 'rude' audience. However, the main effect of this introduction is to establish the figure of Astrophel firmly as a shepherd-poet. This is by no means an obvious association, since most of the poems of *Astrophel and Stella* have a courtly setting; however, the two main exceptions to this are the separately printed 'sonnets of various verse' viii and ix, that is, the two songs that feature 'Astrophel' as the protagonist's name. Placing Astrophel in 'Arcady' strengthens both the pastoral association and the association with Sidney, by merging his two publicly known works (as of 1595).[72]

thou liuedst, madest the forrests ring, | And fields resownd, and flockes to leap and daunce, | And shepheards leaue their lambs vnto mischaunce, | To runne thy shrill *Arcadian* Pipe to heare' (C2ᵃ–C2ᵇ).
70 Though it had of course been written in a very different context, Sidney's phrase from the opening of *Defence of Poesie* would have been particularly resonant with the public perception of Sidney when it was published in 1595. Initially, it may simply have referred to his acquiring a reputation as an accomplished judge of poetry among people like Spenser and Harvey, who were aware of but had not necessarily read his works. In the wake of the success of *Astrophel and Stella* and the two *Arcadia* editions, however, Sidney's phrase appeared like a comment from beyond the grave on his unexpected transformation from public hero to print author.
71 The three stanzas are visually set apart through italics and through the fact that the first line of the next stanza (printed on the same page) begins with a new initial.
72 *Arcadia* is also visually evoked on the first page of 'Astrophel', which features the same decorative device as the first page of the 1590 *Arcadia* (Bᵃ).

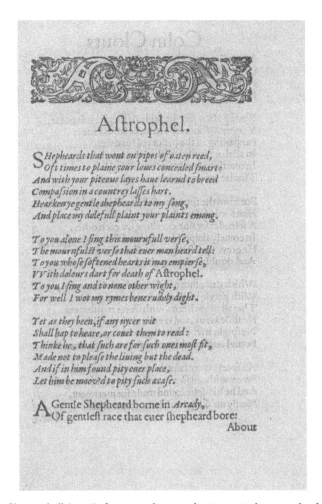

7 First page of 'Astrophel' (1595), featuring the introduction in italic type, the decorative device shared with *Arcadia* and the wrong running title on the verso (show-through)

The introduction of 'Astrophel', then, not only uses the figure of Astrophel as an alter ego for Sidney, it also adapts the figure in a manner that makes it especially suitable for portraying Sidney as a poet (and, more specifically, as a print poet). Within Spenser's poem, Astrophel is presented as an exemplary shepherd who particularly excels at composing songs and poems of various kinds. While the poem does portray Astrophel's martial side, it is not represented as being at odds with his nature as a 'Gentle Shepheard' (l. 19). Even his penchant for hunting 'great troups' (l. 118) of wild beasts is introduced as a suitable occupation for a shepherd, as it is merely an extension of the shepherd's triathlon (consisting of running, swimming and shooting), at which Astrophel competed with his fellow shepherds and 'vanquisht euery one' (l. 95). Similarly, while the poem gestures towards the circumstances of Sidney's death, Spenser deliberately fictionalises and mythologises this death by having Astrophel charge at his quarry like Adonis charges at the boar: Astrophel's weapon of choice is a 'sharp borespear' (l. 126), and like Adonis he receives his mortal wound by having his thigh pierced by the tooth of a 'cruell beast' (l. 134).[73] The subsequent death of Stella – who in this version is Astrophel's wife – and their joint metamorphosis into a flower further serve to blur any factual elements and to enhance a poetic reading of Astrophel's life. His lack of good fortune (l. 30) refers to his unfortunate encounter with the 'cruell beast' rather than rejection by Stella (or any real person she might represent).[74]

The consequences of Astrophel's death are also described in poetic terms by restricting the circle of mourners to 'the sheapheards all' (l. 218) – his fellow poets, who express their grief in a chorus of elegies, or 'dolefull lays'. In this context it is important to bear in mind that although the 'Lay of Clorinda' has become almost synonymous with the phrase due to the critical attention it has received, it is not the only 'dolefull lay' of the collection. In fact, all poems contained in *Astrophel* are introduced as 'dolefull lays'. In order to illustrate this point, it is useful to compare the two stanzas that immediately follow the poem 'Astrophel' and the 'Lay of Clorinda'. The latter two stanzas are usually reprinted as part of the 'Lay', because they are written in the same metre, but they do not form part of the lay proper (which concludes with the line 'Mourning in others, our owne miseries'). The 1595 edition sets them apart through the lack of the decorative border that frames the rest of the 'Lay'. The purpose of the two stanzas within *Astrophel* is to provide a link between the 'Lay of Clorinda' and the five poems generally omitted from modern editions, just as the final two stanzas of the poem 'Astrophel' serve to link it to the 'Lay'. In both cases, the poems that follow are introduced in very similar terms, that is as examples of the 'dolefull lays' 'deviz'd' by the shepherd community as an expression of their collective mourning.

Why, then, did Spenser choose to accompany his own tribute to Sidney the 'new Poete' with poems by other authors, some of which had already appeared in print? I would like to suggest that Spenser was not only interested in Sidney as a poet, but also in the unprecedented posthumous emergence of a poet figure, which was accompanied by a shift in attitude towards Sidney. That shift is reflected in the prefaces to early editions of his works, as well as in the poetic tributes of *The Phoenix Nest* (1593). By combining his own poetry with earlier poems by other writers in *Astrophel*, Spenser is placing himself among a chorus of poetic voices that are at least as much in response to Sidney's rebirth in print as to his death. Consequently, they portray Sidney as a semi-fictionalised figure and narrativise his death by providing him with a fictional life derived partly from mythology and partly from his own works. Yet the inclusion of the earlier elegies also allows Spenser to make an ingenious poetic double-move

---

73 The Adonis analogy must have seemed particularly appropriate, since Sidney also died of a wound to the thigh.
74 Stella 'follow[s] her make like a Turtle chaste | To proue that death their hearts cannot diuide' (ll. 178–9), an image of conjugal love.

through documenting the poetification of Sidney during the years since his death, while simultaneously contributing to that poetification himself.

By grouping them among the chorus of 'dolefull lays', together with Bryskett's poems, as well as his own, Spenser recontextualises the three *Phoenix Nest* poems while still preserving them as a unit. All three poems are reprinted exactly as they originally appeared in *The Phoenix Nest*. Just as Spenser succeeds in bridging the gap between his own poems and earlier poems by other authors, which had not been devised for the *Astrophel* collection, he also succeeds in bridging the gap between the two Sidneys to an extent. *Astrophel* views Sidney's life from the angle of a deliberately fictionalised narrative of Sidney the pastoral poet. Although Spenser repeatedly uses Sidney's life as a point of reference common to all contributors to the collection, all traces of biographical 'fact' contained within individual poems are merged into the chorus of poetic voices mourning a fellow poet.

Roydon's possible identification of Stella as Penelope Rich, for example, loses any special significance it may originally have held in the context of the several different (and irreconcilable) Stellas being presented to the reader in the volume. Similarly, the key geographic locations connected to Sidney's life that are identified by Ralegh are set against the pastoral setting of Roydon's 'ampitheater' contained within 'these woods of *Arcadie*' (l. 91) as well as Bryskett's and Spenser's references to Irish geography, which bears no direct relation to Sidney's death.[75] Not even the name of Sidney's fictional alter ego remains fixed across all of the 'dolefull lays': in addition to 'Astrophel', he is variously called 'Philip', 'Phillisides' or 'Astrophill', making the volume resemble the early volumes of commemorative poetry, which had also referred to Sidney by a variety of names.[76]

The one point on which all 'dolefull lays' agree, however, is that they conceive of Sidney as a 'shepherd' – that is, as a poet – who needs to be mourned by a community of shepherds. The national hero, who still resonates in the sub-title and in the titles of the individual poems, is thus transformed into a poets' poet. As a collection, then, *Astrophel* depicts Sidney's death as a defining moment for poetry by outlining the grief of what Spenser in 'Colin Clouts Come Home Againe' terms 'the shepheards nation'. While *Astrophel* and 'Colin Clouts Come Home Againe' are connected through their pastoral setting and some of their protagonists (Colin, Thestylis, Astrophel and Stella all appear in both halves of the volume), the strongest link between the two is in this idea of a 'nation' of poets.[77]

By placing his alter ego Colin Clout at the centre of the chorus of shepherds mourning Astrophel with their 'dolefull layes', Spenser is in a sense declaring himself

---

75 The places mentioned in Ralegh's epitaph occur in l. 21: 'Kent thy birth daies, and Oxford held thy youth' and ll. 49–50: 'England doth hold thy lims that bred the same | *Flaunders* thy valure where it last was tried'.

76 In 'The mourning Muse of Thestylis', 'A pastorall Aeglogue', and Roydon's 'Elegie'. Of the two remaining *Phoenix Nest* poems, Ralegh's only refers to Sidney as 'thou', while the second 'Epitaph' refers to him as 'Phillip' in the penultimate stanza.

77 One of the few scholars to have noted this link is Michelle O'Callaghan, who observes that 'The "shepheards nation" of *Colin Clouts Come Home Againe* is complemented by the elegiac pastoral community of *Astrophel*'. Michelle O'Callaghan, *The 'shepheards nation': Jacobean Spenserians and Early Stuart Political Culture* (Oxford: Clarendon Press, 2000), p. 12.

to be the heir to the role of chief poet and a counterpart figure to the chief mourner Clorinda.[78] Yet, perhaps more significantly, he is also showing an awareness of the process that had led Sidney to emerge posthumously as the chief poet figure of the 1590s only a few years earlier, which is demonstrated by his grouping of 'Astrophel' with earlier poems that had been part of this phenomenon. As a result, Spenser is offering readers of *Astrophel* an intriguing double perspective: on the one hand, he is contributing to the second wave of responses to Sidney's death, while on the other he is commenting on this second wave as an unprecedented poetic phenomenon. This in turn is a crucial step within the sophisticated argument about the nature of authorship and the social role of the poet that Spenser is proposing in the 1595 quarto.

'Colin Clouts Come Home Againe' is in many ways a poem for which McCabe's observation that Spenser is given to 'auto-fabrication' and his personae are 'persistently auto-referential [...] [but] never truly autobiographical' rings especially true.[79] While it is clear through the geographical references that Colin's 'Home' is located in the vicinity of 'my house of *Kilcolman*' which Spenser pointedly mentions in his dedicatory epistle to Ralegh, the most thoroughly autobiographical element of the poem occurs on a fictional level. In 'Colin Clouts Come Home Againe', Spenser is revisiting the catalogue of his own published works through this fictional poet persona, making it a 'homecoming' to his own fictional spaces as well as a physical return to a place which is clearly intended to be recognised as Ireland. In addition to the evident links to *The Shepheardes Calender*, it refers to *Daphnaïda*, as well as all the dedicatees of the *Complaints* (except the dead Leicester). In a sense, it even pre-empts some themes of book VI of *The Faerie Queene* and the Mutabilitie Cantos, such as court and courtesy, pastoral as a form of refuge, as well as the identifiably Irish setting on Spenser's own doorstep.[80]

While the theme of the fictionalised but loosely recognisable life-narrative for a poet figure 'vnder whose person the Authour selfe is shadowed' is of course something that links 'Colin Clouts Come Home Againe' and *Astrophel*, I would suggest that the association goes further than that. Rather than merely standing side by side, the two halves of the 1595 quarto complement each other. Together, they form a composite narrative whose true interest lies perhaps not so much in narrating the life of a specific poet (either Spenser or Sidney) as in setting out the life of *a* poet in terms of its poetic impact. While the figures of Colin Clout and Astrophel act as a frame of reference throughout, the first half of the volume examines the living poet, whose role as a poet outside a patronage context is defined through the central part that he plays within the community of shepherds. The second half portrays the afterlife of the dead poet who continues to generate poetry via the poetic responses which his death prompts within the same 'shepheards nation'.

---

78 Lawrence Lipking compared the poetic responses to Sidney's death to poetic wars of succession (after which, he argued, Spenser emerged as the victor). Lawrence Lipking, *The Life of the Poet: Beginning and Ending Poetic Careers* (Chicago: University of Chicago Press, 1981).
79 *The Shorter Poems*, p. xvii.
80 Stanza 40 of the first of the Mutabilitie Cantos contains an alternate version of Colin's song to the Shepherd of the Ocean which he summarises for his audience in ll. 100–55.

The 1595 quarto offers the views of different members of this 'shepheards nation', and the complex chorus of voices becomes an integral feature of the text. In this, the volume in fact resembles *The Shepheardes Calender*. In 1986, Jonathan Goldberg demanded 'a poetics of the book that throw the proper name in question', 'however much it may strain criticism and its abiding fictions of "the Author selfe"'.[81] Criticism appears to have taken the strain, so that now it is unusual for readings of *The Shepheardes Calender* not to acknowledge the different 'voices' that it contains. However, the same cannot be said of the 1595 quarto, which in fact takes the multiplicity of authorial voices and the play on authorial identity even further, by featuring not only different personae but texts written by different authors. In this it blurs the boundaries between the two into an identifiable semi-anonymity (as with Thestylis/Bryskett). With minor modifications, some important observations that have been made about the role of anonymity and the interplay between glosses and eclogues, as well as between the different personae of the eclogues, in *The Shepheardes Calender* could be equally applied to the 1595 quarto. Take, for example, Richard McCabe's observation in 'Annotating Anonymity' that attributions to the anonymous 'Immeritô' and the equally shadowy editor figure 'E. K.' are 'made within, and by, the text itself, and are therefore best regarded as rhetorical functions of an obsessively self-reflexive work'.[82] Much of this also holds true for the 1595 quarto, which is just as 'obsessively self-reflexive' as *The Shepheardes Calender*. Although it initially presents itself as a single poem by a named author, the 1595 quarto disintegrates into a series of 'dolefull lays' halfway through. Those 'lays' are attributed to various pastoral personae, which are perhaps also best described as 'rhetorical functions' of the text. To an extent, critical responses to the 'Lay of Clorinda' that argue against the Countess of Pembroke's authorship take an approach which is similar to McCabe's reading of 'E. K.' and 'Immeritô', in that it treats the poem's attribution to Astrophel's sister as a rhetorical strategy by Spenser.[83] However, this is not extended to the other elements of the volume, possibly due to the erroneous assumption that a poem which really has been written by another author could not be deployed to serve a rhetorical function.

Colin and Astrophel share two key characteristics. First, they are both poet figures who play an integral role within this 'shepheards nation'. Second, in the absence of patronage structures, the two poets are defined through their social roles, which revolve around the process of composing poetry as an everyday activity, transforming the life of the poet into an 'active' life. The story of composition is narrativised in both parts of the volume, and in 'Colin Clouts Come Home Againe' is given so much

---

81 Jonathan Goldberg, *Voice Terminal Echo: Postmodernism and English Renaissance Texts* (London: Methuen, 1986), p. 39.

82 Richard McCabe, 'Annotating Anonymity, or Putting a Gloss on *The Shepheardes Calender*', in Joe Bray, Miriam Handley and Anne C. Henry (eds), *Ma(r)king the Text: The Presentation of Meaning on the Literary Page* (Aldershot: Ashgate, 2000), pp. 35–54 (p. 35).

83 See particularly Pamela Coren, 'Spenser, Mary Sidney and the "Dolefull Lay"', *Studies in English Literature*, 42 (2002), 25–41. Coren's essay summarises the authorship debate surrounding the 'Lay of Clorinda' and argues that 'The *Lay* [...] completes the fiction with a "womanish" burst of feeling and orthodox otherworldly direction' (p. 39). Arguably, O'Connell's 'double elegy' reading also treats 'Clorinda' as a rhetorical function within the text.

attention it is almost made to substitute for the poetry itself. In his initial narrative, Colin tells of his poetic dialogue with the Shepherd of the Ocean purely by describing the piping and singing of two well-matched poets, 'by chaunge of turnes, each making other mery' (l. 77). When Cuddy demands to hear the poetry they exchanged, Colin initially replies with a brief synopsis, which is even shorter than its corresponding stanza in the first of the Mutabilitie Cantos.[84] Only when further pressed to repeat the poem itself does Colin agree to give his audience 'the tenor of [his] tale,' (ll. 100–1), implying that what follows is again only a paraphrase.

The sense of detachment in 'Astrophel', then, can be explained through the fact that its purpose is not an elegy written purely to commemorate Sidney. Spenser is not directly responding to Sidney's death as the early elegists were, but envisaging it in poetic terms, by examining the resonance of Astrophel's death within the 'shepheards nation' as part of a conceptual life-narrative of *a* poet. Within this narrative, Sidney/Astrophel as well as Spenser/Colin act as points of reference rather than as joint subjects. The death of Astrophel, which is portrayed primarily via the poetry it gives rise to, thus becomes a moment of birth. The 'shepheards nation' offers a form of poetic survival that is an alternative to merely being remembered through poetry originally written for a patron.[85] While the 'shepheards nation' is of course a fictional concept, it is interesting to note that William Camden's famous description of Spenser's funeral echoes this concept, almost making it sound like a re-enactment of *Astrophel*. According to Camden, Spenser 'was buried at *Westminster* neere *Chawcer* [...] all Poets carrying his body to Church, and casting their dolefull Verses, and Pens too, into his graue'.[86] Spenser's burial near Chaucer's tomb also marked the beginning of 'Poets' Corner' in Westminster Abbey, regarded by the next generation of poets as a sort of physical manifestation of the community of English poets that Spenser had originally invoked.

This idea of a community of (dead) poets in Westminster Abbey is also the subject of William Basse's 'Epitaph on Shakespeare', which begins by imagining a fictitious tomb for Shakespeare in Westminster Abbey: 'Renowned *Spencer* lye a thought more nye | to learned *Chaucer*; and Rare *Beaumond* lye | A little nearer *Spencer*, to make roome | For *Shakespeare* in your threefold fowerfold tombe'.[87] Given the poem's topic – the proximity of poets' tombs as a physical manifestation of interrelations and literary networks – it is revealing that when a version of it was first printed, it was wrongly attributed to John Donne, in a collection of poetry published shortly after his own death, *Poems by J.D. With Elegies on the Authors Death* (1633). The inclusion

---

84 '[O]f my riuer *Bregogs* loue I soong, | Which to the shiny *Mulla* he did beare, | And yet doth beare, and euer will, so long | As water doth within his bancks appeare' (ll. 92–5).

85 Colin describes this more conventional form of poetic survival in ll. 640–7: 'And long while after I am dead and rotten: | Amōgst the shepheards daughters dancing rownd, | My layes made of her shall not be forgotten. | But sung by them with flowry gyrlonds crownd. | And ye, who so ye be, that shall surviue: | When as ye heare her memory renewed, | Be witnesse of her bountie here aliue, | Which she to *Colin* her poore shepheard shewed'.

86 Quoted after the English translation: William Camden, *The historie of the life and reigne of that famous princesse Elizabeth* (1634), p. 232.

87 E. K. Chambers, *William Shakespeare: A Study of Facts and Problems*, 2 vols (Oxford: Clarendon Press, 1930), II, p. 226.

On the duke of Richmond.
Are all diseases dead, or will Death say
He could not kill this Prince the common way,
It was even soe; and Time with Death conspir'd
To make his End as was his life admir'd.
The Comons were not somon'd now, I see,
Merely to make lawes, but to mourne for thee
Nor lesse then all the Bishops could suffice,
To waite upon so great a sacrifice.
The Court the Altar was, the Wayters Peers,
The Mirhe and Frankincense Great Caesars crow...
...brauer offring with more pompe and State,
Nor time nor Death did ever celebrate.
Upon Poet Shakespeare
Renowned Spencer lye a thought more nigh
To learned Chaucer, and rare Beaumont lye
A little neerer Spencer, to make roome
For Shakespeare in your threefold fourefold Tombe.
To lodge all foure in one bed make a shift
Untill Doomesday, for hardly will a fifte
Betwixt this day and that by Fate bee slaine,
For whom the Curtaine may bee drawne againe.

8 Basse's epitaph on Shakespeare (lower part of page), from a manuscript miscellany compiled *c.* 1630

of Donne in this 'shepheards nation' of laureates though this misattribution represents a strong claim for his pre-eminence in the field of poetry by his contemporaries, and provides an intriguing insight into how early readers of manuscript miscellanies may have perceived Donne as a poet. That the 'Epitaph on Shakespeare' had been circulated in manuscript form long before its publication is evident in Ben Jonson's retort in 'To the memory of my beloued, THE AVTHOR MR. WILLIAM SHAKESPEARE: and what he hath left vs', published ten years before *Poems by J.D.* in the 1623 folio edition of Shakespeare's plays. In the relevant passage of his (much longer) poem, Jonson responds though echoing the rhymes of the first quatrain of the 'Epitaph on Shakespeare', while turning its imagery on its head by raising Shakespeare again from the imaginary tomb which the 'Epitaph' had placed him in: 'My *Shakespeare*, rise; I will not lodge thee by | *Chaucer*, or *Spenser*, or bid *Beaumont* lye | A little further, to make thee a roome: | Thou art a Moniment, without a tombe'.[88]

Spenser's 1595 quarto is a text that in its entirety explores the nature of authorship in an innovative manner. It offers a fictional narrative not so much for the life of a specific poet – either Spenser or Sidney – but of the poet in the abstract, who, in death as well as in life forms an integral part of the fictional 'nation' of poets, which Spenser proposes as an alternative to the traditional patronage model. *Astrophel* in fact appropriates Sidney the poet figure of the 1590s in order to make a wider statement about authorship and the role of the poet. As such, the relevance of the 1595 quarto extends beyond the projected image of Spenser as a laureate poet and the portrayal of Sidney as a pastoral poet figure. It is an important poetological text, whose significance has yet to be fully recognised, and which shows Spenser to be keenly aware of, as well as contributory to, changes in thinking about authorship and the role of the dead poet that took place during the 1590s. The 1595 quarto offers an original approach to narrativising the life and afterlife of a poet as a life that might be regarded as 'active'. In simultaneously considering the poetic impact of the living and the dead poet and using two of the most iconic poet figures of the decade as points of reference, Spenser is in a sense bridging the gap between late sixteenth-century poets' *vita activa* and their works, exemplified in the responses to Sidney.

88 *Mr William Shakespeares Comedies, Histories & Tragedies* (1623), A4ᵃ.

Interlude:
'After I am dead and rotten' –
Spenser's missing afterlife

What of Spenser's own literary afterlife? There is no evidence to suggest that when Spenser himself died just four years after publishing 'Astrophel', anyone doubted his status as one of the major contemporary English poets. Nevertheless, his death was a relatively unspectacular affair in terms of the literary responses it provoked. While Spenser's significance as a poet second only to Chaucer was symbolically confirmed by his being buried in an adjacent tomb, and Camden's description of the funeral in terms that echoed (and were perhaps derived from) the funeral of Sidney's fictional counterpart Astrophel in Spenser's poem, evokes a certain sense of low-key spectacle, there seems to have been very little reaction in print to the death of England's greatest print author.

There were some elegies, of course, but the collective grief of the – unnamed – surviving poets implied by Camden's account did not culminate in the publication of a commemorative poetry collection (possibly featuring Latin eulogies by 'Hobbinol', who had eagerly seized the chance to reclaim his position as 'Colin's' friend in styling himself his chief mourner). No enterprising publisher regarded Spenser's death as an opportunity to announce the publication of genuine or spurious works of his that had slept in silence, or even just to republish his two best-known works – perhaps an indication that in 1599 copies of both the 1596 *Faerie Queene* and the 1597 fifth edition of *The Shepheardes Calender* were still readily available at the respective bookshops of William Ponsonby and John Harrison the younger.[1] Examples of early modern publishers taking advantage, or trying to take advantage, of events likely to generate an increased interest in certain books are numerous and include one of Spenser's own works. John Harrison, who held the rights to *The Shepheardes Calender* after Hugh Singleton, published at least two strategically timed reprints: the third edition of 1586 was published shortly after Sir Philip Sidney's death, possibly in the hope that the word 'entitled' on the title page would mislead book-buyers into thinking it was a work attributed rather than dedicated to Sidney.[2] Harrison's next edition of the

---

1 *A View of the State of Ireland*, which had been entered into the Stationers' Register in 1598, was not published until much later, when James Ware included it as the third part of *The Historie of Ireland, Collected by Three Learned Authors* (Dublin, 1633).

2 While the epistle to Gabriel Harvey at the beginning of *The Shepheardes Calender* is never explicitly referred to as an 'epistle dedicatorie', it is positioned at a point in the book where early modern readers would have expected to find dedications, so it is not hard to see how this set-up might have fooled some readers into thinking Sidney was the author and Harvey the dedicatee. If the 1586 edition of *The Shepheardes Calender* was hastily put together by printer John Wolfe in order to meet a sudden surge

Calender, published in 1591, was clearly timed to coincide with an increased interest in works by Spenser (who had officially claimed authorship of the book one year
earlier in his proem to the first book of *The Faerie Queene*) following the withdraw-
ing of the *Complaints* because of 'Mother Hubberds Tale'. If Harrison published the
fifth edition because he was counting on Ponsonby's publication of the 1596 *Faerie
Queene* to generate another surge of interest in Spenser's first book, however, the
gamble may have failed to pay off. At any rate, Harrison let the occasion of Spenser's
death pass without having yet another edition printed. Ponsonby, on the other hand,
who owned the rights to Spenser's remaining titles, may have been reluctant to run
the financial risk of another *Faerie Queene*, yet he also passed up the opportunity to
publish a second edition of 'Colin Clouts Come Home Againe' and 'Astrophel' with
their fitting themes of poets' lives and afterlives.[3]

Likewise, no texts purporting to be previously unknown fragments of the remaining six books of *The Faerie Queene* appear to have circulated and found their way
into print in the wake of Spenser's death, introduced by a preface containing a possibly doubtful account of how the printer had acquired those elusive parcels of verse.[4]
None of those hypothetical publishing events – a collection of poetic tributes by
other poets, the reissuing of his most famous works, or the publication of (genuine
or dubious) newly discovered works or previously unpublished works – would have
been out of place following a major poet's death. What is surprising, then, is that
Spenser's death was such a non-event in publishing terms.

The elegies for Spenser that were printed are not particularly remarkable. John
Weever's 'Epig. 23 In obitum Ed. Spencer Poetae prestantiss.', published in his
Epigrammes (1599), the only poem on Spenser's death known to have been printed

in demand for Sidney-themed books, this would also explain the sloppiness of the book's layout. The
edition features several instances where the compositor has clearly misjudged the amount of available
space and ended up using too large or too small type (including, embarrassingly, in one of the most
conspicuous places of the entire book, the first page of 'Ianuarie'), as well as wrong catchwords, and
'Colins Embleme' awkwardly tagged on to the end of 'Nouember' without a space, so it appears like
a cross between a speech prefix and a gloss. All of those things can of course be found in other early
printed books, but the frequency with which those sloppy printer's errors occur in the 1586 *Calender*
suggests either a remarkably inept compositor or a rush job.

3 The 1595 quarto would of course have been the low-risk option for Ponsonby. A much riskier – but
potentially lucrative – move would have been to republish the scandalous *Complaints*, taking advantage of the fact that Burghley had died in 1598. When Matthew Lownes, who had bought the rights to
Spenser's works from Ponsonby's successor, eventually decided to reprint 'Mother Hubberds Tale' in
1612 (following the death of Burghley's son, the Earl of Salisbury), he opted to separate it from the rest
of the *Complaints* – either an indication that he expected 'Mother Hubberds Tale' to sell particularly
well because of its history, or an indication that he also wanted to cater to Burghley-friendly book-
buyers by giving them the option of buying a cleaned-up, non-slanderous version of the collection.

4 In his essay 'Spenser's Last Days' (in J. B. Lethbridge ed., *Edmund Spenser: New and Renewed Directions*
(Madison: Fairleigh Dickinson University Press, 2006), pp. 302–36), J. B. Lethbridge presents a strong
case that the 'missing' books were written but the manuscripts were lost, and it seems plausible that
this is also what Spenser's contemporaries believed (after all, what else could England's greatest poet
have been doing up there in Ireland all those years). Considering that accounts of Spenser's flight from
Ireland after rebels had burnt down his house appear to have circulated following, perhaps even preceding, his death, publishers could reasonably have expected that fragments of the lost *Faerie Queene*
manuscripts advertised as having been spectacularly saved from the flames would generate interest,
whether they were real or forged. This makes it all the more surprising that no such fragments were
published.

in the same year, is not an elegy but an epigram. The poem's most prominent characteristic are its puns on the word 'ruines', as Weever is eager to demonstrate his knowledge of the fact that the *Complaints* were 'cal'd in' – an event that had taken place when he was in his teens:

> *Colin*'s gone home, the glorie of his clime,
> The Muses Mirrour, and the Shepheards Saint;
> *Spencer* is ruin'd, of our latter time
> The fairest ruine, Faëries foulest want:
> Then his *Time-ruines* did our ruine show,
> Which by his ruine we vntimely know:
> *Spencer* therefore thy *Ruines* were cal'd in,
> Too soone to sorrow least we should begin.[5]

It is odd that Weever chose to make 'The Ruines of Time' the central conceit of his poem, considering that *Complaints*, the title of Spenser's book, would have offered just as much potential for witticisms and perhaps seemed more appropriate in the context of a poet's recent death (as would references to 'Colin Clouts Come Home Againe', which Weever briefly mentions in the first line but then abandons). The focus on the 'Ruines' almost makes it sound as though Weever thought it was the title of the entire book (as well as the reason why it was 'cal'd in').[6] Overall, the effect of the poem is satirical rather than commemorative – rather as if a poem on the death of Shakespeare were to feature multiple puns on *All's Well That Ends Well*. Yet to fault Weever for his running jokes about 'ruines', which through the frequency in which they occur seem ever so slightly tasteless, would be as wrong as to fault Spenser for the supposed 'coldness' of 'Astrophel'; to borrow Winbolt's phrase, Weever's heart was not in the work. Nor was it supposed to be – above all, 'In obitum Ed. Spencer Poetae prestantiss.' is a witty poem from a collection of witty poems, and as with the other poems in the collection, its main aim was not to praise its subject but to show off the poet's own cleverness and satirical skill. This it does achieve, even if it is hardly the kind of poem fit for throwing into a poet's grave, but it still reveals little about Weever's reading of Spenser's life and works.

Nicholas Breton's 'Epitaph vpon Poet Spencer', by contrast, which concludes his *Melancholike Humours* (1600), is a more serious commemorative effort. Despite its title, it is not so much an epitaph as a funeral song of five stanzas, which could be read as the culmination of the passions, humours, conceits and fancies (variously described as 'dolefull', 'vnhappy', 'solemne', 'straunge' or 'odde') that make up the titles of the preceding poems.[7] 'Epitaph vpon Poet Spencer' is the only poem in the

---

5 John Weever, *Epigrammes in the oldest cut, and newest fashion* (London, 1599), G3ᵃ.

6 One possible explanation for the apparent conflation of the poem and the collection would be that Weever did not own a copy of *Complaints* and that 'Ruines of Time' was the only poem from the collection that he knew. Note, however, that Andrew Hadfield argues the exact opposite in his biography of Spenser, suggesting that the repeated references to 'Ruines of Time' indicate that 'the volume that Weever really knew was the *Complaints* – perhaps he possessed a copy' (Andrew Hadfield, *Edmund Spenser: A Life* (Oxford: Oxford University Press, 2012), p. 395).

7 The first and last stanzas both contain references to singing, and the first line of the first stanza, 'Mournfull Muses, sorrowes minions' (F3ᵃ), arguably evokes 'The mourning Muse of Thestylis', one of the 'dolefull lays' for Astrophel.

collection to reference a name and occasion, but there is nothing to suggest that Spenser's death is supposed to be the occasion of the poet's 'melancholike humours' – the dedication merely refers to the contents of the book as 'certain odde pieces of Poetry'.[8] Like Weever's epigram, the third stanza of Breton's 'Epitaph' contains a catalogue of Spenser's works:

> Fairy Queene, shew fairest Queene,
> How her faire in thee is seene.
> Sheepeheards Calender set downe,
> How to figure best a clowne.
> As for Mother *Hubberts* tale,
> Cracke the nut, and take the shale:
> And for other workes of worth,
> (All too good to wander forth)
> Grieue that euer you were wrot,
> And your Author be forgot. (F3[b])

At first sight, those lines look like Breton's observations about individual works, yet on closer inspection, they turn out to be little more than quibbles on titles and rhymes that seem to have been chosen mainly for the sake of convenience. The play on 'Fairy Queene' and 'fairest Queene' in the first couplet does seem particularly apt in the context of a poem that claims to portray the queen 'in mirrours more then one', although it is not much more profound than similar mirrored phrases that can be found in other poems of the collection, such as 'Farewell conceit: Cōceit no more wel fare', 'Kindely true, and truly kinde', or 'Sweetely deare, and dearely sweete'.[9] On the other hand, the second couplet's 'how to figure best a clowne' is not a particularly good description of *The Shepheardes Calender,* and the third couplet's puzzling substitution of the nut's 'shale' for its kernel makes even less sense considering that this instruction, like all the others in this stanza, is in fact addressed to the poem rather than its reader.[10] Overall, then, the stanza amounts to little more than a statement that Spenser wrote those three texts, as well as several others, and that none of them deserves to be forgotten (which is more likely to be a trope than an indication that Spenser's works were genuinely in danger of being forgotten in 1600).[11] As a retrospective evaluation of 'Poet Spencer's' works and their significance, however,

---

8   Nicholas Breton, *Melancholike Humours* (London, 1600), A3[a].
9   These are lines from 'A farewell to conceipt' (D4[a]), 'An odde humour' (F[b]) and 'An odde conceipt' (F2[a]), but there are several more examples, which suggests that it was a device Breton was particularly fond of.
10 Richard Danson Brown points out the oddness of the image, which appears to reverse a proverb meaning 'hard work will reap rewards', which was routinely applied to the interpretation of poetry, but adds that to interpret it as deliberately subversive would mean to credit Breton's poem with too much subtlety. *The New Poet* (Liverpool: Liverpool University Press, 1999), p. 170, n.8. Perhaps Breton simply substituted the word because he needed a rhyme for 'Mother *Hubberts* tale' other than the most obvious one, given the poem's history: 'not for sale'.
11 The absence of any interpretive attempts on Breton's part is particularly noticeable when the stanza is compared to Gabriel Harvey's take on 'Mother Hubberds Tale' as an ill-conceived venture into satire, or Thomas Nashe's attempt to regard it as a text unfairly used to slander Spenser (see Chapter 2).

Breton's 'Epitaph' is just as inadequate as it is as an account of Spenser's life: the only biographical detail the poem mentions is that he is dead.[12]

'Spencers Fayrie Queene', Francis Thynne's commemorative effort in his poetic miscellany *Emblemes and Epigrames* (presented to Sir Thomas Egerton in 1600), is perhaps the most peculiar, however:

> Renowmed Spencer, whose heavenlie sprite
> eclipseth the sonne of former poetrie,
> in whom the muses harbour with delighte,
> gracinge thy verse with Immortalitie,
> Crowning thy fayrie Queene with deitie,
> the famous *Chaucer* yealds his Lawrell crowne
> vnto thy sugred penn, for thy renowne.
>
> Noe cankred envie cann thy fame deface,
> nor eatinge time consume thy sacred vayne;
> noe carping zoilus cann thy verse disgrace,
> nor scoffinge Momus taunt the with disdaine,
> since thy rare worke eternall praise doth gayne;
> then live thou still, for still thy verse shall live,
> to vnborne poets, which light and life will give.

The peculiarity of 'Spencer's Fayrie Queene' lies not so much in the poem itself but in the fact that its final couplet is almost identical to that of another poem by Thynne, with which it forms a unit, although there is no record of the two occurring in sequence in either printed or manuscript form. While the final couplet of 'Spencer's Fayrie Queene' reads: 'then live thou still, for still thy verse shall live | to vnborne poets, which light and life will give', the second poem, 'Vpon the picture of Chaucer', printed in Speght's second edition of Chaucer's works in 1602, switches the order of 'light' and 'life':

> What *Pallas* citie owes the heauenly mind
> Of prudent *Socrates*, wise Greeces glorie;
> What fame *Arpinas* spreadingly doth find
> By *Tullies* eloquence and oratorie;
> What lasting praise sharpe witted Italie
> By *Taßo's* and by *Petrarkes* penne obtained;
> What fame *Bartas* vnto proud France hath gained,
> By seuen daies world Poetically strained:

12 R. M. Cummings's compilation *Spenser: The Critical Heritage* (London: Routledge, 1971) lists a handful of additional pieces of 'obituary verse' for Spenser, but many of them are little more than passing references to Spenser's (or Colin's) death in pastoral works – such as the stanzas from William Basse's *Anander Anetor and Muridella* (1602) (pp. 111–12). Others, such as Iudicio's 'judgement of Spencer' in the second part of the *Returne from Parnassus* (pp. 116–17), occur in a context in which it is doubtful that elegising Spenser is the main purpose of the passage. 'Enuies Scourge and Vertues Honour' (*c.* 1605), a poem that has recently been proposed as an elegy for Spenser by Richard Peterson, is certainly a tribute to Spenser in the sense that it is 'Spenserian' in its diction and imagery, but Spenser's actual death is mentioned in passing at best, and he himself is never mentioned by name, not even as his alter ego 'Colin'. Consequently, Peterson's argument that it is an elegy for Spenser rests principally on the poem's 'Spenserian' nature. See Richard Peterson, '*Enuies Scourge and Vertues Honor*: A Rare Elegy for Spenser', in *Spenser Studies*, 25 (2010), 287–325.

What high renoune is purchas'd vnto Spaine,
Which fresh *Dianaes* verses do distill;
What praise our neighbour Scotland doth retaine,
By *Gawine Douglas*, in his *Virgill* quill;
Or other motions by sweet Poets skill,
The same, and more, faire England challenge may,
By that rare wit and art thou doest display,
In verse, which doth *Apolloes* muse bewray.
Then *Chaucer* liue, for still thy verse shall liue,
T'unborne Poëts, which life and light will giue.

Despite their near-identical final couplets, the two poems are otherwise different in terms of their content, although they use a similar stanza form. 'Spencer's Fayrie Queene' praises 'Renowmed Spenser' (l. 1) as the new Chaucer and depicts the latter ambiguously yielding 'his Lawrell crowne' (l. 6) to either Spenser himself or to *The Faerie Queene* and concludes by pointing out the enduring nature of Spenser's 'rare worke' (l. 13).[13] 'Vpon the picture of Chaucer', by contrast, considers Chaucer's significance as a national poet, comparable both to the classics of ancient Greece and ancient Rome (Socrates and Cicero) and to the more recent Italian, French, Spanish classics (Tasso, Petrarch, du Bartas and de Montemayor), as well as Gawain Douglas, who had translated the *Aeneid* into Scots. The poem concludes by stating that England has a poet of similar – if not greater – significance in Chaucer, who will continue to inspire other English poets to strive towards greatness.

Although the composition of neither poem can be reliably dated, the most plausible scenario is that 'Vpon the picture of Chaucer' was written first. Following the 1598 publication of Speght's works of Chaucer, Thynne, who was the son of William Thynne, a previous editor of Chaucer's works, began to prepare his own edition, allegedly based on notes he had inherited from his father, who had died when Francis was one year old.[14] Thus it is likely that when Spenser died, Thynne, who had spent the past year scrutinising Speght's Chaucer edition for inaccuracies, was prompted by Spenser's burial next to Chaucer to write a poetic sequel to an existing poem (perhaps intended to preface his future edition). When this poem was subsequently included in Speght's second edition, after the two editors had resolved their differences, Thynne decided to expand the poem by adding the aphoristic final couplet of 'Spencer's Fayrie Queene' to the original final couplet. While this scenario is of course speculative, it is supported by the fact that the second stanza of 'Vpon the picture of Chaucer'

13 It is unclear whether it is Spenser or his work being crowned, because the corresponding lines (ll. 5–7) are ambiguously worded: 'Crowning thy fayrie Queene with deitie | the famous *Chaucer* yealds his Lawrell crowne | vnto thy sugred penn, for thy renowne.' Francis Thynne, *Emblemes and Epigrames* (London: Early English Text Society, 1876), p. 71. While the image of Chaucer handing over his laurel crown to his poetic successor like a baton is striking, the underlying idea of Spenser as Chaucer's heir was already conventional in 1599.

14 Thynne's edition was never completed, although he wrote a letter to Speght in 1599, generally known as the *Animaduersions* and published by the Early English Text Society in 1865, pointing out a number of inaccuracies. Speght's second edition of 1602 incorporated his suggested changes. See Megan L. Cook's article 'How Francis Thynne Read his Chaucer', *Journal of the Early Book Society*, 15 (2012), 215–43 for the links between the *Animaduersions* and Speght's edition. Cooke also notes that there is no evidence of Thynne's supposed edition prior to the publication of Speght's (p. 216).

has two additional lines: the final couplet. Regardless of which poem was written first, however, Thynne's self-referential recycling of two lines he evidently considered particularly successful nevertheless suggests that 'Spencer's Fayrie Queene' was never primarily concerned with celebrating Spenser.[15] Together, the two poems form a celebration of Thynne's own happy turn of phrase, which he only modified by changing 'life' to 'light' and vice versa in the second version.

The relative scarcity of elegies on Spenser might be explained through the fact that elegies – especially those published in collections – are not purely expressions of personal grief but at one level also a self-serving bid for attention on the poets' part. Unlike Sidney, Spenser did not leave behind a family of potential patrons, so there was less to be gained from elegising him. What is harder to explain is why there seems to have been no summary response to his life and works following his death. When Matthew Lownes published the folio edition of Spenser's works more than a decade after the poet's death, it contained no preface, dedication or commemorative sonnets, and the title page did not even indicate that 'England's Arch-Poët' was no longer alive. The addition of the 'Two Cantos of Mutabilitie' was not announced by the publisher as an important discovery or used as an incentive to lure prospective book-buyers – despite the fact that they really had been 'neuer before imprinted'.[16] Instead, they were tucked away at the end of *The Faerie Queene* almost as an afterthought, so that readers who failed to read to the end of the poem could easily miss them. The most puzzling omission, however, is that of a prefatory Life. While there is evidence to suggest that the contents of Lownes edition of Spenser's works were sold separately, to be bound up according to the book-buyer's wishes, it is clear from the title page that the publisher did not expect them to be bound up in wholly random order: the largest letters on the page are reserved for 'THE FAERIE QVEEN', followed by 'The Shepheards Calender', suggesting either that those were the compulsory components customers had to purchase, or that those were the works Lownes expected every customer would want at the beginning of the book. Either way, a biographical preface inserted at the beginning of *The Faerie Queene* could reasonably have been expected to work as an introduction to the whole works in the finished book, so the fact that the book was a 'Build-It-Yourself Edition', as Galbraith termed it, does not in itself explain the absence of a prefatory Life of Spenser from the Lownes edition.

When the first prefatory Life of Spenser was eventually published in Jonathan Edwin's edition of *The Works of that Famous English Poet, Mr. Edmond Spenser* in 1679, a full century after *The Shepheardes Calender*, the addition was highlighted on the title page, which contains the words 'Whereunto is added, An ACCOUNT

---

15 This is supported by the context in which the poem occurs in *Emblemes and Epigrames*, framed not by other commemorative poems but by epigrams with titles such as 'That one thinge Produceth annother', 'A longe nose', 'Martin' and 'Vsurers' ('Spencer's Fayrie Queene' is epigram 38 in the volume, the other titles are epigrams 36, 37, 39 and 40 respectively).

16 Andrew Zurcher has persuasively argued that at Lownes's first printing of *The Faerie Queene* in 1609, the Cantos were temporarily misidentified as the conclusion to Book IV (see 'The Printing of the *Cantos of Mutabilitie* in 1609', in Jane Grogan (ed.), *Celebrating Mutabilitie* (Manchester: Manchester University Press, 2010), pp. 40–60). Nevertheless, this does not fully explain why the title page for the collected edition, printed several years later, fails to mention the fact that it contains additional material.

of his LIFE; With other new ADDITIONS Never before in PRINT'.[17] The Words
'ACCOUNT' and 'LIFE' are printed in the same size as 'FAERY QUEEN' four
lines above, suggesting this rather than the new additions (including the notorious
'Mother Hubberds Tale') was what Edwin considered the edition's greatest selling-
point.[18] This account, titled 'A Summary of the Life of Mr. Edmond Spenser', contains only two dates – the years of Spenser's birth and death, cited after an epitaph
reproduced facing the title page instead of the author's portrait – both of which are
wrong.[19] The 'Summary' was in fact not the first Life of Spenser to appear in print.
Both Fuller's *Worthies of England* (1662) and Phillips's *Theatrum Poetarum* (1675)
had previously featured entries on Spenser. Fuller's and Phillips's Lives of Spenser
both contained the mix of biographical or bibliographical facts, and dubious anecdotes commonly found in such compilations. As with other entries in biographical
compilations, the interest of the anecdotes lies not so much in the question whether
those stories are genuine (for the most part they are not) but the way in which they
are being deployed. Fuller's version begins by describing Spenser as learned, but sadly
prone to archaisms, without which his works would have been more 'salable' (p. 219),
before moving on to 'a story commonly told' (p. 220): a version of the 'I receiv'd nor
rhyme nor reason' anecdote.[20] Fuller then has Spenser move to Ireland with Lord
Grey, from where he returns destitute and dies soon afterwards in 1598.[21] Phillips's
version begins by praising Spenser for his achievements in the field of 'Heroic Poesie',
and then traces the beginnings of his career to *The Shepheardes Calender*, which so
impressed Philip Sidney that he recommended the poet to the queen, who appointed
him secretary to Philip's 'brother' Sir Henry Sidney and sent him to Ireland.[22] After
his return, Spenser, 'having lost his great Friend *Sir Philip*, fell into poverty' and, in
a different spin on the anecdote, threw himself onto the mercy of the queen, whose
generosity was cut short by Burghley, because he '[owed] him a grudge for some

17 James Ware's preface to *A View of the State of Ireland* (1633) had included a few biographical snippets
    about Spenser, for example his association with Lord Grey, and the year of his death (which Ware
    insisted was 1599, although 'others have it wrongly 1598' (¶3ᵇ)). Nevertheless, the main purpose of
    Ware's preface was to place the *View* in its historical context.
18 Edwin appears to have been correct about the appeal of the Life of Spenser: the Folger Library owns
    a copy of the Lownes edition of Spenser's works (STC 23084 copy 1) at the end of which a late seven-
    teenth-century owner has written out the entire text of the 'Summary' (see figure 9).
19 While the year of death is only off by a few years (1596 for 1599), the dating of Spenser's birth to 1510
    is puzzling, as it would have made the 'new Poete' rather ancient when he began his flight to fame – as
    well as making him more than three times Lancelot Andrewes's age when he supposedly competed
    with him for the fellowship at Pembroke. Aubrey's notes on Spenser's life contain the same inaccurate
    dates.
20 This highly popular biographical anecdote involving Spenser exists in two main variants. The premise
    to both is that the queen promised Spenser a generous sum of money and ordered Burghley (then her
    treasurer) to give it to him, but Burghley objected, claiming that it was too much. In the first version,
    the queen goes on to tell Burghley to give the poet 'what is reason'. Burghley gives Spenser a signifi-
    cantly smaller sum, and a disappointed Spenser composes the lines 'I was promis'd on a time, | To
    have reason for my rhyme; | From that time unto this season, | I receiv'd nor rhyme nor reason.' In the
    second version of the anecdote, Burghley exclaims 'what, all this for a song?' and so moves the queen
    to reduce the payment to Spenser.
21 Spenser died in January, so Fuller's date is correct according to the old style of dating.
22 Sir Henry Sidney, Lord Grey's predecessor as Lord Deputy of Ireland, was Philip's father, not his
    brother.

9 'A Summary of the Life of Mr. Edmond Spenser' (1679) added to a copy of the Lownes edition by a late seventeenth-century owner

reflections in *Mother Hubbards Tale*' (p. 35). According to Phillips's account, Spenser was so upset by this, he died of melancholy soon afterwards.

Fuller's and Phillips's versions both evidently use the anecdote in order to make sense of what little they could find out about Spenser's life – featuring the common themes of success at court, a secretarial career in Ireland and subsequent poverty followed by a sudden death in England – and arranged the elements into a logical sequence. In Fuller's version, the anecdote's function is primarily to show Spenser as a successful courtier whose poetry moves the queen to be generous to him and snub her treasurer, who was merely being prudent and acting as a 'good Steward'. Spenser's going to Ireland is consequently framed by Fuller as a reward for the success of his poetry but also the beginning of his poverty ('his office under his Lord was lucrative, yet got he no estate'), which Fuller presents as the cause of Spenser's death. Phillips's Life of Spenser, by contrast, is above all an attempt to connect Spenser's works to biographical events, and to explain biographical events as having been indirectly caused by Spenser's writings. In Phillips's version, therefore, Spenser's career at court fittingly begins with his first published work, while Philip Sidney turns from the dedicatee of *The Shepheardes Calender* into Spenser's patron, the driving force behind his going to Ireland, as well as the reason for his subsequent poverty. Spenser's poverty as a result of losing his patron in turn provides Phillips with a context for the anecdote, while 'Mother Hubberds Tale' is used to explain Burghley's meanness, which in this version proves fatal for the poet.

Like the two Lives written before it, the 'Summary of the Life of Mr. Edmond Spenser' that prefaces the 1679 *Works* also turns to anecdotes in order to derive a coherent narrative from what are evidently scattered pieces of information about the author. For example, the anonymous author of the 'Summary' (who, like Fuller and unlike Phillips, begins his Life with Spenser's education at Cambridge), adds that when a fellowship became available at Pembroke Hall, Spenser lost out to Lancelot Andrewes, forcing him to change his career plans:

> Thus defeated of his hopes, unable any longer to subsist in the College, he repair'd to some Friends of his in the North, where he staid, fell in Love, and at last (prevail'd upon by the perswasions, and importunities of other Friends) came to London.[23]

As Hadfield points out in his recent biography, the story of Spenser as Andrewes's competitor for the fellowship was factually wrong and subsequently corrected in a later prefatory life by Thomas Birch.[24] Yet like the anecdotes about Burghley's preventing the queen's excessive generosity towards Spenser in Fuller and Phillips, the anecdote of Spenser's unsuccessful bid for the fellowship at Pembroke is used to explain something that for the author of the 'Summary' evidently needed explaining: why Spenser left Cambridge instead of pursuing a university career, like Gabriel Harvey – or Lancelot Andrewes. At the same time, it also establishes the themes of failed ambition and poverty, both of which seventeenth-century writers appear to

23 *The Works of that Famous English Poet Mr. Edmond Spenser* (London: 1679), A³.
24 Hadfield, *Edmund Spenser*, p. 422.

have considered central to Spenser's life, and explains Spenser's subsequent appearance in London, his turn to poetry and his need for a patron.[25]

Once the author of the 'Summary' has relocated Spenser to London, he offers another anecdote, whose purpose is to explain Spenser's rise to fame as a poet: according to this anecdote, Spenser the unsuccessful scholar and unsuccessful lover of the Girl from the North began to write poetry and, after having impressed his poetically inclined acquaintances, to look for a suitable patron. He shrewdly chose Philip Sidney as 'the Person, to whom he design'd the first Discovery of himself' and headed to Leicester house, armed with a sample canto from *The Faerie Queene* (Canto ix of Book I).[26] As soon as Sidney had reached the mid-point of the canto, he ordered a puzzled servant to give fifty pounds to the poem's author and, after reading two more stanzas, twice doubled that amount, despite the servant's objection that the man who had brought the poem looked as though he would be happy with five pounds. At the second doubling of the amount, Sidney urged the reluctant servant to hurry up and give Spenser his money before he could read any further and 'hold himself oblig'd to give him more than he had' (a sensible decision, because continuing to double the promised amount at each stanza would eventually have left Sidney owing the poet some three billion pounds by the end of the canto).[27]

The main appeal of the 'Summary's' account of the memorable first encounter between Spenser and Sidney lies in two points: the delightful absurdity of the notion that Sidney was very nearly bankrupted by Spenser's poetry and the contrast between the connoisseur of good poetry and the sober servant who considers five pounds an adequate reward for what he prosaically terms 'the Paper'.[28] At the same time, however, the anecdote also serves three important narrative functions: it establishes Spenser as an exceptionally talented poet even at the start of his career, it creates a connection between Spenser and Sidney (another staple of seventeenth-century Lives of Spenser), and it acts as a transition to the next important episode in his life – winning the queen as his patron and being made Poet Laureate. The meagre financial reward Spenser received from his royal patron – at least compared to the much more generous reward from Sidney that had supposedly preceded it – is explained by means of an ironic pun on the expression 'poetical justice' and a highly condensed version of the Burghley anecdote:

> But in this, his Fate was unkind; for it prov'd only a *Poetical Grant*, the payment, after a very short time, being stopt by a *great Councellour*, who studied more the Queen's Profit

---

25 The reasons for Spenser's detour via the North are less clear, although the author of the 'Summary' may have been thinking of Colin Clout's unrequited passion for the 'countrie lasse called Rosalinde' there. In Aubrey's account of Spenser's life, Rosalind's real-life counterpart is 'identified' as a member of the Dryden family, who hailed from Canons Ashby in Northamptonshire – not strictly part of 'the North', but at least somewhat to the north of Cambridge (see Bodleian MS Aubr 8, f. 41).

26 The entire episode of Spenser's encounter with Sidney is contained on a single page of the 'summary' (A^a), so all further quotations from it refer to that page.

27 Aubrey records a variation of the anecdote, in which Spenser left a presentation copy of *The Faerie Queene* that Sidney did not read at first, but when he did, he sought out the poet and rewarded him handsomely with an unspecified amount, despite his servant's protests (see Conclusion for a more detailed account of Aubrey's anecdotes involving Spenser and Sidney).

28 Sidney, in his initial instructions to the servant, refers to the canto as 'the Verses'.

than her Diversion, and told Her, 'twas beyond Example to give so great a Pention to a *Ballad-maker*. (A^a–A^b)

As in Fuller's version, then, Burghley's behaviour is being blamed on habitual mean-ness, possibly stemming from a misguided desire to be prudent with the queen's money. What is peculiar about this version, however, is that while it paraphrases the known anecdote, it refrains from reproducing either of the two punchlines that it generally gives to Burghley or Spenser.[29] Instead, the anonymous author of the 'Summary' changes Burghley's disparaging 'What, all this for a song?' to the insulting but less punchy '*Ballad-maker*' and swaps the apocryphal (and rather un-Spenserian-sounding) quatrain for a stanza of genuine Spenser:

> O Grief of Griefs! O Gall of all good Hearts!
> To see that Vertue should despised be,
> Of such, as first were rais'd for Vertue's parts,
> And now broad-spreading, like an aged Tree,
> Let none shoot up that nigh them planted be!
> O let not those of whom the Muse is scorn'd,
> Alive, nor Dead, be of the Muse adorn'd! (A^b)

In the 'Summary', the stanza is framed as a belated response by 'the grieved Poet' to Burghley's stopping of his royal pension and wrongly identified as part of 'Teares of the Muses' (it is in fact a stanza from 'Ruines of Time').[30] After the stanza, the anonymous author adds, 'How much deeper his resentment wrought in *Mother Hubbard's Tale*, may appear to those that list to read it with reflection'. This passage in the 'Summary', then, not only reverses the standard order of events, it also seeks to provide a context and a justification for the poet's 'resentment', possibly because such a sentiment is at odds with the idea of Spenser as a man 'of a temper strangely tender and amorous' (A^b). Additionally, framing the stanza from 'Ruines of Time' as the poet's response to ill treatment by Burghley allows for an apologetic reading of 'Mother Hubberds Tale' by making it an act of retaliation rather than an aggressive attack on Burghley fuelled by Spenser's seemingly unprovoked hatred.

In addition to the anecdotes, the 'Summary' contains several pieces of biographical information that have been culled from the paratextual materials of Spenser's works. So, for example, Spenser's presence at Leicester House is derived from one of the *Familiar Letters*, which are appended to the biographical account 'as a Testimonial of

29 William Winstanley, who drew on a variety of sources for the compiled Life of Spenser he included in his 1687 *Lives of the Most Famous English Poets*, even included both punchlines.

30 The stanza is cited in the revised version of the poem that was first included in the 'Mother Hubberd'-less edition of the *Complaints* printed by Lownes (and reprinted in the *Works*, which also follows Lownes's edition in separating 'Mother Hubberds Tale' from the rest of the *Complaints*). While the change may not have been authorial, the switch from 'him' to 'such' above all serves to correct a metri-cal error in the original version. In the 1591 edition, the final couplet had saved the negation for the last line of the stanza, resulting in an extra syllable: 'O let the man, of whom the Muse is scorned, | Nor aliue, nor dead be of the Muse adorned' (*Complaints*, C4^b). Richard McCabe argues that the revi-sions to this and the preceding stanza in the Lownes edition were made 'in order to eliminate personal allusions to Burghley' (in *The Shorter Poems*, p. 590). Yet the pronoun switch from the singular to the plural is effectively the only change, and it hardly eliminates the allusions; the fact that the 'Summary' quotes the edited version of the stanza in this context suggests it continued to be understood.

his Familiarities with the most Ingenious and Learned men of those Times' (A2ᵃ) and the location of his own house 'in Kincolman' has been taken from the epistle to 'Colin Clouts Come Home Againe'.[31] Similarly, the anonymous author refers to several of Spenser's 'lost' works, such as *The Dying Pelican* or the *Nine Comedies*, which are only alluded to in prefaces, and attempts to explain the fact that there is no other record of them by speculating that they must have been 'embezill'd when he was in Ireland' (Aᵇ).[32] Additionally, the 'Summary' selectively interprets Spenser's dedicatory verses as evidence that he was 'in great esteem, and good favour with many of the Nobility'.

Of course dedications and prefaces are generally read as non-fiction elements of a text. One point in which the 'Summary' differs from the accounts of Spenser's life that preceded it, however, is the extent to which it draws on Spenser's *poetry* as a source for his life. Thus Spenser's success as a poet is contrasted to his lack of success as a lover, but the evidence the author cites for it is peculiar because it is taken from a fictional source:

> A Poet indeed, without a Rival, but not so successful a Lover, for tho' *Hobbinol* as a Gentleman, rather lov'd in Concert with him, than to his grievance, yet *Menalcas* put him to't, whose treachery, together with the Apostacy of his Mistress, gave him occasion bitterly to complain, and having eas'd himself that way, he apply'd himself to Business. (Aᵇ)[33]

This sentence is in fact a paraphrase of the argument to the June eclogue of *The Shepheardes Calender*.[34] While the paraphrase renders the names of Colin's friend and Colin's rival as '*Hobbinol*' and '*Menalcas*', thus remaining within the fictionalised sphere of the *Calender*, Colin himself is only referred to as 'he', leading to a conflation between the fictional character and Spenser himself (who is referred to as 'he' for most of the 'Summary').[35] This effect is heightened by the fact that the paraphrase is framed by unambiguous references to Spenser: the comment on Spenser's good connections to patrons and the account of his going to Ireland.

Arguably, this biographical reading of the June eclogue is not too surprising, because *The Shepheardes Calender* actively encourages readers to think of Colin as the poet's alter ego, but it is peculiar to find it integrated so seamlessly into a biographical account. Even more remarkable are the two instances in which the 'Summary' refers directly to Spenser's poetic works and connects them to specific moments in his life: the canto associated with the Sidney anecdote and the stanza from 'Ruines

---

31 The spelling mistake in the place name is only in the 'Summary'. In the epistle, which is reproduced later in the volume, it is correctly spelt as 'Kilcolman'.

32 The wording leaves it unclear whether the 'embezill'd' works were located in Ireland or in England, and even the verb itself is ambiguous: according to the *OED*, 'embezzle' may variously refer to theft or to the destruction of documents, both of which are possible readings in this context. As a result, the phrase allows for several scenarios ranging from a raid on Spenser's desk during his absence to careless destruction by undiscerning Irish rebels.

33 The 'Business' refers to Spenser's going to Ireland as Lord Grey's secretary.

34 'This Aeglogue is wholly vowed to the complayning of Colins ill successe in his loue. For being (as is aforesaid) enamoured of a Country lasse Rosalind, and hauing (as seemeth) founde place in her heart, he lamenteth to his deare frend Hobbinoll, that he is nowe forsaken vnfaithfully, and in his steede Menalcas, another shepheard receiued disloyally.' Edmund Spenser, *The Shepheardes Calender* (London: 1579), F2ᵇ.

35 Spenser's name is only mentioned three times in the 'Summary'.

of Time' associated with his unjust treatment by Burghley. The latter is an interesting choice, because it replaces the familiar 'nor rhyme nor reason' quatrain, which anecdotes usually frame as an impromptu witticism, with a far less aphoristic stanza supposed to have been written sometime after the event. One effect of this change is to make Spenser's grudge against Burghley appear less superficial: in the 'nor rhyme nor reason' version, Spenser's complaint is purely about the withholding of a promised payment without blaming anyone in particular, whereas Verlame's words from 'Ruines of Time' in this context appear to accuse Burghley of despising virtue and scorning the muse. Moreover, quoting a stanza of genuine, attributable poetry by Spenser is a way of allowing Spenser to speak for himself, and the way in which it is introduced serves to enhance this. The phrase 'the grieved Poet thus complains' establishes a direct biographical link both to the particular stanza (which begins with the words 'O Grief of Griefs!') and to the title of the collection in which it was published (*Complaints*). The inaccurate reference to 'Teares of the Muses' may simply have been a mistake on the author's part, yet its appearance in the text at this point has the function of establishing an additional biographical connection that strengthens the 'Summary's' point that this stanza represents the voice of 'the Authour selfe' complaining of a personal grievance.

While anecdotes of Spenser winning patronage from Sidney or the queen after presenting or reading from a sample of his poetry exist in several variations, the 'Summary' contains the only version of the anecdote to identify a particular piece of poetry as the one that moved Spenser's patron. At first sight, the canto named in the 'Summary' appears to be an oddly random choice: the ninth canto of Book I occurs at a point in *The Faerie Queene* at which all the main protagonists of Book I have already been introduced. On the other hand, however, Canto ix is the canto that contains the description of Arthur's dream vision of Gloriana, which marks the beginning of his quest, that is, the true beginning of *The Faerie Queene*. As an introduction to the poem as a whole (as opposed to just Book I), it is consequently a very fitting choice – as can be seen from the fact that when Spenser himself sketched out the plot of *The Faerie Queene* in his 'Letter to Raleigh', he began not with Una and Redcrosse but with a paraphrase of a passage from Canto ix:

> So much more profitable and gratious is doctrine by ensample, then by rule. So haue I laboured to doe in the person of Arthure: whom I conceiue after his long education by Timon, to whom he was by Merlin delivered to be brought vp, so soone as he was borne of the Lady Igrayne, to haue seene in a dream or vision the Faery Queen, with whose excellent beauty rauished, he awaking resolued to seeke her out, and so being by Merlin armed, and by Timon throughly instructed, he went to seeke her forth in Faerye land.[36]

The author of the 'Summary' (or his source) may have been thinking of this passage from the 'Letter to Raleigh' when they let Spenser submit this particular canto to Sidney's scrutiny. Nevertheless, his account contains no reference to Arthur or the poem as a whole or the author's 'whole intention'; instead, it highlights 'the Twenty-eighth *Stanza* of *Despair*' as the one by which Sidney is 'much affected' (A[a]), prompting

---

36 *The Faerie Queene* (1590), pp. 592–3. This corresponds to stanzas 3–15 of the canto.

his initial decision to give the poet a generous reward, and the subsequent two stanzas that lead Sidney to double the amount are the ones in which Sir Trevisan vividly outlines how Despair affected Sir Terwin and him, culminating in his companion's suicide. The implication of the scene, then, is that in reading the canto, Sidney took the description of the knights trapped by Despair to reflect the poet's own desperate patron-less situation and was moved by pity as well as the quality of the poetry. The fact that the 'Summary' points out that Spenser selected that particular canto and chose to target Sidney specifically also implies that this may have been his plan all along – which could be read either as a sign he was genuinely desperate for patronage or as a sign that Spenser was being deliberately manipulative. The latter reading would perhaps be too uncharitable, however – it is more likely that the author of the 'Summary' intended the scene to serve as an example of what the concluding paragraph of the Life presents as the final evaluation of Spenser's special abilities as a poet:

> Where he is passionate, he forces commiseration and tears from his Readers [...]. His Descriptions are so easie and natural, that his Pen seems to have a power of conveying *Idea's* to our mind, more just, and to the Life, than the exquisite Pencils of *Titian*, or *Raphael* to our eyes. (Aᵇ–A2ᵃ)

'A Summary of the Life of Mr. Edmond Spenser' is in many ways a fascinating prefatory Life. Nevertheless, it is evidently not a response to the recent death of a poet by his contemporaries but the written Life of a poet whom the author of the 'Summary' regarded as belonging to a hazy past age – rather like sixteenth-century editors viewed the age of Chaucer. This explains the inaccurate dates, which demonstrate a lack of awareness of historical context in turning Spenser into a Henrician poet and letting him attend Cambridge in his mid-sixties (albeit understandable at a time when few people still remembered living under a Tudor monarch and the distinctions between them were perhaps beginning to blur), as well as a lack of awareness of when his works had first been published. It also explains the reliance on anecdotes that portray Elizabethan patronage structures as a system based on meritocracy and friendship, and the barely concealed distaste when the author introduces *Familiar Letters* as 'a *Specimen* of what kind of Wit was then in Vogue amongst [the men of those times]' (A2ᵃ). By 1679, Spenser had very much become 'the prince of poets in his time', as the epitaph that faces the title page puts it.

At the same time, the features that make the 'Summary' such an interesting text are connected to the fact that it is so clearly a late seventeenth-century Life. Specifically, its use of printed works as a source of biographical information and its attempt to let Spenser speak for himself through quotation from a poetic work show the influence of the major biographer of the seventeenth century: Izaak Walton. As a result, Spenser's missing literary afterlife in the wake of his death is not counterbalanced, but at least mitigated through a somewhat adequate Life written in the wake of Walton's *Lives*.

4

Walton's literary *Lives*:
from Donne to Herbert

An adequate Life

R. C. Bald's introduction to his seminal biography *John Donne: A Life* (1970) begins with a bold claim: 'Donne must be the earliest major poet in English of whom an adequate biography is possible'.[1] Biographers of earlier English poets, such as Spenser or Sidney, might beg to differ. Nevertheless, Bald's reasoning merits some closer examination, not so much for what it reveals about Donne, as for what it reveals about the links between twentieth-century expectations of biography (particularly literary biography) and modern notions of what constitutes 'a Life':

> The life of Chaucer can only be pieced together from fragmentary records. Records likewise are the basis of any account of Shakespeare's life; one letter addressed to him has survived, but none of those he wrote himself. A life of Shakespeare is usually filled out with copious descriptions of the age in which he lived and with an autobiographical reading of the works. [...] Some remnants of the private correspondence of [Spenser and Dryden] have survived, but it is so fragmentary as to be relatively unilluminating. Milton's state papers are available in some bulk, and a number of other Latin letters, but of intimate communications in his native tongue to his friends there is a mere handful. After the year 1700 the bulk of such biographical materials increases enormously; the letters of Addison, Swift, Pope, and Dr. Johnson have survived in quantity to supplement their published works, not merely by telling us what passed through their minds in their less formal moments, but also by affording a guide to their daily activities and by illuminating their relations with many of their friends.[2]

Two things are particularly noticeable in this passage: Bald's emphasis on letters and personal documents as prerequisites for 'adequate' biography, and his use of phrases implying privacy. For Bald, the value of letters to a biographer clearly lies in the extent to which they represent 'private correspondence' and 'intimate communications' of his subjects and therefore 'illuminate their relations with [...] their friends'.[3] In other

---

1 R. C. Bald, *John Donne: A Life* (Oxford: Clarendon Press, 1970), p. 1.
2 Bald, *John Donne*, pp. 1–2.
3 A number of recent studies have highlighted the problems involved in treating early modern 'familiar' letters in general and Donne's letters in particular as 'private correspondence' or 'intimate communications' in the modern sense. Margaret Maurer's essay on 'The Prose Letters', in Jeanne Shami, Dennis Flynn and M. Thomas Hester (eds), *The Oxford Handbook of John Donne* (Oxford: Oxford University Press, 2011), pp. 348–61 stresses that Donne's letters were valued for their style and notes that, for this reason, the first letters to be published were included with the 1635 edition of Donne's poems, a fact that puzzled nineteenth-century critics. Judith Rice Henderson's essay 'On Reading the Rhetoric

words, he believes that 'adequate' biography is only possible if the biographer can access sources documenting his subject's private, inner life – the person behind the poet, as it were.

While this may be a common element of modern biographies, the same cannot be said for their sixteenth- and seventeenth-century counterparts. As I set out in Chapter 1, these tend to emphasise their subjects' *vita activa* and exemplariness rather than focusing on their inner lives and individual traits. This may partly explain why the surviving information about the lives of early modern poets often does not account for their private experience to the extent that a modern biographer might wish for. The clash between modern notions of individuality and early modern biographical practice is illustrated by some of the critical responses to Izaak Walton, one of the first English biographers to become known in that function. Allan Pritchard's *English Biography in the Seventeenth Century* (2005) contains a chapter on Walton's *Lives* which is for the most part a perceptive analysis of Walton's strategy of emphasising the similarities rather than the differences between his subjects, in order to portray them as conforming to an Anglican ideal.[4] Yet there is one point about which Pritchard cannot help sounding distinctly critical – Walton's apparent failure to do justice to the 'complex individuality of his characters':

> Rather than revealing the complex individuality of his characters, Walton drastically oversimplifies them to make them conform to his primitive Christian ideal. His subjects were in reality men of unusual complexity and sophistication. He no more conveys the wide-ranging culture, polished urbanity, and fine wit of Wotton, who has been termed 'the most widely cultivated Englishman of his time', than he deals adequately with his diplomatic career. [...] Nowhere does Walton's oversimplification and reduction of the individuality of his characters appear more than in his handling of their speech and writing.[5]

Like Bald, Pritchard is evidently using the term 'adequate' to describe biography as it ought to be. However, it is equally clear that his idea of 'adequacy' is one that post-dates Walton's *Lives* by a considerable margin – even the quotation to support

of the Renaissance Letter', in Heinrich Plett (ed.), *Renaissance Rhetoric* (Berlin: de Gruyter, 1993), pp. 143–62 examines the role of rhetoric in the humanist tradition of (published) collections of letters. She concludes that because they were perceived as exercises in rhetoric, and that since rhetorical considerations could lead to substantial changes being made, such letters should not necessarily be looked at as soul-baring on the part of their writers or as sources of factual biographical information. Lynne Magnusson's *Shakespeare and Social Dialogue* (Cambridge: Cambridge University Press, 1999), on the other hand, argues for early modern letter-writing as a form of enacted social discourse, within which 'familiarity' functions as a mode.

4 Jessica Martin provides a useful outline of this phenomenon in the third chapter ('Godly Prototypes') of her monograph *Walton's Lives* (Oxford: Oxford University Press, 2001). Martin groups the 'commonplaces' of clerical Lives into four categories: 'the description of clerical subjects according to scriptural precept', 'the portrayal of subjects in terms of books, texts or engraved edifices', 'the visible signs of virtue read into the face and body, and into gesture and dress' and 'deathbed decorum' (p. 71). All of these can also be found in Walton's *Lives*, but as I shall argue in this chapter, the second commonplace, that is the portrayal in terms of books and texts, is deployed by Walton in a special manner that evolves over time.

5 Allan Pritchard, *English Biography in the Seventeenth Century* (Toronto: University of Toronto Press, 2005), p. 82. Although Pritchard mainly bases this observation on the four later lives (that is those of Wotton, Hooker, Herbert and Sanderson), much the same could be said for Walton's accounts of Donne's life.

Pritchard's view of Wotton's complex character is taken from an early twentieth-century biography.[6] This illustrates an epistemological problem intrinsic to the study of early modern biography: 'individuality' and 'character' are concepts that are central to modern definitions of biography, yet the terms were charged with very different meanings at the time. Although it would be wrong to claim that there was no concept of character or individuality at all, the terms need to be viewed in their historical semantic context.

'Individuality', a seventeenth-century coinage that is scarce between 1600 and 1700 (a search of the Early English Books Online corpus produces a mere 116 results in 33 texts), is used almost exclusively in a highly literal sense, which is equivalent to 'indivisibility', usually in reference to body and soul. A search for 'individual' produces 6,350 results in 1917 texts (only 840 results in 384 texts occur during the first half of the century). Of these, about 85 per cent are used adjectivally, in the sense of 'indivisible', with 'individual companion' and 'holy individuall Trinity' being particularly common phrases during the earlier decades, and 'individual person' steadily gaining prominence. 'Individual' as a noun is especially rare before 1650 (39 occurrences in 32 texts). To begin with, it is predominantly used in the sense of 'single element of a group' and 'object within a species' (see meanings 2a and 2b in the OED). During the 1660s, 'individual' in the sense of 'single (person)' becomes the most common usage, while during the final two decades, the noun acquires a more specific meaning, inclining towards the meaning of 'self', especially in theological and philosophical works. While this may not be a fully representative account of the history of the term, it nonetheless gives an indication of its evolution and demonstrates that at the time Walton was writing, 'individuality' in the modern sense was not a universal concept.

'Character' is an even more complex case. In the seventeenth century, the term has a variety of meanings, but underlying them all is the idea of a distinctive symbol or sign of something.[7] Nevertheless, the emphasis is on identifiability and classifiability rather than on uniqueness. One reason for this lies in the influence of the Theophrastan idea of character, which, as the following extract illustrates, seeks to identify typical traits about groups of people rather than the defining traits of a particular person:

> [H]auing conuersed with all sorts of natures bad and good, and comparing them togither: I took it my part to set down in this discourse their seuerall fashions and maners of life. [...] I will begin with those which delight in cauilling. And first I will define the vice it self: Then I will describe the Cauiller by his fashion and manners.[8]

---

6 Logan Pearsall Smith, *The Life and Letters of Sir Henry Wotton* (Oxford: Clarendon Press, 1907).

7 The OED entry lists fifteen different meanings, twelve of which contain examples from seventeenth-century texts (the remaining three are only contain examples from the eighteenth century onwards). The meanings current in the seventeenth century include: 1a 'A distinctive mark impressed, engraved, or otherwise made on a surface; a brand, stamp', 4b 'A particular person's style of handwriting; an example of handwriting', 7a 'A distinctive indication, a visible token, evidence [...] a feature, trait, characteristic', 10 'The face or features as identifying a person; personal appearance as indicative of something', and 11 'Recognized official rank or position; status, capacity established function, role; position occupied in relation to other people or things'.

8 Quoted after the first English translation, purported to be by John Healey, in *Epictetus manuall. Cebes table. Theophrastus characters* (1616), pp. 2–3.

The second semantic influence is the use of the concept in Aristotelian rhetoric.[9] In the only monograph-length study of early modern notions of 'character', Edward Burns observes that the rhetorical concept of 'Ethos' – frequently rendered as 'character' in English rhetorical manuals – played a significant role in shaping the early modern meaning of the term.[10] Burns's book is primarily concerned with 'character' in the dramatic sense and the emergence of eighteenth-century acting theory. Nevertheless, the majority of his observations about the semantic shift towards a more 'substantive' concept of character during the the seventeenth century are equally applicable to 'character' in the biographer's sense.[11]

'Individuality' and 'character', then, are concepts whose application to early modern biography must needs be problematic. Nevertheless, although the accuracy of Bald's claim that only biography which considers its subject's private life can be 'adequate' is debatable, his observation that there are more surviving documents of this nature from the late seventeenth century onwards is largely accurate. This reflects a shift in the concept of an exemplary life from one favouring the *vita activa* to one which places increasingly more emphasis on the private, introspective life. It is this shift that prepared the ground for the literary lives of the eighteenth century, which are the direct ancestors of modern literary biography. The text which best illustrates the beginning of this shift is Izaak Walton's *Life of Donne*.

There are two major sources for Donne's private life: his letters, of which a large number were also collected and published shortly after his death, and Walton's *Life of Donne*, which exists in four different versions, written over the course of thirty-five years. As one might expect, the letters contain some biographical information, although the way in which they were edited by Donne's son, John Donne the younger, makes it somewhat problematic to regard them exclusively as Donne's 'private correspondence'. Some of the editorial changes made to the letters suggest that *Letters to Severall Persons of Honour* (1651, reissued in 1654) was intended as a collection of stylistically exemplary letters rather than as a faithful reproduction of letters written by Donne.[12]

Izaak Walton's *Life of Donne* has had an even more profound influence on biographers as a source of first-hand evidence of Donne's private life than the letters. Originally written as a preface to Donne's *LXXX Sermons* (1640), a 'corrected and enlarged' version was republished separately in 1658, before the *Life of Donne* was included in the two collected editions of Walton's *Lives*, published in 1670 and 1675 respectively, each time with further modifications. The success of Walton's Lives and

---

9 This is reflected in Sir Thomas Elyot's dictionary, which defines the term as 'a token, a note made with a pen, a fygure, *a style or fourme of speakynge*' (emphasis added). Sir Thomas Elyot, *The dictionary of Syr Thomas Eliot Knyght* (1538), D[a].

10 Edward Burns, *Character: Acting and Being on the Pre-Modern Stage* (London: Macmillan, 1990).

11 Burns, *Character*, p. 6.

12 See Bald, *John Donne*, pp. 3–4 for a comparison between the surviving letters in manuscript and print and an overview of the changes made to the sequence of the letters and the omission or modification of dates and addressees' names. Although Bald notes that the *Letters to Severall Persons of Honour* appear to have been edited to resemble a letter-writing manual, he insists on trying to read the letters as private correspondence, prompting a revealing outburst of biographer's frustration: 'In spite of the gratitude to the younger Donne for having salvaged a large quantity of his father's correspondence, it is difficult in trying to use it not to feel frequent exasperation. [...] [T]here was almost no attempt to arrange the letters in any useful order' (p. 3).

their influence on later biographers reflect the growing interest in the personal lives of poets during the latter half of the seventeenth century. This especially applies to the *Life of Donne*, for reasons I shall explain below.

Walton's *Lives* follow on from the tradition of exemplary lives, and arguably, even the personal elements, such as anecdotes, mainly serve the purpose of illustrating his subjects' exemplarity. However, the precise nature of that exemplarity is nevertheless very different from that presented in earlier exemplary lives, such as Roper's *Life of Syr Thomas More* or Greville's *Life of Sidney*. While there have been a number of studies concerned with the shift towards inwardness and the rise of autobiography, little work has been done on how this affected the emerging of literary biography.

At its most fundamental, literary biography means juxtaposing a poet's life and works in a way in which the two inform each other and form a unified whole. Consequently, two things are necessary for a literary biographer: belief in the existence of an inner life of the poet, and the assumption that it filters down into the works, which can then be used as a key to unlock this inner life. In this chapter, I hope to show that Izaak Walton's most profound impact on biography lay in the innovative use which the *Life of Donne* made of Donne's writings, leading Walton to pioneer 'modern' biographical methods. Through a combination of his unusual background for an early modern biographer, his belief in a 'private' spiritual life, and his interest in poetry, Walton stumbled upon an approach to Donne's works that enabled him to treat them as a reflection on Donne's inner thoughts. This in turn provided him with the tools for accomplishing a task which might otherwise have proved impossible: writing the *Life of Herbert*, which is possibly the earliest life of an English poet that truly portrays its subject's life *as* a poet. While Walton's primary concern was to write Anglican hagiography rather than the lives of poets, and while his discovery of those biographical methods may have been accidental, the different versions of the *Life of Donne* and *Life of Herbert* are nevertheless formative texts for the genre of literary biography. Therefore, if Bald's statement holds true, and John Donne is 'the earliest major poet in English of whom an adequate biography is possible', part of the credit should go to Izaak Walton, for having been the first biographer to think about Donne's life in an 'adequate' manner and leaving a path for later biographers, such as Bald, to follow.

The structure of Walton's *Life of Donne*

Izaak Walton is a writer who has generally been underappreciated by criticism and whose influence on the development of biography tends to be noted in passing rather than fully acknowledged by modern scholarship. Because Walton is now most frequently turned to by Donne scholars for supporting evidence from a first-hand witness, it is considered good scholarly practice to approach him with extreme caution. One recent example of this is the *Oxford Handbook of John Donne* (2011), whose editors are at pains to highlight in their introduction the caution and 'discretion' with which the contributors refer to Walton's *Life of Donne*.[13]

---

13 Shami, Flynn and Hester (eds), *Oxford Handbook of John Donne*, p. 6. See also Steven W. May's essay in the same volume, 'Donne and Egerton: The Court and Courtship', which speaks of Walton's 'always-suspect testimony' (p. 456). However, in his essay 'Donne's Family Background and Early Years', Flynn

The scepticism of Donne scholars regarding Walton as a first-hand source of biographical facts is of course justified. However, since this use of Walton's *Life of Donne* reduces it to the status of a frustratingly unreliable eyewitness account, Walton is undervalued as a consequence. The real contribution of the *Life of Donne* is not in providing an account of Donne's life by someone who was acquainted with him during his later years.[14] Instead, a more useful – and perhaps less judgemental – way of reading Walton's *Life of Donne* would be to view it as an early reader's response to Donne's works and his attempt to account for them all in biographical terms. If viewed as a biographical reader (rather than just an error-prone biographer), Walton turns out to be not only of interest to modern biographers of Donne but worthy of study himself.

Over the past few decades in particular, there has been a relative dearth in Walton scholarship, especially regarding Walton's *Lives*. The three seminal studies on the subject were published between 1930 and 1966 (though the latter is based on an earlier lecture series).[15] Additionally, there has as yet been no critical edition of the complete *Lives*. The Oxford University Press edition of *The Lives of John Donne, Sir Henry Wotton, Richard Hooker, George Herbert & Robert Sanderson*, with an introduction by George Saintsbury (1927) is still the edition most commonly cited, but it contains no annotations, is entirely based on the 1675 text (with the 1678 *Life of Sanderson* added to it) and acknowledges no textual differences between the different versions. *The Compleat Walton* (1929), edited by Geoffrey Keynes, only has eleven pages of bibliographical notes, of which only four refer to the *Lives*. *The Compleat Angler* has fared slightly better in this respect; an excellent critical edition by Jonquil Bevan was published in 1983, but this too was the first of its kind. On the whole, Walton has been consigned to critical footnotes that are often dismissive of his biographical efforts.

More recently, however, Jessica Martin's *Walton's Lives: Conformist Commemorations and the Rise of Biography* (2001) has made a strong case for the importance of Walton's *Lives* for establishing biography as a genre. Walton's biographical practice, Martin argues, played a crucial part in shaping readers' expectations in terms of content, form, and the presence of the biographer within the text. While Martin's study examines the *Lives* in the light of what Walton intended to achieve – to write Anglican hagiography as a layman – this chapter will focus on an aspect of the *Lives* that is effectively a by-product of Walton's endeavours: the accidental emergence of literary biography.

Walton's engagement with his subjects' works might easily pass unnoticed today, except for the dismay that his 'manipulation' of sources has caused to critics like

---

nevertheless acknowledges that '[Walton's] influence in Donne studies remains incalculably great' (p. 394).

14 As John Butt has pointed out in *Biography in the Hands of Walton, Johnson, and Boswell* (Los Angeles: University of California Press, 1966), when Donne died in 1631, Walton had only known him for seven years and there are no surviving letters by Donne or Walton to support the idea that they were friends (p. 4).

15 Donald Stauffer's *English Biography Before 1700* (1930), David Novarr's *The Making of Walton's 'Lives'* (Ithaca, NY: Cornell University Press, 1958) and John Butt's *Biography in the Hands of Walton, Johnson, and Boswell* (1966).

John Butt, who regarded it as an 'offense to modern sensibilities'.[16] Quoting from an author's works and seeking connections between the life and the works has become a staple of modern literary biography, as is aptly illustrated by biographers' responses in cases where this cannot be done easily.[17] Among his contemporaries, however, Walton stands out as highly unusual not only in the extent to which he refers to his subjects' works but also in the way in which he uses them. He extensively quotes, paraphrases and reshapes his subjects' writings (including their poetry) and weaves them into his narrative. Underlying this is an assumption that we would perhaps more readily associate with the eighteenth than with the mid-seventeenth century: that literary works are reflective of their author's inner thoughts and present a picture of his frame of mind at the time of writing.[18] What R. C. Bald called a lack of respect for 'the sanctity of a quotation' is in fact part of a sophisticated technique, which Walton perfected over the course of his revisions of the *Life of Donne*, and whose aim was to ventriloquise the voice of his subject.[19]

I have chosen to focus on two of Walton's *Lives*, the *Life of Donne* and the *Life of Herbert*, because they are the ones for which he relied particularly heavily on the written works of his subjects. Furthermore, they stand at opposite ends of Walton's career as a biographer. The 1640 *Life of Donne* marks the beginning of Walton's life-writing and is the one among his *Lives* which underwent the most – and the most substantial – revisions. In its different versions, the *Life of Donne* reflects Walton's growing interest in reading Donne's works biographically and using them in his *Life*. In the following, I shall particularly highlight the differences between the 1640 and the 1658 version, because they illustrate this development most clearly. The *Life of Herbert*, on the other hand, represents the late phase of Walton's life-writing. It underwent comparatively minor changes in its different versions and is the culmination of Walton's technique of accessing his subject's life via his writings.

Since the seventeenth century, attitudes towards Walton as a biographer have shifted from admiration for his style to criticism bordering on hostility directed against his methods. Critical appreciation of Walton has perhaps been hampered by the fact that he has mostly been labelled a predecessor rather than heralded as an innovator. Paradoxically, despite their critical attitude towards him, Walton has remained hard to avoid for his successors. For example, although modern biographers of Donne tend to – and are probably right to – question Walton's reliability for

---

16 Butt, *Biography*, p. 9.
17 See for example Duncan-Jones's observation regarding the 'wide gap' in Sir Philip Sidney's life, in the preface to her 1991 biography, which I have discussed in Chapter 2.
18 See Leon Edel, *Writing Lives: Principia Biographia* (New York: Norton, 1987): 'The interest in the personal and the private life, the life of the inner man, dates [...] from the eighteenth century: certainly it was a harbinger of Romanticism' (p. 37).
19 R. C. Bald, 'Historical Doubts Respecting Walton's *Life of Donne*', in Millar MacLure and F. W. Watt (eds), *Essays in English Literature from the Renaissance to the Victorian Age, Presented to A. S. P. Woodhouse* (Toronto: University of Toronto Press, 1964), pp. 69–84 (p. 70). John Butt, in *Biography*, even goes as far as to suggest Walton's ventriloquising is tantamount to a crime, as he notes that Walton has been '*convicted* of using both Herbert's *Temple* and his *Country Parson* in evidence of Herbert's thoughts and behaviour' (pp. 9–10, emphasis added). Alan Stewart's terminology is less hostile than that of earlier scholars, referring to ventriloquised passages in the Life of Donne as 'rewritings', 'fabrications' and 'appropriations' (*Oxford History of Life-Writing* vol. II, p. 229).

certain episodes of Donne's life, such as his early life or his last days, they are forced to rely on his account for those very episodes due to a lack of other sources. Similarly, although they are sceptical of Walton's use of anecdotes in his *Life*, few of them can altogether resist the temptation to retell them (with the story about Donne's vision of his wife and dead child being a particular favourite).[20]

In its earliest version, Walton's *Life of Donne* is similar in structure to other prefatory lives, including Speght's *Life of Chaucer*, written two generations earlier. Naturally, there are some structural differences between the two: Walton does not discuss the lives of Donne's children, and his account of Donne's 'service' is divided into two phases – before and after Master Donne became Dr Donne. With some minor modifications, however, Speght's table of contents could almost be attached to the 1640 *Life of Donne*. Like Speght, Walton begins with his subject's parentage and education. Then he moves on to the topics of Donne's marriage, service, friends at court and finally his poetry and his death and posthumous reputation. The earlier sections of Walton's 1640 *Life of Donne* are also similar to the corresponding sections of Speght's *Life of Chaucer* in terms of content. The parallels are particularly close in the sections on Chaucer's and Donne's education: both Speght and Walton stress their subjects' extraordinary diligence and their achievements across all areas of learning as well as their travels to foreign countries. None of this is altogether surprising, of course, as they are both prefatory lives, so similarities in structure are only to be expected.

Nevertheless, as the 1640 *Life of Donne* progresses, Walton begins to diverge from the pattern of the late sixteenth-century prefatory life by placing his emphases in different places. The first point at which this becomes clear is the section on Donne's marriage. In the *Life of Chaucer*, Chaucer's marriage primarily has a dynastic function. Speght uses it to cast his subject in the role of head of family (the section is followed by a family tree and a brief account of the lives of Chaucer's children) and to highlight the distant link to John of Gaunt.[21] By contrast, in Walton's 1640 *Life*, the section on Donne's marriage has a very different function and is disproportionately long. Walton uses it to bridge the years between Donne's education and his becoming a minister. As David Novarr has pointed out, this allows Walton to gloss over the years of Donne's life which might not suit the life of *Dr* Donne, and to present his subject in a favourable manner even while describing 'the remarkable error of his life'.[22]

---

20 John Carey's *John Donne: Life, Mind and Art* (London: Faber and Faber, 1981) and George Parfitt's *John Donne: A Literary Life* (Basingstoke: Macmillan, 1989), two otherwise very dissimilar studies, both question Walton's reliability but build an argument on this anecdote about Donne's 'vision'. One offers a reading of what Donne's vision may reveal about his mindset at the time, while the other refers to it in order to illustrate a point about Donne's character. Alan Stewart also cannot resist the appeal of this anecdote, but, unlike his predecessors, focuses on how the introduction of a 'supernatural' element changes Walton's *Life of Donne* (*Oxford History of Life-Writing* vol. II, p. 231).

21 After admitting that he does not know the name of Chaucer's wife and is uncertain whether she was an attendant of John of Gaunt's wife, Speght brushes away the uncertainty in concluding the section 'But howsoeuer it was, by this marriage he became brother in law to John of Gaunt Duke of Lancaster, as hereafter appeareth' (b.iii.ᵇ).

22 Novarr, *The Making of Walton's 'Lives'*, p. 51. Jessica Martin makes a similar point when observing that Walton's view of autobiography as the goal towards which a biographer strives means that '[a] perfect *Life* cannot include details its subject might prefer suppressed' (*Walton's Lives*, p. 172).

While this may have been one of Walton's considerations, the account of Donne's marriage also has an important structural function within the *Life*, and it is the first indication that, unlike Speght, Walton is aiming to turn his subject's life into a structured narrative. He goes to some lengths to present this episode in the life of Master Donne as a prefiguration of the life of Dr Donne. This is achieved by means of a forced biblical parallel and a – probably apocryphal – quotation: a gloss to Genesis 29 (the first of several glosses to biblical passages in the 1640 *Life*) and Sir George More's statement that 'he thought [Donne] a Secretary fitter for a King then a Subject' (A6^b).

Just after Donne's release from prison, Walton considers his subject's state of mind, and concludes with a biblical comparison:

> He was now at liberty, but his dayes were still cloudie, and being past this trouble, others did still multiply, for his Wife (to her extreme sorrow) was detained from him. And though with *Iacob* he endured not a hard service for her, yet he lost a good one. (A6^b)

In this description of Donne's 'cloudie dayes', the parallels between Donne's dismissal and Jacob's having to work for his future father-in-law for fourteen years are not immediately obvious. In fact, Walton himself admits as much in this passage. Yet his wording – 'though with Iacob he endured not [...] yet'[23] – nevertheless highlights the words 'with' and 'yet' (rather than the 'not') and, together with the marginal gloss, establishes a first link between Donne and Jacob, albeit on a somewhat shaky pretext.

Throughout the 1640 *Life*, Walton keeps drawing comparisons between Donne and Jacob, all of which are glossed, and all of which seem strangely laboured.[24] Some of them seem to be tailoring the biblical passages to his needs in order to apply them to Donne's life, while at the same time drawing the reader's attention to the incongruity of the comparison by providing the respective Bible passage in the gloss. Walton's Jacob-analogies merit closer examination, because they form the first instance of his strategy of appropriating quotations and reshaping them into a narrative. This is a particularly Waltonian technique that was to become even more significant for his way of looking at his subject's life as he turned to applying it not only to the Bible but to Donne's own writings, in order to recreate Donne's voice for his readers. The latter is especially prominent in the later versions of the *Life of Donne*, but the germ of this technique, which Walton refined in his later *Lives*, lies in making the marriage episode the starting-point for his narrative of Donne the biblical patriarch in the 1640 *Life of Donne*.[25]

---

23 See also the 1670 *Life* on Donne's dismissal by Egerton, which uses a similar strategy of establishing a parallel by denying it: 'And though the *Lord Chancellor* did not at Mr. *Donnes* dismission, give him such a Commendation as the great Emperour *Charles* the fifth, did of his Secretary *Eraso*, when he presented him to his Son and Successor *Philip* the Second; saying, *That in his* Eraso, *he gave to him a greater gift then all his Estate, and all the Kingdomes which he then resigned to him*: yet he said, He parted with a Friend, and such a Secretary as was fitter to serve a King then a subject' (p. 19).

24 The 1640 *Life* has more references to Jacob than to the two other, more predictable biblical counterparts for Donne, King David (as the first 'religious poet') and St Paul (as the charismatic preacher figure and late convert – a particularly fitting counterpart for the Dean of St Paul's).

25 Philip West notes in his study of biblical references in Henry Vaughan's *Silex Scintillans* (a collection of poetry in imitation of Herbert's *The Temple*) that Jacob is the patriarch who was most closely associated with the Anglican church. See the chapter 'Patriarchs and Pilgrims', in Philip West, *Henry Vaughan's 'Silex Scintillans': Scriptural Uses* (Oxford: Oxford University Press, 2001), pp. 23–62.

The second reference to Jacob occurs when Donne is at last persuaded to take orders. Walton includes a scene in which he attempts to portray Donne's inner conflict through a series of biblical scenes, which he blends together into the imagined voice of Donne's inner monogue:

> And doubtlesse (considering his own demerits) did with meek *Moses* humbly aske God, *Who am I?* [...] But God who is able to prevaile, wrastled with him, as the Angel did with *Iacob*, and marked him for his owne, marked him with a blessing [...]; And then as he had formerly asked God humbly with *Moses*, *Who am I?* So now (being inspired with the apprehension of Gods mercies) he did ask King *Davids* thankfull question, *Lord who am I that thou art so mindfull of me?* So mindfull of me as to move the learnedst of Kings to descend to move me to serve at thine Altar? So merciful to me as to move my heart to embrace this holy motion? Thy motions I will embrace, take the cup of salvation, call upon thy Name, and preach thy Gospell. (B1ᵇ)

Walton might have added a number of glosses to this passage, ranging from Exodus 3 (the story of the burning bush) to Psalm 8, or indeed Donne's sermons which repeatedly refer to the 'Who am I?' motif. However, the only gloss is 'Gen. 32.', highlighting the somewhat incongruous comparison between Donne's inner struggle and Jacob's fight with the angel. In the biblical version of the story, Jacob prevails and gains the blessing as a reward. In Walton's version, however, God (through his representative, James I) prevails over Donne's doubts, so if Donne is to be seen as Jacob it is really his defeat that proves to be the blessing. Walton is consequently changing the outcome of the biblical wrestling match by allowing his 'Jacob' to lose, while still insisting on an analogy.

At other points, Walton himself weakens his comparison between Jacob and Donne, either by qualifying it or by providing the biblical context of a passage that evidently does not suit the context in which he is quoting it. For example, Walton notes that Donne's friends welcomed his going on the diplomatic mission to Germany shortly after his wife's death, because they had 'feared his studies, and sadnesse for his wives death, would as *Iacob* says, *make his dayes few*, and (respecting his bodily health) *evill too*' (B2ᵇ, glossed 'Gen. 47.'). In fact, Jacob says nothing of the sort. In the passage alluded to, the elderly Jacob, after being asked his age, tells the Pharaoh that his days *have been* short and evil. There is of course no mention of excessive study or the death of either of his wives as the suggested cause of this, nor is there any indication that the 'evil' is referring to Jacob's health, as Walton's added parenthesis implies.[26] Similarly, after Donne's appointment as Dean of St Paul's, Walton has him decline his father-in-law's quarterly allowance, saying:

---

26 Since it is crucial to the context of the line that Jacob has in fact reached a ripe old age (130 years), it is traditionally read as a comment referring to the fleeting nature of mortal life. See Donne's funeral sermon for Lady Danvers (George Herbert's mother): '*God* cals vpon man, euen in the consideration of the name of *God*, to consider his *future state.* [...] *God* hath beene *God*, as many millions of millions of generations, already, as hee shall be hereafter; but if we consider *man* in the *present*, to day, now, how short a *forenoone* hath any man had; if 60. if 80. yeeres, yet *few and euill haue his daies beene.*' John Donne, *A Sermon of Commemoration of the Lady Danvers* (1627), pp. 75–6.

(as good *Iacob* said when he heard *Ioseph* his sonne lived) *It is enough*, you have been
kinde to me and carefull of mine, I am, I thanke my God, provided for, and will receive
this money no longer. (B3ᵃ, glossed 'Gen. 45.')

Here it is Walton's own mention of the quotation's original context that draws
attention to the fact that it bears no relation to the situation he is describing. Jacob's
gratefulness at the unexpected news that his son is alive is clearly very different from
Donne's gratefulness for his father-in-law's financial support. Again, Walton seems
to be deliberately directing attention to the flaw in the analogy, but he is nevertheless
intent on drawing it.

The episode of Donne's marriage, then, acts as the starting-point for a whole series
of comparisons between Donne and Jacob. Walton's references to those passages and
his attempts to present them as particularly relevant to crucial moments in Donne's
life mark the beginning of his move towards narrative, and away from an antiquarian
collation of biographical and bibliographical facts, which characterises early prefatory lives. The two aspects that most gain in importance in Walton's revisions of
the 1640 *Life of Donne* are the role of narrative, and Donne's writings as a source of
information about his state of mind at certain points of his life. I shall return to these
two aspects in both this and the next section of this chapter.

The Jacob analogies might be best read as a not entirely successful attempt by
Walton to shape the structure of his narrative in an extension of the traditional
method of figural reading.[27] This second structuring device in the 1640 *Life of Donne*
is also first introduced in the marriage episode, in Sir George More's seemingly pro-
phetic praise of Donne as a 'Secretary fitter for a King then a Subject'. The narrative
of Donne's special relationship with another 'Jacob', who acted as a patron to Donne
and promoted his clerical career, is far more prominent in the 1640 *Life of Donne*
than it is in any of the later versions. This can be explained partly through its structuring function and partly through the context in which the first version of the *Life
of Donne* was published.

LXXX Sermons does not immediately begin with Walton's *Life* but with the dedication to Charles I by John Donne the younger. Donne Junior refers to the volume
as 'some Monument', not just to his father, the author of the sermons, but also to
Charles's father, the late James I. Throughout the text, the younger Donne stresses the
impact that James had on the life and works of his father, to the point of almost giving
James full credit for the sermons themselves. His main aim in writing the dedication
seems to be to prove his own royalist credentials and his loyalty towards Charles I by
presenting his father's sermons as essentially the product of royalist sentiments:

In this rumor of Warre I am bold to present to your sacred Majestie the fruits of Peace,
first planted by the hand of your most Royal Father, then ripened by the same gracious
influence, and since no lesse cherisht and protected by your Majesties especiall favour

---

27 Erich Auerbach's famous definition of this method of Bible reading is: 'Figural interpretation estab-
   lishes a connection between two events or persons, the first of which signifies not only itself but also the
   second, while the second encompasses or fulfills the first.' Erich Auerbach, 'Figura' in *Scenes from the
   Drama of European Literature* (New York: Meridian Books, 1959), pp. 11–76 (p. 53). Thus the figure of
   Dr Donne pervades the 1640 *Life* even during passages that strictly describe stages in the life of Master
   Donne.

vouchsafed to the Author in so many indulgent testimonies of your good acceptance of his service. (A3ᵃ)[28]

The younger Donne's gardening imagery in the first sentence of his dedicatory epistle so firmly attributes all the credit to James (and, to a lesser extent, Charles) that readers may be forgiven for wondering whether Donne was even involved in the process. The 'fruits of Peace' are anything but the fruits of Donne's labour. It is James who plants the seeds and makes the fruit ripen under his care. Even the soil of peace in which the fruits grow is clearly of James's making, in allusion to James's motto, *Beati Pacifici* ('blessed are the peace-makers').[29] Donne, on the other hand, becomes merged into his works as part of the 'fruits'.

John Donne the younger's curious strategy of praising 'the Author' in a manner that effectively dissolves his identity is continued in his avoiding to mention his father's name. It is of course clear from the context that 'that learned and reverend divine, Iohn Donne' of the title page is likely to be related to 'your Majesties most humble and most dutifull Subject, Jo: Donne' who signs the dedicatory epistle. Nevertheless, in the epistle the younger Donne only refers to his father as 'the Author' without even claiming personal acquaintance, let alone kinship.

To some extent, the younger Donne's failure to acknowledge his father may simply be due to modesty: he is acting as his father's executor and is consequently at pains to show he does not intend to take credit for works that are not his own. However, it is also part of an orchestrated bid for patronage. By stressing the close association between the author of the sermons and the late king, the dedicatee's father, he is establishing an indirect link between the present king and himself, turning *LXXX Sermons* into a joint monument set up by the sons to commemorate the fathers. At the same time, he is subtly hinting at the possibility of a similarly close patronage relationship between the sons in the future. In this context, actually using the phrase 'my father' may have appeared an unsubtle turn of phrase and transformed a tentative bid for patronage into a demand.

Additionally, the exaggerated emphasis the dedicatory epistle places on James's 'coauthorship' of Donne's works introduces a theme that reappears in Izaak Walton's *Life of Donne*, which follows directly after the dedication. James figures at several crucial moments in Walton's account: first he encourages Donne to write his *Pseudo-Martyr* and subsequently predicts him a brilliant career in the church, while at the same time actively preventing him from having any other career. Then he 'recommend[s] him to be made Doctor in Divinity' (and the University of Cambridge is happy to oblige). Later, he sends Donne to Germany in a delegation in order to restore his mental health after the death of his wife and grants him his wish of a position in London by appointing him Dean of St Paul's over dinner. Finally, following a

---

28 See also the Latin epitaph facing the first page of the table of contents (incorporated by Walton into the *Life* proper in later editions). This epitaph stresses that Donne took up orders not only 'instinctu et impulsu spir: Sᵗⁱ', but also 'monitu et hortatu Regis Iacobi'. The words 'Regis Iacobi' are printed in the same large font size as 'Iohannes Donne' (Cᵇ).

29 See Walton, *Life of Donne* (1640), 'King *Iames*, whose Motto, *Beati Pacifici*, did truly characterize his disposition, endeavoured to compose the differences of [Germany]' (B2ᵇ).

misunderstanding concerning Donne's loyalty, James makes a public declaration of his pleasure in 'making him a Divine'.

Although James's involvement in Donne's clerical career was indeed unusual, Walton's highly personalised anecdotes about it are either deliberate misreadings or adaptations of existing anecdotes.[30] For example, R. C. Bald has pointed out that the misunderstanding due to which Donne was temporarily 'clouded with the Kings displeasure' is more likely to have occurred in 1627, which would make it the displeasure of Charles I.[31] Bald has also questioned the authenticity of the other anecdotes involving James in the 1640 *Life of Donne*. However, the main interest of those anecdotes lies not in the stories they tell, but in the question of why Walton chose to include them and what part they perform within the text. At one level, his depiction of James as the driving force behind Donne's career is of course intended to flatter (whether to flatter the King or Donne is a matter of perspective). Yet it also has a clear function within the 1640 *Life of Donne*. Walton is using the anecdotes about Donne's personalised patronage-relationship with the king as a substitute for Donne's *vita activa*, which is otherwise absent from the *Life*. Thus he renders the most public aspect of Donne's life personal, almost private. Walton even goes as far as to write five years of Charles I's reign – corresponding to most of the period during which Walton himself was Donne's parishioner – out of Donne's *Life*, in order to stress the personal aspect of Donne's loyalty as James's subject.

A particularly interesting episode in terms of Walton's privatisation of the patronage-relationship is Donne's justification after briefly falling out of favour. It begins as a highly formal situation, with James sending for him and 'requiring his answer to the accusation' but ends with Donne having a curiously private moment with the king, who 'with his own hand did, or offered to raise him from his knees' before calling in his lords and declaring that '*My Doctor is an honest man*'. It is the uncertainty about whether James really did raise the kneeling Donne that turns a formal gesture into a private one, since it implies that there was no-one else present to relate the story exactly and this was a moment shared only by Donne and the King. In the later editions, in which the patronage-relationship with James figures less prominently as a structuring device, this ambiguity disappears.

As a structuring device, the patronage-relationship with James told in anecdotes is more successful than its counterpart, the figural association of Donne with Jacob. One of the reasons for this is that it adds a personalised, private dimension to Donne's life. Yet this too has its limitations, as it can only be related to Donne's career as Dean of St Paul's, which according to Walton's reading is only one aspect of Donne's exemplarity. This may explain why, in his revisions, he increasingly turned away from those more established models for structuring a written life and began to develop his own, which allowed him to explore Donne's inner life as well as his clerical career.

30 Peter McCullough notes in his essay 'Donne and Court Chaplaincy' that 'the effort that James put into creating Donne [royal chaplain and doctor of divinity], and in such rapid succession, is without precedent in the period as an example of royal promotion of a clerical career. [...] Donne went from laity to clergy, from no degree to doctorate, from unemployment to royal chaplaincy, in no more than a few weeks'. *Oxford Handbook of John Donne*, pp. 558–9.
31 Bald, 'Historical Doubts Respecting Walton's *Life of Donne*', pp. 73–6.

In the following section, I shall outline the origins of Walton's idea of a private life, before examining how Walton used Donne's works as sources for his inner life by trying to derive a personal voice from them.

Walton and the 'private' life

Walton differs from other early modern biographers in two crucial points. The first of these is his creation of a biographer-figure who is noticeable, precisely because he is ostensibly at pains to remain unobtrusive. The second is his unusual social and educational background. In *Walton's Lives*, Jessica Martin observes that Walton's approach to clerical biography owes much to the fact that he was a layman himself. Additionally, Walton is perhaps the first early modern biographer who was not university educated. In the preface to his 1640 *Life of Donne*, Walton voices his own doubts concerning his suitability for the task, pre-empting similar doubts on his readers' part. He does so by echoing an episode from Plutarch's 'Life of Pompey', casting himself in the role of the 'poore Bondman' and self-consciously expressing an awareness of his comparative lack of classical humanist education through an allusion to a classical text – in English translation:[32]

> If I be demanded, as once *Pompeys* poore Bondman was, (whilest he was alone on the Sea shore gathering the pieces of an old Boat to burne the body of his dead Master) What art thou that preparest the funeralls of *Pompey* the great? Who I am that so officiously set the Authors memorie on fire? I hope the question hath in it more of wonder then disdaine.
> Wonder indeed the Reader may. (A5ᵃ)

It would be wrong to take Walton's self-deprecation entirely at face value. To some extent, his repeated professions of unworthiness and simplicity are merely a rhetorical device. They serve to elevate his subject even further, and act as an ingenious way of claiming truthfulness without appearing boastful, 'for he that wants skill to deceive, may safely be trusted' (A5ᵃ), while also strategically lowering readers' expectations, making it easier for Walton to exceed them. Yet it would be equally wrong to regard this episode merely as a modesty topos. In order to understand Walton's uniqueness as a biographer, it is important to bear in mind that Walton's expectation to be met with doubt and 'wonder' by his contemporary readers was justified.

In a sense, his 1640 *Life of Donne* was creating a precedent. Most early lives in English were not only written about subjects who had led public, 'active' lives (and had had the education to go with it), they were also written by people who moved within the same sphere as their subjects. William Roper, author of the *Life of Syr Thomas More* was More's son-in-law and had been 'continually resident in his House for the space of sixteene yeares and more'.[33] Like his father-in-law, Roper had been educated at university and had later trained as a lawyer at Lincoln's Inn. Fulke Greville, though

---

32 The question asked of the bondsman is taken almost verbatim from Thomas North's 1579 translation.
33 William Roper, *The Life of Syr Thomas More Knight* (Paris, 1626), *4ᵇ. See also Hugh Trevor-Roper, 'Roper, William (1495 × 8–1578)', *Oxford DNB*.

not related to Sidney, had known him since childhood. They had received a similar education and both had tried – and failed – to secure a career at court.

Walton, by contrast, was the son of a tippler, trained as a draper after having finished his formal education at the age of sixteen and seems to have ended up associating with poets and divines almost by accident.[34] Anthony Wood dedicates a short passage in *Athenae Oxonienses* (1691) to Walton, drawing his readers' attention to the discrepancy between Walton's own background and that of the people he associated with:

> *Isaac Walton*, of whom I desire the Reader to know, that he was born in the ancient Borough of *Stafford* in *Aug.* 1593. that he was by Trade a Sempster in *Chancery-lane* in *London*, where continuing till about 1643. (at which time he found it dangerous for honest men to be there) he left that city and lived sometimes in *Stafford*, and elsewhere but mostly in the Families of the eminent clergy-men of *England*, of whom he was much beloved. He hath written the lives of Dr. *Joh. Donne*, Sir *Hen. Wotton*, Mr. *Rich. Hooker*, Mr. *George Herbert*, and of Dr. *Rob. Sanderson* sometime B. of *Lincoln*: All of which are well done considering the education of the author; as also *The compleat Angler, or the contemplative Man's recreation*, &c.[35]

Wood's assessment of Walton may be taken either as thinly veiled snobbery or a response which 'hath in it more of wonder then disdaine'. Jessica Martin favours the former reading, calling Wood's 'the first of many class-governed judgements [...] masquerading as critical assessment'.[36] However, regardless of any class-conscious undertones, the passage from *Athenae Oxonienses* above all shows one thing: that Wood found Walton's background a remarkable enough fact to record it in a context in which it was not strictly necessary to mention Walton at all. In a biographical compilation, whose subjects are linked through their educational background (i.e. their association with the University of Oxford), the inclusion of any biographical information on Walton, who evidently did not share that background, is surprising.[37] Thus the most significant point about the passage is not Wood's mildly patronising tone when he writes about Walton's education, but the fact that Wood chose to write about Walton in the first place – with more wonder than disdain.

The fact that Walton's background was so remarkable to his contemporaries matters in this context because, as Martin has noted, it is one of the reasons he was forced to develop his own approach to life-writing. Henry Wotton, who had initially been asked to write the prefatory life to Donne's *LXXX Sermons* would have been a much more obvious choice of biographer than Walton, who only took over the task when Wotton died shortly after agreeing to write the life. As Walton remarks in his preface, 'it was a Work worthy [Wotton's] undertaking, and he fit to undertake it; betwixt whom and our Author, there was such a friendship contracted in their

---

34 Jessica Martin, 'Walton, Izaak (1593–1683)', *Oxford DNB*. Of course, the fact that he attended school until the age of sixteen still meant that Walton had an above-average level of education among his contemporaries.

35 Anthony Wood, *Athenae Oxonienses* (1691), pp. 264–5.

36 Martin, *Walton's Lives*, p. 300.

37 The passage occurs at the end of the section on Richard Hooker, where it follows a description of Hooker's monument, on which the portrait reproduced in Walton's 1665 *Life of Hooker* was based.

youths, that nothing but death could force the separation' (A5ª). As well as having been a close friend of Donne, Wotton had had a similar education (they were contemporaries at Oxford) and had afterwards gone on to have the kind of diplomatic career that Donne may have aspired to during his youth.[38] Finally, Wotton – like Donne – was an ordained minister, and thus had the religious authority and theological background to write an author's life to be prefixed to a collection of sermons.[39]

Walton would not have been able to write the kind of author's life that Wotton might have written, and he said as much in his preface. As a result, he gradually turned away from the *vita activa*, and was forced to develop a new approach, which involved crafting a narrative of his subject's inner, personal life. Walton's concept of a 'private' life, which became more pronounced through the Civil War and the restrictions it imposed on Anglicans, is closely linked to his idea of personal faith.[40] This idea can of course be found in *The Compleat Angler*'s presentation of angling as a contemplative art and a form of private worship, epitomised in its motto from 1 Thessalonians: 'Study to be quiet, and to do your own business'. The passage that best summarises Walton's idea of the private life, however, can be found in a relatively unknown pamphlet called *Love and Truth*, published anonymously in 1680.[41] *Love and Truth*, the most political of Walton's writings, consists of two letters, allegedly written by a 'quiet and conformable citizen of London, to two busie and factious shop-keepers of Coventry'. Throughout the pamphlet, the letter-writer 'R. W.' is admonishing the seditious shopkeepers, highlighting the harm that one person's 'sin of *Schism* or *sedition*' (p. 5) will bring to other people. 'R. W.' himself advocates conformism and encourages the shopkeepers to adopt a new motto: 'study to be quiet, and to do your own business'.[42] In one particularly interesting passage, 'R. W.' speaks out vehemently against 'extempory Prayer' in public, as practised by nonconformist minister Hugh Peters during the Civil War, countering it with a description of what prayer ought to be like:

> God forbid, that private Christians should be so tied to set Forms of Prayer, as not in their retired and private devotions to make their private Confession of their private sins to the searcher of all hearts: and beg their pardon of him and pray extempore for such a measure of his assisting grace so to strengthen them, that they may never relapse into those, or the like sins: This doubtless is to honour and to serve God, but this is but to honour and serve him privately: And if I be mistaken in my private Prayers my mistakes

38 For the educational similarities between Wotton and Donne, see Alexandra Gajda's essay 'Education as a Courtier', in *Oxford Handbook of John Donne*, pp. 395–407, which mainly focuses on examining the impact of Donne's Catholicism on his education yet notes that in many ways, Donne's educational journey 'mirrors the experience of Wotton, or the Bacon brothers' (p. 407).

39 For a more detailed overview of Wotton's life, see A. J. Loomie, 'Wotton, Sir Henry (1568–1639)', *Oxford DNB*.

40 See Jonquil Bevan's *Izaak Walton's 'The Compleat Angler': The Art of Recreation* (Brighton: Harvester, 1988). Bevan proposes that *The Compleat Angler* was written partly as a book of consolation for his Anglican clergy friends who had been forced into – inner or actual – exile during the Commonwealth, by conveying their shared values via the angling narrative, as well as using the pun on angler / Anglican and stressing the parallels to early Christianity through the apostles who were fishermen by profession.

41 The attribution to Walton is based on parallel passages in Walton's other writings and annotations by William Sancroft, one of Donne's successors as Dean of St Paul's and later Archbishop of Canterbury.

42 The phrase is repeated four times in the pamphlet.

concern only my self and end there. But it is not so in your *Publick extemporary Prayers*, the mischief is not ended when the Prayers are.[43]

This passage from *Love and Truth* illustrates how essential an inner, 'private' self is to Walton's idea of the contemplative life led by those who practice the 'primitive piety' he considers the ideal form of worship. His *Lives* too are modelled on this ideal of 'primitive piety', and aim to present their subjects as exemplary in terms of their faith. This private dimension of 'primitive piety', then, may explain why, when forced to explore new ways of approaching Donne's life, Walton became so interested in Donne's personal voice.

Walton's aim is to present Donne's personal life not so much in a domestic as in a spiritual sense. This focus on spiritual life and private faith is another point in which Walton's approach to his subject radically differs from earlier prefatory lives. It is particularly visible in Walton's reading of Donne's works as sources and his attempts to discover the personal voice of Donne in his poetic voice. He then aims to recover this voice by means of a curious ventriloquising technique that he perfected over the course of his revisions.

The 1640 *Life of Donne* is the version in which Donne's works, specifically his poetic works, figure least prominently, but Walton's interest in them is already discernible. In his later revisions of the *Life*, particularly the 1658 version, which contains the most significant additions, this is one of the aspects that change most, and each version contains more references to Donne's works than the previous one.

One of the expanded passages in the 1658 *Life of Donne* which indicate an increased interest in Donne's writing on Walton's part is the section concerning the 'Hymne to God the Father', as an example of Donne's 'heavenly Poetry'. Whereas the 1640 *Life* only briefly states the circumstances of the *Hymne*'s composition (claiming that it was written during Donne's serious illness), the 1658 version belatedly provides a reason for its inclusion:

I have the rather mentioned this *Hymne*, for that he caus'd it to be set to a most grave and solemn tune, and to be often sung to the *Organ* by the *Choristers* of that *Church*, in his own hearing, especially at the Evening Service. (pp. 77–8)

Walton's explanation for the inclusion of the *Hymne* is peculiar, because in a sense his anecdote raises more questions than it answers. For example, why does Walton provide no explanation for dedicating almost an entire page in the *Life* to a poem that is not overtly autobiographical? One might have expected Walton to give some justification for his decision to use a poem to illustrate how Donne was affected by his illness. However, his use of 'the rather' in the passage cited above, suggests that these are merely his reasons for mentioning this particular hymn, not an explanation as to why he is discussing a religious poem in this context. Walton appears to consider the information that the 'Hymne to God the Father' was composed 'on [Donne's] former sick bed' sufficient to justify his reading of it as evidence of 'the great joy that then possest his soul' (p. 76). The phrase 'possest his soul', added in the 1658 version,

---

43 Izaak Walton, *Love and truth in two modest and peaceable letters concerning the distempers of the present times* (1680), p. 35.

creates a closer analogy to the description of Donne's *Devotions*, as a manifestation of 'the most secret thoughts that then possess his soul' (see above), which could be read as evidence that Walton's interest in reading the poem biographically has increased. From this passage, then, it seems that in 1658 Walton already perceives no need to defend the principle of treating Donne's poetry as a valid source for his *Life*. Instead, he merely highlights the particular relevance of a specific poem for the life of its author to explain the reasons for its selection.

The second question raised by Walton's anecdote about the *Hymne to God the Father* concerns his motivations for adding it in the 1658 version. If he trusted his readers to understand his reasoning without further explanation in 1640, why not in 1658? One possible reason is suggested by the digressive passage following the anecdote about Donne's hymn. In that passage, Walton likens the hymn to those written by early Christians, as acts of 'primitive piety':

> After this manner did the Disciples of our Saviour, and the best of Christians in those Ages of the Church nearest to his time, offer their praises to the Almighty God. And the reader of St *Augustines* life may there find, that towards his dissolution he wept abundantly, that the enemies of Christianity had broke in upon them, and prophaned and ruin'd their *Sanctuaries*, and because their *Publick Hymns* and Lauds were lost out of their Churches. (pp. 78–9)

The parallel Walton has chosen here is merely a projection, however. Since part of his point is that the early Christians' hymns had already been irretrievably lost in Augustine's time, he cannot know whether those lost hymns were at all similar to the *Hymne to God the Father*. In fact, the early Christian hymns almost serve as a pretext for Walton to mention the 'enemies of Christianity' and the destruction wrought by them. It is therefore possible that one of Walton's reasons for including the anecdote about the hymn was that it allowed him to express his regret at the persecution of early Christians (whom he frequently associates with the more recent suppression of Anglicanism) through the tears of Augustine.[44]

Yet above all, Walton uses the anecdote to strengthen his biographical reading of Donne's *Hymne*. One important function of the story is to show Donne's life as a poet blending seamlessly into his life as a divine. He is portrayed making arrangements to have his poem turned into a church hymn, by having it set to music and sung at the evening service in his church. The anecdote also describes the hymn's progress from a personal experience of God's grace to poetry, and finally a shared expression of praise (which simultaneously creates a heightened personal experience of God's grace for the poet). This is achieved through the unusual device of letting Donne himself offer a biographical reading of his hymn:

> [He] did occasionally say to a friend, *The words of this Hymne have restored to me the same thoughts of joy that possess my soul in my sicknesse when I composed it. And, Oh the power of Church-musick! that Harmony added to it has raised the affections of my heart,*

---

44 See Novarr, *The Making of Walton's 'Lives'*, p. 95. Novarr reads the incomplete sentence 'But now oh Lord –', which concludes the passage in the 1658 version, as a politically charged comment expressing oblique criticism of the Puritans. See also Bevan's reading of *The Compleat Angler* as a text that explores this topic.

and quickned my graces of zeal and gratitude; and I observe, *that I alwaies return from paying this publick duty of* Prayer *and* Praise *to* God *with an unexpressible tranquillity of mind*, and a willingnesse to *leave the world*. (p. 78)

This passage illustrates Walton's ventriloquising technique particularly well: it appears to be a coherent speech that confirms Walton's portrait of Donne, yet there are several indications that the speech is Walton's rather than Donne's. The first of these is his vagueness regarding the situation in which Donne is supposed to have spoken those words. Donne is not only shown addressing an unspecified friend, even Walton's carefully chosen word 'occasionally' is ambiguous. It may equally refer to one particular occasion (implying that what follows are Donne's exact words) or a number of different occasions (implying that it is a paraphrase of what Donne said on several occasions, to several people, which would make it an imitation of Donne's speech).[45]

The second indication that Walton is attempting to recreate Donne's voice rather than quoting him is the lack of italics in the phrase 'and I observe'.[46] Logically, the phrase should be part of Donne's speech, and as there is no reason to suspect a deliberate emphasis here, it should consequently be italicised along with the rest of the passage. The lack of italics, however, creates the impression of Walton speaking and attempting to link two separate quotations, which are only loosely connected via the theme of church music. This reading is supported by the fact that there is no direct link between Donne's first and second observation. 'This public duty' is unlikely to refer to listening to the choristers' singing. The most logical conclusion from the missing italics and the unclear reference in Donne's second observation would be that Walton merged two different passages or witness accounts into a single speech. His aim may have been to express a point more concisely and present his readers with a speech that was perhaps more 'typical' of Donne than anything he actually said.

There is a similar instance of this ventriloquising technique in one of the few additions of the 1670 version of the *Life of Donne*. Here Walton condenses several letters written by Donne at several points during his life, to create one letter to exemplify Donne's state of mind during his time at Mitcham. Walton does not attempt to conceal the fact that the letter is not a single letter quoted verbatim and introduces this ventriloquised letter (which follows a similarly modified extract introduced as 'an extract collected out of some few of his many Letters') with the words 'Thus he did bemoan himself: And thus in other letters' (both p. 29). Walton concludes: 'By this you have seen a part of the picture of his narrow fortune, and the perplexities of his generous minde' (p. 32), making it clear that he is creating a character sketch from several letters to form a 'picture' rather than simply quoting one example.

The best way of understanding Walton's ventriloquising technique would be in terms of considering Walton as part of a commonplace book culture. Walton's contemporaries were taught that reading ideally involved both meticulous note-taking and the identification of universally applicable 'sentences' or aphorisms to be grouped

---

45 See meanings 2 and 3 in the *OED* entry for 'occasionally', both of which were current in 1658.

46 The peculiar use of italics, which often seems excessive, is a characteristic of Walton's *Lives*; they are consistently used to differentiate between Walton's words and those of his sources.

under thematic headings (or *loci*) in ever-expanding notebooks.[47] Adam Smyth, in his study of early modern commonplace books as a form of autobiography, defines this as 'the sum of expectations, textual practices, and approaches to language that the commonplace book – as theory, process and text – created and encouraged', and outlines its key characteristics.[48] While Smyth's outline of the features of commonplace book culture occurs in the context of his argument that seventeenth-century commonplace books can be read as an early form of autobiography, it also illustrates why it is a useful concept for explaining the technique used by Walton in his *Lives*.[49]

Somewhat paradoxically, the idea of a commonplace book culture is useful for explaining not so much Walton's participation in as his deviation from it. Several of the thought patterns and approaches to topics that Smyth compiles in his list of typical ways in which commonplace-book culture manifested itself can be found in Walton's *Lives*. For example, Walton's aim of moulding all of his subjects into model Anglican clergymen, instead of focusing on what Pritchard would call 'the individuality of his characters', could be regarded as the 'pursuit of similarity more than difference'. The paraphrasing and merging of quotations as part of his ventriloquising technique certainly indicates 'a willingness to rework material; a tendency to cut, add, or alter text'. Similarly, his prefaces and digressions reveal 'self-reflexivity [and] an interest in method'.[50]

Humanist education played a crucial role in the dissemination of commonplace book culture and was instrumental in shaping pupils into future readers and writers.[51] Thus Walton supports his claim that Donne was a diligent student and never wholly lost his way even 'in his most unsetled youth', by pointing to 'the visible fruits of his labours: some of which remain to testifie what is here written: for he left the resultance of 1400 Authors, most of them analyzed with his own hand' (B4[b]). His word choice, especially his use of the words 'resultance' and 'analyzed', indicates that Walton is speaking of a collection of commonplace-book-like excerpts rather than 1,400 complete volumes with annotations. This becomes even clearer in the 1658 version, in which 'analyzed' is amended to 'abridged and analyzed' (p. 88), placing

---

47 For more detailed accounts of the practice of commonplacing and its different manifestations and implications see Richard Yeo, 'Notebooks as Memory Aids: Precepts and Practices in Early Modern England', in *Memory Studies*, 1 (2008), 115–36 and chapter seven in William Sherman, *Used Books: Marking Readers in Early Modern England* (Philadelphia: University of Pennsylvania Press, 2008), which is dedicated to one of the most prolific commonplace book writers, Sir Julius Caesar.

48 Adam Smyth, *Autobiography in Early Modern England* (Cambridge: Cambridge University Press, 2010), p. 127. Smyth suggests this concept as a way of considering commonplace books in broadly generic terms while accounting for the discrepancy between 'neat' theoretical templates for commonplace books and their often much 'messier' reality (p. 123).

49 See also Jonquil Bevan's observation that in its different editions, *The Compleat Angler* 'develops from an angling manual-cum-pastoral into a kind of prose anthology or commonplace-book'. Izaak Walton, *The Compleat Angler, 1653–1683*, ed. Jonquil Bevan (Oxford: Clarendon Press, 1983), p. 15.

50 Adam Smyth, *Autobiography in Early Modern England*, p. 128-9.

51 See Mary Thomas Crane, *Framing Authority* (Princeton, NJ: Princeton University Press, 1993) and Peter Mack, 'Humanist Rhetoric and Dialectic', in Jill Kraye (ed.), *The Cambridge Companion to Renaissance Humanism* (Cambridge: Cambridge University Press, 1996), pp. 82–99. Crane argues that the practice of using commonplace-books offered an 'influential model for authorial practice' (Crane, *Framing Authority*, p. 3), while Mack suggests that the extensive use of commonplace-books in classrooms helped to shape future reading habits (Mack, 'Humanist Rhetoric', p. 90).

Donne firmly within an educational context in which meticulous note-taking and the subsequent thematic organisation of knowledge formed an integral part of the process of reading, as well as composition. In Walton himself, however, commonplace-book culture does not appear to be as deeply ingrained as in his university-educated contemporaries.[52] He is not writing in an aphorism-based commonplace-book style and in several points, especially concerning his use of quotation, he seems almost diametrically opposed to the criteria outlined by Smyth.

Walton's deviation from the standard of commonplace-book culture is particularly apparent in his approach to Donne's writings, which does not suggest that he is working with an 'idea of literary creativity resistant to post-nineteenth-century expectations of "self-expression" [and] "voice"' – or at least not as much as we might expect from a writer born towards the end of Elizabeth's reign.[53] In fact, Walton's reading of Donne's works hardly resembles a commonplace-book writer's mining of a text for memorable, reusable aphorisms. Instead, it rests on the assumption that literary expression is a form of personal expression and that Donne's 'voice' is consequently discernible in his poetry. In making this assumption, Walton differs radically from his predecessors in his use of quotation. Texts such as Abraham Fraunce's *Arcadian Rhetorike* (1588), Francis Meres' *Palladis Tamia* (1598), Robert Allot's *Englands Parnassus* (1600) or John Bodenham's *Englands Helicon* (1600) make ample use of literary quotation. However, those quotations function as decontextualised aphorisms and examples of poetic style (or, in the case of *Arcadian Rhetorike* as examples of various rhetorical devices), not as a reflection on the poet's person or thought processes. While this may to some extent be expected from compilations that imitate commonplace-books in terms of structure, even William Drummond's records of Jonsonian aphorisms, which are all from a single source, arguably fall into the same category.[54] Drummond records Jonson's comments about various fellow writers and their works, and even quotes a poem in full, but there is no sense that the witticisms are intended to add up to Jonson's 'voice' or offer the reader – or indeed Drummond himself – access to his thoughts. They are merely a collection of quotable, aphoristic snippets that show off Jonson's knowledge and wit (which is presumably the effect Jonson himself intended).

To his seventeenth-century readership, Walton's *Life of Donne* thus offered an approach that was familiar in principle, yet innovative in its application, which may

---

52 A particularly remarkable example for this ingraining of commonplace-book culture through education is Walter Bagot (1557–1623), a county official in Staffordshire and recipient of several hundred letters now held at the Folger Shakespeare Library, some of which he endorsed with aphoristic quotes from the classics. Walter Bagot had most likely not distinguished himself as a scholar – his quotes from Ovid in particular contain a number of obvious mistakes – and does not appear to have thought very much about the original context of the lines he was quoting or cared about them as poetry. This makes it all the more interesting that he nevertheless chose to reach for those half-remembered lines several decades later, as a way of sarcastically commenting on yet another letter from his demanding brother-in-law. For a more detailed account of Bagot's aphoristic endorsements, see the blog article 'Aphorism therapy, or, How to cope with dishonest relatives' by Heather Wolfe, the Folger Library's curator of manuscripts (*The Collation*, 21 March, 2014).

53 Smyth, *Autobiography in Early Modern England*, p. 128.

54 Those notes, originally written by Drummond in 1619, survived only via a later transcript. This was subsequently edited for the Shakespeare Society as *Conversations with William Drummond* in 1842.

go some way towards explaining Walton's instant success as a biographer. He uses excerpts from Donne's works and letters not for their aphoristic value but in order to ventriloquise Donne's voice. In order to achieve this, rather than decontextualising the passages he quotes and making them more universally applicable, Walton is keen to contextualise them and highlight their specific application to Donne's life (which accounts for some of his factual errors).

The purpose of Walton's ventriloquising the voice of Donne is, to borrow the terminology of *The Compleat Angler*, the re-creation of the contemplative man. His technique of creating his subject's voice through quotation from several works is remarkable, not only because it was an innovative approach and had a significant impact on his life-writing contemporaries and successors.[55] In addition to its novelty and influence, Walton's ventriloquising technique reveals his belief in autobiography as the ideal form of life-writing towards which the life-writer should strive. This interest in the autobiographical form is already indicated in the 1640 *Life of Donne*, grows more apparent in the 1658 version and finally culminates in Walton's preface to the collected *Lives* of 1670:

> And now, I wish that as *Josephus* (that learned *Jew*) and others, so these men had also writ their own lives: and since 'tis not the fashion of these times; that their friends would do it for them, before delayes make it too difficult. And I desire this the more: because 'tis an *honour due to the dead*, and *a debt due to those that shall live, and succeed us.*[56]

Walton's unique position when writing the 1640 *Life of Donne*, then, led him to develop a new method of life-writing, which was based on the concept of a 'private' inner life existing beyond the *vita activa*. His ventriloquising technique proved highly influential, especially for writers of poets' Lives, because it offered a way of overcoming the gap between the private life and the *vita activa* by treating poetic works as products of – and sources for – the life.

Walton's use of a sustained biographical reading of Donne's works is his major contribution to the genre of biography. It created a precedent for other biographers, through its way of treating an author's life and works as informing each other. This, in essence, is what a literary biographer aims to do, and Walton should therefore be credited with having (unwittingly) pioneered English literary biography over the course of writing the *Life of Donne*. The following section examines precisely how Walton uses biographical interpretation to tie his narrative together and to blend Dr Donne the divine and John Donne the divine poet into the same person, creating the basis for what Bald termed 'adequate biography'. The final section of this chapter will then focus on the *Life of Herbert*, and propose that the technique that Walton developed over the course of his revisions of the *Life of Donne* enabled him to write the *Life of Herbert* as the life of a poet.

---

55 See for example the Life of Abraham Cowley in Gerard Langbaine's *English Dramatick Poets* (1691), discussed in Chapter 1. Although most of Langbaine's Lives are compiled from earlier compilations, the Life of Cowley is singled out as meriting a special biographical approach – and that approach is Waltonian ventriloquism.

56 Izaak Walton, *The lives of Dr. John Donne, Sir Henry Wotton, Mr. Richard Hooker, Mr. George Herbert* (1670), 'Epistle to the Reader', A5b.

'In which the reader may see the most secret thoughts': paraphrase and biographical readings in the *Life of Donne*

In the absence of an autobiography by Donne, Walton in the 1640 *Life of Donne* at first turns to the most overtly autobiographical passages in the preface of *Pseudo-Martyr*, and he is keen to signal to his readers that he is quoting, by putting the passage in italics and adding '(they be his owne words)' (A6ᵃ). 'His owne words' should not be taken to mean verbatim quotation, however. In fact, it is the first instance of Walton's ventriloquising technique – and one of the rare occasions on which he appears to disguise the fact that he is paraphrasing, or at least rearranging Donne's 'owne words' into new sentences.

Yet the question of whether Walton is quoting Donne (or trying to suggest that he is) is perhaps less important than the significance that he attributes to his recreation of Donne's voice speaking about his own life. This can be seen from the fact that although Walton modifies and rearranges this passage slightly in later version, the phrase 'they be his owne words' remains unchanged. The paraphrased passage itself, which refers to Donne's spiritual 'search' has evidently been chosen as a substitute for an account of Donne's conversion to Anglicanism, perhaps because Walton was unable to find any evidence regarding how and when it took place.[57]

What may initially just have been a device to cover Walton's own vagueness about the exact circumstances of an important event in Donne's life by letting his subject speak for himself, later became a significant aspect of the *Life*, however, as it forms the starting-point of Walton's biographical readings of Donne's works. In the later versions of the *Life*, Walton resorts more and more frequently to Donne's writings as evidence for his state of mind at the time of writing, using them as sources for, as well as citing them in support of, his account of Donne's life.[58] This attempt to link the author's life and works is something that does not strike us as particularly remarkable today. However, a comparison with Fulke Greville's *Life of Sidney*, which only precedes the first version of Walton's *Life of Donne* by one generation, shows that this was not common practice during the first half of the seventeenth century. Greville had vehemently denied any meaningful links between Sidney's life and Sidney's works, but for Walton there seems to be little doubt that there is a link between the life and works of Donne.

The differences betweeen the 1640 and the 1658 versions of the *Life of Donne* are mainly linked to added material, which frequently results in changes of

---

57 Walton was not the only biographer of Donne to find Donne's conversion an unexpectedly tricky issue. Brian Cummings notes that although the narrative of Donne's conversion has held a persistent appeal for biographers, they have all 'hunted in vain for definitive signs for [it]'. Cummings also points out that readings that profess to see it reflected in his works (such as the *Holy Sonnets*) will not bear closer scrutiny. Brian Cummings, *The Literary Culture of the Reformation: Grammar and Grace* (Oxford: Oxford University Press, 2002), p. 384.

58 This includes a peculiar reference to *Biathanatos*, which uses the text to establish Donne's legal credentials by calling it a 'laborious Treatise concerning Self-murther [...], wherein all the Lawes violated by that act, are diligently survayed, and judiciously censured' (B4ᵇ). This is usually read as an attempt to gloss over a text that might otherwise have been regarded as an inappropriate work for the Dean of St Paul's, although it could also be read as an attempt to find a text to associate with the period of Donne's legal training.

emphasis.[59] One aspect that gains in prominence in the 1658 edition is the role of Donne's works within the *Life*. Several of the expanded and added passages refer to Donne's writings and are concerned with linking them to particular episodes in his life. One example that illustrates Walton's closer engagement with Donne's works in the 1658 *Life* particularly well is a passage concerning the publication of Donne's *Devotions*, after his recovery from a serious bout of illness. In the 1640 version, this passage reads:

> As his health increased, so did his thankfulnesse, testified in his booke of Devotions, A book that may not unfitly be called *A composition of holy Extasies*, occasioned and applicable to the Emergencies of that sicknesse, which booke (being Meditations in his sicknesse) he writ on his sicke bed; herein imitating the holy Patriarchs, who were wont in that place to build their Altars where they had received their blessing. (B3ᵇ)

In this version, Walton mainly seems to refer to the *Devotions* in order to liken Donne to the patriarchs once again: there are glosses to 'Gen. 12.7.8' and 'Gen. 28.18' (Abraham building an altar after arriving in Canaan and Jacob building an altar at Bethel). While the *Devotions* are a form of spiritual autobiography, Walton's use of the phrase 'occasioned and applicable to the Emergencies of that sicknesse' illustrates his attempts to ground them in concrete biographical fact by stressing the moment of composition, and, by extension, to treat them as a potential source of biographical information. Additionally, there are indications that he conflates the confessional 'I' of the *Devotions* with Donne's private voice. In the 1658 version, several lines have been added after the title of the book, so that the passage now reads: 'testified in his *book of Devotions*, which he published at his recovery. In which the reader may see, the most secret thoughts that then possest his soul, Paraphrased and make [*sic*] publick.'[60] Although the connection between Donne's recovery from his illness and the publication of the *Devotions* is of course clear from Donne's introduction, Walton's claim that the *Devotions* contain the author's secret thoughts 'paraphrased and made publick' goes one step further towards biographical interpretation.

Perhaps the most interesting term in this added passage is the word 'paraphrased'. As the *OED* entries for the verb and noun 'paraphrase' show, it is a word that during the mid-seventeenth century was associated both with the idea of clarification and getting closer to the paraphrased original through explanation, and with the idea of moving away from the original by providing an increasingly free rendition of it.[61] The fact that Walton in the 1658 *Life of Donne* regards the *Devotions* as 'secret thoughts [...] paraphrased', then, indicates that he regards the text as a snapshot of Donne's

---

59 The corrections of the 1658 edition are mostly minor, and the account of Donne's early life, that is, up to his marriage, is almost unchanged. Throughout the different editions of the *Life of Donne*, this is the section that changes least.

60 1658 *Life of Donne*, p. 72. The lines that follow it have also been rephrased and expanded from the 1640 version, but the insertion quoted above is the most significant change within the passage.

61 In order to express this apparent contradiction, the first two editions of the *OED* cited Abraham Cowley's note on one of the *Pindaric Odes*, '[It] could not be rendred without much Paraphrase' as evidence of a distinct meaning of the noun 'paraphrase': 'a process or mode of literary treatment'. In the latest version of the dictionary, the same example is included under the main definition, which now reads: 'A rewording of something written or spoken by someone else, esp. with the aim of making the sense clearer; a free rendering of a passage'.

state of mind at a particular moment of his life, as it were. Nevertheless, although those 'secret thoughts' are in slightly fictionalised form, Walton implies that they can be accessed by readers through an act of biographical interpretation in order to get past the 'paraphrase'.

Kate Gartner Frost, in her study of the *Devotions*, has argued that there is a discrepancy between the ways in which the text was read by Donne's contemporaries and by 'modern' readers since the nineteenth century. The latter, Frost claims, were inclined to overlook the *Devotions*' place within a confessional tradition and their function as a devotional text, and instead searched it for evidence of 'Donne's private self'.[62] In particular, she criticises the way in which Sir Edmund Gosse's *Life and Letters of John Donne, Dean of St Paul's* (1899), the most influential Donne biography for most of the twentieth century, mined the *Devotions* for autobiographical information.[63] To an extent, however, Walton defies Frost's division of readers into contemporaries on the one hand and 'modern' readers on the other, by approaching the text in a manner that is not wholly unlike the one she attributes to late nineteenth- and twentieth-century readers.[64] Walton's 1658 *Life of Donne* contained an added passage, which suggests that as he read the *Devotions*, Walton was attempting to strip away the paraphrase in order to get to Donne's 'secret thoughts'. In the passage in question, Walton is ventriloquising Donne's gladness at having found his true calling:

> [A]nd now, such a change was wrought in him, that he could say with David, *Oh how amiable are thy Tabernacles, O Lord God of Hosts!* Now he declared openly, *that when he required a temporal, God gave him a spiritual blessing.* (p. 45)

The source of Donne's 'open declaration' that Walton is paraphrasing here is a passage from the *Devotions*. In this passage, Donne is praising not God but James I, thanking him for the part he played in his ordination by acting as an instrument of divine providence and persuading him to become a minister:

> and I who was sicke before, of a vertiginous giddines, and irresolution, and almost spent all my time in consulting how I should spend it, was by this *man of God*, and *God of men*, put into the poole, and recouerd: when I asked, percha[n]ce, a *stone*, he gaue me *bread*, when I asked, percha[n]ce, a *Scorpion*, he gaue me a *fish*; whe[n] I asked a temporall *office*, hee denied not, refused not that, but let mee see, that hee had rather I took this.[65]

Walton's ventriloquising of this passage, then, reveals his interpretive effort, resulting in his own paraphrase of what he believes to be Donne's thoughts.

In the 1640 *Life*, Walton's digression between Donne's final illness and the account of his death is almost entirely reserved for discussion of his poetry. After returning to Donne's marriage – calling it 'the remarkable error of his life' (B3ᵇ) – Walton

62 Kate Gartner Frost, *Holy Delight: Typology, Numerology, and Autobiography in Donne's 'Devotions Upon Emergent Occasions'* (Princeton, NJ: Princeton University Press, 1990), p. 16.

63 Sir Edmund Gosse, *Life and Letters of John Donne, Dean of St Paul's*, 2 vols (London: W. Heineman, 1899).

64 See also David Novarr's comparison of Walton to Lytton Strachey (*The Making of Walton's 'Lives'*, p. 493).

65 John Donne, *Devotions Vpon Emergent Occasions, and seuerall steps in my Sicknes* (1624), pp. 193–4. The imagery used by Donne is an inversion of Matthew 7.11–12, where it serves as an illustration to the phrase 'ask and it shall be given you', which directly precedes those lines.

moves on to Donne's poetry. Although he initially labels it 'the recreations of his youth', implying another 'remarkable error' (which, unlike his marriage, Dr Donne did regret and feel embarrassed about), Walton is keen to distinguish between the different categories of poetry and to stress that Donne never forsook 'heavenly poetry'. In order to illustrate his point, he then quotes one of Donne's poems, 'A Hymne to God the Father' in full, adding that it was written 'on his former sick bed' (i.e. in 1623) and expresses 'the great joy he then had in the assurance of Gods mercy to him' (all B4ᵃ). In this case, however, the link between the text itself and its biographical context is less evident than with the more overtly autobiographical *Devotions* or the preface of *Pseudo-Martyr*, requiring a greater interpretive effort on Walton's part.

As David Novarr, R. C. Bald and others have observed, Walton's dating of events is often inaccurate, and there are several points at which this can be proven. While this has frequently been regarded as one of his shortcomings as a biographer and as a source of first-hand information about Donne's life, it is important to bear in mind that Walton prioritises narrative over accurate dating. For him, the main function of dates is ancillary and lies in strengthening the narrative by creating a supporting sequence of events, but they do not form the starting-point for his narrative.[66] It is unlikely that he anticipated that his *Lives* might ever be used to confirm the exact time at which events in his subjects' lives took place.

Walton's dating of the 'Hymne to God the Father' may therefore not be correct. In fact, the only other poem mentioned by title in the 1640 *Life of Donne*, 'A Hymne to God my God in my Sickness', which Walton dates to Donne's '[sick-bed] which was his Death-bed' (B4ᵃ) is now generally believed to have been written during Donne's earlier period of sickness, after which he also wrote the *Devotions*. However, while scepticism of Walton's dating of the poems is justified, the crucial point is not so much the question whether he dates them correctly as the fact that he is attempting to date them at all. Walton is trying to associate the hymns, which he probably encountered for the first time when they were published alongside Donne's other poetry in 1633, with particular points in Donne's life, at which he believes Donne may have been in the right frame of mind to voice such thoughts. Walton's (mis)attribution of Donne's two *Hymnes* to his two major periods of illness is therefore a first step towards a biographical reading of his works. It represents the first instance of something that was to increase with every new version of the *Life of Donne*: Walton's attempts to locate the personal voice of his subject in his authorial and poetic voice.

The *Life of Herbert*

The *Life of Herbert* in several ways represents the culmination of Walton's technique of using his subject's works to access his life.[67] Yet the most persuasive reason for regarding the *Life of Herbert* as the culmination of Walton's biographic technique

---

66 Cf. also the seventeenth-century biographical compilers, who privilege the titles of works over dates, or the 1679 'Summary of the Life of Mr. Edmond Spenser' (discussed in the Interlude), which uses only two dates from Spenser's life and gets them both wrong.

67 See Clayton D. Lein, 'Art and Structure', in Walton's *Life of Mr George Herbert*', *University of Toronto Quarterly*, 46 (Winter 1976/7), 162–72, which argues that the *Life of Herbert* is the most tightly

may be that Walton himself thought of it in those terms. In his preface to the 1670 collected *Lives*, Walton briefly looks back on his unexpected career as a biographer, into which he stumbled as others might 'into a *Law-sute*, or a *quarrel*' (A5ᵇ). Among the four *Lives*, he singles out the *Life of Herbert*, devoting nearly as many lines to it as to the other three combined. This is partly to draw attention to the circumstances of publication – the 1670 *Lives* were published shortly after the first edition of the *Life of Herbert*, which left Walton little time for revision.[68] Yet the preface also singles out the *Life of Herbert* as the one among the four that was written entirely out of choice, not because Walton felt (in one way or another) compelled to write it.

It may be wrong to conclude from Walton's description of the *Life of Herbert* as 'writ, chiefly to please my self' (A6ᵃ), that the others were all written chiefly to please others. However, the fact that Walton assigns the special status of a 'free-will offering' which was 'not writ in haste' (A6ᵃ–A6ᵇ) to the *Life of Herbert* indicates that it was the *Life* that presented him with the blankest canvas yet, and that he regarded this as an opportunity. When writing the *Life of Herbert*, Walton was restricted neither by the prefatory format nor by any personal obligations to the subject's memory.[69] This gave him free rein to explore his idea of biography as a portrait of the private life in the subject's own voice, which he had developed over the course of twenty years.

Compared to the *Life of Donne* (both in its earliest version and in its revisions), the *Life of Herbert* shows signs of development in three areas: method, style and content. Whereas the *Life of Donne* contains remnants of structural false starts, as I have discussed above, the *Life of Herbert* is more successfully and more methodically structured. Clayton D. Lein, in his analysis of the structure of the *Life of Herbert*, notes that Walton's 'subtlety of artistic manipulation' is evident in his use of balanced parallel structures.[70] The elements Lein particularly highlights are twofold. First, Walton's portrayal of Puritans and Anglicans as polar opposites (exemplified in the two contrasting figures of Andrew Melville and George Herbert).[71] Second, Lein highlights what he calls the 'two mothers' motif – Walton's strategy of making Herbert's submission to his mother one of the focal points during the first half of the *Life*, while his equal submission to the church plays a similarly prominent part during the second half.[72] Nevertheless, Lein adds, 'the most original creative dimension of

structured and that Walton wrote it 'as if to demonstrate what biography in his hands could now achieve' (p. 162).

68 After the minor revisions for the publication in the 1670 collected *Lives*, the *Life of Herbert* was revised twice more, first for publication in the tenth edition of *The Temple* (1674) and then for the second collection of Walton's *Lives* (1675). However, the changes are less significant than those between the 1640 and the 1658 *Life of Donne*, and they do not substantially affect the structure of the *Life* and the way in which Walton uses Herbert's works. In the present section, the title *Life of Herbert* refers to the first edition, unless otherwise specified, but the points made regarding its structure and technique equally apply to the later versions.

69 The *Life of Herbert* was the first of Walton's *Lives* to be written for separate publication.

70 Lein, 'Art and Structure', p. 162.

71 Some of the inaccuracies in Walton's depiction of Melville (whom he calls 'Melvin' throughout) can be explained through his function as an antagonist to Herbert.

72 Cf. Herbert's poem 'The British Church', which begins with the lines 'I joy, deare Mother, when I view | Thy perfect lineaments, and hue | both sweet and bright'. Helen Wilcox (ed.), *The English Poems of George Herbert* (Cambridge: Cambridge University Press, 2007), p. 390.

the *Life of Herbert* [...] has little to do with balance; instead it lies with Walton's personal response to Herbert'.[73]

Yet Walton's response to Herbert is not purely 'creative'; there is also a marked structural component to it. Partly because he lacked personal acquaintance with his subject, Walton's personal response to Herbert is extrapolated from his response to Herbert's works. He makes extensive use of Herbert's poetry, and assigns to it an even more integral part within his narrative than Donne's poetry had played in the *Life of Donne*. As a result, Herbert's writings in the *Life of Herbert* set a paradigm for Herbert's life and Walton shapes his narrative around various pieces of poetry.

Each significant episode of Herbert's life is associated by Walton with one or more of his poetic works, turning the *Life of Herbert* into a record of a body of works as well as a life. Herbert's Cambridge years and the earliest phase in his writing are represented by the letter and sonnet sent to his mother and his verses in response to Andrew Melville (which are not reproduced but only alluded to). The episode of the anchor poems – a different version of which had already appeared in the 1658 *Life of Donne* – is used to explain the friendship between the two divine poets, which Walton seems to date to some point after Herbert had left Cambridge. The *Temple* poems, particularly 'Affliction I', are used by Walton to illustrate Herbert's spiritual conflict. The verses written on the chimney at Bemerton in conjunction with his prose work *A Priest to the Temple* (1652) represent Herbert's time as an exemplary 'countrey parson'. Finally, 'Sunday' becomes emblematic of Herbert's final days, which, according to Walton, he spent meditating and singing his own hymns and accompanying himself on 'one of his instruments' (p. 77). It is worth noting in this context that Walton persistently refers to *A Priest to the Temple* by its subtitle, *The Countrey Parson*. Both titles were added to the text by Barnabas Oley, a minister who had first edited it as part of *Herbert's Remains* (also 1652), and they are illustrative of two very different readings which the text offers. The archaic-sounding 'A Priest to the Temple' presents the text as a prose counterpart to the views expressed in *The Temple*, whereas 'The Countrey Parson' has rural associations and encourages readers to draw parallels between Herbert's account of the qualities an ideal parson ought to possess and his own life at Bemerton. Walton's decision to use the subtitle rather than the main title reflects his attitude to the text: he is less interested in using *A Priest to the Temple* to explain *The Temple* than in mining it for information about Herbert's life.

In addition to a more adept handling of structuring devices, the *Life of Herbert* also shows an advancement in terms of biographical method in Walton's treatment of his sources. Herbert, as Walton points out in his introduction, was to him 'a stranger as to his person' (p. 12). Possibly as a result of this, Walton appears far more at pains to lay open his sources than in the *Life of Donne*. Although Walton does not use exact citations, he takes care to name all of his major written sources (as well as some of the parishioners whose accounts he cites) within the text. In the case of Herbert's *A Priest to the Temple*, he even names the editor Barnabas Oley, whose 'most conscientious and excellent Preface' (p. 72) he used as one of his sources, as well as the price at which

---

73 Lein, 'Art and Structure', p. 170.

the book can be bought.[74] Walton also adds an appendix of letters written by Herbert to his step-father and by Donne to Herbert's mother, which support his account of Herbert's time at Cambridge and Donne's friendship with Magdalen Herbert.

Yet the fact that he did not know Herbert personally still does not fully explain Walton's eagerness in the *Life of Herbert* to draw attention to the soundness of his methods and to 'assure the Reader, that I have used very great diligence to inform my self, that I might inform him of what follows' (p. 61). After all, the situation of not being able to draw on personal knowledge of his subject was not an altogether unfamiliar one for Walton. Having only known Donne during his final seven years, Walton would already have had to use 'great diligence' to recover the material for most episodes of Donne's life, especially since Wotton, his most obvious source, was no longer available to him. Similarly, Walton had never met Richard Hooker, the subject of his third *Life* – which is hardly surprising, considering that Hooker had died when Walton was just seven years old.[75] In his introduction to the *Life of Hooker* (1665), he had highlighted the methodological difficulties of the task:

> And though I have undertaken it, yet it hath been with some unwillingness; foreseeing that it must prove to me, and especially at this time of my Age, a work of much labour to enquire, consider, re-search, and determine what is needful to be known concerning him. For I knew him not in his Life, and must therefore not onely look back to his Death, now 64 years past; but almost 50 years beyond that, even to his Childhood and Youth, and gather thence such Observations and Prognosticks, as may at least adorn, if not prove necessary for the completing of what I have undertaken.
>
> This trouble I foresee; and foresee also that it is impossible to escape Censures; against which I will not hope my well-meaning and diligence can protect me (for I consider the Age in which I live) and shall therefore but intreat of my Reader a Suspension of them.[76]

The real difference between the earlier lives and the *Life of Herbert* lies not so much in the fact that Walton had to research his account of Herbert's life, but in the confidence with which he handled the task and revealed his sources and methods to his readers. Although in his introduction to the *Life of Hooker*, Walton had presented the passage of time since his subject's death as the main cause for his evident unease, his situation as a biographer forced to 'enquire, consider, re-search' was not so very different when writing the *Life of Herbert* in 1670, thirty-four years after Herbert's death. This time, however, his doubts concerning the feasibility of the task seem to have diminished considerably. In the *Life of Herbert*, Walton demonstrates greater awareness of, and confidence in, his methods for producing a documentary account of his subject's life.

Stylistically, the *Life of Herbert* also shows signs of evolution. Compared to the *Life of Donne*, especially in its earlier forms, it is more unified. This is particularly evident in his treatment of Herbert's poetry. In the 1640 and 1658 *Life of Donne*, Walton treats Donne's poetry almost exclusively during the death-bed digression. In the *Life*

---

74 'A book so full of plain, prudent and useful rules, that, that *Countrey Parson*, that can spare 12 *d*. and yet wants it, is scarce excusable' (pp. 71–2).

75 The first version of the *Life of Hooker* appeared in 1665, placing it between the second version of the *Life of Donne* (1658) and the first version of the *Life of Herbert* (1670).

76 Izaak Walton, *The Life of Mr Rich. Hooker* (1665), pp. 1–2.

of Herbert, however, Herbert's poetry is blended into the account of his life much more seamlessly, and Walton repeatedly cites extracts from *The Temple* as autobiographical texts in order to support his points. For example, the last five stanzas of 'Affliction I' are presented to the reader as evidence of Herbert's inner conflict at a particular moment of his life. After describing Herbert's ill health, his desire to leave Cambridge and his reluctance to 'prove an undutiful Son to so affectionate a Mother' (p. 41), Walton refers his readers to *The Temple*:

> And what I have now said, may partly appear in a Copy of verses in his printed Poems; 'tis one of those that bears [*sic*] the title of *Affliction*: And it appears to be a pious reflection on Gods providence, and some passages of his life. (pp. 41–2)

Although Walton associates 'Affliction I' with a specific phase of Herbert's life, it is worth noting that he does not claim that this was when the poem was written. Instead, his interpretation goes one step further, by implying that the poem echoes Herbert's state of mind during his time of 'affliction' as well as his state of mind during a later point in his life, when he was remembering and reflecting on that time.

Here Walton is clearly identifying individual words and phrases from the poem as potentially applicable to Herbert's situation at Cambridge, such as 'I was intangled in a World of strife, | Before I had the power to change my life', '*Academick* praise' and 'I could not go away, nor persevere'.[77] Partly through his selection of those particular stanzas, Walton is suggesting to his readers that these can be positively identified as references to Herbert's first major spiritual conflict. In doing so, he is not only asserting that Herbert's poetic voice and personal voice are one and the same, he is also using some of Herbert's more ambiguous phrases to blur the distinctions between his physical and spiritual life, as for example in 'thou throwest me | Into more sicknesses'.[78]

The result of Walton's selection of stanzas and the reading that he offers for them is to create a more unified Herbert, who is using the same voice in composing his divine poetry and in speaking of his life. David Novarr lists several passages in which Walton appears to be converting ideas from Herbert's poetry into prose and presenting the result as Herbert's own words, in order to support points which Walton has derived from them. For example, he argues that the passage in which Walton has Herbert compare his wit to '*a Pen-knife in a narrow Sheath, too sharp for his Body*' (p. 41) is 'an obvious reworking of "Affliction IV"', which in turn was one of his sources for Herbert's ill health.[79] Novarr's observation is an important one: first, because it illustrates Walton's use of Herbert's poetry as sources in a circular argument; and second, because it also shows his adoption of a more unified style of writing as he attempts to extract Herbert's voice from works and perhaps even imitate it, in order to write the quasi-autobiographical text he is envisioning in the preface to the 1670 collected *Lives*.[80]

---

77 *Life of Herbert*, p. 42. These correspond to ll. 41–2, 45 and 48 in 'Affliction I' as it appears in *The English Poems of George Herbert*.

78 *Life of Herbert*, p. 43. These correspond to ll. 51–2 of the poem.

79 Novarr, *The Making of Walton's 'Lives'*, p. 333. Novarr also claims to have identified direct borrowings from 'Content', 'The Pearl', 'The Odour' and 'The Priesthood' in the *Life of Herbert*.

80 See, for example, the phrase 'such conflicts, as they only can know, that have endur'd them' which is first used by Walton to describe Herbert's situation at Cambridge (p. 45) and later reappears as a

Additionally, the *Life of Herbert* succeeds in blending the life and the works more seamlessly into its narrative. An example of this is the Mary Magdalen motif which merges biography- and poetry-related aspects. Walton uses it to allude to 'S. Mary Magdalen', one of the *Temple* poems, as well as to enhance the quasi-saintly figure of Magdalen Herbert (reinforced by quoting Donne's poem 'To the Lady *Magdalen Herbert, of St. Mary Magdalen*'). He also uses this motif to create an unusual image for his activity as a biographer by likening 'her Alablaster box of precious oyntment [...] by her dedicated to embalm and preserve [Christ's] sacred body from putrefaction' to his own efforts to 'preserve the memory of my two deceased friends, Dr. *Donne*, and Sir *Henry Wotton* by declaring the various employments and accidents of their Lives' (pp. 11–12).[81]

Walton's readings of his subject and his subject's works have also become more unified in the *Life of Herbert*, in that he presents life and work as informing each other to a greater extent than in his earlier *Lives*. This is particularly apparent in the 'letter and sonnet' format, which is unique to the *Life of Herbert*. On two occasions in the *Life*, Walton juxtaposes a letter with a poem that not only echoes the sentiments expressed in the letter but also acts as a key to reading it. Walton suggests that in both cases letter and sonnet were written (or at least sent) simultaneously. Yet there are indications that they may be particularly skilful examples of Walton ventriloquising the voices of Donne and Herbert respectively and the 'letter and sonnet' format is to some extent his invention. Donne's letter carries the same date and is signed in the same manner as the first of three letters to Magdalen Herbert appended to the *Life of Herbert* in a separate section, suggesting some degree of modification to the letter. This cannot be verified, however, as Walton is the only source for both letters (as well as both sonnets).[82]

Although both 'letters and sonnets' are addressed to Magdalen Herbert, their context is arguably very different. Without Walton's introduction, which also links the poem 'Autumnal' to the first encounter between the letter-writer and the addressee, Donne's 'letter and sonnet' would read like a bid for patronage, although this is a term Walton avoids, perhaps intentionally. Instead, he is anxious to define their relationship as one characterised by a spirit of '*Amity*' (using the word '*amity*' six times in just over a page). In doing so, he turns what would otherwise have seemed merely a piece of coterie poetry into a token of intimate friendship. At the same time, · this transforms the voice of Donne the poet, speaking to his patroness in a received

---

quotation, indicated by italics, as Herbert's own description of his hesitation about whether to become rector of Bemerton: '*He endured*, (as he would often say) *such spiritual Conflicts, as none can think, but only those that have endur'd them*' (p. 58).

81 Interestingly, the comparison also introduces an element of self-interest, because it may imply that Walton is viewing his *Lives* as a way of cementing his own fame as a biographer, just as Mary Magdalen's act 'so far preserve[d] her own memory, that these demonstrations of her sanctified love, and of her officious, and generous gratitude, should be recorded and mentioned' (p. 11).

82 Robin Robbins, in the Longman edition of Donne's poems states that 'To the Lady *Magdalen Herbert*' is 'not precisely datable, since Walton evidently transferred the entire ending from the first of three other letters from D. to Mrs Herbert'. *The Poems of John Donne*, ed. Robin Robbins, 2 vols (Harlow: Pearson Education, 2008), i, 27. Helen Wilcox's Cambridge edition of Herbert's poems divides the 'sonnet' and includes it under the titles 'New Year Sonnet (I)' and 'New Year Sonnet (II)'. *The English Poems of George Herbert*, p. 3.

mode of address, into a personal expression of 'sacred Indearment' (p. 26). The combination of letter and sonnet, then, has the effect of interweaving the poetic and the
personal voices of Donne more closely than in any version of the *Life of Donne*. Letter
and sonnet mutually inform each other's reading in the manner that Walton is trying
to encourage: the letter by providing a specific context for the sonnet's composition
and the sonnet by illuminating the poet's relationship with the addressee.

Similarly, the second 'letter and sonnet', by George Herbert, are presented in a way
which makes them mutually explanatory. The recipient is again Magdalen Herbert.
However, through his selection of a letter-fragment that concerns Herbert's resolution to reject love poetry for divine poetry, Walton assimilates the situation to the one
he presented for the first 'letter and sonnet'. With the letter-writer sending poetry for
the recipient's approval, while making her the audience for his views on divine poetry,
the situation perhaps resembles that of a poet speaking to a friend (and patroness)
more than that of a son speaking to his mother. At the same time, through being
paired with Herbert's declaration to consecrate his 'poor abilities in *Poetry*' (p. 28) to
God, the poem becomes highly personalised and is turned into an illustration of of
Herbert's private faith.

Although Herbert's letter and sonnet are introduced as testimony of Herbert's
'vertue and [...] serious study of learning' during his youth, their main function within
the *Life of Herbert* is to document the birth of Herbert the divine poet, whose poetry
represents a unique form of personal expression. While the poems of *The Temple*
invite a personalised reading, it is important to note how much further Walton goes
in his interpretive efforts than his predecessor. Barnabas Oley had written a meander-
ing triple Life of Dr Jackson, Nicholas Ferrar and George Herbert, prefixed to *A Priest
to the Temple*. In this Life, Oley only went as far as to say that Herbert's poetry indicates that he was well informed on religious matters and did not make a rash choice
in becoming a minister: '[He] knew full well what he did when he received Holy
orders, as appears by every page in this Book, and by the Poems call'd *Priesthood*, and
Aaron' (B8ᵃ–B8ᵇ).

In terms of content, the *Life of Herbert* shows a development of Walton's idea
of private life. It is not only the one among his *Lives* that has the most pronounced
domestic focus, it also portrays Herbert as making a conscious choice in favour of
leading a private life and against a *vita activa*. Walton is keen to stress that, unlike
Donne, Herbert was not denied a court career but actively decided against it. Thus he
begins by outlining the family background of 'our *George*' (as he incongruously refers
to him) over nearly five pages, stating that the Herberts were 'a family, that hath been
blest with men of remarkable wisdom and with a willingness to serve their Countrey'
(p. 13). He supports this claim through devoting more space than might be expected
to the careers of Herbert's six brothers: two soldiers, one captain of 'fortunate and
true English valour' (p. 17), one diplomat, one Master of the Revels, as well as one
fellow of New College, who only receives a perfunctory mention. Walton is eager to
suggest to his readers that, initially at least, Herbert looked set to pursue a similarly
active life. He presents Herbert's appointment as public orator at Cambridge as the
stepping-stone to a promising political career and reminds his readers that previous
university orators had gone on to achieve great things:

His two precedent Orators, were Sir *Robert Nanton*, and Sir *Francis Nethersoll*: The first
was not long after made Secretary of State; and, Sir *Francis*, not long after his being
Orator, was made Secretary to the Lady *Elizabeth* Queen of *Bohemia*. (p. 32)

Even Walton's description of the deaths of Herbert's two most influential friends
at court, followed by the death of the King, as putting an end to 'all Mr *Herbert*'s
Court-hopes' (p. 45) serves not so much as an explanation for Herbert's change of
heart, but as a reminder that Herbert was entertaining those hopes with some justification.[83] Walton, then, is stressing that Herbert would have had the opportunity
to choose a *vita activa*, and that it would have been the natural path for him to take.
Simultaneously, he is expressing his approval for Herbert's choice to become one of
the 'Domestick Servants of the King of Heaven' (p. 46) instead. By doing so, Walton is
implicitly assigning a significant role to the private life, elevating it to a higher status
than the *vita activa* – in direct contrast to the traditional model – and citing Herbert
himself in support of this view.

The *Life of Herbert* has a strong domestic focus, partly because the private life
and Herbert's withdrawal from public life to become God's 'Domestick Servant' are
shown as taking precedence over the *vita activa*. This is apparent both in the prominent roles that Walton gives to Herbert's mother and wife and in the disproportion-
ate amount of space that he devotes to Herbert's time as an ideal 'countrey parson'
at Bemerton.[84] Although Herbert was only rector of Bemerton for about three years,
more than half of the *Life of Herbert* (59 out of 106 pages) is dedicated to this time
span. Herbert's relationship with his parishioners is given particular attention, which
is reflected in the selection of chapter-headings from *A Priest to the Temple*. They are
used by Walton to support his notion of Herbert's life as a 'practical Comment' on
his writings (p. 71) – a phrase that is revealing of Walton's reading of Herbert as a
priest to *The Temple*.

Walton's use of Herbert's poetry to set a pattern for the *Life*, his handling of
sources, his close interweaving of Herbert's life and works and his elevating of the
domestic life above the *vita activa*, all contribute to make the *Life of Herbert* not only
a piece of Anglican hagiography but also the literary life of a poet. Although this was
perhaps not Walton's main intention in writing the *Life of Herbert*, it is clear that he
regarded Herbert as a poet. As early as 1653, in his first mention of Herbert, he had
let Piscator, one of the characters of *The Compleat Angler*, refer to him as 'that holy
Poet Mr. *George Herbert*' (p. 19).[85] While the full title of the *Life of Donne* (in all versions) reminds readers of his office as dean of St Paul's, the 1670 *Life of Herbert* was
published with the title page facing a portrait of Herbert, titled 'The Effigies of Mr
George Herbert: Author of those Sacred Poems called The Temple'.[86]

---

83 Shortly afterwards, Walton has Herbert contemplate a return to 'the painted pleasures of a Court-life'
    (p. 45), implying that although those three deaths halted the Secretary of State fast-track, they had not
    destroyed Herbert's prospects of a court career entirely.
84 After the conclusion of the *Life* proper, Walton dedicates two and a half pages to the 'Debt justly due
    to the memory of Mr *Herberts* vertuous wife' (p. 117).
85 Note, however, that Piscator quotes Herbert's poetry purely for the piety expressed in it, without apply-
    ing it to Herbert's life.
86 *Life of Herbert*, p. 2.

In an addition to his 1658 *Life of Donne*, Walton had even invoked Herbert and *The Temple* during his account of the anchor poems, an episode that aims to establish Donne as a divine poet as well as a celebrated divine. According to Walton's version of the story, Donne had a number of seals carved with the emblem of Christ crucified on an anchor shortly before his death and bequeathed the seals to his closest friends. One of those seals was sent to Herbert, along with a poem, and Herbert wrote a poem in response.[87] As Helen Gardner observed in 1952, Walton's account is inaccurate and may have been based on a number of false assumptions because the poems and the seal were found together among Herbert's papers.[88]

However, the crucial question regarding Walton's account of the anchor poems is not whether he misunderstood the occasion of the poems and merged them by accident (as Gardner suggests), or whether this is merely another example of Walton's adapting his sources to suit his purposes.[89] The most important question has to be why Walton chose to insert the episode – and Herbert – into the 1658 *Life of Donne* and what purpose the poems might serve within this context.

Walton introduces the story of the anchor poems directly after the story of the 'Hymne to God the Father', with the words 'Before I proceed further, I think fit to informe the reader' (pp. 79–80). In other words, it is a digression within the digression that interrupts the account of Donne's final illness and death in order to draw attention to his poetic works. What is peculiar about the anchor poems episode is that its focal point is neither the emblem itself nor the nobility of Donne's gesture but rather 'that man of primitive piety Mr. *George Herbert*' (p. 81).

Walton's decision to interrupt the narrative of his 1658 *Life of Donne* and dedicate a whole page to a brief analysis of *The Temple* (first published two years after Donne's death, and in the same year as the first edition of *Poems by J. D.*) is surprising. Arguably, there was no pressing reason to mention Herbert in a life of Donne at all. Although Walton is keen to present Donne and Herbert as particularly close friends, there is little evidence beyond the anchor poems themselves to support this claim. Of the 129 letters in Donne's *Letters to Severall Persons of Honour* (1651), only one letter mentions Herbert by name, in a request to Sir Henry Goodere to pass on the message that 'all of *Uvedall* house are well' to Herbert.[90] In addition to this, only one short letter has a heading that suggests that it may have been addressed to Herbert.[91] This letter, dated 12 December 1600, when Herbert was seven years old, is a friendly note in which Donne jokingly apologises for the long delay in dispatching a 'little businesse' for his friend because 'these small things make as many steps to

---

87 Donne's poem had first been published in the revised edition of his poems in 1650.
88 Gardner argues that Donne's poem was most likely written at his ordination, when he first adopted the new seal, and that Herbert's response is a composite of lines written in reply to Donne's poem and a second poem, which Herbert wrote when he received the seal after Donne's death. For a more detailed account, see John Donne, *The Divine Poems*, ed. Helen Gardner (Oxford: Clarendon Press, 1952), Appendix G, 'Donne's Latin Poem to Herbert and Herbert's Reply', pp. 138–47.
89 Cf. Novarr, *The Making of Walton's 'Lives'*, p. 504: '[Walton] was interested in the poems only insofar as they were testimonies of friendship. It is quite likely that he did not particularly care for the poems as poems'.
90 *Letters to Severall Persons of Honour*, p. 236.
91 'To my good friend G. H.', in *Letters to Severall Persons of Honour*, pp. 206–7.

their end, and need as many motions for the warrant, as much writing of the Clerks, as long expectation of a Seal, as greater' (p. 206).[92] The jocular tone of the letter, and specifically Donne's remark 'but Sir, even in Princes and Parents, and all States that have in them a naturall Soveraigny, there is a sort of reciprocation', are consistent with a letter sent to a young child, so it is possible that Herbert really was the recipient.[93] Nevertheless, this is clearly not the type of 'happy friendship' between the two poets that Walton has in mind.

Similarly, Oley's prefatory life of Herbert only contains one brief mention of Donne, which makes their relationship sound rather less close and cordial than it appears in Walton's version in merely naming Donne as one of Herbert's many eminent admirers who wrote dedications to him:

> [Herbert's] Art of Divine Poesie, and other polite learning [...] so commended him to persons most Eminent in their time, that *Doctor Donne* inscribed to him a paper of Latine verses in print; and the *Lord Bacon* having translated some Psalmes into English meetre, sent them with a Dedication prefixed, To his very Good friend, Master GEORGE HERBERT.[94]

Of course this is not to suggest that the friendship between Donne and Herbert never existed. Their friendship may well have been just as 'long and dear' as Walton claims, but if it was, it did not manifest itself very prominently in their surviving works or letters. Consequently, it would have made perfect sense for Walton to write his *Life of Donne* without any mention of Herbert. Yet he chose to include him and to stress the 'Sympathy of inclinations' between Herbert and Donne rather more than his sources would seem to merit.[95] This indicates that Walton may have added the digression about *The Temple* and the anchor poems for reasons other than just his personal admiration for Herbert.

As well as emphasising the private element of Donne's life by means of outlining a close friendship, the episode of the anchor poems serves to establish Herbert not only as Donne's friend but as his spiritual and poetic equal. It is this affinity between them, Walton argues, which formed the basis for their friendship:

---

92 Donne was secretary to the Lord Keeper at the time, which may explain the joke about administrative procedures.

93 Towards the end of a roughly contemporary letter in the Folger's collection (dated 8 August 1597), Richard Broughton adopts a similarly jocular tone when he sends his regards to his children and nephews, complimenting his son and oldest nephew for having proved 'so profound schollers in so short a tyme' and singling out his youngest nephew, six-year-old Harvey Bagot, for special praise, 'who in time may proue so profound a clerk as his Diocesan' (Folger MS L.a.279, fol. 1r).

94 George Herbert, *A Priest to the Temple, or, The Country Parson his Character, and Rule of Holy Life* (1652), b12ᵃ.

95 A similar idea of a 'friendship' between two (apparently) like-minded poets can be found in a passage in Speght's 'Life of Chaucer'. Speght considered Spenser to be 'most worthy to be Chaucer's friend, for his like naturall disposition that Chaucer had' (c.iii.a) and modifies lines from book IV of *The Faerie Queene* in order to make Spenser declare the same. The difference between the two biographers' strategies, however, is that Speght could not possibly have been trying to convince readers of the 'Life of Chaucer' that Spenser was Chaucer's 'friend' in anything but a metaphorical sense, while Walton used the idea of a personal friendship between Herbert and Donne to express his notion of a 'Sympathy of inclinations' derived from what he considered to be similarities between their works.

Betwixt [them] there was a long and dear friendship, made up by such a sympathy of inclinations, that they coveted and joyed to be in each others company; and this happy friendship was still maintained by many sacred indearments. (pp. 82–3)[96]

While Walton's account of the friendship may be essentially truthful, it still needs to be treated with a degree of caution, because of the circularity in Walton's use of quotations that David Novarr has noted (see above). The anchor poems as they are printed in the 1658 *Life* have not only been modified by Walton, they are also offered to the reader as 'some Testimony' of the 'many sacred indearments' Donne and Herbert exchanged, though they appear to be the only such 'indearments' whose existence can be proved. Why, then, does Walton go to such lengths to insert George Herbert into the *Life of Donne* and introduce a seven-page digression merely to prove the existence of this friendship for which there seems to be no other evidence?

Walton evidently read *The Temple* as a spiritual autobiography of sorts. As with Donne's *Devotions*, he read the text as a reflection of the author's state of mind at the time of writing, although in this case the emphasis is not on sickness but on spiritual conflict.[97] The other aspect that Walton's analysis of *The Temple* stresses is its use-fulness as a book of instruction to the reader that allows him to trace and relive the author's personal conflicts, as well as their resolution:

[*The Temple* is] *a book*, in which by declaring his own spirituall Conflicts [Herbert] hath raised many a dejected and discomposed soul, and charmed them into sweet and quiet thoughts: *A book*, by the frequent reading whereof, and the assistance of that Spirit that seemed to inspire the Author, the Reader may attain habits of *peace* and *piety*, and all the gifts of the *Holy Ghost* and *Heaven*. (pp. 81–2)

This is very similar to the terms in which Walton speaks of Donne's writing, spe-cifically of his religious poetry. It may well have been this perceived similarity, along with the simultaneous publication of Donne's and Herbert's poetry, that first sug-gested the 'Sympathy of inclinations' to him.[98]

The anchor poems and their presentation on the page in the 1658 *Life of Donne*, which gives them the appearance of letters, show Donne and Herbert engaged in a poetic and theological dialogue, giving them the appearance of humanist men of letters engaged in a written exchange. Yet the 'dialogue' in this case is purely imagi-nary. Herbert's poem could never have been received by Donne in the shape in which Walton presents it, because it implies that Donne was already dead at the time of writing.[99] This notion that Herbert wrote his reply after Donne's death also allows Walton to make the transition to Donne's alleged death-bed composition, which

96 Note the similarities between this and the '*sympathy of souls*' between Donne and his wife in the 1675 version.
97 Spiritual conflict is an aspect of Donne's life that is given greater prominence in the 1658 version. However, this only applies to one particular phase of Donne's life, that is his hesitation to take orders (see pp. 29, 32 and 41). At the same time, Walton all but removes it from Donne's earlier life, so as to avoid the issue of his conversion (as a result, Walton's Master Donne almost appears to have been a closet Anglican all along).
98 Both *The Temple* and the first collection of Donne's poems were published in 1633.
99 The final quatrain contains the phrases 'his hand could write no more' and 'he gave his soul, and then gave o're'. The fact that the poem as it is reproduced in the 1658 *Life* is likely to be a blend of two different poems, can be ignored here.

concludes the digression about his poetry. Although the 1658 *Life of Donne* (like the 1640 version) only cites the title of the 'Hymn to God my God in my Sicknesse', the added date, 'March 23. 1630' (p. 85) has clearly been chosen to suggest that this was the very last thing Donne wrote before 'his hand could write no more'.[100]

The main function of Herbert's inclusion in the 1658 *Life of Donne*, then, is to help Walton to portray Donne as a religious poet, by associating him with the other eminent religious poet of his generation. In a sense, he is not so much likening Herbert to Donne as Donne to Herbert. Emphasising – and perhaps exaggerating – the personal and poetic affinity between the two divine poets allows Walton to present Donne as a primarily religious poet.[101] This strategy is both more subtle and more effective than his earlier one, which had been simply to assert that Donne 'scattered' all of his non-religious poems during his youth and regretted them afterwards.

Although the *Life of Donne* is unlikely to have been received by Walton's contemporaries as primarily the life of a poet, there is some evidence that the *Life of Herbert* was (perhaps contrary to Walton's original intentions). The commendatory poem by Samuel Woodforde is dated to Herbert's seventy-seventh anniversary (3 April 1670) and was published in the first edition of the *Life of Herbert*. Woodforde's poem celebrates Herbert as a religious poet and praises Walton for 'eternizing' him as such.[102] Similarly, the commendatory poem by Wotton's son Charles, dated 1672 and (unlike Woodforde's poem) a response to the 1670 collected *Lives*, refers to Herbert as having been 'fitted for a Court' (A8ᵃ) but sees the culmination of his life in his death as a divine poet:[103]

> with a soul compos'd of Harmonies,
> Like a sweet Swan, he warbles, as he dies
> His makers praise, and, his own obsequies. (A8ᵃ)

Finally, although the *Life of Herbert* was not intended as a prefatory life to accompany his works, a version of it, with Walton's preface removed, was added to all subsequent early modern editions of *The Temple*.[104] The fact that for an entire generation of readers Walton's *Life of Herbert* was an inseparable feature of *The Temple* illustrates not only its success and popularity, but also the continued influence it had on biographical interpretations of Herbert's poetry. It is tempting to view the *Life of Herbert* in isolation, as an unprecedented text that makes the transition from clerical

---

100 While it would be a very fitting conclusion to Donne's life, this story not only clashes with the critical consensus that the 'Sicknesse' in question was not Donne's death-bed, but also with Walton's own claim that directly before his death, Donne 'lay fifteen dayes earnestly expecting his hourly change' (p. 116).

101 For a more detailed analysis of Walton's strategy of turning Donne and Herbert into 'friends', see my article 'Shaping Living Memory: John Aubrey, Izaak Walton, and the idea of poetic friendship', in *South Atlantic Review*, 83 (2018), 139–57.

102 'To his very worthy and much honoured Friend, Mr. *Izaack Walton*, upon his Excellent Life of Mr. *George Herbert*' (pp. 5–9).

103 'To my Old, and most Worthy Friend, Mr Izaak Walton, on his Life of Dr. Donne, &c', A6ᵇ–A8ᵇ.

104 The tenth edition (published in 1674) was the first to appear after Walton's *Life of Herbert*. After the thirteenth edition (1709), Herbert's poetry seems to have gone out of fashion. The ESTC lists no further editions until 1799. Although this edition makes no mention of Walton either on the title page or in the introduction, it contains an (unattributed) version of the *Life of Herbert*, which has been renamed to 'A Biographical Sketch of the Author'.

biography to a Life of a religious poet and thus comes closer to being literary biography than any other early modern Life. Nevertheless, elements of Walton's technique of biographical reading and soliloquising of his subject's inner voice in his *Life of Herbert* can already be traced in the different versions of the *Life of Donne*, written several decades earlier.

Conclusion:
brief lives and lives of the poets

One question that remains to be answered is what the 'pre-history' in the early modern period sketched out in the preceding chapters was building up to. Two names that tend to figure prominently in histories of literary biography have so far not featured in this book: John Aubrey and Samuel Johnson. In Johnson's case, this may be easily explained through the scope – none of the texts discussed so far were written after 1700. Aubrey, on the other hand, is a special case, partly because of his greater distance to the early modern poets whose lives he wrote, and partly because he was not associated with the medium of print.

The key premise of this study has been that it is possible to trace the emergence of biographical narratives for authors who died between the 1580s and the 1630s from evaluations of their works and their lives that were written in the immediate wake of their deaths. For this reason, I have focused on texts written about dead authors by contemporaries or writers of the following generation. The bulk of the authorship debate surrounding the figure of Robert Greene played out within a year of his death. Edmund Spenser incorporated the pastoral poet 'Astrophel' into his imagined poet nation just a few years after the publication of Sidney's works. Even Walton's *Life of Donne* was written less than a decade after Donne's death in 1631. Aubrey, by contrast, was writing his biographical sketches of Sidney, Spenser, Shakespeare and Jonson from a much greater distance. Ben Jonson, the only poet on that list to die within Aubrey's own lifetime, died when Aubrey was just ten years old, some forty years before he started compiling a 'brief life' of Jonson.[1] With Sidney, the distance was nearly a century. Aubrey may have witnessed Sidney's second funeral after viewing his coffin, which had been unearthed by the 'firing of Paules' in 1666. Nevertheless, his vivid description of the first funeral and the 'wonderfull great state' of the funeral procession is owed to his having caught a glimpse of Lant's Roll as a young boy, almost fifty years after the event.[2] Aubrey's practice, therefore, is a historical and biographical project that seeks to empirically recover truths about authors' lives, drawing on records and interviews with eyewitnesses wherever possible (as is evident by numerous 'quaere' notes on the margins). My objective in this

---

1 Aubrey's short biographical sketches, which survive in three manuscript volumes at the Bodleian Library, are usually referred to as 'Aubrey's "Brief Lives"', after the short title of the first critical edition, whose full title was *'Brief Lives', Chiefly of Contemporaries*, 2 vols, ed. Andrew Clark (Oxford: Clarendon Press, 1898).
2 MS Aubr. 6, fol. 82v.

book has been to study a set of textual events that fall short of this and thus constitute a 'pre-history' consisting of texts by writers who were less self-conscious than Aubrey about the process of biographical recovery.

Perhaps more significantly, while this study is centred on print responses to authorial afterlives in print, Aubrey's ambitious 'Brief Lives' project is firmly rooted in an antiquarian manuscript context that formed a deliberate counterculture to print. In her articles on editing Aubrey's works and on the close links between those works and his collection of 'rarities', Kate Bennett has demonstrated that Aubrey was not writing for print publication and chose an unusual format for his 'Brief Lives' partly out of a sense of disillusionment with the inadequacies of print in conveying biographical truth.[3] Strictly speaking, the 'Brief Lives' as we tend to think of them today were created by Andrew Clark's 1898 edition, which, like all modern editions, selectively compiled passages, so that some of the resulting 'lives' looked quite unlike the way they had appeared in Aubrey's manuscripts. Ironically, even the source that Clark gave for the title 'Brief Lives' can no longer be traced: in his introduction, he described one of the Aubrey manuscripts at the Bodleian Library (MS Aubr. 6) as bearing the title 'Σχεδιάσματα. Brief Lives part i'. Today, however, the manuscript has no such title. Perhaps it was lost in a later rebinding, or perhaps it never existed. Either way, the missing title serves as a fitting illustration of the discrepancy between the 'Brief Lives' and the manuscripts containing the results of Aubrey's ambitious project.

Aubrey's antiquarian approach led to two things: first, a body of manuscript texts that cannot be converted into print without major editorial interventions (which inevitably means sacrificing important features of the manuscripts), and second, a materialist focus within the 'Brief Lives' themselves.[4] For these reasons, Aubrey needs to be treated separately from the contemporary 'biographers' who are the subject of this study. At the same time, however, his 'Brief Lives' represent a step further towards texts that are governed by a coherent sense of the literary life, and thus towards literary biography. Given Aubrey's greater distance to his subjects and his ethos in writing biography, which differed dramatically from that of his contemporaries, it is particularly revealing to see how his materialist focus manifests itself in the lives written of people of whom he had no first-hand knowledge, forcing him to rely heavily on anecdotes.[5] Additionally, it led him to include elements such as a diagram of Sidney's horoscope, which is reproduced in the manuscript, although its

---

3 'Editing Aubrey', in Joe Bray, Miriam Handley and Anne C. Henry (eds), *Ma(r)king the Text* (Aldershot: Ashgate, 2000), pp. 271–90 and 'John Aubrey's Collections and the Early Modern Museum', *Bodleian Library Record*, 17.3–4 (2001), 213–34.

4 Even Bennet's excellent critical edition of the 'Brief Lives' (Oxford: Oxford University Press, 2015), which takes great pains to flag up all sorts of features of the manuscript to readers and even tries to reproduce images, cannot quite convey the character of the Aubrey manuscripts themselves.

5 Walton's belief in autobiography as the ideal form of biography meant that he considered it the biographer's duty not to include information the subject would not have been likely to include had he written his own life (Thomas Sprat, in his 'Life of Cowley' took a similar approach). Aubrey, by contrast, subscribed to the principle that biography should above all be truthful, even if it meant that it would have to remain hidden and unread 'till about 30 yeares hence; for the author & the Persons (like Medlars) ought to be rotten first' (letter to Anthony Wood, MS Aubr. 6, fol. 12). For this reason, Aubrey included even pieces of juicy – and unsubstantiated – gossip among his notes, some of which

significance or its relation to the other pieces of information that Aubrey compiled about Sidney are not explained in the text.

It is evident that Aubrey systematically collected information about the personal lives of the major poets and playwrights of the late sixteenth and early seventeenth century – Sidney, Spenser, Shakespeare and Jonson – from their contemporaries wherever possible. Nevertheless, a number of elements from Aubrey's accounts of the lives of those authors have been shown to be factually incorrect. The general consensus among modern scholars has been that, much like Walton, Aubrey was not one to let mere facts get in the way of a good story, yet as with Walton, the interest of the anecdotes lies perhaps less in the stories themselves than in how they aim to illuminate the lives of their subjects. Here Aubrey's antiquarian interest in the material object becomes significant, as his fascination with two aspects of authors' lives is particularly evident: the idea of literary networks on the one hand, and narratives that locate the process of creation and illuminate the factual basis of literary texts by the means of 'keys' (thus portraying the author at work) on the other.

Aubrey's interest in networks and his desire to find patterns and establish connections between his notes may be traced not only to his antiquarian background but also to his scientific interests (he was an early and ardent member of the Royal Society).[6] Thus he notes links not only between poets and their patrons, citing dedications and poems, but also records 'friendships' among poets. This is also partly reflected in the sequence in which the Lives occur in his manuscripts. For example, the 'Life of Shakespeare' follows the 'Life of Jonson' in the manuscript (MS Aubr. 6), but there is also a logical link between the two authors, because both Lives highlight the parallels between them and effectively portray them as moving in similar circles and using similar methods for seeking out material to use in their plays.

The Lives of Sidney and Spenser are joined in a similar manner: the 'Life of Spenser' is effectively inserted into a cluster of Lives of members of the Sidney-Herbert family. One episode that is particularly interesting in this respect occurs in the 'Life of Sidney' and describes an apocryphal scene: according to Aubrey's account, Sidney was so 'cloyed and surfeited with the Poetasters of those dayes' that when Spenser delivered a copy of *The Faerie Queene* to him, he merely 'layd it by' and did not receive the poet.[7] Once he had read it, however, he was 'so exceedingly delighted with it' (fol. 82v) he had the poet tracked down, summoned him back and gave him a handsome reward, despite a servant's protests that it was too generous.[8] It is needless to say

are discussed in Alan Stewart's chapter 'John Aubrey's Minutes of Lives', in *Oxford History of Life-Writing* vol. II, pp. 233–52.

6 Michael Hunter, who conducted a detailed survey of the activity of early Royal Society fellows as recorded through minutes, lists Aubrey as one of the most active early members, while noting that he was among a small minority of active fellows who were never elected council members, although 'the reasons for this are not entirely clear'. Michael Hunter, *The Royal Society and its Fellows 1660–1700: The Morphology of an Early Scientific Institution* (Chalfont St Giles: British Society for the History of Science, 1982), p. 77.

7 MS Aubr. 6, fol. 82 and 82v.

8 This precise version of the anecdote does not appear elsewhere, although it evidently shares characteristics with the Spenser anecdotes discussed above in the Interlude. Unlike the other biographers, however, Aubrey uses his anecdote primarily to provide a logical starting-point for the special relationship between Spenser and Sidney, which he also attempts to trace at other points in his manuscripts.

that this scene almost certainly never took place. In fact, the first person to question the authenticity of this episode was the person for whom Aubrey had written it down: Anthony Wood added the sceptical marginal note 'qu. wh. this be true' at this point in the manuscript (fol. 82v). Nevertheless, the anecdote is illuminating, partly because it provides a glimpse of how writers of Aubrey's generation may have imagined Elizabethan patronage structures (poets showing up unannounced at their prospective patrons' homes to deliver their offerings in person), and partly because it reveals Aubrey's eagerness to associate Sidney and Spenser. He records the story of the beginnings of their 'great friendship' (fol. 82v) although he has no authority for it – generally, Aubrey names his sources for anecdotes of this nature – and although he leaves a gap in his account for the sum of money Spenser supposedly received, there is no accompanying 'quaere' note indicating his intent to verify this information. Perhaps, then, the episode was included by Aubrey not only because it is a great story (which it unquestionably is) but because it provided him with a convenient way of linking the lives of two people who he felt ought to be linked: the 're-viver of Poetry in those darke times' and the 'Prince of Poets of his tyme'.[9]

In addition to noting friendships and patronage links, Aubrey occasionally 'identifies' people on whom some of their fictional characters were said to have been based.[10] This aspect feeds into his interest in the process of literary creation, which is perhaps most evident in his collecting of information that might provide a 'key' to literary works. At the beginning of a letter 'identifying' several of the characters of *Arcadia* and *Astrophel and Stella*, Dorothy Tyndale expresses her regret that she cannot 'giue you the Key you desire, but all I know of it is not worth any thing', implying that Aubrey had specifically asked her to provide a key to Sidney's works.[11] Aubrey evidently disagreed with Tyndale's judgement and added her letter to the 'Life of Sidney', effectively making it act as the key that the letter-writer had denied it was. While there are no similarly detailed 'keys' to the works of Spenser and Shakespeare, the identification of Spenser's 'Mistris Rosalind' as a distant relative of John Dryden's and the seemingly trivial anecdote of the Grendon constable who provided 'the Humour of ...... the constable, in Midsomernights Dreame' essentially serve the same function.[12] In both cases the anecdotes attempt to contextualise the work by establishing a direct link to the poet's own life – in the latter case, Aubrey even goes as far as to venture a guess that the story of the memorable constable might explain the title of the play: 'I thinke it was Midsomer night that he happened to lye there' (that is 'at Grendon in Bucks wch is [on] the roade from London to Stratford').[13] Similarly, he

---

9 MS Aubr. 6, fol. 82 and 83.
10 Even the proximity of poets' graves is recorded by Aubrey; one of the things he notes about Michael Drayton is that he lies buried 'neer Spencer' (MS Aubr. 8, fol. 8v).
11 MS Aubr. 6, fol. 82B (letter inserted between the pages). Although Tyndale was not a member of the Wilton circle herself, she was nevertheless 'conversant among [Sidney's] relations'.
12 MS Aubr. 8, fol. 41 and MS Aubr. 6, fol. 109. The ellipses are Aubrey's and indicate he was unable to verify the name of the character – which is not surprising, because there is no constable in *A Midsummer Night's Dream*. Most probably, Aubrey's source had confused his Shakespeare comedies, and the constable with the memorable character was really Dogberry from *Much Ado About Nothing*.
13 Both MS Aubr. 6, fol. 109. The sentence that begins 'I thinke it was Midsomer night...' is an insertion added on the margin of the page and marked with an asterisk.

traces the origins of Spenser's poetry to the 'delicate sweet ayre' of Hampshire, where, according to Aubrey's source, Mr Samuel Woodford (coincidentally a resident of Hampshire) he 'enjoyed his Muse: & writt good part of his verses'.[14]

Finally, Aubrey records anecdotes about the four poets that portray them at work. Most famously, this includes the story of Sidney's habit of carrying a 'Table booke' while hunting so he could 'write downe his notions as they came into his head, when he was writing his Arcadia'.[15] Spenser, Jonson and Shakespeare are likewise portrayed in the act of composition in Aubrey's anecdotes. In Spenser's case, one anecdote hints at a draft version of *The Faerie Queene*, written on 'an abundance of Cards' during his time at Cambridge, where they were discovered 'lately, at ye coll. takeingdowne the wainscot of his chamber' – at least according to the poet John Dryden, Aubrey's source for this episode.[16] Of Shakespeare and Jonson, Aubrey notes that they 'did gather Humours of men dayly where ever they came', that is they went hunting for characters to use in their plays.[17] He supports this claim by identifying several of the people supposed to have inspired characters in Shakespeare's and Jonson's plays. Those 'identifications' include John Dee as the model for Jonson's 'Alkimist' (MS Aubr. 6, fol. 38), Charles Chester as 'Carlo Buffono' in *Every Man Out of His Humour* (MS Aubr. 6, fol. 76), Thomas Sutton as the title character of *Volpone*, as well as the Grendon constable already mentioned above. Jonson is also shown systematically compiling a 'Cataloge' of typical Yorkshire phrases by observing the linguistic habits of fellow actor and playwright John Lacy, to use as 'his hint to Tale of a Tub for clownery'.[18]

The individual biographical sketches that constitute Aubrey's larger 'Brief Lives' project may not be 'adequate' literary biography as postulated by R. C. Bald. Yet in their focus on locating the process of literary creation and portraying the author at work, the anecdotes Aubrey chose to collect nevertheless reflect a shift towards a more marked emphasis on the literary lives of authors at the end of the seventeenth century – a shift brought about partly by the influence of Walton's *Lives*. This growing interest in the literary life was concomitant with an idea of authorship that assumed the presence – and the decipherability – of the author's thoughts in the written text.

By the early eighteenth century, this notion – which had been an uncommon enough feature in Walton's *Lives* for him to draw his readers' attention to it repeatedly – had gained in significance, owing to innovations in editing practice that highlighted the importance of situating literature in the historical moment of writing. This movement of historically grounded editing, spearheaded by Richard Bentley and Shakespeare editor Lewis Theobald, thus rested on the implicit assumption that

---

14 MS Aubr. 6, fol. 83.
15 MS Aubr. 6, fol. 82.
16 MS Aubr. 8, fol. 41. Neither Dryden nor Aubrey provided any explanation why Spenser should have wanted to hide his early drafts in the wall panelling of his college room, however.
17 MS Aubr. 6, fol. 109.
18 MS Aubr. 8, fol. 45v. Aubrey records this anecdote twice – the other mention of it is in MS Aubr. 6, fol.108 – which indicates either that the long-lived Mr Lacy (Aubrey's most valuable contemporary source for the lives of several playwrights) was particularly fond of telling this story, or that Aubrey considered it a particularly good illustration of what he believed to be Jonson's method of working (or perhaps both).

contextual knowledge of an author's life and circumstances of writing was conducive to (and indeed necessary for) a full understanding of the text. These innovations in editing, which implied a privileging of the author's life as a key to the text, were not necessarily welcomed by authors themselves, however. Perhaps the greatest opponents of this new way of reading and editing literary texts were Jonathan Swift and Alexander Pope. They not only satirised Bentley and Theobald and the ideas they stood for in *The Battle of the Books* and *The Dunciad Variorum* but also went to remarkable lengths to frame their own works in a ludic manner to foil any attempts of directly associating the author with his work. One of the earliest examples of their practice of deliberately planting false biographical trails for readers to follow can be found in Swift's preface to *A Tale of a Tub*:

> Whatever Reader desires to have a thorow Comprehension of an Author's Thoughts, cannot take a better Method, than by putting himself into the Circumstances and Postures of Life, that the Writer was in, upon every important Passage as it flow'd from his Pen; For this will introduce a Parity and strict Correspondence of Idea's between the Reader and the Author. Now, to assist the diligent Reader in so delicate an Affair, as far as brevity will permit, I have recollected, that the shrewdest Pieces of this Treatise, were conceived in Bed, in a Garret: [...] and in general, the whole Work was begun, continued, and ended, under a long Course of Physick, and a great want of Money. Now, I do affirm it will be absolutely impossible for the candid Peruser to go along with me in a great many bright Passages, unless upon the several Difficulties emergent, he will please to capacitate and prepare himself by these Directions. And this I lay down as my principal *Postulatum*.[19]

The principal target of Swift's satire is a particular type of preface that offers 'Circumstances of Time, Place and Person' (p. 17) as information that is potentially crucial for gaining a full understanding of the text that follows. Yet while Swift is primarily mocking 'Modern' authors for excessively contextualising their own works in their introductions, the phenomenon he ridicules also presupposes a way of reading that privileges the author's biography and the moment of composition and treats them as 'keys' to the text.

Swift's secondary target, then, is the practice of biographical reading. The satire of the preface lies not so much in the underlying assumption that readers will strive for a 'thorow Comprehension of an Author's Thoughts', if not a 'Parity and strict Correspondence of Idea's'. This assumption is something that Swift takes for granted in his quest to take 'candid perusers' like Bentley to task for what he considered a ridiculous manner of approaching literary texts. Instead, Swift's satire lies in the suggestion that it is impossible for a reader to understand a text unless he 'goes along' with the author by exactly replicating the circumstances of its composition while reading – biographical reading taken to ludicrous extremes, that is.

The practice of biographical reading also underpins a later work, which is generally referred to as marking the true beginning of 'adequate' literary biography: Samuel Johnson's *Lives of the Poets*. By the time Johnson was writing those *Lives* (in the late

---

19 Jonathan Swift, *A Tale of a Tub* (1704), pp. 18–19.

1770s and early 1780s), the literary life had become an established category – and indeed a commercial one.

On the one hand, Johnson's *Lives of the Poets* illustrated how much authors' lives had gained in importance since the late seventeenth century. Roger Lonsdale stresses that the *English Poets* series for which Johnson's *Lives* were originally commissioned was a commercial project, and Johnson himself was enlisted not so much because the booksellers behind the project appreciated his critical contributions as because they were interested in his 'literary "brand name" [...] which would in itself confirm the edition's superiority to anything [rival publishers] might produce'.[20] Lonsdale goes on to argue that the publishers of the *English Poets* were 'virtually forced' (p. 13) to include a biography for each of the authors featured because John Bell, whose *Poets of Great Britain* series it was intended to rival had announced the inclusion of Lives in his editions. Yet while Lonsdale's point about the booksellers' commercially oriented mindset and their view of Johnson's name as an additional selling-point for their edition is a valid one, it would be wrong to conclude that the biographies merely served as a pretext for attaching Johnson's name to the project. While they foresaw the commercial appeal the name 'Johnson' would have and exploited it in their advertisements, the booksellers also evidently regarded biographical prefaces as a valuable selling-point for an edition and considered it a worthwhile investment to commission new Lives rather than reprint or collate existing ones (as Bell's editions did).

The innovations in editing practice, which had served to assign greater significance to the lives of authors for an understanding of their works, had taken place before the background of a growing commercialisation of the book market during the eighteenth century. This in turn had led to a wider audience for literature – and thus arguably a greater need for authors' lives to make texts more accessible. By the late 1770s there was evidently a market for literary lives, which prompted the booksellers involved with the *English Poets* series to make biographical prefaces an integral feature of their editions. The subsequent popularity of Johnson's *Prefaces*, which far exceeded that of the series to which they were appended and whose publication they had delayed, eventually led to their separate reissuing as *Lives of the Poets*.[21] While this may have been partly due to a demand for the 'brand name' Johnson, it also indicates that there was now a significant readership willing to buy (and read) biographical prefaces even when they were dissociated from the context of the works they were meant to introduce.

Perhaps most importantly, however, Johnson's *Lives of the Poets* illustrates just how natural it had become by the end of the eighteenth century to connect the biographical record of a poet's life with his literary output and to materially locate the act of creation. This is particularly apparent in Johnson's 'Life of Cowley', which was

20 Samuel Johnson, *The Lives of the Most Eminent English Poets, with Critical Observations on their Works*, 4 vols, ed. Roger Lonsdale (Oxford: Clarendon Press, 2006), i, 12.
21 Although Johnson's *Lives* had been originally planned as short prefaces added to each individual volume of the series, Johnson took considerably longer to write them than anticipated. As a consequence of this, the 'prefaces' were published in separate, supplementary volumes, which could only be bought with the entire series, a policy that for two years frustrated early buyers who tried – and failed – to purchase just the volumes of *Prefaces*.

among the first to be published.[22] In this Life, Johnson's approach differs significantly from that of Thomas Sprat or Gerard Langbaine discussed in Chapter 1. Sprat,
Cowley's first biographer, had told the story of Cowley's *vita activa*, while Langbaine
had attempted to emulate Izaak Walton's methods by tracing Cowley's biography
through referring almost exclusively to his works. Johnson's 'Life of Cowley', by contrast, is characterised by the way in which it blends the 'active' and the writing life of
its subject into a single flowing narrative. Unlike its two predecessors, Johnson's 'Life
of Cowley' is concerned with outlining Cowley's political and poetic careers simultaneously, which makes it an 'adequate' example of literary biography. However, in his
frequent transitions from Cowley's political life to his works and back, Johnson is in
fact pursuing a peculiar agenda. Rather than merely seeking to combine the two into a
unified portrait of Cowley, Johnson appears to be actively looking for inconsistencies
between the author and the works. Again, Lonsdale's observations are instructive:

> At times, Johnson's biographies recall the disparity between the impressive 'book' and
> its disappointing 'author' discussed in his early essays. [...] He confronts Cowley's love
> poetry with the triumphant claim that 'he in reality was in love but once, and then never
> had resolution to tell his passion' [...] and later deflates the belief that 'an author's life is
> best read in his works' by contrasting what a reader might deduce about the poet from
> *The Seasons* and the known facts about Thomson the man. (p. 98)

The 'contrasting' technique described by Lonsdale in this passage not only illustrates
Johnson's scepticism towards taking a poet's poetic voice to be identical with his personal voice, it also shows that linking the two had become the norm. By the time
Johnson was writing his 'Life of Cowley', the belief that a poet can be found in his
works had become so ingrained that he felt he had to make a conscious critical effort
to 'deflate' it and draw attention to its fallacies. Johnson's critical approach towards
the poets whose Lives he was writing was in turn the product of an eighteenth-
century phenomenon that had emerged alongside the desire of readers to 'have a
thorow Comprehension of an Author's Thoughts'. That phenomenon was the rise of
the learned critic.

What Lonsdale terms Johnson's 'brand name' (later consolidated by his becoming
the subject of the first extensive literary biography of a living author) and the *English
Poets* series itself stood at the end of wider developments over the course of the eighteenth century. Part of these developments was the idea of a 'modern' – meaning an
English – canon of literature to match that of the 'ancients' in terms of quality and
significance, which was reflected in new editions of the collected works of English
authors, with the multi-volume editions published by Jacob Tonson being the most
influential.[23]

Tonson's editions included Nicholas Rowe's 1709 edition of Shakespeare's works,
the first of many modern Shakespeare editions. It is best remembered for its preface,

---

22 Abraham Cowley was the earliest of the authors featured in the *English Poets* series.
23 For the significance of Tonson's editions and their visual appearance, see John Barnard's essay 'Creating
    an English Literary Canon, 1679–1720: Jacob Tonson, Dryden and Congreve', in Simon Eliot, Andrew
    Nash and Ian Willison (eds), *Literary Cultures and the Material Book* (London: The British Library,
    2007), pp. 307–21.

in which Rowe considered 'the greatness of [Shakespeare's] Genius' in relation to 'the Antient Poets' and attempted to assess as his knowledge of their works.[24] One of the consequences of assigning a degree of importance to English classics that equalled that of the 'Antients' was that they could be evaluated by means of the same critical tools. Since Shakespeare was the author whose 'genius' was the most undisputed, it was no coincidence that his works were subjected to particular scrutiny. While Rowe was not the first to comment on 'the Liberties of his Writing' (p. xxiii) – that is, the apparent failure of Shakespeare's plays to observe the Aristotelian unities of time, place and action – his preface proved to be one of the most influential pieces of early Shakespeare criticism and was reprinted in nearly all subsequent editions until 1821.[25] Yet perhaps the most interesting aspect about Rowe's preface is how it combines literary judgements with a biographical narrative that is at least partially derived from the works. So, for example, Rowe progresses from a speculative account of Shakespeare's education to his seeming ignorance of ancient writers, before going on to praise 'the natural Bent of his own Great *Genius*' as nevertheless comparable to that of the ancient authors, albeit not directed by their influence. The sequence is revealing, because it effectively reverses the process of Rowe's critical analysis by placing the conclusions drawn from the structure and contents of the plays first: that the 'Liberties' must be the result of ignorance of the classics, which in turn must be the result of an incomplete education.

While literary criticism had not been considered essential for earlier Lives of poets – as can be seen in Langbaine's reluctance to pass any form of judgement on Cowley's works – it had evidently become an integral part of them now. Johnson certainly did not share Langbaine's reservations, but even before he began writing the *Lives*, they had been announced in the advertisements for the *English Poets* series as 'Preface[s], Biographical *and Critical*' (emphasis added). In a sense, then, Johnson's views of authorship and his judgements regarding the literary merits of authors' works, which underpin his accounts of poets' lives, were what his readership expected. Perhaps this aspect constituted part of the appeal of the *Lives of the Poets*, since earlier printed Lives were lacking in this respect.

The shared ancestry of literary criticism and literary biography reflected in Johnson's *Lives of the Poets* can still be felt today. As the examples from twentieth- and twenty-first-century biographies that have featured in the preceding chapters illustrate, biography is now so central to our notion of authorship that its absence is perceived as inherently problematic. Since the phenomenon of literary biography is so closely interwoven with how we conceive of authorship, there are two particular pitfalls in the study of early modern authors, because there is a disjunction between the life and the works caused by the absence of literary biography and its associated assumptions.

---

24 Nicholas Rowe, 'Some Account of the Life &c of Mr. *William Shakespear*', in *The Works of Mr. William Shakespear*, 6 vols, ed. Nicholas Rowe (1709), vol. 1, pp. i–xl (p. xxiii and p. iii).
25 R. B. McKerrow, 'The Treatment of Shakespeare's Text by his Earlier Editors, 1709–1768', in Peter Alexander (ed.), *Studies in Shakespeare: British Academy Lectures* (London: Oxford University Press, 1964), pp. 103–31. McKerrow also observes that 'its admitted importance, in spite of the vast number of statements contained in it which have since been discredited, seems to some extent to have distracted attention from Rowe's treatment of the plays themselves' (both p. 108).

The first of those pitfalls lies in naive readings that implicitly assume it is possible to recover 'intimate' accounts of early modern lives either from the literary works themselves (as in Dowden's attempt to trace the progress of Shakespeare's 'mind' in his plays) or from non-literary documents, such as wills or account books. This assumption that writing the lives of early modern authors is essentially a matter of finding the right 'key' can lead to a speculative approach and result in biographies that attempt to bridge the gap between life and works imaginatively.[26] For obvious reasons, this approach is particularly widespread in the field of Shakespeare biography – arguably, even the numerous studies questioning the identity of 'Shakespeare' are in themselves a product of the keenly felt lack of a 'complete Shakespeare'.

The second pitfall, however, lies in concluding that since the literary life as a category does not exist during the sixteenth and seventeenth century, 'the opportunity was missed', as Harold Nicolson put it.[27] It would be wrong to imagine the emergence of literary biography in the way Brian Tuke envisioned the arrival of Chaucer in English literary history – instantaneous, unprecedented and defying the spirit of the (dark) age in which it occurred, 'as it were nature repugnyng'. Although there is no single, linear pre-history that unfolds during the period investigated, there is a series of faltering events of authorship. Each of the writers who have featured in Chapters 1–4 – though perhaps it would be more accurate to refer to them as 'readers' in this context – had his own motivations for considering a dead author's life through his writings. Equally, each had his own method of doing so, and some were more successful than others. Collectively, however, the texts I have examined show an attempt to comment on lived life in relation to literary works, and an inclination towards biographical reading that is greater than one might expect to find in texts written before the eighteenth century. This pre-history of literary biography, which coincides with the growing professionalisation of print authorship and the print industry, and which has yet to be explored fully, forms an intriguing counternarrative to the established idea of authorial emergence through self-fashioning.

As well as presenting a counternarrative to the idea of the self-fashioning author, the afterlives of dead early modern poets that have been outlined in this study also point to a counterdynamic to living poets' striving for 'possessive authorship': readers and print professionals displaying possessive attitudes towards dead authors in their desire for definitive readings, editions and life-narratives. Thus Robert Greene's death prompted several publishers to compete for the final say on his life and career by claiming ownership of the last pamphlet he had written, supposedly at the very moment of his death, while Gabriel Harvey and Thomas Nashe competed for the final verdict on Greene as an author. The posthumous publication of Sidney's works death can likewise be regarded as a series of struggles for ownership of the dead poet and his works by different agents with different aims. In addition to the Countess of Pembroke's attempts to control her brother's afterlife, there was publisher William

---

26 Recent examples include two imaginative Shakespeare biographies: Stephen Greenblatt's *Will in the World* (2004) and Katherine Duncan-Jones's *From Upstart Crow to Sweet Swan* (2011). While there is nothing inherently wrong with the imaginative approach, it does mean the resulting biographies cross over into fiction.

27 Nicolson, *The Development of English Biography*, p. 38.

Ponsonby, who secured the printing rights to *Arcadia* through his shrewd move of deferring to the family's ownership of the book. He then went on to publish not one but two editions of the text, in which two editors competed not only for the definitive authorised version of *Arcadia* but also for the definitive version of Sidney to which his newly expanded readership should be introduced. By contrast, in the preface to *Astrophel and Stella*, Thomas Nashe, a print professional with a clear commercial interest in the text, distinguishes between the Countess of Pembroke's dead brother and 'Astrophel', the author contained in the poetry, and frames his claim of ownership as one made on behalf of the general reading public. Finally, Edmund Spenser's posthumous revival of 'Astrophel' in a pastoral landscape of his own creation was arguably not so much a tribute to as an appropriation of Sidney.

At first sight, Izaak Walton's self-effacing 'who am I?' attitude towards his role as a biographer would seem to make him less concerned about ownership of John Donne and George Herbert – despite beginning his elegy for the former with the words 'Our *Donne* is dead' and occasionally lapsing into calling Herbert 'our *George*'. Yet he did shape their biographical narratives to correspond to his personal reading of their poetic works, especially in introducing his idea of a friendship between the two based on a 'Sympathy of inclinations' and in defining Donne not as a poet and a divine but as a divine poet. While Walton may never have consciously sought to control the life-narratives of Donne and Herbert, he effectively continued to 'own' them long after his own death. Even as contemporary Donne and Herbert scholars frequently voice their scepticism about the factual accuracy of Walton's *Lives*, or express their intentions to rely on Walton's testimony as little as possible, they nevertheless struggle to avoid him entirely. This is not only proof of the true ingeniousness of Walton's approach to life-writing, it also serves as a useful reminder that while Walton's attempts to recover the private voice of the author from his works may now strike us as naïve, the quest for a 'complete' author, whose life and works add up to a consistent whole, continues to be a driving force of literary scholarship.

Bibliography

Manuscripts

Bodleian Library MS Aubr. 6 [Aubrey, 'Brief Lives' part I]
Bodleian Library MS Aubr. 8 [Aubrey, 'Brief Lives' part III]
Folger Shakespeare Library MS H.b.1 [scribal version of the unrevised 'old' *Arcadia*]
Folger Shakespeare Library MS L.a.279 [Letter from Richard and Anne Broughton to Walter Bagot]
Folger Shakespeare Library MS V.a.125 [miscellany containing William Basse's epitaph for Shakespeare]
University of Edinburgh MS De.5.96 [Drummond MS of *Astrophel and Stella*]

Primary texts

Allot, Robert, *Englands Parnassus* (1600).
Anon, *The Cobler of Caunterburie* (1590).
Anon, *An Elegie on the death of that late incomparable poet, Robert Wild, D.D. who departed this life August the 12th, 1679* (1679).
Anon, *An Elegy on the most celebrated poet of the age, John Dryden Esq. who departed this life, May the 1st. 1700* (1700).
Anon, *An Elegy upon the most ingenious Mr. Henry Care who departed this life on the eighth day of August, 1688, and in the two and fortieth year of his age* (1688).
Anon, *Merie tales newly imprinted [and] made by Master Skelton Poet Laureat* (1567).
Anon, *Merrie conceited iests of George Peele Gentleman, sometimes a student in Oxford VVherein is shewed the course of his life how he liued: a man very well knowne in the Citie of London and elsewhere* (1606).
Anon, *Wits Recreations. Selected from the Finest Fancies of Moderne Muses* (1640).
Anon, *Tarlton's Jests and News out of Purgatory*, ed. James Orchard Haliwell (London: Shakespeare Society, 1844).
Anon, *The Three Parnassus Plays (1598–1601)*, ed. J. B. Leishman (London: Ivor Nicholson & Watson, 1949).
Aubrey, John, *Aubrey's Brief Lives*, ed. Oliver Lawson Dick (London: Secker and Warburg, 1949).
Aubrey, John, *Brief Lives*, 2 vols, ed. Kate Bennett (Oxford: Oxford University Press, 2015).

Aubrey, John, *Brief Lives and Other Selected Writings*, ed. Anthony Powell (London: Cresset Press, 1949).

Aubrey, John, *'Brief Lives', Chiefly of Contemporaries*, 2 vols, ed. Andrey Clark (Oxford: Clarendon Press, 1898).

Aubrey, John, *Letters Written by Eminent Persons in the Seventeenth and Eighteenth Centuries: To which are Added ... Lives of Eminent Men by John Aubrey Esq*, 2 vols (London: Printed for Longman, Hurst, Rees, Orme, and Brown, ... and Munday and Slatter, Oxford, 1813).

B. R., *Greenes News from Both Heauen and Hell* (1593).

Bacon, Francis, *Resuscitatio, or, Bringing into publick light severall pieces of the works, civil, historical, philosophical, & theological, hitherto sleeping, of the Right Honourable Francis Bacon, Baron of Verulam, Viscount Saint Alban according to the best corrected coppies: together with His Lordships life / by William Rawley* (1657).

Baldwin, William, *A Myrroure for Magistrates* (1559).

Bale, John, *Illustrium Maioris Britanniae Scriptorum* (1548).

Behn, Aphra, *The Histories and Novels of the Late Ingenious Mrs Behn in one Volume. Together with The Life and Memoirs of Mrs Behn, written by One of the Fair Sex* (1696).

Blount, Thomas Pope, *De Re Poetica* (Menston: Scolar Press, 1972) [facsimile of the 1694 edition].

Bodenham, John, *Englands Helicon* (1600).

Breton, Nicholas, *Brittons Bowre of Delights* (1591).

Breton, Nicholas, *Melancholike Humours* (1600).

Burnet, Gilbert, *Some passages of the life and death of the right honourable John, Earl of Rochester who died the 26th of July, 1680 / written by his own direction on his death-bed by Gilbert Burnet* (1680).

Camden, William, *The historie of the life and reigne of that famous princesse Elizabeth* (1634).

Chaucer, Geoffrey, *The Workes of Geffray Chaucer Newly Printed*, ed. William Thynne (1532).

Chaucer, Geoffrey, *The Workes of our Antient and Learned English Poet, Geffrey Chaucer*, ed. Thomas Speght (1598), *The Workes of our Antient and Learned English Poet, Geffrey Chaucer*, ed. Thomas Speght (1602).

Chettle, Henry, *Kind-Harts Dreame* (1592).

Cleveland, John, *The works of Mr. John Cleveland containing his poems, orations, epistles, collected into one volume, with the life of the author* (1687).

Cowley, Abraham, *The Works of Abraham Cowley*, ed. Thomas Sprat (1668).

Daniel, Samuel, *The Whole Works of Samvel Daniel Esquire in Poetrie* (1623).

Daniel, Samuel, *The Works of Samvel Daniel* (1601).

Day, Angel, *Vpon the Life and Death of the Most Worthy, and Thrise Renowned Knight, Sir Phillip Sidney: A Comemoration of his Worthines* (c. 1586).

Dekker, Thomas, *A Knights Conjuring Done in Earnest: Discouered in Iest* (1607).

Dickenson, John, *Greene in Conceipt* (1598).

Donne, John, *Deaths Duell* (1632).

Donne, John, *Devotions Vpon Emergent Occasions, and Seuerall Steps in my Sicknes* (1624).

Donne, John, *Devotions Vpon Emergent Occasions, and Seuerall Steps in my Sicknes* (1638).

Donne, John, *Letters to Severall Persons of Honour* (1651).

Donne, John, *LXXX Sermons* (1640).

Donne, John, *Poems by J.D. With Elegies on the Authors Death* (1633).

Donne, John, *Poems by J.D. With Elegies on the Authors Death, to which is Added Divers Copies Under his Own Hand Never Before in Print* (1635).

Donne, John, *A Sermon of Commemoration of the Lady Danvers* (1627).

Donne, John, *The Divine Poems*, ed. Helen Gardner (Oxford: Clarendon Press, 1952).

Donne, John, *The Poems of John Donne*, ed. H. J. C. Grierson (London: Oxford University Press, 1933).

Donne, John, *The Poems of John Donne*, ed. Robin Robbins, 2 vols (Harlow: Pearson Education, 2008).

Donne, John, *Selected Letters*, ed. P. M. Oliver (Manchester: Fyfield, 2002).

Drayton, Michael, *Poly-Olbion* (1612).

Elyot, Sir Thomas, *The Dictionary of Syr Thomas Eliot Knyght* (1538).

Fell, John, *The Life and Death of Dr. Thomas Fuller* (1661).

Foxe, John, *Actes and Monuments* (1583).

Fraunce, Abraham, *Arcadian Rhetorike* (1588).

Fuller, Thomas, *A History of the Worthies of England* (1662).

Gager, William (ed.), *Exequiae Illustrissimi Equitis, D. Philippi Sidnaei, Gratissimae Memoriae ac Nomine Impensae* (Oxford, 1587).

Gascoigne, George, *A Hundreth Sundrie Flowres Bound vp in One Small Poesie* (1573).

Gascoigne, George *The Posies of George Gascoigne Esquire* (1575).

Gascoigne, George *The Whole Woorkes of George Gascoigne Esquyre: Newlye Compyled into One Volume* (1587).

Gosson, Stephen, *The Schoole of Abuse* (1579).

Greene, Robert, *The Blacke Bookes Messenger* (1592).

Greene, Robert, *Greenes Groats-worth of Witte* (1592).

Greene, Robert, *Greenes Mourning Garment* (1590).

Greene, Robert, *Greenes Neuer Too Late* (1590).

Greene, Robert, *Greenes Vision* (1592).

Greene, Robert, *Menaphon* (1589).

Greene, Robert, *A Notable Discouery of Coosenage* (1591).

Greene, Robert, *Philomela* (1592).

Greene, Robert, *A Quip for an Vpstart Courtier* (1592).

Greene, Robert, *The Repentance of Robert Greene Maister of Artes* (1592).

Greene, Robert, *The Second Part of Conny-Catching* (1591).

Greene, Robert, *Greene's Groatsworth of Wit*, ed. D. Allen Carroll (Binghamton, NY: Center for Medieval and Early Renaissance Studies, State University of New York at Binghamton, 1994).

Greville, Fulke, *The Life of the Renowned Sr Philip Sidney* (1652).

Greville, Fulke, *Greville's Life of Sir Philip Sidney*, with an introduction by Nowell Smith (Oxford: Clarendon Press, 1907).

Guilim, John, *A Display of Heraldry* (1610).

Harington, John, *Orlando Furioso in English Heroical Verse* (1591).

Harvey, Gabriel, *Foure Letters and Certeine Sonnets* (1592).

Harvey, Gabriel, *Pierces Supererogation* (1593).

Harvey, Richard, *Philadelphus* (1593).

Healey, John, *Epictetus Manuall. Cebes Table. Theophrastus Characters* (1616).

Heath, James, *Flagellum, or the Life and Death, Birth and Burial of Oliver Cromwell* (1663).

Herbert, George, *Herbert's Remains*, ed. Barnabas Oley (1652).

Herbert, George, *A Priest to the Temple, or, The Country Parson his Character, and Rule of Holy Life* (1652).

Herbert, George, *The Temple* (1633).

Herbert, George, *The Temple* (1799).

Herbert, George, *The English Poems of George Herbert*, ed. Helen Wilcox (Cambridge: Cambridge University Press, 2007).

Herbert, George, *The Works of George Herbert*, ed. F. E. Hutchinson (Oxford: Oxford University Press, 1941).

Johnson, Samuel, *The Lives of the Most Eminent English Poets, with Critical Observations on their Works*, 4 vols, ed. Roger Lonsdale (Oxford: Clarendon Press, 2006).

Johnson, Samuel, *The Lives of the Poets*, ed. John H. Middendorf, *The Yale Edition of the Works of Samuel Johnson*, vols xxi–xxiii (New Haven, CT: Yale University Press, 2010).

Jonson, Ben, *Discoveries (1641), Conversations with William Drummond of Hawthornden (1619)* (Edinburgh: Edinburgh University Press, 1966).

Jonson, Ben, *The Workes of Beniamin Ionson* (1616).

Langbaine, Gerard, *An Account of the English Dramatick Poets* (1691).

Langbaine, Gerard, *The Lives and Characters of the English Poets* (1698).

Lant, Thomas, *'Lant's Roll'* (1587).

Lloyd, John (ed.), *Peplus, Illustrissimi Viri D. Philippi Sidnaei Supremus Honoribus Dicatus* (Oxford, 1587).

Lyly, John, *Euphves: The Anatomy of Wyt* (1578).

Lyndsay, Sir David, *The Warkis of the Famous and Vorthie Knicht Schir Dauid Lyndesay of the Mont* (Edinburgh, 1568).

Machiavelli, Niccolò, *I Discorsi di Nicolo Machiavelli* (1584).

Machiavelli, Niccolò, *Il Prencipe* (1584).

Machiavelli, Niccolò, *Libro dell'arte della Guerra* (1587).

Meres, Francis, *Palladis Tamia* (1598).

Milton, John, *A complete collection of the historical, political and miscellaneous works of John Milton ... to which is prefix'd the life of the author, containing besides the history of his works, several extraordinary characters of men and books, sects, parties, and opinions* (1698).

Milton, John, *Letters of state written by Mr. John Milton ... to which is added, an account of his life ; together with several of his poems, and a catalogue of his works, never before printed* (1694).

Moffet, Thomas, *Nobilis: Or a View of the Life and Death of a Sidney, and Lessus Lugubris* (San Marino, CA: The Huntington Library, 1940).

More, Sir Thomas, *The Workes of Sir Thomas More Knyght, sometym Chauncellourof England, Written by him in the Englysh Tonge*, ed. William Rastell (1557).

Munday, Anthony, *The Death of Robert, Earl of Huntington* (1601).

Munday, Anthony, *The Downfall of Robert, Earl of Huntington* (1601).

Munday, Anthony, and others, *Sir Thomas More*, ed. Vittorio Gabrieli and Giorgio Melchiori (Manchester: Manchester University Press 1990).

Nashe, Thomas, *Pierce Penilesse his Supplication to the Diuell* (1592).

Nashe, Thomas, *Strange Newes* (1592).

Nashe, Thomas, *Works of Thomas Nashe*, 5 vols, ed. R. B. McKerrow (London: Sidgwick & Jackson, 1910).

Neville, Alexander (ed.), *Academiae Cantabrigiensis Lachrymae Tumulo Nobilissimi Equitis, D. Philippi Sidneij Sacratae* (1587).

Phillips, Edward, *Theatrum Poetarum* (1675).

Phillips, John, *The Life and Death of Sir Phillip Sidney* (1587).

Pope, Alexander, *The Dunciad Variorum* (1729)

Pope, Alexander, *The Dunciad: In Four Books*, ed. Valerie Rumbold (London: Longman, 1999).

R. B., *Greenes Funeralls* (1594).

Roper, William, *The Mirrour of Vertue in Worldly Greatnes. Or the Life of Syr Thomas More Knight, sometime Lo. Chancellour of England* (Paris, 1626).

Rowe, Nicholas, 'Some Account of the Life &c of Mr. *William Shakespear*', in *The Works of Mr. William Shakespear*, ed. Nicholas Rowe, 6 vols (1709), vol. 1, pp. i–xl.

Rowlands, Samuel, *Greenes Ghost Haunting Coney-Catchers* (1602).

R. S. (ed.), *The Phoenix Nest* (1593).

R. S. (ed.), *The Phoenix Nest, Reprinted from the Original Edition* (London: Shakespeare Head Press, 1926).

R. S. (ed.), *The Phoenix Nest, 1593*, ed. Hyder Edward Rollins (Cambridge, MA: Harvard University Press, 1931).

Shakespeare, William, *Mr William Shakespeares Comedies, Histories & Tragedies* (1623).

Shakespeare, William, *Mr William Shakespeares Comedies, Histories & Tragedies* (1632).

Shakespeare, William, *Poems Written by Wil. Shake-speare Gent.* (1640).

Shakespeare, William, *The Complete Sonnets and Poems*, ed. Colin Burrow (Oxford: Oxford University Press, 2002).

Sidney, Sir Philip, *An Apologie for Poetrie* (1595).

Sidney, Sir Philip, *Arcadia* (1590).

Sidney, Sir Philip, *Arcadia* (1593).

Sidney, Sir Philip, *Syr P.S. His Astrophel and Stella [...] to the End of which are Added, Sundry and Rare Sonnets of Diuers Noble Men and Gentlemen* (Q1) (1591).

Sidney, Sir Philip, *Sir P.S. his Astrophel and Stella. Wherein the Excellence of Sweete Poesie is Concluded* (Q2) (1591).

Sidney, Sir Philip, *Syr P.S. his Astrophel and Stella. Wherein the Excellence of Sweete*

Poesie is Concluded. To the End of which are Added, Sundry other Rare Sonnets of Diuers Noble Men and Gentlemen (Q3) (*c.* 1597).

Sidney, Sir Philip, *The Defence of Poesie* (1595).

Sidney, Sir Philip, *The Poems of Sir Philip Sidney*, ed. William Ringler (Oxford: Clarendon Press, 1962).

Sidney, Sir Philip, *The Prose Works of Sir Philip Sidney*, ed. Albert Feuillerat, 4 vols (Cambridge: Cambridge University Press, 1963–1968).

Skelton, John, *Pithy Pleasaunt and Profitable Workes of Maister Skelton, Poete Laureate*, ed. John Stow (1568).

Skelton, John, *The Complete English Poems*, ed. V. J. Scattergood (Harmondsworth: Penguin, 1983).

Spenser, Edmund, *Colin Clouts Come Home Againe* and *Astrophel* (1595).

Spenser, Edmund, *Complaints* (1591).

Spenser, Edmund, *The Faerie Queene* (1590).

Spenser, Edmund, *The Faerie Queene* (1596).

Spenser, Edmund, *The Shepheardes Calender* (1579).

Spenser, Edmund, *The Shepheardes Calender* (1581).

Spenser, Edmund, *The Shepheardes Calender* (1586).

Spenser, Edmund, *The Shepheards Calender* (1591).

Spenser, Edmund, *The Shepheards Calender* (1597).

Spenser, Edmund, *Three Proper and Wittie Familiar Letters / Two Other Very Commendable Letters* (1580).

Spenser, Edmund, *A View of the State of Ireland*, in *The Historie of Ireland, Collected by Three Learned Authors*, ed. James Ware (Dublin, 1633).

Spenser, Edmund, *The Works of that Famous English Poet, Mr. Edmond Spenser, viz. The Faery Queen, The Shepherds Calendar, The History of Ireland, &c. whereunto is Added an Account of his Life, with other New Additions Never before in Print* (1679).

Spenser, Edmund, *Edmund Spenser: The Shorter Poems*, ed. Richard McCabe (London: Penguin, 1999).

Spenser, Edmund, *The Works of Edmund Spenser: A Variorum Edition*, ed. Edwin Greenlaw, Charles Osgood and Frederick Padelford, 11 vols (Baltimore, MD: Johns Hopkins University Press, 1932–57).

Swift, Jonathan, *A Tale of a Tub* (1704).

Thynne, Francis, *Animaduersions uppon the annotacions and corrections of some imperfections of impressiones of Chaucer's workes (sett downe before tyme and nowe)* (London: Early English Text Society, 1865).

Thynne, Francis, *Emblemes and Epigrames* (London: Early English Text Society, 1876).

Tottel, Richard (ed.), *Songes and Sonettes Written by the Right Honorable Lorde Henry Haward Late Earle of Surrey, and other* (1557).

Walton, Izaak, *The Compleat Angler, Or the Contemplative Man's Recreation* (1653).

Walton, Izaak, 'The Life and Death of Dr. *Donne*, Late Deane of St Pauls London', in Donne, *LXXX Sermons* (1640), A5^a–C^a.

Walton, Izaak, *The Life of John Donne* (1658).

Walton, Izaak, *The Life of Mr. George Herbert* (1670).

Walton, Izaak, *The Life of Mr. Rich. Hooker* (1665).

Walton, Izaak, *The Lives of Dr. John Donne, Sir Henry Wotton, Mr. Richard Hooker, Mr. George Herbert* (1670).

Walton, Izaak, *The Lives of Dr. John Donne, Sir Henry Wotton, Mr. Richard Hooker, Mr. George Herbert* (1675).

Walton, Izaak, *Love and Truth in Two Modest and Peaceable Letters Concerning the Distempers of the Present Times* (1680).

Walton, Izaak, *The Complete Angler*, ed. Jonquil Bevan (Oxford: Clarendon Press, 1983).

Walton, Izaak, *The Compleat Walton*, ed. Geoffrey Keynes (London: Nonesuch Press, 1929).

Walton, Izaak, *The Lives of John Donne, Sir Henry Wotton, Richard Hooker, George Herbert & Robert Sanderson*, with an introduction by George Saintsbury (Oxford: Oxford University Press, 1927).

Walton, Izaak, *The Lives of John Donne, Sir Henry Wotton, Richard Hooker, George Herbert & Robert Sanderson*, with an introduction and notes by S. B. Carter (London: Falcon Educational, 1951).

Walton, Izaak, *Selected Writings*, ed. Jessica Martin (Manchester: Fyfield, 1997).

Ware, John (ed.), *The Historie of Ireland* (Dublin, 1633).

Weever, John, *Epigrammes in the oldest cut, and newest fashion* (1599).

Whetstone, George, *A remembraunce of the wel imployed life, [and] godly end, of George Gaskoigne Esquire who deceassed at Stalmford in Lincolnshire the 7. of October. 1577. The reporte of Geor. Whetstons gent. an eye witnes of his godly and charitable end in this world* (1577).

Whetstone, George, *Sir Phillip Sidney, his honorable life, his valiant death, and true vertues A perfect myrror for the followers both of Mars and Mercury* (1587).

Winstanley, William, *The Lives of the Most Famous English Poets* (1687).

Witney, Geffrey, *A Choice of Emblemes, and other Deuises, for the Moste Parte Gathered out of Sundrie Writers, Englished and Moralized* (1586).

Wood, Anthony, *Athenae Oxonienses* (1691).

Secondary texts

Alexander, Gavin, *Writing After Sidney* (Oxford: Oxford University Press, 2006).

Altick, Richard D., *Lives and Letters: A History of Literary Biography in England and America* (New York: Alfred A. Knopf, 1965).

Anderson, Judith H., *Biographical Truth: The Representation of Historical Persons in Tudor-Stuart Writing* (New Haven, CT: Yale University Press, 1984).

Anderson, Judith H., Donald Cheney and David A. Richardson (eds), *Spenser's Life and the Subject of Biography* (Amherst: Massachusetts Studies in Early Modern Culture, 1996).

Arendt, Hannah, *The Human Condition* (Chicago: University of Chicago Press, 1958).

Auerbach, Erich, 'Figura', in E. Auerbach, *Scenes from the Drama of European Literature* (New York: Meridian Books, 1959), pp. 11–76.

Austin, Warren B., *A Computer-aided Technique for Stylistic Discrimination: The Authorship of 'Greene's Groatsworth of Wit'* (US Department of Education, 1969).

Baines, Paul and Pat Rogers, *Edmund Curll, Bookseller* (Oxford: Clarendon Press, 2007).

Baker, J. H., 'Rastell, William (1508–1565)', *Oxford Dictionary of National Biography*.

Bald, R. C., 'Historical Doubts Respecting Walton's *Life of Donne*', in Millar MacLure and F. W. Watt (eds), *Essays in English Literature from the Renaissance to the Victorian Age, Presented to A. S. P. Woodhouse* (Toronto: University of Toronto Press, 1964), pp. 69–84.

Bald, R. C., *John Donne: A Life* (Oxford: Clarendon Press, 1970).

Barker, W. W., 'Rhetorical Romance: The "Frivolous Toyes" of Robert Greene', in George M. Logan and Gordon Teskey (eds), *Unfolded Tales: Essays on Renaissance Romance* (Ithaca, NY: Cornell University Press, 1989), pp. 74–97.

Barnard, John, 'Creating an English Literary Canon, 1679–1720: Jacob Tonson, Dryden and Congreve', in Eliot, Nash and Willison (eds), *Literary Cultures and the Material Book*, pp. 307–21.

Bauman, Zygmunt, *Mortality, Immortality and other Life Strategies* (Cambridge: Polity Press, 1992).

Beal, Peter, *In Praise of Scribes: Manuscripts and their Makers in Seventeenth Century England* (Oxford: Clarendon Press, 1998).

Bedford, Ronald, Lloyd Davis and Philippa Kelly, *Early Modern Autobiography* (Ann Arbor: University of Michigan Press, 2006).

Bedford, Ronald, Lloyd Davis and Philippa Kelly, *Early Modern English Lives: Autobiography and Self-Representation 1500–1660* (Aldershot: Ashgate, 2007).

Bednarz, James P., *Shakespeare & the Poets' War* (New York: Columbia University Press, 2001).

Bennett, Kate, 'Editing Aubrey', in Bray, Handley and Henry (eds), *Ma(r)king the Text*, pp. 271–90.

Bennett, Kate, 'John Aubrey's Collections and the Early Modern Museum', *Bodleian Library Record*, 17.3–4 (2001), 213–34.

Berger, Thomas L. and William C. Bradford, *An Index of Characters in English Drama to the Restoration* (Englewood: Microcard Editions Books, 1975).

Berger, Thomas L. and Sidney L. Sonderberg, *An Index of Characters in Early Modern English Drama: Printed Plays, 1500–1660* (revised ed.) (Cambridge: Cambridge University Press, 1998).

Berry, Edward, *The Making of Sir Philip Sidney* (Toronto: University of Toronto Press, 1998).

Bevan, Jonquil, *Izaak Walton's 'The Compleat Angler': The Art of Recreation* (Brighton: Harvester, 1988).

Bloom, Harold, *The Anxiety of Influence: A Theory of Poetry* (Oxford: Oxford University Press, 1973).

Boureau, Alain and Roger Chartier (eds), *The Culture of Print: Power and the Uses of*

Print in Early Modern Europe, trans. Lydia G. Cochrane (Cambridge: Polity Press, 1989).

Bradley, A. C., *Shakespearean Tragedy: Lectures on Hamlet, Othello, King Lear, Macbeth* (London: Macmillan, 1929).

Bray, Joe, Miriam Handley and Anne C. Henry (eds), *Ma(r)king the Text* (Aldershot: Ashgate, 2000).

Brennan, Michael, 'William Ponsonby: Elizabethan Stationer', *Analytical & Enumerative Bibliography*, 7 (1983), 91–110.

Brink, Jean R., '"All his Minde on Honour Fixed": The Preferment of Edmund Spenser', in Anderson, Cheney and Richardson (eds), *Spenser's Life and the Subject of Biography*, pp. 45–64.

Brown, Cedric and Arthur F. Marotti (eds), *Texts and Cultural Change in Early Modern England* (Basingstoke: Macmillan, 1997).

Brown, Georgia, *Redefining Elizabethan Literature* (Cambridge: Cambridge University Press, 2004).

Brown, Richard Danson, *The New Poet* (Liverpool: Liverpool University Press, 1999).

De Bruyn, Frans, *Eighteenth-Century British Literary Scholars and Critics* (Detroit, MI: Gale Cengage Learning, 2010).

Burns, Edward, *Character: Acting and Being on the Pre-Modern Stage* (London: Macmillan, 1990).

Butt, J. E., 'Walton's Copy of Donne's *Letters* (1651)', *Review of English Studies*, 8 (1932), 72–4.

Butt, John, *Biography in the Hands of Walton, Johnson, and Boswell* (Los Angeles: University of California Press, 1966).

Buxton, John, 'On the Date of Syr P.S. His Astrophel and Stella...', *Bodleian Library Record*, 6 (1960), 614–16.

Carey, John, 'Is the Author Dead? Or, The Mermaids and the Robot', in Kozuka and Mulryne (eds), *Shakespeare, Marlowe, Jonson*, pp. 43–54.

Carey, John, *John Donne: Life, Mind and Art* (London: Faber and Faber, 1981).

Chaghafi, Elisabeth, 'Shaping Living Memory: John Aubrey, Izaak Walton and the Idea of Poetic Friendship', *South Atlantic Review*, 83 (2018), 139–57.

Chamberlain, Richard, *Radical Spenser: Pastoral Politics and the New Aestheticism* (Edinburgh: Edinburgh University Press, 2005).

Chambers, E. K., *William Shakespeare: A Study of Facts and Problems*, 2 vols (Oxford: Clarendon Press, 1930).

Chartier, Roger, *The Order of Books: Readers, Authors, and Libraries in Europe Between the Fourteenth and Eighteenth Centuries*, trans. Lydia G. Cochrane (Cambridge: Polity Press, 1994).

Cheney, Patrick, 'Biographical Representations: Marlowe's Life of the Author', in Kozuka and Mulryne (eds), *Shakespeare, Marlowe, Jonson*, pp. 183–204.

Cheney, Patrick, *Marlowe's Republican Authorship: Lucan, Liberty, and the Sublime* (Basingstoke: Palgrave Macmillan, 2009).

Cheney, Patrick, *Shakespeare's Literary Authorship* (Cambridge: Cambridge University Press, 2008).

Cheney, Patrick, *Spenser's Famous Flight: A Renaissance Idea of a Literary Career* (Toronto: University of Toronto Press, 1993).

Cheney, Patrick and Frederick A. de Armas (eds), *European Literary Careers: The Author from Antiquity to the Renaissance* (Toronto: University of Toronto Press, 2002).

Cheney, Patrick and Lauren Silberman (eds), *Worldmaking Spenser: Explorations in the Early Modern Age* (Lexington: University Press of Kentucky, 2000).

Clark, Sandra, *The Elizabethan Pamphleteers: Popular Moralistic Pamphlets 1580–1640* (London: Athlone Press, 1983).

Colclough, David (ed.), *John Donne's Professional Lives* (Cambridge: D. S. Brewer, 2003).

Coleman, Patrick, Jayne Lewis and Jill Kowalik (eds), *Representations of the Self from the Renaissance to Romanticism* (Cambridge: Cambridge University Press, 2000).

Collinson, Patrick, *The Birthpangs of Protestant England: Religions and Cultural Change in the Sixteenth and Seventeenth Centuries* (Basingstoke: Macmillan, 1988).

Collinson, Patrick, *The Religion of Protestants: The Church in English Society 1559–1625* (Oxford: Clarendon Press, 1982).

Conrad, F. W., 'Manipulating Reputations: Sir Thomas More, Sir Thomas Elyot, and the Conclusion of William Roper's *Lyfe of Sir Thomas Moore, Knighte*', in Mayer and Woolf (eds), *The Rhetoric of Life-Writing*, pp. 133–61.

Cook, Megan L., 'How Francis Thynne Read his Chaucer', *Journal of the Early Book Society*, 15 (2012), 215–43.

Corbett, Margery and Lightbown, Robert, *The Comely Frontispiece* (London and Boston, MA: Routledge and Kegan Paul, 1979).

Coren, Pamela, 'Edmund Spenser, Mary Sidney and the "Dolefull Lay"', *Studies in English Literature*, 42 (2002), 25–41.

Corns, Thomas N., 'The Early Lives of John Milton', in Sharpe and Zwicker (eds), *Writing Lives*, pp. 75–89.

Cory, H. E., *Edmund Spenser: A Critical Study* (Berkeley: University of California Press, 1917).

Craig, Hugh and Arthur F. Kinney (eds), *Shakespeare, Computers, and the Mystery of Authorship* (Cambridge: Cambridge University Press, 2009).

Crane, Mary Thomas, *Framing Authority* (Princeton, NJ: Princeton University Press, 1993).

Creswell, Catherine J., 'Giving a Face to an Author: Reading Donne's Portraits and the 1635 Edition', *Texas Studies in Literature and Language*, 37 (1995), 1–15.

Crupi, Charles W., *Robert Greene* (Boston, MA: Twayne Publishers, 1986).

Cummings, Brian, *The Literary Culture of the Reformation: Grammar and Grace* (Oxford: Oxford University Press, 2002).

Cummings, R. M., *Spenser: The Critical Heritage* (London: Routledge, 1971).

Dabbs, Thomas *Reforming Marlowe* (London: Associated University Presses, 1991).

Dimmick, Jeremy, 'Gower, Chaucer and the Act of Repentance in Robert Greene's Vision', *Review of English Studies*, 57 (2006), 456–73.

Dobranski, Stephen B., *Readers and Authorship in Early Modern England* (Cambridge: Cambridge University Press, 2005).

Dollimore, Jonathan, *Radical Tragedy: Religion, Ideology and Power in the Drama of Shakespeare and his Contemporaries* (Brighton: Harvester Press, 1984).

Donaldson, Ian, *Ben Jonson: A Life* (Oxford: Oxford University Press, 2011).

Donaldson, Ian, 'Looking Sideways: Jonson, Shakespeare and the Myths of Envy', in Kozuka and Mulryne (eds), *Shakespeare, Marlowe, Jonson*, pp. 241–57.

van Dorsten, Jan, Dominic Baker-Smith, and Arthur F. Kinney (eds), *Sir Philip Sidney: 1586 and the Creation of a Legend* (Leiden: Sir Thomas Browne Institute, 1986).

Dowden, Edward, *Shakespeare: A Critical Study of his Mind and Art* (London: Henry S. King, 1875).

Downie, J. A., 'Marlowe: Facts and Fictions', in Downie and Parnell (eds), *Constructing Christopher Marlowe*, pp. 13–29.

Downie, J. A. and J. T. Parnell (eds), *Constructing Christopher Marlowe* (Cambridge: Cambridge University Press, 2000).

Duncan-Jones, Katherine, '*Astrophel*', in Hamilton (ed.), *The Spenser Encyclopedia*, pp. 74–6

Duncan-Jones, Katherine, 'Philip Sidney's Toys', in Dennis Kay (ed.), *Sir Philip Sidney*, pp. 61–80.

Duncan-Jones, Katherine, *Shakespeare: Upstart Crow to Sweet Swan, 1592–1623* (London: Arden Shakespeare, 2011).

Duncan-Jones, Katherine, *Sir Philip Sidney, Courtier Poet* (London: Hamish Hamilton, 1991).

Duncan-Jones, Katherine, *Ungentle Shakespeare: Scenes from his Life* (London: Thomson Learning, 2001).

Edel, Leon, *Writing Lives: Principia Biographia* (New York: Norton, 1987).

Eliot, Simon, Andrew Nash and Ian Willison (eds), *Literary Cultures and the Material Book* (London: The British Library, 2007).

Epstein, William H., *Recognizing Biography* (Philadelphia: University of Pennsylvania Press, 1987).

Erne, Lukas, *Beyond 'The Spanish Tragedy': A Study of the Works of Thomas Kyd* (Manchester: Manchester University Press, 2001).

Erne, Lukas, *Shakespeare as a Literary Dramatist* (Cambridge: Cambridge University Press, 2003).

van Es, Bart, ' "Johannes fac Totum?": Shakespeare's First Contact with the Acting Companies', *Shakespeare Quarterly*, 61 (2010), 551–77

Falco, Raphael, *Conceived Presences: Literary Genealogy in Renaissance England* (Amherst: University of Massachusetts Press, 1994).

Falco, Raphael, 'Instant Artifacts: Vernacular Elegies for Philip Sidney', *Studies in Philology*, 89 (1992), 1–19.

Falco, Raphael, 'Spenser's "Astrophel" and the Formation of Elizabethan Literary Genealogy', *Modern Philology*, 91 (1993), 1–25.

Ferguson, Margaret, 'Nashe's *The Unfortunate Traveller*: The "Newes of the Maker" Game', *English Literary Renaissance*, 11 (1981), 165–82.

Ferrell, Lori Anne and Peter McCullough (eds), *The English Sermon Revised: Religion,*

Literature and History 1600–1750 (Manchester: Manchester University Press, 2000).

Fitzpatrick, Joan, *Shakespeare, Spenser and the Contours of Britain: Reshaping the Atlantic Archipelago* (Hatfield: University of Hertfordshire Press, 2004).

Fleck, Andrew, 'The Father's Living Monument: Textual Progeny and the Birth of the Author in Sidney's "Arcadias"', *Studies in Philology*, 107 (2010), 520–47.

Flynn, Dennis, 'Donne's Family Background and Early Years', in Shami, Flynn and Hester (eds), *Oxford Handbook of John Donne*, pp. 383–94.

Fowler, Elizabeth, *Literary Character: The Human Figure in Early English Writing* (Ithaca, NY: Cornell University Press, 2003).

Foxell, Nigel, *A Sermon in Stone: John Donne and his Monument in St Paul's Cathedral* (London: Menard Press, 1978).

Frost, Kate Gartner, *Holy Delight: Typology, Numerology, and Autobiography in Donne's 'Devotions Upon Emergent Occasions'* (Princeton, NJ: Princeton University Press, 1990).

Gâcon, Gérard, 'A Cartographer of Seventeenth-Century Selves: John Aubrey's *Brief Lives*', in Frédéric Regard (ed.), *Mapping the Self: Space, Identity, Discourse in British Auto / Biography* (Saint-Etienne: Publications de l'Université de Saint-Etienne, 2003).

Gajda, Alexandra, 'Education as a Courtier', in Shami, Flynn and Hester (eds), *Oxford Handbook of John Donne*, pp. 395–407.

Galbraith, Stephen K, 'Spenser's First Folio: The Build-It-Yourself Edition', *Spenser Studies*, 11 (2006), 21–49.

Genette, Gérard, *Paratexts: Thresholds of Interpretation*, trans. by Jane E. Lewin (Cambridge: Cambridge University Press, 1997).

Gieskes, Edward, *Representing the Professions: Administration, Law and Theater in Early Modern England* (Newark: University of Delaware Press, 2006).

Gittings, Clare, *Death, Burial and the Individual in Early Modern England* (London and Sydney: Croom Helm, 1984).

Gittings, Robert, *The Nature of Biography* (London: Heineman, 1978).

Goldberg, Jonathan, *Voice Terminal Echo: Postmodernism and English Renaissance Texts* (London: Methuen, 1986).

Goldberg, Jonathan, *Writing Matter: From the Hands of the English Renaissance* (Stanford: Stanford University Press, 1990).

Gondris, Joanna (ed.), *Reading Readings: Essays on Shakespeare Editing in the Eighteenth Century* (London: Associated University Press, 1998).

Gosse, Sir Edmund, *Life and Letters of John Donne, Dean of St Paul's*, 2 vols (London: Heineman, 1899).

Gould, Warwick and Thomas F. Staley (eds), *Writing the Lives of Writers* (London: Macmillan, 1998).

Gouws, John, 'Fact and Anecdote in Fulke Greville's Account of Sidney's Last Days', in van Dorsten, Baker-Smith and Kinney (eds), *Sir Philip Sidney: 1586 and the Creation of a Legend*, pp. 62–82.

Grafton, Anthony, *Defenders of the Text: The Tradition of Scholarship in an Age of Science, 1450–1800* (Cambridge, MA: Harvard University Press, 1991).

Grafton, Anthony, 'The New Science and the Traditions of Humanism', in Kraye (ed.), *Cambridge Companion to Renaissance Humanism*, pp. 203–23.

Grafton, Anthony and Lisa Jardine, *From Humanism to the Humanities: Education and the Liberal Arts in Fifteenth- and Sixteenth-Century Europe* (London: Duckworth, 1986).

Granqvist, Raoul, 'Izaak Walton's *Lives* in the Nineteenth and the Early Twentieth Century: A Study of a Cult Object', *Studia Neophilologica*, 54 (1982), 247–61.

de Grazia, Margreta, *'Hamlet' Without Hamlet* (Cambridge: Cambridge University Press, 2007).

de Grazia, Margreta, *Shakespeare Verbatim* (Oxford: Clarendon Press, 1991).

Greenblatt, Stephen, *Renaissance Self-Fashioning* (Chicago: University of Chicago Press, 1980).

Greenblatt, Stephen, *Sir Walter Ralegh* (New Haven, CT: Yale University Press, 1973).

Greenblatt, Stephen, *Will in the World: How Shakespeare Became Shakespeare* (London: Jonathan Cape, 2004).

Greetham, D. C., *Theories of the Text* (Oxford: Oxford University Press, 1999).

Greg, W. W. (ed.), *Henslowe's Diary*, 2 vols (London: A. H. Bullen, 1904–8).

Greg, W. W. and William A. Jackson (eds), *Records of the Court of the Stationers' Company, 1576 to 1602* (London: Bibliographical Society, 1930).

Griffiths, Jane, *John Skelton and Poetic Authority: Defining the Liberty to Speak* (Oxford: Oxford University Press, 2006).

Guibbory, Achsa (ed.), *The Cambridge Companion to John Donne* (Cambridge: Cambridge University Press, 2006).

Hadfield, Andrew, *Edmund Spenser: A Life* (Oxford: Oxford University Press, 2012).

Hadfield, Andrew, ' "Secrets and Lies": The Life of Edmund Spenser', in Sharpe and Zwicker (ed.), *Writing Lives*, pp. 55–73.

Hager, Alan, 'The Exemplary Mirage: Fabrication of Sir Philip Sidney's Biographical Image and the Sidney Reader', in Kay (ed.), *Sir Philip Sidney*, pp. 45–60.

Hamilton, A. C. (ed.), *The Spenser Encyclopedia* (Toronto: University of Toronto Press, 1997).

Hampton, Timothy, *Writing from History: The Rhetoric of Exemplarity in Renaissance Literature* (Ithaca, NY: Cornell University Press, 1990).

Hannay, Margaret P., 'The Countess of Pembroke's Agency in Print and Scribal Culture', in George L. Justice and Nathan Tinker (eds), *Women's Writing and the Circulation of Ideas* (Cambridge: Cambridge University Press, 2002), pp. 17–49.

Harvey, Elizabeth, 'Nomadic Souls: Pythagoras, Spenser, Donne', *Spenser Studies*, 22 (2007), 257–79.

Haskin, Dayton, 'Donne's Afterlife', in Guibbory (ed.), *Cambridge Companion to John Donne*, pp. 233–46.

Helgerson, Richard, *The Elizabethan Prodigals* (Berkeley: University of California Press, 1976).

Helgerson, Richard, *Forms of Nationhood: The Elizabethan Writing of England* (Chicago: University of Chicago Press, 1992).

Helgerson, Richard, *Self-Crowned Laureates* (Berkeley: University of California Press, 1983).

Henderson, Judith Rice, 'On Reading the Rhetoric of the Renaissance Letter', in Heinrich Plett (ed.), *Renaissance Rhetoric* (Berlin: de Gruyter, 1993).

Heninger, S. K., *Sidney and Spenser: The Poet as a Maker* (University Park: Pennsylvania State University Press, 1989).

Hirschfeld, Heather, 'Early Modern Collaboration and Theories of Authorship', *Publications of the Modern Language Association of America*, 116 (2001), 609–22.

Holland, Peter, 'Shakespeare and the *DNB*', in Kozuka and Mulryne (eds), *Shakespeare, Marlowe, Jonson*, pp. 139–49.

Hood, Edwin Paxton, *The Uses of Biography: Romantic, Philosophic and Didactic* (London: Partridge and Oakey, 1852).

Hughes, Richard E., *The Progress of the Soul: The Interior Career of John Donne* (New York: William Morrow, 1968).

Hunter, Michael, *John Aubrey and the Realm of Learning* (London: Duckworth, 1975).

Hunter, Michael, *The Royal Society and its Fellows 1660–1700: The Morphology of an Early Scientific Institution* (Chalfont St Giles: British Society for the History of Science, 1982).

Ingrassia, Catherine, 'Dissecting the Authorial Body: Pope, Curll, and the Portrait of a "Hack Writer"', in Catherine Ingrassia and Claudia N. Thomas (eds), *'More Solid Learning': New Perspectives on Alexander Pope's 'Dunciad'* (Lewisburg, PA: Bucknell University Press, 2000), pp. 147–66.

Jardine, Lisa, *Erasmus, Man of Letters: The Construction of Charisma in Print* (Princeton, NJ: Princeton University Press, 1993).

Jardine, Lisa and Anthony Grafton, '"Studied for Action": How Gabriel Harvey Read His Livy', *Past & Present*, 129 (1990), 30–78.

Jardine, Lisa and Alan Stewart, *Hostage to Fortune: The Troubled Life of Francis Bacon* (London: Gollancz, 1998).

Jenkins, Harold, 'On the Authenticity of *Greene's Groatsworth of Wit* and *The Repentance of Robert Greene*', *Review of English Studies*, 11 (1935), 28–41.

Johnson, Francis R., *A Critical Bibliography of the Works of Edmund Spenser Printed Before 1700* (Baltimore, MD: Johns Hopkins University Press, 1933).

Jones, H. S. V., *A Spenser Handbook* (New York: F. S. Crofts, 1930).

Jones, Richard F., *Lewis Theobald, his Contribution to English Scholarship* (New York: Columbia University Press, 1919).

Jowett, John, 'Henry Chettle: "Your old Compositor"', *Text*, 15 (2003), 141–61.

Jowett, John, 'Johannes Factotum: Henry Chettle and *Greene's Groatsworth of Wit*', *Papers of the Bibliographical Society of America*, 87 (1993), 453–86.

Judge, Cyril Bathurst, *Elizabethan Book-Pirates* (Cambridge, MA: Harvard University Press, 1934).

Kay, Dennis, 'Sidney – A Critical Heritage', in Kay (ed.), *Sir Philip Sidney*, pp. 3–41.

Kay, Dennis (ed.), *Sir Philip Sidney: An Anthology of Modern Criticism* (Oxford: Clarendon Press, 1987).

Kennedy, William J., *Authorizing Petrarch* (Ithaca, NY: Cornell University Press, 1994).

Kinney, Arthur F., *Humanist Poetics: Thought, Rhetoric, and Fiction in Sixteenth-century England* (Amherst: University of Massachusetts Press, 1986).

Kirkley, Harriet, *A Biographer at Work: Samuel Johnson's Notes for the 'Life of Pope'* (Lewisburg, PA: Bucknell University Press, 2002).

Klein, Lisa M., *The Exemplary Sidney and the Elizabethan Sonnetteer* (Newark: University of Delaware Press, 1998).

Kliman, Bernice W., 'Samuel Johnson and Tonson's 1745 Shakespeare: Warburton, Anonymity, and the Shakespeare Wars', in Gondris (ed.), *Reading Readings*, pp. 299–317.

Kozuka, Takashi and J. R. Mulryne (eds), *Shakespeare, Marlowe, Jonson: New Directions in Biography* (Aldershot: Ashgate, 2006).

Kraye, Jill, *The Cambridge Companion to Renaissance Humanism* (Cambridge: Cambridge University Press, 1996).

Kristeller, Paul Oskar, 'The Active and the Contemplative Life in Renaissance Humanism', in Brian Vickers (ed.), *Arbeit, Musse, Meditation: Betrachtungen zur 'Vita activa' und Vita contemplativa'* (Zürich: Verlag der Fachvereine, 1985), pp. 133–52.

Kumaran, Arul, 'Print, Patronage and the Satirical Pamphlet: The Death of Robert Greene as a Defining Textual Moment' (unpublished PhD thesis, University of Saskatchewan, 2001).

Larner, John, 'Traditions of Literary Biography in Boccaccio's *Life of Dante*', *Bulletin of the John Rylands Library*, 72 (1990), 107–17.

Lavin, J. A., 'The First Two Printers of Sidney's *Astrophel and Stella*', *Library*, 26 (1971), 249–55.

Lee, Hermione, *Body Parts: Essays in Life-Writing* (London: Chatto & Windus, 2005).

Le Goff, Jacques, *History and Memory* (New York: Columbia University Press, 1992).

Lein, Clayton D., 'Art and Structure in Walton's *Life of Mr George Herbert*', *University of Toronto Quarterly*, 46 (Winter 1976–77), 162–72.

Lethbridge, J. B., 'Spenser's Last Days', in J. B. Lethbridge (ed.), *Edmund Spenser: New and Renewed Directions* (Madison, NJ: Fairleigh Dickinson University Press, 2006), pp. 302–36.

Levao, Ronald, *Renaissance Minds and their Fictions: Cusanus, Sidney, Shakespeare* (Berkeley: University of California Press, 1985).

Lindenbaum, Peter, 'Sidney's *Arcadia* as Cultural Monument and Proto-Novel', in Brown and Marotti (ed.), *Texts and Cultural Change*, pp. 80–94.

Lipking, Lawrence, 'The Birth of the Author', in Gould and Staley (ed.), *Writing the Lives of Writers*, pp. 36–53.

Lipking, Lawrence, *The Life of the Poet: Beginning and Ending Poetic Careers* (Chicago: University of Chicago Press, 1981).

Loewenstein, Joseph, *The Author's Due* (Chicago: University of Chicago Press, 2002).

Loewenstein, Joseph, *Ben Jonson and Possessive Authorship* (Cambridge: Cambridge University Press, 2002).

Loewenstein, Joseph, 'Spenser's Retrography: Two Episodes in Post-Petrarchan Bibliography', in Anderson, Cheney and Richardson (eds), *Spenser's Life and the Subject of Biography*, pp. 99–130.

Loomie, A. J., 'Wotton, Sir Henry (1568–1639)', *Oxford DNB*.

Loretelli, Rosamaria, 'Trial by Cheap Print', in Rosamaria Loretelli and Roberto De Romanis (eds), *Narrating Transgression of the Criminal in Early Modern England* (Frankfurt am Main: Europäischer Verlag der Wissenschaften, 1999), pp. 27–50.

Love, Harold, *Attributing Authorship: An Introduction* (Cambridge: Cambridge University Press, 2002).

Love, Harold, *The Culture and Commerce of Texts* (Amherst: University of Massachusetts Press, 1998).

Love, Harold, 'Gossip and Biography', in Sharpe and Zwicker (eds), *Writing Lives*, pp. 91–104.

Love, Harold, *Scribal Publication* (Oxford: Clarendon Press, 1993).

Mack, Peter, 'Humanist Rhetoric and Dialectic', in Kraye (ed.), *Cambridge Companion to Renaissance Humanism*, pp. 82–99.

Magnusson, Lynne, *Shakespeare and Social Dialogue* (Cambridge: Cambridge University Press, 1999).

Mallette, Richard, 'Spenser's Portrait of the Artist in *The Shepheardes Calender* and *Colin Clouts Come Home Againe*', *Studies in English Literature*, 19 (1979), 19–41.

Marcus, Leah S., *Unediting the Renaissance: Shakespeare, Marlowe, Milton* (London: Routledge, 1996).

Marotti, Arthur F., *John Donne, Coterie Poet* (Madison: University of Wisconsin Press, 1986; repr. Eugene, OR: Wipf and Stock, 2008).

Marotti, Arthur F., *Manuscript, Print, and the English Renaissance Lyric* (Ithaca, NY: Cornell University Press, 1995).

Marshall, Gerald, 'Time in Walton's *Lives*', *Studies in English Literature*, 32 (1992), 429–42.

Marshall, Peter, *Beliefs and the Dead in Reformation England* (Oxford: Oxford University Press, 2002).

Martin, Jessica, 'Izaak Walton and the "Re-Inanimation" of Dr Donne', in Colclough (ed.), *John Donne's Professional Lives*, pp. 246–59.

Martin, Jessica, 'Walton, Izaak (1593–1683)', *Oxford DNB*.

Martin, Jessica, *Walton's Lives: Conformist Commemorations and the Rise of Biography* (Oxford: Oxford University Press, 2001).

Masten, Jeffrey, 'Representing Authority: Patriarchalism, Absolutism and the Author on Stage', in *Textual Intercourse: Collaboration, Authorship and Sexualities in Renaissance Drama* (Cambridge: Cambridge University Press, 1997), pp. 63–112.

Maurer, Margaret, 'The Prose Letter', in Shami, Flynn and Hester (eds), *Oxford Handbook of John Donne*, pp. 348–61.

May, James M., *Trials of Character: The Eloquence of Ciceronian Ethos* (Chapel Hill: University of North Carolina Press, 1988).

May, Steven W., 'Tudor Aristocrats and the Mythical "Stigma of Print"', *Renaissance Papers* (1980), 11–18.

Mayer, Thomas and D. R. Woolf (eds), *The Rhetoric of Life-Writing in Early Modern Europe* (Ann Arbor: University of Michigan Press, 1995).

McCabe, Richard, 'Annotating Anonymity, or Putting a Gloss on *The Shepheardes Calender*', in Bray, Handley and Henry (eds), *Ma(r)king the Text: The Presentation of Meaning on the Literary Page*, pp. 35–54.

McCabe, Richard, '"Thine owne Nations Frend / And Patrone": The Rhetoric of Petition in Harvey and Spenser', *Spenser Studies*, 22 (2007), 47–72.

McCrea, Adriana, 'Whose Life Is It, Anyway? Subject and Subjection in Fulke Greville's *Life of Sidney*', in Mayer and Woolf (eds), *The Rhetoric of Life Writing*, pp. 299–320.

McCullough, Peter, 'Donne and Court Chaplaincy', in Shami, Flynn and Hester (eds), *Oxford Handbook of John Donne*, pp. 554–65.

McCullough, Peter, 'Donne as preacher', in Guibbory (ed.), *Cambridge Companion to John Donne*, pp. 167–81.

McElderry, B. R., 'Walton's *Lives* and Gillman's *Life of Coleridge*', *PMLA*, 52 (1937), 412–22.

McGann, Jerome J., *The Textual Condition* (Princeton, NJ: Princeton University Press, 1991)

McKenzie, D. F., David McKitterick and I. R. Willison (eds), *The Cambridge History of the Book in Britain* (Cambridge: Cambridge University Press, 1999–).

McKenzie, D. F., *Making Meaning: 'Printers of the Mind' and Other Essays*, Peter D. McDonald and Michael F. Suarez (eds) (Amherst: University of Massachusetts Press, 2002).

McKerrow, Ronald B., 'The Treatment of Shakespeare's Text by his Earlier Editors, 1709–1768', in Peter Alexander (ed.), *Studies in Shakespeare: British Academy Lectures* (London: Oxford University Press, 1964), pp. 103–31.

McLaughlin, Martin, 'Biography and Autobiography in the Italian Renaissance', in Peter France and William St. Clair (eds), *Mapping Lives: The Uses of Biography* (Oxford: Oxford University Press, 2002), pp. 37–65.

Melnikoff, Kirk and Gieskes, Edward (eds), *Writing Robert Greene: New Essays on England's First Notorious Professional Writer* (Aldershot: Ashgate, 2008).

Mentz, Steven, 'Forming Greene: Theorizing the Early Modern Author in the *Groatsworth of Wit*', in Melnikoff and Gieskes (eds), *Writing Robert Greene*, pp. 115–31.

Mentz, Steven, *Romance for Sale in Early Modern England: The Rise of Prose Fiction* (Aldershot: Ashgate, 2006).

Mentz, Steven, 'Selling Sidney: William Ponsonby, Thomas Nashe, and the Boundaries of Elizabethan Print and Manuscript Cultures', *Text*, 13 (2000), 151–74.

Miller, Edwin H., *The Professional Writer in Elizabethan England: A Study of Nondramatic Literature* (Cambridge, MA: Harvard University Press, 1959).

Mills-Court, Karen, *Poetry as Epitaph: Representation and Poetic Language* (Baton Rouge: Louisiana State University Press, 1990).

Montrose, Louis, 'The Elizabethan Subject and the Spenserian Text', in Patricia Parker and David Quint (eds), *Literary Theory/Renaissance Texts* (Baltimore, MD: Johns Hopkins University Press, 1986), pp. 303–40.

Montrose, Louis, 'Interpreting Spenser's February Eclogue: Some Contexts and Implications', *Spenser Studies*, 2 (1981), 67–74.

Montrose, Louis, 'Spenser's Domestic Domain: Poetry, Property, and the Early Modern Subject', in Margreta de Grazia, Maureen Quilligan and Peter Stallybrass (eds), *Subject and Object in Renaissance Culture* (Cambridge: Cambridge University Press, 1996).

Mulryne, J. R., 'Where We Are Now: Directions and Biographical Methods', in Kozuka and Mulryne (eds), *Shakespeare, Marlowe, Jonson*, pp. 1–19.

Murphy, Andrew, *Shakespeare in Print: A History and Chronology of Shakespeare Publishing* (Cambridge: Cambridge University Press, 2003).

Murphy, Andrew (ed.), *The Renaissance Text: Theory, Editing, Textuality* (Manchester: Manchester University Press, 2000).

Murray, Peter B., *Shakespeare's Imagined Persons: The Psychology of Role Playing and Acting* (Basingstoke: Macmillan, 1996).

Neill, Michael, *Issues of Death: Mortality and Identity in English Renaissance Tragedy* (Oxford: Oxford University Press, 1997; repr., 1998).

Nelson, Alan H., 'Calling All (Shakespeare) Biographers: Or, a Plea for Documentary Discipline', in Kozuka and Mulryne (eds), *Shakespeare, Marlowe, Jonson*, pp. 55–67.

Newcomb, Lori Humphrey, 'Greene, Robert (*bap.* 1558, *d.* 1592)', *Oxford DNB*.

Newcomb, Lori Humphrey, *Reading Popular Romance in Early Modern England* (New York: Columbia University Press, 2001).

Nicolson, Harold, *The Development of English Biography* (London: Hogarth Press, 1927).

Novarr, David, *The Making of Walton's 'Lives'* (Ithaca, NY: Cornell University Press, 1958).

O'Callaghan, Michelle, *The 'Shepheards Nation': Jacobean Spenserians and Early Stuart Political Culture* (Oxford: Clarendon Press, 2000).

O'Connell, Michael, '*Astrophel*: Spenser's Double Elegy', *Studies in English Literature*, 11 (1971), 27–35.

Oliver, H. J., 'Izaak Walton's Prose Style', *Review of English Studies*, 21 (1945), 280–8.

Parfitt, George, *John Donne: A Literary Life* (Basingstoke: Macmillan, 1989).

Paris, Bernard J., *Imagined Human Beings: A Psychological Approach to Character and Conflict in Literature* (New York: New York University Press, 1997).

Pask, Kevin, 'The "Mannes State" of Philip Sidney: Pre-scripting the Life of the Poet in England', *Criticism*, 36 (1994), 163–88.

Pattison, Neil, '"None but Himself": "Tibbald", Theobald, and *The Dunciad Variorum*', *Forum for Modern Language Studies*, 45 (2009), 254–69.

Pearsall, Derek, 'The Problems of Writing a Life of Chaucer', *Studies in the Age of Chaucer*, 13 (1991), 5–14.

Peterson, Richard S., '*Enuies Scourge and Vertues Honor*: A Rare Elegy for Spenser', *Spenser Studies*, 25 (2010), 287–325.

Peterson, Richard S., 'Laurel Crown and Ape's Tail: New Light on Spenser's Career from Sir Thomas Tresham', *Spenser Studies*, 12 (1998), 1–35.

Pigman, G. W., *Grief and English Renaissance Elegy* (Cambridge: Cambridge University Press, 1985).

Pitcher, John, 'Editing Daniel', in W. Speed Hill (ed.), *New Ways of Looking at Old Texts* (Binghamton: Renaissance English Text Society, 1993), pp. 57–73.

Pitcher, John, 'Essays, Works and Small Poems: Divulging, Publishing and

Augmenting the Elizabethan Poet, Samuel Daniel', in Murphy (ed.), *The Renaissance Text*, pp. 8–29.

Poole, William, *John Aubrey and the Advancement of Learning* (Oxford: Bodleian Library, 2010).

Post, Jonathan F. S., 'Donne's Life: A Sketch', in Guibbory (ed.), *Cambridge Companion to John Donne*, pp. 1–22.

Powell, Anthony, *John Aubrey and his Friends* (London: Eyre & Spottiswoode, 1948).

Pritchard, Allan, *English Biography in the Seventeenth Century* (Toronto: University of Toronto Press, 2005).

Proudfoot, Richard, 'Marlowe and the Editors', in Downie and Parnell (eds), *Constructing Christopher Marlowe*, pp. 41–54.

Raleigh, Walter, *Six Essays on Johnson* (Oxford: Clarendon Press, 1910).

Rambuss, Richard, *Spenser's Secret Career* (Cambridge: Cambridge University Press, 1993).

Ray, Robert H., 'Herbert's Words in Donne's Mouth: Walton's Account of Donne's Death', *Modern Philology*, 85 (1987), 186–7.

Rees, Joan, *Samuel Daniel: A Critical and Biographical Study* (Liverpool: Liverpool University Press, 1964).

Richards, Jennifer, *Rhetoric and Courtliness in Early Modern Literature* (Cambridge: Cambridge University Press, 2003).

Richardson, B. E., 'Studies in Related Aspects of the Life and Thought of Robert Greene, with Particular Reference to the Material of his Prose Pamphlets' (unpublished DPhil thesis, University of Oxford, 1976).

Riggs, David, 'The Poet in the Play: Life and Art in *Tamburlaine* and *The Jew of Malta*', in Kozuka and Mulryne (ed.), *Shakespeare, Marlowe, Jonson*, pp. 205–24.

Robson, Mark, 'Writing Contexts in William Roper's *Life of Thomas More*', in Gould and Staley (ed.), *Writing the Lives of Writers*, pp. 79–89.

Roche, Thomas P., 'Autobiographical Elements in Sidney's *Astrophil and Stella*', *Spenser Studies*, 5 (1985), 209–29.

Rogers, Pat, 'Edmund Curll and the Publishing Trade', in Runge and Rogers (ed.), *Producing the Eighteenth Century Book*, pp. 215–34.

Rose, Mark, 'The Author in Court: *Pope v. Curll (1741)*', in Woodmansee and Jaszi (ed.), *The Construction of Authorship*, pp. 211–29.

Ross, Marlon B., 'Authority and Authenticity: Scribbling Authors and the Genius of Print in Eighteenth-Century England', in Woodmansee and Jaszi (eds), *The Construction of Authorship*, pp. 231–57.

Rowe, Katherine, *Dead Hands: Fictions of Agency, Renaissance to Modern* (Stanford, CA: Stanford University Press, 1999).

Runge, Laura L. and Pat Rogers (eds), *Producing the Eighteenth-Century Book: Writers and Publishers in England 1650–1800* (Newark: University of Delaware Press, 2007).

Sanders, Chauncey, 'Robert Greene and his "Editors" ', *PMLA*, 48 (1933), 392–417.

Schmitz-Emans, Monika, 'Überleben im Text? Zu einem Grundmotiv literarischen Schreibens und einigen Formen seiner Reflexion im poetischen Medium', *Colloquia Germanica*, 26 (1993), 135–61.

Scodel, Joshua, *The English Poetic Epitaph: Commemoration and Conflict from Jonson to Wordsworth* (Ithaca, NY: Cornell University Press, 1991).

Scott-Warren, Jason, *Sir John Harington and the Book as Gift* (Oxford: Oxford University Press, 2001).

Seary, Peter, *Lewis Theobald and the Editing of Shakespeare* (Oxford: Clarendon Press, 1990).

Shami, Jeanne, Dennis Flynn and M. Thomas Hester (eds), *The Oxford Handbook of John Donne* (Oxford: Oxford University Press, 2011).

Sharpe, Kevin and Steven N. Zwicker (eds), *Writing Lives: Biography and Textuality, Identity and Representation in Early Modern England* (Oxford: Oxford University Press, 2008).

Sherman, William H., *Used Books: Marking Readers in Early Modern England* (Philadelphia: University of Pennsylvania Press, 2008).

Shore, David R., 'Colin Clouts Come Home Againe', in Hamilton (ed.), *The Spenser Encyclopaedia*, pp. 173–7.

Shrank, Cathy, *Writing the Nation in Reformation England, 1530–1580* (Oxford: Oxford University Press, 2004).

Shuger, Debora, 'Life-writing in Seventeenth-century England', in Coleman, Lewis and Kowalik (eds), *Representations of the Self*, pp. 63–78.

Smallwood, Philip, *Critical Occasions: Dryden, Pope, Johnson, and the History of Criticism* (New York: AMS Press, 2011).

Smith, D. N., 'Raleigh, Sir Walter Alexander (1861–1922)', rev. Donald Hawes, *Oxford DNB*.

Smith, Emma, 'Author v. Character in Early Modern Dramatic Authorship: The Example of Thomas Kyd and The Spanish Tragedy', *Medieval and Renaissance Drama in England*, 11 (1999), 129–42.

Smith, G. C. Moore, 'Izaak Walton and John Donne', *Modern Language Review*, 15 (1920), 303.

Smith, Helen and Louise Wilson (eds), *Renaissance Paratexts* (Cambridge: Cambridge University Press, 2011).

Smith, Logan Pearsall, *The Life and Letters of Sir Henry Wotton* (Oxford: Clarendon Press, 1907).

Smith, Nigel, *Literature and Revolution in England 1640–1660* (New Haven, CT: Yale University Press, 1994).

Smyth, Adam, *Autobiography in Early Modern England* (Cambridge: Cambridge University Press, 2010).

Stanwood, P. G., *Izaak Walton* (New York: Simon & Schuster Macmillan, 1998).

States, Bert O., *Hamlet and the Concept of Character* (Baltimore, MD: Johns Hopkins University Press, 1992).

Stauffer, Donald, *English Biography Before 1700* (Cambridge, MA, Harvard University Press, 1930).

Steinberg, Theodore L., 'Spenser, Sidney, and the Myth of Astrophel', *Spenser Studies*, 11 (1994), 187–201.

Steinberg, Theodore L., 'Weeping for Sidney', *Sidney Newsletter & Journal*, 11 (1991),

3–15 [contains transcriptions and translations for elegies from the Leiden collection].

Stenner, Rachel, Tamsin Badcoe and Gareth Griffith (eds), *Rereading Chaucer and Spenser: Dan Geffrey with the New Poete* (Manchester: Manchester University Press, 2019).

Stewart, Alan, *The Oxford History of Life-Writing*, vol. II: *Early Modern* (Oxford: Oxford University Press, 2018).

Stewart, Alan, *Philip Sidney: A Double Life* (London: Chatto & Windus, 2000).

Strachey, Lytton, 'Shakespeare's Final Period' (1906), in *Books and Characters, French & English* (London: Chatto & Windus, 1922), pp. 47–64.

Stubbs, John, *Donne: The Reformed Soul* (London: Penguin, 2006).

Suarez, Michael Felix and H. R. Woudhuysen (eds), *The Oxford Companion to the Book* (Oxford: Oxford University Press, 2010).

Sullivan, Ernest W., '1633 *Vndone*', *Text*, 7 (1994), 297–306.

Targoff, Ramie, *Common Prayer: The Language of Public Devotion in Early Modern England* (Chicago: University of Chicago Press, 2001).

Targoff, Ramie, *John Donne, Body and Soul* (Chicago: University of Chicago Press, 2008)

Tedder, H. R., 'Newman, Thomas (*c.*1564–1594)', rev. Anita McConnell, *Oxford Dictionary of National Biography*.

Thomson, Peter, 'Tarlton, Richard (*d.* 1588)', *Oxford Dictionary of National Biography*.

Trevor-Roper, Hugh, 'Roper, William (1495×8–1578)', *Oxford Dictionary of National Biography*.

Vickers, Brian, *Shakespeare, Co-Author: A Historical Study of Five Collaborative Plays* (Oxford: Oxford University Press, 2002).

Vickers, Brian (ed.), *Shakespeare: The Critical Heritage*, 6 vols (London: Routledge & Kegan Paul, 1974–81).

Voss, Paul, 'Books for Sale: Advertising and Patronage in Late Elizabethan England', *Sixteenth-Century Journal*, 29 (1998), 733–57.

Walker, Greg, *Writing under Tyranny* (Oxford: Oxford University Press, 2005).

Wall, Wendy, *The Imprint of Gender: Authorship and Publication in the English Renaissance* (Ithaca, NY: Cornell University Press, 1993).

Warkentin, Germaine, 'Patrons and Profiteers: Thomas Newman and the "Violent enlargement" of *Astrophil and Stella*', *Book Collector*, 34 (1985), 461–87.

Warner, J. Christopher, 'Poetry and Praise in *Colin Clouts Come Home Againe*', *Studies in English Literature*, 19 (1979), 19–41.

Waters, William, *Poetry's Touch: On Lyric Address* (Ithaca, NY: Cornell University Press, 2003).

Watson, Robert N., *The Rest is Silence: Death as Annihilation in the English Renaissance* (Berkeley: University of California Press, 1994).

Wendorf, Richard, '"Visible Rhetorick": Izaak Walton and Iconic Biography', *Modern Philology*, 82 (1985), 269–91.

West, Philip, *Henry Vaughan's 'Silex Scintillans': Scripture Uses* (Oxford: Oxford University Press, 2001).

Westley, Richard, 'Computing Error: Reassessing Austin's Study of *Groatsworth of Wit*', *Literary and Linguistic Computing*, 21 (2006), 363–78.

White, Helen C., 'Early Renaissance Saints' Lives', *Annuale Mediaevale*, 4 (1964), 93–123.

Wilson, Christopher, R., 'Astrophil and Stella: A Tangled Editorial Web', *Library* 6 (1979), 336–46.

Wilson, Katharine C., *Fictions of Authorship in Late Elizabethan Narratives: Euphues in Arcadia* (Oxford: Clarendon Press, 2006).

Wilson, Katharine C., ' "The Ironicall Recreation of the Reader": The Construction of Authorship in the Prose Fictions of John Lyly, Robert Greene and Thomas Lodge' (unpublished DPhil thesis, University of Oxford, 2000).

Winbolt, S. E., *Spenser and his Poetry* (London: George G. Harrap, 1912).

Wolfe, Heather, 'Aphorism therapy, or, How to cope with dishonest relatives', *The Collation*, 21 March 2014.

Woodmansee, Martha and Peter Jaszi (eds), *The Construction of Authorship: Textual Appropriation in Law and Literature* (Durham, NC: Duke University Press, 1994).

Woods-Marsden, Joanna, *Renaissance Self-Portraiture: The Visual Construction of Identity and the Social Status of the Artist* (New Haven, CT: Yale University Press, 1998).

Worden, Blair, 'Shakespeare in Life and Art: Biography and *Richard II*', in Kozuka and Mulryne (eds), *Shakespeare, Marlowe, Jonson*, pp. 23–42.

Woudhuysen, H. R., *Sir Philip Sidney and the Circulation of Manuscripts 1558–1640* (Oxford: Clarendon Press, 2000).

Yachnin, Paul and Jessica Slights (eds), *Shakespeare and Character: Theory, History, Performance, and Theatrical Persons* (Basingstoke: Palgrave Macmillan, 2009).

Yates, Frances, *The Art of Memory* (London: Routledge, 1966).

Yeo, Richard, 'Notebooks as Memory Aids: Precepts and Practices in Early Modern England', *Memory Studies*, 1 (2008), 115–36.

Zurcher, Andrew, 'The Printing of the *Cantos of Mutabilitie* in 1609', in Jane Grogan (ed.) *Celebrating Mutabilitie* (Manchester: Manchester University Press, 2010), pp. 40–60.

Zwicker, Stephen N., 'Considering the Ancients: Dryden and the Uses of Biography', in Sharpe and Zwicker (eds), *Writing Lives*, pp. 105–24.

Index

CPSIA information can be obtained
at www.ICGtesting.com
Printed in the USA
LVHW092023130720
660559LV00018B/876